Praise for Linda H. Davis & *Charles Addams*

"Linda Davis has dug deep in her fabulous biography of *The New Yorker*'s most mysterious and spooky (and all-together ooky) artist. The book's a scream."

–Michael Maslin

"A person's charm is difficult for a writer to convey on the printed page, but Linda Davis has managed it. At the close, I found myself feeling terribly cheated that I hadn't had the pleasure of Charlie Addams' company."

–Edward Sorel, *The New York Observer*

"If you don't appreciate martinis with eyeballs in them, this is not the book for you. For the rest of us, here is an irresistible riot of a read, an exhilarating, expertly mixed cocktail of words and images. Charles Addams's life was crowded with women–famous women, smart women, witty women, garden-variety drop-dead beautiful women– but in Linda Davis he has truly met his match."

–Stacy Schiff, Pulitzer Prize-winning author of *Véra*

"Chas Addams remains a commanding presence as one of the iconic artists who contributed to shaping that unique satirical art form– the *New Yorker* cartoon. He was also the only *New Yorker* artist who, because of his brilliant and unorthodox originality, was the object of widespread and thoroughly misplaced fascination about his mental stability. Linda Davis has delved into his work and the brain, hand, and raucous life that shaped it, offering a complex, entertaining and completely riveting portrait of a gentle, loving man, and his passionate and engaged embrace of life."

–Ed Koren, author and political cartoonist for *The New Yorker*

Also by Linda H. Davis

Onward and Upward: A Biography of Katharine S. White

Badge of Courage: The Life of Stephen Crane

Chas
Addams

Linda H. Davis

CHARLES ADDAMS

A CARTOONIST'S LIFE

TURNER

PUBLISHING COMPANY

Turner Publishing Company
Nashville, Tennessee
www.turnerpublishing.com

Library of Congress Cataloging-in-Publication Data
Names: Davis, Linda H., author.
Title: Charles Addams : a cartoonist's life / Linda H. Davis.
Description: Nashville, Tennessee : Turner Publishing, [2021] | Previously published: 2006 |
Includes bibliographiCal references and index.
Identifiers: LCCN 2021021868 (print) | LCCN 2021021869 (ebook) | ISBN
9781684426898 (paperback) | ISBN 9781684426904 (hardback) | ISBN
9781684426911 (ebook)
Subjects: LCSH: Addams, Charles, 1912-1988. | Cartoonists--United

States--Biography.
Classification: LCC NC1429.A25 D38 2021 (print) | LCC NC1429.A25 (ebook)
| DDC 741.5/6973 [B]--dc23
LC record available at https://lccn.loc.gov/2021021868
LC ebook record available at https://lccn.loc.gov/2021021869

Frontispiece by Nancy Crampton
Book design by Barbara M. Bachman
Cover design: Lauren Peters-Collaer

Printed in Canada

For my family—
Chuck, Allie, Randy,
and Mom (Patricia H. Davis)
Johnny and Michael, Cheryl and Lars

With love and laughter

Cartooning "is the ideal work for the uncommitted."

—Ed Koren

Contents

—

FIFTEEN YEARS HAVE PASSED SINCE THE FIRST publication of this biography, and yet Charles Addams still feels close at hand.

The Addams Family remains alive and unwell in worldwide syndication, delighting today's children as it did Baby Boomers, including me. The Family has inspired new animated films, an M&M's candy commercial, a play. Westfield, New Jersey, birthplace of the cartoonist, now honors him with an annual AddamsFest, and the state has inducted him into the New Jersey Hall of Fame.

The Family's presence is felt everywhere. When my friend Bob decided to adopt a rescue cat, his choice owed something to the cat's name, "Morticia." When my middle grandson, Sam, was only two, he would gravitate toward a large reproduction of the Addams ghouls in my house, asking me to repeat the names.

It's rare to encounter someone who doesn't know what's meant by an Addams Family house or an Uncle Fester–type.

To know Charles Addams was to perceive the world as he did. I look at the 1870 Victorian house across the street from my Massachusetts home and see an Addams house. I pass a neighbor's sign saying "Rufus A. Jones, Premier Painting" (I have changed the name)—planted before a house with shingles peeling and weeds overtaking the yard—and see an Addams cartoon. Addams's friends, wives, and lovers were similarly intoxicated: they gave him such gifts as a sewing basket fashioned from a dead armadillo, a bearskin coat, a private viewing of a mummy, a stuffed raven...

It was easy to fall under his spell. During my six years with Charles Addams ("Charlie" to his friends), I began filling my fountain pen with sepia ink, an Addams color, and ceased taking a broom to the cobwebs in my house. When I changed doctors, I chose the one named Gomez. My husband, always an enthusiastic gift giver, became Addams-inspired. Chuck's gifts to me included such treasures as a set of highball-sized "Name Your Poison" glasses: "Arsenic," "Cyanide," "Hemlock," "Curare," and so on. After the Widow Addams gave me Charlie's bearskin coat, I kept it draped over a chair in my home office, next to my desk—as though Charlie had just dropped it there upon entering the room. On cold winter mornings I would drag the nine-pound garment across my lap. "Okay, Charlie, now I've got you where I want you," I'd tell the coat. "Give it up!"

People always ask biographers how they come up with their subjects. Many admit it happens almost by accident. After a long period of considering and discarding ideas following my second biography of a literary figure, I concluded that I would write about an artist, or a cartoonist—Charles Addams. It dawned on me for no particular reason; he was a repressed idea. Though I never met him in the flesh, he became so real to me that I didn't feel deprived.

The years I spent with Addams were some of the happiest of my life. I quickly learned that he was as original and irresistible as his cartoons. (Chuck used to say that when he heard me laughing at my desk, he knew I was working.) And I was lucky in my sources—particularly in the Widow Addams, who had been wanting someone to write a biography when I came along, and opened her home to me.

Perhaps I fell too much in love with my subject. ("If I was your husband, I'd be very jealous of Charlie," my Random House editor, Bob Loomis, observed. "He's not jealous of a dead man," I replied.) Yet I challenge anyone to write about Addams and remain neutral.

Whether my communing with the Addams spirit found its way into the biography is not for me to say. Still, I hope I brought him to life on the page so that readers can have the pleasure of his company too.

Linda H. Davis
Pittsfield, Massachusetts

Chas
Addams

Chapter One

—

Arrested at the
Age of Eight

THEY SAID THAT CHARLES ADDAMS SLEPT IN A COFFIN
and drank martinis with eyeballs in them. They said he kept a guillotine
at his house and received chopped-off fingers in the mail from fans. It
was once reported that he had been given a monogrammed straitjacket as
a birthday gift—a garment that might have come in handy if the other
stories were true, such as the one Patricia McLaughlin told about Addams moving around the living room at a party, "methodically and im-
ponderably depositing" dollops of tooth powder in various corners. "A
charm to ward off cavity-causing vampires?" she wondered. People said
that Addams had married Morticia, the pale dagger in the spidery black
dress from *The Addams Family*, that familiar band of subversives that included Gomez, Lurch, Pugsley, Wednesday, Uncle Fester, Grandma,
Thing, and Cousin Itt.

The story most often heard concerned a Charles Addams cartoon
about a ghoul in a maternity room, come to claim his offspring. "Don't
bother to wrap it; I'll eat it here," he tells the nurse. They said that Addams would have periodic mental breakdowns and begin drawing the
gruesome maternity room cartoon. Or he'd redraw "The Skier," his classic 1940 cartoon showing single ski tracks on either side of a tree, as
though the skier seen vanishing down the hill has passed right through it.
As Addams would begin madly sketching the skier or the maternity

ghoul (depending on which version of the story you heard), his *New Yorker* employer had him carted off in an ambulance to the loony bin.

Everyone from Dick Cavett to medical illustrator Shirley Baty had heard the stories. George Plimpton heard them while he was still a student at Harvard during the 1940s; Wilfrid Sheed was told about them during his school years at Oxford.

And the Addams legend caught up with *New Yorker* staff members and contributors all over the world. What, people wanted to know, was Charles Addams really like? Even in places where people had never heard of *The New Yorker,* said Calvin Trillin, "eventually they'd get around to asking about Addams." James Geraghty, Addams's former art editor at *The New Yorker,* had been asked the question wherever he went. "In Avignon I was asked . . . the French for 'What is Charles Addams really like?' " He had been asked the same question in Italian in Bergamo, and in Greek on the island of Rhodes. And he truly believed that if he had ever visited Timbuktu, he'd have been asked the question in Timbuktuese: "What is Charles Addams really like?"

"Are people ever disappointed when they meet you?" a reporter once asked Addams.

"I suppose they are. Aren't you?" he deadpanned.

Everyone from Cary Grant to the clerk at the Registry of Motor Vehicles had wanted to meet Addams. He had long ago opened his front door to find "a fat little man standing there."

"I've just come to see you in your natural bailiwick," drawled Alfred Hitchcock.

Many years before 1981, when the latest intrepid reporter went in search of answers, the name Chas Addams, as the artist abbreviated it in thick black ink in a lower corner of his cartoons ("Just a matter of design," he explained; "it looks better than writing out 'Charles' "), had become synonymous with black humor. He could make even a chair "scary, grim," said *New Yorker* artist Mischa Richter.

Though much of Addams's work was funny without being dark, and marked by great sweetness, it was the sinister stuff that had made him famous and earned him such sobriquets as "the Van Gogh of the Ghouls," "the Bela Lugosi of the cartoonists," "the graveyard guru," and a purveyor of "American Gothic." His work was compared to that of Shakespeare and Poe.

The Addams name was intertwined with a certain kind of offbeat character and place. One saw a particular type of woman—model-thin, with pale skin and long black hair, wearing a black dress—and thought: "Morticia." Round, bald men brought Uncle Fester to mind. The Addams name also conjured an atmosphere, and a house—a peeling Victorian confection that had come to represent something menacing.

"Well, it looked a bit like a Charles Addams cartoon," Lady Bird Johnson said in 1964, after seeing the property in Johnson City, Texas, that would become the presidential ranch. "And I think that if I'd been told that I was going to buy it and start trying to make it into a home I would have turned and run," she added. It was no coincidence that the notorious Hitchcock movie *Psycho,* released in 1960, had featured an Addamsesque Victorian as the home of the psychopath Norman Bates: Hitchcock had become an Addams friend and owned two of his original cartoons.

Sometimes the Addams delinquents assumed nonhuman form. There was the famous hairball, named Cousin Itt in the television series. There was the grinning, snaggletoothed, grinchy figure who had appeared in *The New Yorker* in 1974 tearing down a wintry mountain slope on a snowmobile, the razorlike hair on his body flying straight back: the Abominable Snowman as winter sportsman. But often Addams's creepiest people were the normal-looking, nondescript types, the people one passes on the street without truly seeing them: the little clerk, the drab housewife, the "purposeful charlady," as Addams called her, who in a memorable 1942 cartoon raises the leg of her bound and gagged employer and continues her mechanical sweeping.

PEOPLE SWORE THAT they had actually seen the maternity room cartoon, but Addams had never drawn it. He had, however, submitted a cartoon rough (an artist's draft) with a similar idea: "I'm worried about Albert," says a wife of her husband in a maternity room. "He eats his young." "It was of course rejected," Addams told his friend Steven M. L. Aronson, a book editor and writer.

Still, people believed what they wanted to believe. A 1978 *New Yorker* Thanksgiving cover by Addams showing a stunned turkey farmer contemplating the flock that has gathered into military formations in the yard provoked some wild reactions by readers who inter-

preted the straightforward drawing as a reference to "Nazi concentration camps."

And yet Addams himself had invited the misperception—if only in jest. Hadn't he once answered his fan mail on a letterhead inscribed "The Gotham Rest Home for Mental Defectives"? Hadn't he worn flaming red pajamas over his clothes to one Manhattan party, and a Knights Templar robe to another? Dressed as Abe Lincoln for an awards ceremony, which wasn't a costume party? Taken to pedaling a tricycle (while smoking a cigar) around another party?

He had long delighted in telling reporters about some of the gifts he had received: a gilded skull, a human thighbone, a frozen beef heart in a box for Valentine's Day. "I woke up the other night and felt like screaming," he once told a reporter. "I thought, 'Why not? No one will ever hear me.' So I let out a long, thin scream, and felt much better."

He visited snake farms. He was known to picnic in graveyards, and he sometimes took souvenirs. Friends of the cartoonist noted that it was always at Charlie's instigation that they found themselves dropping in at the "booby hatch," or the winter home of the Ringling Bros. circus freaks in Sarasota, Florida. "Charlie, what about you? What did you do over the weekend?" cartoonist Mort Gerberg asked Addams over lunch one day when the mundane conversation had turned to the subject of gypsy moths. "Well, it was really such a nice day on Sunday, I decided to take a friend for a drive—to Creedmore," said Addams, referring to the state psychiatric facility in Queens. Gerberg wasn't sure whether he was kidding.

Addams's friend Ralph Fields, a lawyer who had a home on Long Island, as Addams did, recalled the time the cartoonist offered him a ride back to the city. Addams arrived at the appointed hour in his 1926 35C Bugatti (the same model Isadora Duncan was riding in when the fringes of her neck shawl caught in the spokes of a rear wheel) and from there followed a route back to New York that took them by cemeteries "about seventy-five percent of the time," said Fields. "It was a beautiful day for looking at cemeteries."

But Addams's interest in "the aberrations of life," as his friend from Quogue, Walker McKinney, put it, also led to random acts of kindness. Addams took a keen interest in McKinney's brother, who had been brain damaged as a boy, giving him autographed copies of his cartoon collections and spiriting him away for rides in his classic cars, which included a red 1933 Aston Martin, a gleaming 1960 Bentley, and a 1927 Amilcar—"the poor man's Bugatti," Addams called it. He maintained a long correspondence with a fan who had been disabled in childhood by meningitis.

Addams's friends treasured his endless curiosity, and his irreverent, sometimes haunting one-liners: "Okay, let's get out the carving set!" he cried the day a bird hit the big glass window at a friend's barn and was killed. "Well, we'll stab them," he said when the soft-shell crabs another friend had ordered for an Addams birthday dinner turned up alive. (He and his hostess, Axie Whitney, gassed them in the oven instead.) "What a pity," he would sigh at the happy ending of a near-disaster. Was it any wonder that Addams loved W. C. Fields—a perpetrator, as George Carlin would point out, rather than a victim.

Everyone had an Addams story. Emmy and Billie Winburn, Savannah friends through Addams's old flame Odette (Benjamin) Terrel des

"Emily, have you ever put that in the window on a moonlit night?"

Chenes remembered the time Charlie noticed the white plaster horse head sitting on their fireplace mantel—the handiwork of their young daughter, Emily.

"Emily, have you ever put that in the window on a moonlit night?" he asked the girl.

"No."

"Try it," he said.

Though he was known to be a bon vivant and a lover of women (almost everyone had heard about his 1960s romance with actress Joan Fontaine), there was that undeniable dark streak. He saw bats where there were barn swallows. He had an unfortunate tendency to laugh at funerals. Then there were the things he kept in his homes, and in the trunk of his car. There was the woman—make that women—who had tried to kill him . . .

Bennett Cerf, who had published Addams's first cartoon collections at Random House, called him "the gentlest and kindest old schizophrene." A woman who had gone to school with Addams in Westfield, New Jersey, remembered him as an unsmiling "sinister figure prowling the dim halls of old W.H.S." without offering a salutation. (She claimed to have been afraid of him.) "People expected him to look like Lon Chaney, Jr., in *The Werewolf*," said Dick Cavett, who interviewed Addams in 1978 for his television show. Once, Cavett introduced the cartoonist to two women, who "kind of gripped each other" in apprehension before they saw him.

The true Addams was instantly reassuring. A well-dressed, courtly man with silvery backcombed hair and a gentle manner, he bore no resemblance to a fiend. He stood six feet one inch tall, with a head made for caricature: a big round nose, large ears, squinty eyes, and a thin-lipped mouth that never showed his teeth, even when he laughed—a source of endless fascination and second-guessing for children. "Charlie, do you have any teeth?" his wife's daughter had asked when she was little. (When he left the house, he suddenly turned around and made a face at the little girl, using all ten fingers to spread his mouth and expose his perfectly acceptable ivories.)

He had been immortalized in clay, paint, and print. Alexandra "Axie" Whitney, a former girlfriend, did a disarming sculpture of the cartoonist's

Readers interpreted this *New Yorker* cover as a
reference to Nazi concentration camps.

wonderful head. "The eyes aren't squinty enough," he'd told her, and sprang down from his perch to fix them. Artist Everett Raymond Kinstler caught the squinty, "twinkly" eyes perfectly. Though Addams was not a vain man, he liked the result of Kinstler's 1975 oil portrait enough to want to buy it. He was photographed by Bachrach, Beaton, and Penn. Peter DeVries borrowed pieces of Addams for the character of Pete Seltzer in his 1968 novella, *Witch's Milk:* a man whose extensive dental work had given "his smile a rather villainous air, at least until you got used to it." (Addams had seen pictures of himself smiling; he "looked so evil, he couldn't stand it," he told his friend Buddy Davie.)

And yet he walked the streets of Manhattan unrecognized. At newsworthy events, the camera would be trained on someone else. "Thank God no one knows my face," Addams told his wife as the flashes went off on one such occasion.

Addams had long claimed that he looked like the Addams Family's toothless grinning ghoul, Uncle Fester, "only with more hair." But even in the black bearskin coat he wore on the coldest days of a New York winter—a nine-pound garment with thirty-four-inch sleeves, in which the average man would have looked like David Copperfield in Mr. Dick's clothes—he was unthreatening. His coffee-colored eyes twinkled; he looked "like an elf—except that he was 6′ 4″ or so," said Mort Gerberg. (To the people who were surprised that Addams did not seem sinister in the flesh, he said, "I try not to let it show.")

And yet there was something familiar about Addams: People were sure they had seen him somewhere. One evening, he joined a group of cronies from the Vintage Sports Car Club at the Hotel Elysée on Fifty-fourth Street. They were all standing around enjoying a drink before dinner when a call girl entered the room and gravitated toward Addams. After a few moments' chat, she said, "You look like someone. Who are you?"

"I'm Bella Abzug's husband," said Addams.

Strangers sometimes mistook him for Walter Matthau (and once, Lyndon Johnson) because of his bulbous nose and crinkly eyes. "Mr. Matthau," a woman began on the street one day, only to be bitterly disappointed when Addams told her that he was not the actor. Even his voice, with its slow, "side-of-the-mouth delivery," as writer Sidney Offit described it—a faintly lisping drawl that was part New Jersey, part Addams—suggested Matthau. (In a peculiar symmetry, Matthau played Pete Seltzer in the 1972 movie version of *Witch's Milk, Pete 'n' Tillie.*)

And yet, said Offit, Addams had an "innate dignity," which set him apart from Matthau's screen image. Dressed in Brooks Brothers suits and Saks ties, "he looked like someone who once in a while did a cartoon, but had a very interesting and rather sophisticated life somewhere else," said cartoonist Lee Lorenz. Kennedy Fraser, who wrote *The New Yorker*'s "On and Off the Avenue" column, always thought of Addams "as a kind of 1940s and '50s New York figure." And with his faultless tailoring, Italian leather boots, and suave manner, he did seem to belong to that more stylish time of nightclubs and cigarette girls and big bands.

Still the questions and rumors persisted. What must his home be like? In the 1960s, the *New York Herald Tribune* ran a photograph of a fantasy Addams room—the cartoonist's lair as an interior designer had imagined it. The Addams habitat had "Surfwood walls," an "eery [*sic*] skylight," a stuffed snake slithering across a black Chinese desk, "and murky niches hung with such objects as primitive masks, headless puppets, and of course, a Vampira doll," noted the *Tribune*.

But the photograph did not prepare the visitor to the Addams apartment for the real thing.

The Addams dwelling at 25 West Fifty-fourth Street was directly behind the Museum of Modern Art, at the top of the building. It was reached by an ancient elevator, which rumbled up to the twelfth floor. From there, one climbed through a red-painted stairwell where a real mounted crossbow hovered. The Addams door was marked by a "big black number 13," and a knocker in the shape of a vampire.

The apartment consisted of the top two floors of the building. It stood under a leaky ten-thousand-gallon water tank which had flooded the bedroom at least once, destroying the drawings, photographs, papers, and other mementos Addams kept in boxes under the bed, as well as on closet shelves. The layout was equally eccentric. The bedroom, where Addams worked most of the time, was upstairs, accessible to the downstairs living room and kitchen only by outside service stairs.

Inside, one entered a little kingdom that fulfilled every fantasy one might have entertained about its inhabitant. On a pedestal in the corner of the bookcase stood a rare "Maximilian" suit of armor, which Addams had bought at a good price ("a bargain at $700") from the Litchfield Collection at Sotheby's Parke-Bernet gallery thirty years earlier. It was joined by a half suit, a North Italian Morion of "Spanish" form, circa 1570–80, and a collection of warrior helmets, perched on long stalks like decapitated heads: a late sixteenth-century German burgonet; a German trooper's lobster tail pot helmet, circa 1650; and the pointed fore-and-aft helmet from the sixteenth-century Italian suit, which was elaborately etched with game trophies, men-at-arms, monsters, birds. There were enough arms and armaments to defend the Addams fortress against the most persistent invader: wheel-lock guns; an Italian prod; two maces; three swords. Above a sofa bed, a spectacular array of medieval crossbows rose like birds in flight. "Don't worry, they've only fallen down once," Addams once told an overnight guest. The valuable pieces of medieval weaponry, which would ultimately fetch $220,113 at auction, mingled with books, framed cartoons and illustrations, photographs of classic cars, gruesome artifacts, and such inexpensive mementos as a mounted rubber bat.

Everywhere one looked in the apartment, something caught the eye. A rare papier-mâché and polychrome anatomical study figure, nineteenth century, with removable organs and body parts captioned in French, protected by a glass bell. ("It's not exactly another human heart beating in the house, but it's close enough," said Addams.) A set of engraved aquatint plates from an antique book on armor. A lamp in the shape of a miniature suit of armor, topped by a black shade. There were various snakes; biopsy scissors ("It reaches inside, and nips a little piece of flesh," explained Addams); and a shiny human thighbone—a Christmas present from one wife. There was a sewing basket fashioned from an armadillo, a gift from another.

In front of the couch stood a most unusual coffee table—"a drying out table," the man at the wonderfully named antiques shop, the Gettysburg Sutler, had called it. ("What was dried on it?" a reporter had asked. "Bodies," said Addams.) The table had holes in each corner for draining the fluids, a rusted adjustable headrest, and a mechanism for raising and lowering the neck. There was also, Addams genially pointed out, "a rather sinister stain in what would be the region of the kidneys." The table was covered with the usual decorative objects—a Baccarat goblet, a couple of plates, a miniature castle, a bowl of ceramic nesting snakes.

Some years earlier, following an Allman Brothers concert, eighteen-year-old Christopher Benjamin, the son of an old love, had arrived at the Addams apartment at about three in the morning. A lady friend of Charlie's came down the outside stairs from the bedroom to let the boy into the living room to sleep on the sofa bed. Christopher was "wiped out and tired" when he looked around the lamplit room for the first time "to see torture devices, armor, crossbows—a stunning end" to his adolescent adventure. He thought, "It doesn't get better than this."

"There was not a false note in that apartment," said Shirley Baty. Everything harmonized—and yet it was "sort of funny," remembered *New Yorker* cartoonist William Hamilton. "He'd have, say, a Currier & Ives print, but it would be of Siamese twins." And yet there was nothing gimmicky. Addams, for instance, would never have had one of those fancy bathroom chairs disguising a toilet, such as he had seen at the William F. Buckley apartment. "A throne should look like a throne," he protested.

Addams regarded even his grisliest artifacts with an artist's eye. He thought his crossbows—which were made of iron, steel, and walnut and exquisitely detailed with iron scrolling, Gothic slotted ornaments, and ivory and ebony inlays of running hounds, bears, and goats' heads— "quite beautiful." He loved the clean craftsmanship of his papier-mâché anatomical figure; he earnestly demonstrated how the brain came apart "like a walnut." Even "that ghastly table," as *New Yorker* cartoonist James Stevenson called it, once used for human embalming, was elegantly made, with mahogany legs and frame, brass fittings, and a "marvelous" canework top, said Addams. (The workmanship reminded Addams "of the old Rolls-Royces.") The human thighbone, noted Addams, had "taken on a beautiful patina."

By 1981, Addams had not only been trafficking in cartoons for half a century; he had published a dozen book collections, most recently *Creature Comforts,* released that year. Addams illustrations had graced the dust jackets of books by Peter DeVries, Wolcott Gibbs, Evelyn Waugh, and Brendan Gill; Addams cartoons adorned the walls of the Fogg Art Museum, the Metropolitan Museum of Art, the Rhode Island School of Design, the Museum of the City of New York, and the Pennsylvania University Museum. Addams originals were owned by Roald Dahl, Evelyn Waugh, John O'Hara, Ray Bradbury, Herbert Marshall, Ronald Coleman, "a New Haven doctor who specializes in medical humor," and a fortunate few others, including a friend who hung her two classic Addams cartoons on a wall with a Picasso and a Léger. His influence as a cartoonist was worldwide. Such was the Addams fan base that he once got a colonoscopy in exchange for a cartoon. He had won the Humor Award from Yale, an honorary doctorate from the University of Pennsylvania, and a special award from the Mystery Writers of America.

One quickly saw that the Addams wit, unlike that of many comic geniuses, was not confined to his art. Asked by a reporter whether he could fairly be described as "the progenitor of American middle-class macabre humor," Addams had blinked and said, "I have always thought of my family as upper-middle-class." He had told another reporter, "I like to think I've formed some terrible people. Won't people love to hear that I'm just a normal American boy?" And he talked with apparent candor about his claustrophobia and his fear of snakes, his unconventional—and macabre—last wedding, his struggle with cartoon ideas, his secularism.

"If I told you your work was theological, that much of its essence was theological as well as being funny, would you agree?" asked reporter John Callaway.

"Yes," said Addams, nodding. "I might even go into a corner and cry for a little while," he added, blowing his usual deadpan and laughing before he got through the sentence.

Once, said Addams, a priest had asked him about his religion. "Well, I believe in Mother Nature," Addams had told him. And the priest had said, "That's all right. As long as you believe in something." Addams seemed to remember the remark fondly.

Nancy Holmes once told Addams that everyone loved him. He asked how she described him to people. "As very nice," she said. "Lord, you're going to ruin my reputation," he told her. "Why don't you describe me as having the faint scent of formaldehyde?"

Were the crossbows mere props? Was it all a cover, just a gag? After all, fans sent him things. "You're run out of the house by brass lizards and bat door knockers and—you know," Addams had said. And he understood the impulse. People gave him such things "because they want me to be a man who likes shin bones," he said. "People must feel I need a skull." And yet Addams himself obviously delighted in his gruesome curiosities. They were "perhaps childlike enthusiasms," he said, "but I don't mind; it keeps you curious." Was it *vanitas*? Though Addams had described death as "a kind of cozy condition" that he thought shouldn't be too upsetting, he was also a collector; perhaps all the memento mori and the preoccupation with death and violence in his cartoons revealed an attempt to resist the inevitable by literally building a fortress against it.

Or was he working out unhealthy impulses in his cartoons? Was Addams, in fact, the genial man he appeared to be? And if so, how to explain the multiple marriages, and the abundance of cartoons about spousal killing? How to take the persistent, though untrue, story about his mental breakdowns?

Looking around the Addams apartment—the water tower, Addams called it—the observant reporter would note a dog bed on the premises, and various civilized touches—a homey afghan on the couch, fine pieces of furniture. But though Addams in 1981 had recently remarried, there was no sign of a wife on the premises. (The elevator man knew Addams as "the man with the dog.") The kitchen was minute, suggesting that the resident dined out a lot.

An investigation of the tightly packed cream-colored bookshelves backed in scarlet produced such titles as *The Bashford Dean Collection of Arms and Armour in The Metropolitan Museum of Art*, 1933, the three-volume 1842 edition of *A Critical Inquiry into Ancient Armour*—and a first edition of *Charlotte's Web*.

"What kind of a kid were you, aside from your drawing?" asked John Callaway.

"Well, a perfectly good-natured child, and no great problem," said Addams with his mischievous smile. And then he paused. "I was arrested at the age of eight . . ."

—

Chapter Two

A Normal American Boy

NEXT DOOR TO THE UNFORBIDDING ADDAMS HOUSE IN Westfield, New Jersey—a friendly 1907 Colonial Revival with a porch, a rolling lawn, and summer awnings—stood a rambling, irresistible Victorian house under repair, which eight-year-old Charlie had been itching to get inside. One day he got his chance. He broke in with some of the neighborhood kids and did the usual mischief—pulling down window shades, splashing paint around, filling the carpenters' shoes with wet mortar. Charlie (called "Chilly" by his friends for reasons long forgotten) "drew skeletons all over the walls." When the boys tired of their adventure, they drifted outside to play baseball in a nearby field. Then a policeman appeared.

"Are you Charles Addams?" he said.

"Yes," said Charlie, and ran like hell for home. There he hid in the attic until his mother called him downstairs.

"I had never seen a policeman with his hat off before," Addams remembered. "They took me down to the local court with the other children. My father paid the damages. It wasn't really an arrest, but I like to think of it as one."

Addams enjoyed saying that if he hadn't been a cartoonist, he might have been a criminal. But that was the romantic in him talking. His boyhood delinquency had in truth been limited to petty crime such as stealing tomatoes from a neighbor's garden. Later he progressed to freight car jumping—on a train "barely rolling," which suddenly speeded up. As soon as it slowed to about thirty miles an hour, Charlie and the other boy jumped off and "went end over end down an embankment. I think we hitchhiked and took a trolley to get home," said Addams.

Though Charlie Addams was known as something of a rascal around the neighborhood, and though he tried his damnedest to shake things up in Westfield—a conservative, upscale commuting town founded in 1720, which prided itself on its good principles and good roads—he knew that his efforts paled beside the real action going on in town. There was the "local bad boy" who ran off disguised as a woman in a stolen car and ended up on a Georgia chain gang, where he was ultimately stuffed into a barrel, rolled downhill, and suffocated. The story inspired a sensational 1932 book by Robert E. Burns and an Academy Award–nominated movie starring Paul Muni as fugitive James Allen. (Arthur Mallifert, as he was known in Westfield, would find his way into a couple of Addams cartoons, including the 1981 "Mallifert Twins." In the waiting room of A. G. Whincoop, Patent Attorney, sit two lumpy men with close-cropped hair, suspiciously regarding each other. They look exactly alike, down to the pens clipped to their shirt pockets, the eyeglasses dangling from cords around their necks, and their homely inventions. "Separated at birth, the Mallifert twins meet accidentally," reads the caption.) And there was the Addams family dentist, who hanged himself in the swamp near Surprise Lake. "I don't know whether it was the trouble he was having with my teeth, or what," said Addams. In Westfield, he said, "I was always aware of the sinister family situations behind those Victorian façades." His earliest memory, dating from the age of eighteen months, was of an old man getting run over by an automobile.

Addams later claimed that the ideas for his darker cartoons came while he walked the streets of Westfield. He borrowed the town's Rialto Theatre, with its fifties marquee jutting out over the sidewalk, for a 1960 cartoon. The featured film is *The Killer Moth* ("Stark Sheer Terror . . . Most Terrifying Story Ever Filmed!" screams the poster). In the respectable-looking crowd exiting the theater is Uncle Fester, who confides to the hooded figure next to him, "Well, at least it was true to life." Atop the marquee lurks a giant unseen moth.

Addams liked to think of himself as the only native of Westfield who went on to vote for Franklin Roosevelt. A convenient forty-five-minute commute from New York by boat or by rail, with 125 trains running daily, Westfield offered wide, shady streets in well-built neighborhoods. Downtown, "towering masses of brick and stone buildings" were cooled by a river breeze. Here were fine schools, churches of all denominations, and a beautiful eighteen-hole golf course. "We make no attempt to set forth its advantages in the seductive style of the West," boasted *The Westfield Leader.*

If Westfield was, as Addams saw it, King's Row—"a good clean town" teeming with sordid private intrigues and crimes, as in the 1940 Henry Bellamann novel of that name—the shutters at 522 Elm Street had nothing wicked to hide. "I know it would be more interesting, perhaps, if I had a ghastly childhood—chained to an iron bed and thrown a can of Alpo every day," said Addams. But "I'm one of those strange people who actually had a happy childhood."

He came from ordinary beginnings in an ordinary town during a fairly quiet moment in history. World War I was still two years away. Nothing very exciting was happening in the vicinity of Westfield. The year of the cartoonist's birth—1912—was distinguished by the sinking of the *Titanic,* the election of Woodrow Wilson as the nation's twenty-eighth president, and the discovery of the fifty-thousand-year-old Piltdown Man, which later proved to be a hoax.

The beloved only child of Charles Huey Addams, a manager and sometime "commercial traveler" for the Aeolian Company, a premier maker of pipe organs and player pianos, and Grace Spear Addams, a homemaker, Charles Samuel Addams arrived in the world at the considerate hour of one o'clock in the afternoon, on Friday, January 7, apparently in the house his parents were renting at 511 Summit Avenue. He weighed eight pounds. He began smiling at the end of his second month, and never stopped. From infancy he would laugh "for anyone until he became and is known as the most remarkably good-natured baby in the town," wrote Grace in his baby book. "The photographer told me one of his pictures showing the jolly expression was a great drawing card for them and [he] kept it in the window for many weeks," she recorded. There was something else about this exceptionally happy baby. He "crept on his face for some time before he could manage to raise himself," wrote

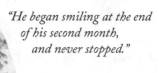

*"He began smiling at the end
of his second month,
and never stopped."*

*Charlie's mother, Grace
Spear Addams, regarded
each new stage of Charlie's
development with
naturalness, irreverence,
and humor.*

*Charles Huey Addams knew
what was "beyond price."*

Grace. The delighted new mother, who was thirty-three years old at her son's birth and had been married some nine years, soon abandoned the baby book entirely in favor of the baby.

At the house with the porch and the summer awnings were a lilac hedge, a dog named Peter, and three doting adults—Charlie's mother and father and Grandma Spear, on whom he later based the Addams Family's grandma. The cartoon grandmother—a humped, goggle-eyed, smiling hag with wispy white hair and a shawl, who makes bat cookies for the children and tells them fairy stories about the dragon who "gobbled up the handsome young prince and lived happily ever after"—"could have been my Grandma Spear in the early morning," Addams reflected. "Just before breakfast," he added with a sly smile.

By the time she came to live with her daughter and son-in-law, at least two years before Charlie was born, she was widowed and presumably wounded by a scandal Charlie seems not to have known about. And yet it is from Grandma Spear—born Emma Louise Tufts in Jersey City, New Jersey, into the old Massachusetts family for whom Tufts University is named—that Addams got his most illustrious collateral ancestors: two American presidents and a signer of the Declaration of Independence. (Emma was directly descended from Anne Adams, a third cousin of President John Adams, thereby linking cartoonist Addams to John Adams and John Quincy Adams.) Through a related branch of the family, he was a distant cousin of Samuel Adams. Emma married Howard Spear, a New York fertilizer merchant, with whom she had three children. And it was here, in the Spear grandfather, that the family history took a disreputable turn.

Howard Spear had no sooner ascended to the position of clerk in the Second District Court in the Bronx than his accounts showed a small irregularity. Though he was not charged with embezzlement, he was formally warned to get his books in order. When fifty-six-year-old Howard Spear died of appendicitis in 1903, he was almost certainly facing the consequences of financial misconduct. His death certificate listed him as married, but with no occupation; his parents' names and birthplaces were "unknown."

And so kindly Grandma Spear, who was sixty-eight and shuffling when Charlie was born and therefore always old in his eyes, occupied the upstairs floor in the house on Elm Street. She fretted about her fifteen-year-old grandson's leaving for summer camp in Ocean Grove without his felt hat. (In a letter, she urged him to get a cheap hat at the shore to wear in the sun.) She loomed large enough in his childhood to secure a place at the top of the list of mostly cryptic names and phrases he scribbled for a memoir he never wrote, "1912–1924: Memoir of a Prepuberty Wasp." ("Grandma Spear" came before "Erection Ring," "Officer Miller and Big Arrest," and "Lowe's Chauffeur and Ku Klux.")

Addams never tired of telling how as a boy he would slide down the laundry chute at home to the pantry where Grandma Spear was making tea or baking a pie—controlling his descent by sticking out his elbows. Then he would jump out and scare the wits out of her. On at least one occasion, she spanked him, proving "stronger than he had expected." But "mostly she was very kind to me," he said. Along with borrowing her for the Addams Family's grandma, Addams clipped both of her surnames—Tufts and Spear—for the tombstones in one of his cemetery cartoons.

If his parents ever touched him except in affection, Addams left no record of it. Even in the various accounts of his "big arrest"—which included a *True Detective*–like version in which the cops traced Charlie by his muddy footprints, and he "wore a different pair of shoes" for a week "to throw them off the track"—Addams mentioned no punishment for his crime. And yet he was not spoiled. The beloved son in the black-and-white Addams family photographs was by every account respectful, devoted, and entirely appreciative. As writer Leila Hadley put it, "Charlie was the only person I ever knew who had only good things to say about each of his parents."

Grace Spear Addams was forty by the time her only child started school, and she responded to motherhood as one accepts a longed-for gift, with gratitude and pleasure. "At three weeks he could follow objects, with a decided intelligence in his eyes," she wrote in the "Our Baby" book. (And his eyes, by the way, were the "deepest blue.") Her own merry eyes, which were wide-set and framed by handsome dark brows, like her son's, seem to have regarded each new stage of Charlie's development, each boyhood antic, with naturalness, irreverence, and humor.

"Little Charlie Addams is a funny cup o' tea," she wrote on the back of a comic photograph of Charlie, about age ten, posing in front of a lake in his belted swimming suit.

Much of the Addams humor—his jokiness, his amused view of the world—came from his mother. To her husband, Grace commented privately on Charlie's nose, which underwent a startling metamorphosis one adolescent summer. "Get a load of the nose," she said when she and Charles picked their son up at camp. She laughed off sexual matters. When she accidentally walked in on Charlie in the bathroom when he had an erection, she reassured him. It was all right, she said; he was just growing. (When he said, "Oh, shit," in front of a prim Westfield matron, she lightly scolded, "Oh, Charlie, you stop that, you stop that.") And when he came home drunk at seventeen, she imitated his muffled speech. "Muff muff," she said, laughing. "Muff muff."

Her husband, like her son, adored her. "Girlie," Charles Sr. called her; "Dollie," "Lovey dove," "Gracie," "my anchor," "my guiding star," "a treasure beyond price," wrote Charles Huey Addams. Once, arriving at a hotel in Wichita and finding not one but two letters from her, he had saved one to read the next day, thereby giving himself the pleasure of hearing from her on both days of his business stay. "You must get tired of reading this so often," he told her in an undated letter, "but I think and keep repeating my great admiration for you."

Dressed in vest and pinstripes and polished shoes, pinching some papers between his fingers, the smiling, attractive, middle-aged man leaning against an ornately carved piano in a formal photograph, who was often obliged to be away from his loved ones on Aeolian Company business, knew what was "beyond price."

It was Isaac Addams, Charles Huey's great-great-grandfather, who set the Addams family apart by adding the second *d* to his surname, presumably to distinguish himself from a neighbor. Isaac's grandson, John Huy Addams, was a prominent Illinois farmer, miller, banker, and politician (Abraham Lincoln called him "My dear Double D'ed Addams"). John Huy was the father of social reformer Jane Addams, "Saint Jane," the second woman to win the Nobel Peace Prize. Jane Addams and cartoonist Charles Addams were therefore first cousins twice removed. But it was Samuel Huy Addams, Charles Huey's father, who added the historical drama to the family and began Addams's abiding interest in the

Civil War. At the age of eighteen, in 1861, the Pennsylvania farm boy joined Rush's Lancers (Company K, 6th Pennsylvania Cavalry) to fight in the Civil War. Captured at Brandy Station and thrown into the notorious Libby prison, he missed his regiment's bloody engagements at Gettysburg and Second Manassas, but was released—miraculously intact—in time to fight in the horrific showdown between Grant and Lee at Cold Harbor. It was Lee's last great victory in the field, in which both sides suffered devastating losses. Spared once again, Samuel Huy Addams mustered out of the Union Army in October 1864 and settled into a long life in Canton, Ohio, marrying twice and prospering with the help of an inheritance, though he applied to the army for an invalid's pension. From his first marriage, to Pennsylvanian Kate Rheinhold, came three children, including Charles Huey, born in Canton in 1873.

Grandpa Addams was deeply religious, as virtually all Civil War soldiers were—an influence that led to the Addams secularism. "I think [my father] saw so much of religion, the old-time Jehovah's Witnesses type of thing, that he'd had enough of it," said Addams, by way of explaining the lack of churchgoing in his own small family. "And I think he didn't want to see the inside of a church again." In the unwritten Addams memoir, his paternal grandfather landed at the bottom of the scribbled list of names and phrases. The suggestion was that Grandpa talked too much of God, and too little of war.

But the old veteran, who had inherited money from his father, saw to it that his children got a good education. Charles Huey Addams was one of the few young men of his working-class community to finish high school. Five years later he became a naval architect and shipbuilder. But about ten years before Charlie's birth, with little call for naval architects during peacetime, Charles took a job as a salesman for the venerable Aeolian Company, and thereafter confined his shipbuilding to graceful wooden boats his son later proudly displayed on the walls of his own home.

Often on the road, Charles moved from hotel to hotel and city to city without complaint. He sent roasted chestnuts back to his family to remind them of him. He had made only one sale, he wrote Grace in an undated letter, but he was trying not to be discouraged. In his frequent letters home, he sympathized with his wife, urging her on during her bouts of loneliness and back trouble, and praised and encouraged his son, whom he called "Skid." "I surely miss you especially in the morning after shaving as I want to go into your room and pull and romp with you," he wrote the summer Charlie was twelve. And he concluded "with lots of love, and a hug and a couple of punches in the stomach from your Daddy."

Charles moved swiftly from salesman to manager of the wholesale department, and from house renter to owner the year Charlie was eight.

In later years, Addams told two stories that summed up his doting

Charlie and his father, who liked to "pull and romp" with him.

parents. The first took place in Chicago, where the little family moved on Aeolian business for a year. It was the only time in Charlie's youth that he lived away from Westfield, and it was his first day of school. His parents had bought him "a dark red coat with a fur collar"—beaver. And he remembered "sitting on a little carousel with some other kids [when] one of the Chicago kids said, 'What is it, a boy or a girl?' And I went back and told my parents. They said, 'Well, you don't have to wear the coat to school anymore.' "

The second story concerned the Iron Maiden of Nuremberg, the life-sized torture chamber shaped like a woman with spikes on the inside to impale its victim, which later turned up among the torture devices in an Addams cartoon about a garage sale, and in other drawings, including one showing smiling Grandma Addams at her old black sewing machine in the attic, making an oversized garment and using an Iron Maiden as a dressmaker's dummy. As a boy, Charlie had once seen an Iron Maiden in an antiques shop, but he hadn't been able to afford it. What would his parents have thought if he'd requested it for his birthday? a reporter later wondered.

"I think they'd have looked at each other and then possibly bought me one," said Addams.

"Ah. They were very understanding in that way?"

"Just what the boy wants."

And such was the closeness between parents and child that six-year-old Charlie included his mother and father on his own Christmas list. Along with "dum bells," ice skates, toy boats, tools, a wristwatch, "a Bee-bee gun," games, and "a wind up engine" for Christmas of 1919, he asked for "some fairy tale books" and "The Book of Knowledge" for "Mama and Daddy and me."

It was "a happy childhood full of boy scouts and *Treasure Island*," summer camp, and imaginary play. "There was always a little group of boys at his house, doing things," remembered a Westfield friend, Allison Mackay. Every year Charlie went to Wilke's Toy Store to buy a ghost mask for Halloween—"I wouldn't have considered being anything but a ghost!" said Addams. The mask had a "cheese-like, pasty smell—it just smelled so much worse than the other masks." There were picnics along the brook with little Norma Hill, and amateur theatricals in the cupola of the spooky Victorian on the corner of Elm. Charlie and Norma invented the plots, wrote the dialogue, and made costumes. (The plays were "very weird," remembered Norma.) At the corner Victorian, "I must have buried 50 treasures," he said. "Dog skulls . . . whatever I had in my pocket." And there was a house on stilts twenty feet high—a "Treehut," which "could be well defended with BB guns"—where Charlie used to sleep. From the roof, where Charlie liked to sit while his father read the paper on the deck below, hung an old-fashioned wooden sign painted with a duck and the words "Duck Inn." Sometimes he'd be Robin Hood, sometimes Running Fox, his camp name. "I lived in my imagination in the backyard," said Addams.

The truth was, his dentist's suicide was the "only exciting thing that ever happened to me," said Addams.

If the Addams childhood offers a clue to the cartoons that came later, and to the man who collected working crossbows, it lies in the claustrophobia that also took hold then. At some point, Charlie became "A Little Apprehensive," he wrote at the top of his list of memoir notes. Then he wrote "Tiny" above "Little." As a boy he feared being locked in a closet. "I wasn't much for the underground huts all the kids were building in those days. And I was always glad to get out," he said.

Though Addams left no record of childhood trauma, he did note that his mother was also claustrophobic.

"She is a wonderful mother, and always planning for your good," Charles Sr. wrote the summer Charlie was twelve. The surviving letters, though written mostly after Charlie had graduated from high school and left home, evoke a woman whose spirits were frequently, even seriously, low. From the grand old Hotel de Soto in Savannah in 1930, where Charles had taken Grace for a few days' holiday after she met him in Charleston, he wrote his son, "Mom came just in time to avoid a breakdown. The loneliness of her situation was almost more than could be expected for a mother to stand. I am glad to say that she is again happy and the only thing to make it complete is to have you with us. . . ."

While Charlie seems never to have felt burdened by his mother's dependency on him, he shared her fearfulness. And he developed something more than the typical childish interest in the spirits of the dead. He haunted the town's old Presbyterian churchyard, where the copper-colored Revolutionary War stones tilted on the sloping, tree-shaded lawn, spending hours alone there, just staring at the graves and "imagining the ghosts inside." He took nothing, and committed no vandalism. He just liked to read the tombstones and "imagine who was lying down there, and what they looked like now." He also speculated that "maybe I was trying to scare myself."

Chapter Three

—

Be Prepared

"THERE'S A LEGEND IN WESTFIELD," SAID ADDAMS. "THEY say instead of locking me in the west wing of the family mansion they gave me a pencil and whipped me until I drew pictures." From almost the moment he could hold a crayon in his chubby baby hand, Charlie had begun drawing with a happy vengeance.

Into the sunny blue childhood, past the town's brick and stone buildings cooled by the river breeze, past the lilac hedge and the dog named Peter, the Great War had arrived. Armed with paper and a fistful of crayons in World War I Westfield, the grinning, doted-upon son "damned the Kaiser and hung him." He ran him over with a train and "had him stabbed, shot, boiled in oil, and torpedoed at sea." At the age of two, Charlie put the Kaiser under a Macy's truck. Though the war ended before Charlie's seventh birthday, it lived on in his imagination. ("The Hun Within," he wrote in his memoir notes.) Flags, a fighter plane, and a parachute festooned the Christmas tree that six-year-old Charlie drew on his 1919 letter to Santa, mingling with the candy canes and stars.

Addams would credit his father for his talent ("I think what talent I have I inherited from him," he said, adding, "Father drew well himself, though his style, like most architects', was rather dry and sparse"), and the great illustrators and storytellers of the day for shaping him as an artist. He soaked up the spectacular dark wood engravings of Gustave Doré, whose work included romantic and often grotesque depictions of

The Inferno, The Raven, and Perrault's fairy tales; he absorbed the powerful black-and-white draftsmanship of John Tenniel, whose illustrations added both humor and dimension to Aesop's fables and *Alice's Adventures in Wonderland,* a book that would inspire a number of Addams cartoons. Arthur Rackham's "moody backgrounds, gnarled trees, [and] grinning witches" infiltrated the nursery, and took hold.

When Charlie was in second grade, he spilled some water in art class. Told by Miss Hunt that he could no longer paint with the class, Charlie said, "I don't care. I'll have more fun my own self." He drew his third-grade teacher "as a sort of pretty harpy with pointy ears." He sketched death's-heads and skeletons until his mother began to worry. The boy who lived in his imagination in the backyard began to live on paper as well.

As an older boy, he came under the spell of Albert Pinkham Ryder, the nineteenth-century "necrophiliac artist," as Addams called him, known for his lyrical, dreamlike paintings. He read Grimm and Poe, Stevenson's *The Black Arrow,* and Conan Doyle—particularly such blood-and-thunder works as *Sir Nigel* and *The White Company,* which propelled him into the middle of the fourteenth century, the Hundred Years' War, and the chivalric world of knights and castles.

By age twelve—knobby-kneed and "freckled to death"—he resolved to make his own suit of armor. And so he wrote a letter to Dr. Bashford Dean, the first curator of arms and armor at the Metropolitan Museum of Art, inquiring how to go about it. Informed by Dr. Dean that apprentice knights were required to put in seven years at an armorer's shop before they were allowed to make their first suit, Charlie decided on a longbow instead. He designed it himself, and made the wooden stock under the supervision of his indulgent father, who provided the materials. Charlie used his longbow to shoot balloons at Surprise Lake, where his dentist had hanged himself.

Always his parents were there, urging him on. "Your map of the lake was so clear and well defined that I know exactly where you are located," his father wrote twelve-year-old Charlie at Eagle Lake one summer. At some point, Grace hand-carried Charlie's drawings to the *New York Herald World* office of the famous H. T. Webster, creator of Caspar Milquetoast. Webster told her to forget about her son's dreams of an art career. He had no talent.

When he was thirteen Charlie won a drawing contest sponsored by a local chain of clothing stores. His winning entry, published in *Ropeco* magazine, showed a Boy Scout coming to the aid of a man being electrocuted on high-tension wires. Wearing rubber boots, the scout stood on a rubber mat. The caption said, "Be Prepared." The prize was ten dollars' worth of store merchandise. Charlie spent it on a baseball mitt and a hunting knife.

The boy with the homemade longbow grew into a slender, dreamy young man whose high school notebook was covered with sketches of knights in armor. He was the kid doodling in class instead of taking notes, the kid drawing "funny-looking people" and handing them to Norma Hill to make her laugh. ("Very careless in Exam," wrote an irritated teacher on a report card.) Classmate Helen Miller recalled the more appreciative Miss Day, who taught high school English. One day she caught sight of Charlie bent over a sketch in class, his face wreathed in a smile. As Miss Day talked about Shakespeare, she drifted to the back of the room to Charlie's chair, looked over his shoulder at his drawing, and laughed outright. "She made class interesting, and he made it funny," said Helen Miller. Filing into homeroom in the morning, his classmates were greeted by an Addams cartoon on the blackboard, typically starring one of them. To them, Charlie was "a neverending source of interest, both flattering and otherwise, in sixth period English."

Charlie would saunter through the corridors of Westfield High School in a patterned V-neck sweater and a smile; he had thick, dark hair, which he wore combed back (he was good-looking, said Dorothy Masenior Bass), and was typically accompanied by one or more of an eclectic army of friends: the smartest girl in the class, the prettiest girl, a football player. Described as "very bright" and quiet, he was by turns friendly and shy, and conspicuous in the best way. "You should have seen him imitate snuff-inhaling English gentlemen and accomplished harpists," said his high school yearbook. "You couldn't help but like him," said Helen Miller. Though he was not much of an athlete, he ran track and served as scrub on the football team. But mostly he gravitated toward the more creative pursuits: the Art Club, the literary magazine (called *The Weather Vane*), and various committees. He was the rare adolescent who belonged—not just to the popular group, but everywhere. ("Chilly" became "Chil.")

—

BY THE TIME Charlie reached high school, he had been working at his scrawlings, as he called them, for a decade or more, and he was serious about them. He served as art editor of *The Weather Vane,* dressing it up with cartoons and illustrations. He even contributed a tender short story, about a black dockworker-turned-actor. In defiance of H. T. Webster, he created a cartoon strip called "Laughs from the School." Filled with inside jokes about the teachers, Senior Day costumes, and the like, "Laughs" was something of an adolescent version of Jefferson Machamer's newspaper strip, "Gags and Gals."

Like all young artists, Addams learned by imitating. While the nursery gods called Doré, Rackham, and Tenniel hovered nearby, Addams absorbed the popular Machamer, whose cartoons were published in *Judge, Life,* and *College Humor,* and took in the deft, fluid lines of Percy Crosby, creator of the nine-year-old street kid Skippy, hero of a full-page cartoon that began in the humorous *Life* in 1923. Another idol was George Herriman, whose *Krazy Kat* strip ran in the Hearst papers from 1913 to 1944. The revered *Krazy Kat*—distinguished in part by strong characters, literary allusions, shifting background scenes, and an outsider quality—was the first comic to win serious critical appraisal. In his 1924 essay, Gilbert Seldes called Herriman "the counterpart of Chaplin."

Charlie was headed for a career as a serious illustrator, but the jokes kept staging a breakout. In class he would race through his mechanical drawing assignment in order to begin a cartoon. Content to be a middling student whose only A was in Drawing II, he seemed to take nothing seriously. Coleridge? He drew a funny ancient mariner. Washington Irving? A Sleepy Hollow schoolmaster, hat flying, astride a galloping, laughing horse. Latin was Caesar doing leg lifts, and Ariovistus on Caesar's knee. In collaboration with his friend Jim Moore, who presumably wrote the Latin text (Charlie having earned a C– in Latin II), he drew a series of Latin cartoons, sometimes "mauling clichés." In translation:

Student: "We come to bury Caesar, not to praise him."
Teacher: "Who said this?"
Student: "Some undertaker."

—

FROM ITS FIRST slender fifteen-cent issues in 1925, *The New Yorker*—the sophisticated weekly magazine founded *not* "for the old lady in Dubuque"—had offered a dazzling display of illustrations, decorative "spot" drawings and headings, caricatures of show people such as the

Chas Addams in high school: "He amazed us."

Marx Brothers and Gloria Swanson—and comic drawings, in a wide range of styles, by some of the most talented artists and illustrators around: Gardner Rea, Helen Hokinson, Al Freuh, Garrett Price, I. Klein, Alice Harvey, and John Held, Jr. Many of the magazine's striking, smart-

looking covers were drawn by the stylish Rea Irvin, a longtime professional cartoonist and art editor whose own work was influenced by the
clean lines of Japanese prints.

But *The New Yorker*'s founder and editor, Harold Ross, had not been
satisfied with the primitive drawings that passed for cartoons—essentially
illustrations with text. In those "he/she" drawings, word and line never
became fully integrated. With Rea Irvin—Ross's artistic conscience at
the magazine—he began guiding *The New Yorker*'s favored artists toward
more lively comic drawings with a single caption. By the fall of 1926,
modern cartoons had begun squeezing out the static "he/she" drawings
and coming into their own. And by the late twenties, the cartoons were
superb, the art in full swing.

The three major artists of the early *New Yorker*—Peter Arno
(Addams thought Arno was incredible), Helen Hokinson, and Gluyas
Williams—were already there. Arno was everywhere: in his series about
a pair of tippling charwomen called "The Whoops Sisters"; in the decorative headings he drew for "The Talk of the Town" or a profile; in *New
Yorker* covers—and best of all in his big, brassy cartoons, drawn in a
razzle-dazzle style with heavy black strokes. Helen Hokinson's timeless,
marvelous matrons—another *New Yorker* staple, top-heavy and frivolous,
and drawn with a unique tenderness—traipsed into the cartoons on their
sensible heels. The peerless full-page drawings of Gluyas Williams—the
Fred Astaire of line—also graced the magazine during this time.

Addams "liked the feeling for the city. And I liked the muted tastes and
the accuracy of it, and of course, I loved the cartoons." As soon as he saw
The New Yorker, he thought, "Well, that's the magazine I want to work for."

With a 1928 cartoon in *The Weather Vane*, the sixteen-year-old cartoonist began inching away from imitation. It shows two small boys approaching a dinosaur skeleton in a museum. As the smaller boy climbs up
the stand to touch the mounted relic, the other shouts, "Look out, Pete!
It might be Lon Chaney!"

But looking back at his *Weather Vane* days, Addams could remember
nothing that hinted at the sinister work to come. It was all "better forgotten," he said. Though he saved his adolescent scrawlings, he couldn't
stand to look at them. "We were drawing pictures, you know, remotely resembling Robin Hood and Ben-Hur—chariot races," said Addams. In

carefully composed scenes titled "When Knights Were Bold" or "When Streets Ran with Blood," Addams knights clashed on horseback in front of a castle; a masked executioner waited by a guillotine as a swarming mob carried human heads on pikes. The class of 1929 even took the me-

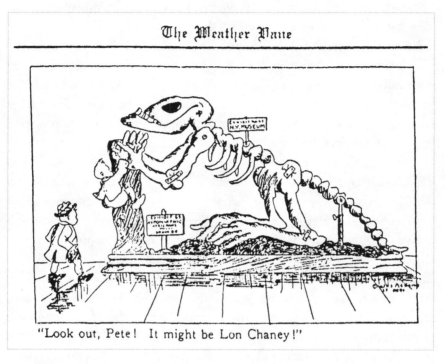

The Weather Vane

"Look out, Pete! It might be Lon Chaney!"

dieval age as its inspiration, dividing itself into knights and ladies. Among those earning a "Distinction"—Class Scribe, Class Bard—was Charles Addams, Class Peintour. His schoolmates knew he would be a success. "He amazed us," said his yearbook legend.

Chapter Four

Sex Fiend Slays Tot

P EOPLE ALWAYS WANTED TO KNOW WHEN THE SINISTER stuff began. "I would think when I first started working for *The New Yorker*, I stumbled across something," said Addams. He couldn't "remember that there was a real beginning to it," and he preferred not to look under the hood. As he put it elsewhere, "Like everyone else, I suppose, I had some perfectly outrageous and evil ideas and I fooled around for a long time trying to transform them into humor." Asked where he picked up "his interest in the bizarre," he said, "That's like asking a bird how he learned to sing."

The truth was, the ideas had always come hard—so hard, Addams wasn't eager to be reminded of it. Asked what it was like to be a young cartoonist, he said, "It was a very tough business, and it still is." He had a lingering image of himself at his boyhood home in New Jersey "looking out the window and trying to think up things."

It was an indication of how painful he had found the fledgling years that he remembered the period from his first cartoon sale to *The New Yorker* until his work began appearing regularly there as about six years, though his journey out of obscurity had in fact been fairly swift.

First a stint at Colgate, because "practically everyone in Westfield went to Colgate," where he entertained his classmates by sketching "voluptuous nudes" in his notebook during English Lit and drawing cartoons in the manner of the popular Rube Goldberg—whose work featured ludicrously elaborate inventions to meet mundane needs such as keeping a man from forgetting to mail his wife's letter, or sharpening a pencil—which Addams mimeographed and passed around.

"I hope Charlie is making progress in his studies and drawing," Charles Sr. wrote Grace from the road.

In her own letters to Charlie, Grace urged him to eat breakfast, write as often as he could—"as that helps a lot"—and "be sure to get plenty of cartoons in the next issue" of the college paper.

Grandma Spear was gone now; she had died in 1928, when Charlie was sixteen. With Charlie away at school, Grace was now utterly alone during Charles's business trips. "I dread to have Daddy leave so soon again and would go with him if it were not so expensive—as it really is very lonely at times," she wrote Charlie at school.

After a year at Colgate, Charlie transferred to the University of Pennsylvania. He was under the impression that he could study art there, but art turned out to be first-year architecture. There followed a drifting year of hilarious times spent with seven roommates crammed into the top floor of the Theta Chi fraternity off campus. He remembered hazy Prohibition nights in nearby Camden, drinking the powerful grappa—"a foul distillation of wine, of the dregs of wine"—followed by raucous games of frat-house pool which left the felt tabletop in tatters. And yet by October 1930, he was coming home every weekend to be with his mother. He left Penn after a year, passing all but two of his courses, for which he took incompletes, and moved on to the Grand Central School of Art.

The school was situated at the top of Grand Central Terminal on East Forty-second Street. In this unlikely setting Addams at last found a real art school, with fifteen hundred students and an accomplished faculty composed of painters, watercolorists, sculptors, illustrators, a designer of stained glass windows, a muralist, and a costume designer, some of them award winners, some with international reputations. "They didn't let you touch color until you'd done a million black and whites," said Lyda Barclay Hall, who, as Lyda Barclay, met Addams there when they were both nineteen. They took one class together, Miss Hilton's design and commercial art course.

Lyda was freshly arrived from Georgia, and so pretty she might have been taken for a film star; Charlie was thin and frightening-looking, thought Lyda, with bad skin—and irresistible charm. He was always joking; she was very gullible. She believed every story he told her, including the one about the dog he kept in his school locker, whom he pretended to feed. One night Lyda was walking alone on Third Avenue when she heard a gruff voice behind her: "Hello, White Girl," Charlie said. He was the first friend she made in New York.

When he should have been in class, he was in the bustling Beaux Arts terminal downstairs, watching people. Or he would ride the double-decker open-air buses on Fifth Avenue and study the architecture—a sweep of Gothic Revival, limestone, Art Deco, Gilded Age town-houses, and neo-Renaissance apartment buildings, grand in scale and offering ornamental moldings and Art Nouveau touches. One day in 1931, he did a sketch of a window washer on a tall building—an airy bird's-eye view—and dropped it off at the *New Yorker* offices at 25 West Forty-fifth Street, neglecting to include a return envelope. When he went back for the sketch months later, he was surprised to learn that it had been accepted as a decorative spot (a drawing used by *The New Yorker* as an end-of-column or space filler). He swept into Grand Central waving his $7.50 *New Yorker* check at Lyda. She thought he had forged it.

The unsigned Addams window washer ran at the bottom of the "Among the Books" section in the February 6, 1932, issue of the magazine, felicitously placed in the middle of a capsule review of Christopher Morley's *Swiss Family Manhattan.*

And so at the age of twenty Addams got his toehold, albeit a tenuous one, at *The New Yorker.* By now, James Thurber was there. William Steig was drawing "Small Fry," a popular series about the adventures of a beguiling city urchin in knickers and cap. George Price, who would become another Addams favorite, was just starting to contribute, drawing mostly spots. Helen Hokinson's frequent cover paintings showing her familiar sentimental matron attended by servants and waiters as she travels the world with her uneasy-looking Scottie, impervious to the stock market crash, was giving *The New Yorker* some of the best cover art it would ever publish. Along with the full-scale black-and-white Gluyas Williams illustrations of the party scene and the industrial crises, the magazine ran big drawings by William Crawford Galbraith that looked like paintings.

Also running at this time was a witty but short-lived series by Richard Decker which suggested the future Addams, in humor if not in style: a striped convict in his cell reads various letters—from the IRS; the Court of the City of New York, calling him to jury duty; and his mother, saying that her son Otto has been absent from school for six days.

Addams liked that in cartoons "the idea is important." He was learning that he could be serious about his art without drawing serious subject matter. And anyway, he reasoned, as he continued to work on his cartoons, it seemed that everything he drew came out funny.

"I DON'T KNOW if I'm happy with the direction that Charlie's mind is taking," said Charles Sr. upon learning that his son wanted to be a cartoonist. Grace worried about Charlie's ability to make a living. Still, whatever their misgivings, his parents remained supportive. Charlie was their "golden boy," said Lyda Barclay. Anyone could see it.

Three months after Charlie's big break in *The New Yorker,* his father died at home. It was about nine-thirty one evening in May 1932, two months after Charles had suffered a brain hemorrhage. He was just fifty-eight years old, and he had been battling arthritis and hypertension. Charlie now "thought he'd better get on with his art development," said his former Colgate roommate, Ralph Jones. And so he left the Grand Central School and got a job retouching crime scene photographs at *True Detective* magazine in New York.

Hired at $15 a week, "terrible" money even during "the nadir of the Depression," said Addams, he did lettering, diagrammed crime scenes re-creating "how the murderer moved about the room," drew "the X where the body was found," and painted the blood out of some of the grislier police shots that ran with the stories—an exercise that might be compared to blotting stains from a suit of clothes with benzene. It required skill rather than talent. Addams personally liked the pictures the way they were, "with just a tad more blood and gore," he said.

"This was just a job, just a job, but ya know, it didn't hurt me," Addams later told Steven Aronson.

"As an exercise in technique?" asked Aronson.

"Absolutely."

"But didn't it also nourish your imagination in some way?" asked Aronson.

"Not a bit," said Addams.

It was the era captured in a flashbulb. Here were the glory days of organized crime and mythical figures such as Al "Scarface" Capone and Lucky Luciano. Sinister figures in pearl-gray homburgs cruised the city streets in big Packards. Bonnie and Clyde, John Dillinger and his gang, tore around the dirt roads of the Midwest, robbing banks and bumping off anyone who got in their way. As the Depression wore on well into the 1930s and prosperity was no longer just around the corner, criminal executions soared, reaching their zenith in 1935 with 199. William Edward Hickman was put to death for the kidnapping and dismembering of a two-year-old child; Bruno Richard Hauptmann got the chair for the kidnapping and murder of the Lindbergh baby. The *Daily News* served up a grainy photograph of Ruth Snyder "just as they turned the juice on," recalled Addams, in the electric chair at Sing Sing for the murder of her husband. As Addams remembered it, a reporter had hidden a tiny camera in his fly to get the shot. The result "looked a little trembly, but it would anyway," he said. "Because when the current hits you, you jump a foot in spite of all the straps."

In landing a job at *True Detective*, Addams had virtually assured himself of steady employment at a time when nearly a quarter of the workforce was unemployed. In New York alone, men and women of all ages roamed the streets looking for work and shelter. People jammed the Criminal Courts Building for the privilege of serving on jury duty, which paid $4 a day. Some seven thousand "shine boys" lined the sidewalks, scrutinizing the passing shoes. The unemployed sold apples for five cents apiece on the street. But the pulp magazines, which flooded the magazine racks, did a thriving business.

Along with motion pictures, humor magazines, and comic strips such as the popular *Blondie* and *Krazy Kat*, the pulps fed the public's appetite for escape. Here in the crime magazines one could read such lurid tales as "The Mutilation Monster" and "Tragedy of the Passionate Paramour."

True Detective was the brainchild of the indefatigable Bernarr Macfadden—"the health nut," Addams called him. "Married Marie 'the body'

McDonnall. She was always doing that, too—exercising and trotting, the original jogger, I suppose."

Long before tabloid journalism entered the mainstream, Macfadden had been practicing it in his best-known paper, *The New York Evening Graphic,* dubbed the "Evening Pornographic." Now, in *True Detective,* which sold two million copies a month in its heyday, Macfadden had set the standard for true crime reporting. Macfadden, said a competitor, could "work romance into a hanging."

At first *True Detective* ran fictionalized accounts of actual crimes. But it soon dropped the disguise for terse factual reporting pieces, some of which were written by the young Dashiell Hammett and other talented unknowns.

When Addams wasn't prettying up Macfadden's blood-spattered photographs and learning a few things about magazine work in the process, he drew cartoons. Tall and wolfish-looking, he arrived back at the Westfield train station day after day, as his father had done for so many years before him, one of the stream of commuters in suits and hats. The next morning the routine began again. The train carried him to the Jersey City waterfront, where he caught a ferry to New York City. From there he took a subway to the big Macfadden building at 1926 Broadway. The trip took forty-five minutes each way. A monthly commuter ticket cost $10, two thirds of his weekly earnings.

With the $7.50 he'd earned from his decorative spot still burning in his memory, he submitted "an unfortunate scene" to *The New Yorker,* done in the line style that was popular then. It was so slight, and seemed so unfunny to him later, he couldn't imagine why *The New Yorker* accepted it. Published in the magazine's January 4, 1933, issue in stellar company—alongside cartoons by William Steig, Helen Hokinson, and James Thurber and writing by E. B. White and Ring Lardner—the unassuming drawing bearing the name "Addams" in modest capitals depicts a bashful hockey player in stocking feet who has just stepped onto the ice. "I forgot my skates," he tells his teammates.

Though the Addams cartoon was not in the league of *The New Yorker*'s star artists, it might easily have been mistaken for the work of one of the magazine's capable though unstellar second-string talents. Addams remembered being paid about $30 for the drawing—half a month's salary at *True Detective.* He kept the little pen-line drawings coming. "I think the money went to my head," he said.

"Why, hello, Otto," says the bearded man standing over the artist sculpting horse heads on the studio floor, one after another, each smaller

"I forgot my skates."

than the last. "They *told* me you were getting an inferiority complex." This and three other modest cartoons were published in *The New Yorker* in 1933, after the Addams hockey player.

He began to be noticed. But after five published cartoons, Addams also hit a wall. He managed to place only one cartoon in *The New Yorker* in 1934.

From the beginning, he labored to come up with ideas. "He was always worried that he was going to run out of funny things," said Guy Fullerton, a Westfield friend. At the end of each day spent retouching crime scene photographs, Addams arrived back at the Westfield train station, "always in need of a ride," said Fullerton, who was there to pick up his father—though Addams had a car that Fullerton remembered as a 1929 Ford roadster, and the Addams house on Elm Street was an easy walk of five blocks, including a loop around the cemetery. Addams was after not just a ride, but cartoon ideas. "Guy, have you got anything for me? I'm sterile," he would say. He agreed to pay Fullerton for gags he was able to turn into salable cartoons.

If Addams stood out in Westfield, it was because "his sense of humor was a little different from everybody else's," Fullerton remembered. How else to explain Addams's passing on the name Fullerton to another cartoonist for use in a desert island cartoon—as though the name "Fullerton" were funny? Or the time Charlie saw a newspaper photograph of men in Rome bare-chested at the ocean, after which he proceeded to remove the tank top of his own bathing suit on the beach at Asbury Park, and got arrested. Riding to the Jersey shore in a convertible packed with friends, Addams soon found himself in another predicament. At some point during the party, he and pretty Peggy Hall became hungry, and they conceived the plan of going to the dinner party next door and pretending to be invited guests. They had gotten as far as the fruit cocktail when their consciences overtook them. To the astonishment of the two hostesses, the young strangers confessed their prank, apologized, and left.

One never knew quite how Addams would react to things. He was, for instance, entranced by the Fullertons' black maid, Mahala, a very agreeable woman who weighed perhaps 350 pounds. Charlie would dine at the Fullerton home, his eyes following Mahala as she served. "Magnificent creature," he would say. At which point Mrs. Fullerton would admonish him, "Charlie, you stop that."

Sometimes he even drove Mahala home in the rumble seat of his little Ford. The family watched as the maid climbed in, sinking the car—then off it went.

"But she *is* magnificent," Charlie told his mother. "Look at her. Do you know anyone else who looks like that?"

—

FROM THE "NERVOUS PENMANSHIP" of an unhappily married humorist doodling in his *New Yorker* office instead of writing had come the accidental cartoonist—and something altogether new in cartoon art.

While other cartoonists drew children acting like grown-ups, James Thurber's grown-ups looked as though they'd been drawn by a child, though not quite: doughy little men and lumbering women with short, manly, crudely cut hair, all with homicide on their minds. "Have you forgot our little suicide pact?" a Thurber woman asks a man in a 1932 cartoon. "There was no anger in what he did, just exasperation," said Addams in admiration. "Anger isn't funny; exasperation is."

One day in early 1935, without warning, Addams submitted a sketch of newspapers rolling off a printing press. In the midst of a line of *Herald Tribune*s a tabloid appears with the headline "Sex Fiend Slays Tot." *The New Yorker*'s editors approved the idea, but asked Addams to change the *Tribune* to *The New York Times* and to draw a more authentic-looking press. Addams made the revisions, drawing a meticulous reproduction of the *New York Times* nameplate. The finished cartoon was published on March 23, 1935.

It was then, as if the sex fiend had released Addams from some restraint, that he began working in a more adventurous, sometimes lascivious style. The cartoons signed "Chas Addams"—in controlled capitals at first—included a racy, laugh-out-loud drawing showing an African tribesman in lusty pursuit of a naked native woman. "Geographic readers don't *want* that sort of thing, I tell you!" says a white man to a photographer. In another cartoon, a YMCA lecturer stands aghast before an audience watching a pornographic film on a movie screen. "Something must be wrong, Mr. Mulligan," says the man working the projector. "*This* isn't the story of the incandescent lamp." The world taking shape on paper was marked by unexpected juxtapositions: A man's parachute turns out to be crocheted by his wife; an Indian suggests a pillow fight—with a bed of nails. Unlike that of anyone else drawing for *The New Yorker*, the Addams cartoon world owed much to the presence of magic in everyday life: A museum janitor is startled to see milk and a newspaper outside the mummy's tomb.

Though Addams continued to draw mostly in pen-line, he began experimenting with wash—ink diluted with water and artfully applied to heavy paper with a brush—"trying to develop a technique that was suitable for what I thought I wanted to be," he said later. The change in style came about at a time when *The New Yorker*'s editors were asking Addams for "better drawing" on his roughs, and more variety. The art notes on an Addams rough showing beavers obstructing a man-made dam requested "better drawing; water level should be lower; smaller beavers; debris out of river bed."

Three months after the publication of the newspaper tabloid drawing, *The New Yorker* bought a second macabre Addams cartoon. The idea for it had come to him on a date. Addams was at an amusement park with Guy Fullerton's pretty sister, Jane, and Fullerton, whom he had invited to tag along. They had arrived at the roller coaster, "an ordinary Ride Playland," when suddenly Guy noticed a flock of pigeons overhead. "Charlie, I think we're in trouble: vultures!" he joked. The Addams cartoon published in the August 17 issue of *The New Yorker* shows a roller-coaster car filled to capacity. In the front row, a woman gestures up. "Alfred, look! Vultures!" she tells the man sitting next to her.

The more realistic wash style better delineated the man at the controls, the crowd below, and the steep track the car was ascending. The vultures were high up, and so subtly drawn they might have been gulls— a technique that heightened the impact of the gag. For this first Addams cartoon that married the richer style to macabre subject matter, he was paid $40. He earned an additional $10 for it the following month— probably because *The New Yorker* ran it at a larger size or asked him to redraw it—making it the most he had earned on a cartoon to date.

That January, Addams turned twenty-three, and he began keeping a notebook to record all his art sales. At the end of each month he entered the figure for his total earnings: $75 in January, $145 in February, and so on—$130, $125, $85, $150, he wrote in his pretty hand in the five-by-seven-inch black leather spiral notebook, indicating cartoons sold primarily to *The New Yorker*. (A few had gone to *Collier's* and elsewhere.) He even sold two of his original drawings—one for $15, the other for a whopping $50.

After a year and a half or two years—Addams was vague about it—he left *True Detective*. "I gave up any thought of having a job," he said. And

"Alfred, look! Vultures!"

by June 1935, nearly every issue of *The New Yorker* carried one or two Addams cartoons. He could now consider himself a *New Yorker* artist.

In attaining that longed-for status, he did not, however, join the staff, which consisted of a small group of editors, secretaries, "Talk" reporters, and others. At *The New Yorker,* creative writers and artists were contributors, most of them working from home. And all the cartoonists, illustrators, and painters were called "artists"; cartoons were called "drawings." Addams received no salary, and no guarantee that the magazine would buy his drawings. His earnings depended entirely on the quality and quantity of his contributions—and a certain amount of luck.

Under the payment scheme devised by Harold Ross, *The New Yorker* paid $10 for spots, while cartoons were paid for by the square inch—which translated into significantly more money for such artists as Peter Arno and William Crawford Galbraith, who usually drew to full-page dimensions, and Gluyas Williams, whose drawings were conceived as full-page illustrations. Though an artist could earn additional payment if he was asked to redraw, it was an unpredictable business, and a shaky way to earn a living. Raises and bonuses were given at the editors' discretion, or as motivation. One simply couldn't count on making money.

Nor could one be sure what the editors would accept. During the mid-thirties, some of *The New Yorker*'s best cartoonists tried their hands at black humor, with very mixed results. Whitney Darrow, Jr., along with Helen Hokinson, drew in a gentler style that worked better with dark subject matter—though one Darrow cartoon, showing a man carrying a big bundle under his arm as he's confronted by a cop, landed in *The New Yorker*'s pages with a thud: "It's nothing at all, really—just an old mutilated corpse." George Price, who had not yet found his own cartoon world of misfits and cranks, turned in two good drawings. A 1935 Price series of a levitating man ended with a gunshot. "He never knew what hit him," the man's wife tells the cops, with the smoking rifle still in her hand.

The New Yorker's unsuccessful offerings included a heavy-handed cartoon from the father of "Small Fry." "Now will you stop that damned Southern drawl?" demands the Steig character as he strangles a woman. Some were way over the top. A 1940 Carl Rose panel drawing of a reporter struggling to write an article about the Germans eating dog meat was, well, in bad taste. When he fails to find the information he's looking for, he leaves the library for the pet store and has a dog cooked to order at a restaurant: "Tough, gamy, strong-flavored," he types.

And when Addams submitted a cover idea showing "a storm cloud hovering over the weather bureau," editor Katharine White winced, calling it "ghastly in both thought and execution."

Though freelancing offered no security, it did, for that very reason, keep the pressure on, which Addams, like most artists and writers, needed. Pressure alone could not, of course, solve the problem of creating ideas, but here *The New Yorker* gave him some help.

Chapter Five

Who's Talking?

"Boo! (n.yrkr)," addams recorded in early april of 1935, noting a payment of $35 for a desert island cartoon. (It showed a castaway in the ocean sneaking up on another luckless soul on a blip of land barely big enough for two.) Though Addams's output remained modest compared to that of the magazine's big producers, the quality of his work and his willingness to redraw made him a valued artist. In 1935 Addams was rewarded with a $5 raise per drawing—an increase he found "most encouraging."

Addams, who was living at home, felt so encouraged that despite earning only $10 for all of July, and nothing at all in August, he took a vacation to Cuba—a trip he was less than candid in describing to Wolcott Gibbs, Katharine White's assistant. "Dear Mr. Gibbs," he wrote from Westfield on August 16, "I have to go out of town on a rather important matter, so I won't be able to submit any drawings for a couple weeks or so."

Why, as a freelancer, he felt the need to cover for the lack of submissions is uncertain. But the surge in his productivity—which would result in twenty-one published *New Yorker* cartoons in 1935, along with sales to *Collier's* and others, compared to only one *New Yorker* cartoon published in 1934—suggests that by now *The New Yorker* was feeding Addams at least some of his cartoon ideas, and that he was feeling indebted to them.

As Harold Ross had conceived it, *The New Yorker* was an inherently "collaborative effort." Most of the magazine's cartoon gags, as well as the subjects for text, were cooked up by the staff and various writers and artists, who flooded the magazine with as many as two thousand sketches and written ideas a week. "We looked at 839 idea pictures this PM and Gibbs read about 500 art ideas this morning," the dedicated Katharine White had written to her husband, E. B. White, in 1934. The magazine's editors generally matched ideas to talent. If, for instance, a full-page illustration of a crowd scene was needed, Carl Rose was one artist who could draw it wonderfully; but if the editors wanted a certain elegant-yet-complex crowd, Gluyas Williams would be tapped to do it. If the editors had a gag about a matron, any one of a number of cartoonists might be asked to draw it, but certain matrons belonged to particular talents. A Mary Petty dowager—who belonged to a hushed interior world of drawing rooms and butterfly-like aproned maids—was to a Helen Hokinson matron what a hothouse flower was to a garden perennial.

Or a cartoon submitted by one artist might be redrawn by another. When Carl Rose turned in a drawing of a fencer slicing off his opponent's head—"Touché!"—Ross asked Thurber to redraw it. "Thurber's people have no blood," he explained. "You can put their heads back on and they're as good as new." And the Rose cartoon became a famous Thurber cartoon. A 1939 Addams cartoon based on an idea by Richard McCallister would be similarly effective. It showed a headless man leaving a barbershop. "Next?" says the benign-looking barber as two stricken customers take in the scene. Like Thurber, Addams was bloodless, the violence always implied.

The New Yorker had long functioned as a family in which everyone shared the chores. (In keeping with the homey atmosphere, the editors used knitting needles to point at the drawings under consideration.) E. B. White—who was better known for his writing than his drawing—once painted a *New Yorker* cover illustration based on his own idea, a delicate watercolor of a sea horse eating oats from a bag. He also polished and wrote captions, including the caption for a famous 1928 cartoon by Carl Rose depicting a mother and her small boy at the dinner table. "It's broccoli, dear," says she. "I say it's spinach, and I say the hell with it," says the moppet.

The concept of a writer working in partnership with an artist was hardly original. As cartoonist Lee Lorenz later noted, the use of gagmen in cartooning could be traced to "the illustrated anecdote popular in comic magazines at the turn of the century." With the exception of William Steig, who worked entirely from his own ideas, and Thurber, who drew most of his own gags, almost every *New Yorker* artist, including Arno and Hokinson and Gluyas Williams, was handed ideas by the staff. Helen Hokinson had her own collaborator, James Reid Parker. George Price drew entirely from outside suggestions.

Such was the overflow of ideas that gagmen would amuse themselves and the cartoonists with unpublishable gags. (Desert island: man sees box floating toward him, opens it, finds twelve dozen condoms.)

For all the abundance of *New Yorker* art coming in and enlivening its pages—in the thirties, the art was the best thing in *The New Yorker*—the magazine's staff remained small. There was no art department or art editor; all cartoons and illustrations were handled by the fiction department, under Katharine White, Harold Ross's "literary conscience" and right arm at *The New Yorker* almost since its beginning. *The New Yorker* bought more art than they could immediately use, storing it in a "bank" which included as many as five thousand spots; they kept a careful account of their subject matter—"NO Book drawings, 30 animal drawings on hand" read the typed notes from December 31, 1934—and kept track of their artists' various specialties or obsessions. "ALAIN is tending toward religious drawings (priests, etc.). DUNN toward low-life (cops, thugs, etc.)." From the weekly art conference came the call for "more high-life, winter-sports and small drawings (not animal)."

The artists' day of reckoning fell on Tuesdays, when *The New Yorker* bought cover illustrations and cartoons. The art conference took place in a smoke-filled room in the magazine's small building at 25 West Forty-fifth Street. Gathered around the table supplied with ashtrays and knitting needles were, among select others, forty-three-year-old Harold Ross—loud, brilliant, profane, his porcupine hair tamed and parted on the side—and Katharine White ("Mrs. White," as Ross and nearly everyone else at the magazine called her), also forty-three, an aristocratic woman of supreme self-assurance whom Peter Arno reduced to chignon and cigarette in a caricature she loved. Hour after hour, the comments and suggestions flew. "Who's talking?" Ross would ask of a sketch in which a character's mouth was closed. "Where am I in this drawing?"

"Is that funny?" asks the Thurber man in the artist's rendering of the art conference, perhaps speaking for Harold Ross, as the Thurber woman representing Mrs. White regards the proceedings with arms folded in disapproval.

Also present was writer Wolcott Gibbs, Mrs. White's thirty-three-year-old assistant in fiction—silent and high-strung, a handsome, blond, cerebral executioner in the dust jacket illustration Addams later drew for a collection of Gibbs's *New Yorker* writing and criticism, *More in Sorrow*. From Mrs. White, Gibbs had inherited the task of working directly with the artists, encouraging them, handing out checks and ideas.

The lone artist in the room was Rea Irvin, who left his imprint all over the look of *The New Yorker*—in the graceful and distinctive headline type, called Irvin type, which he had designed; in the Regency dandy known as Eustace Tilley, whom he drew for *The New Yorker*'s inaugural cover, and who appears to this day on nearly every anniversary issue; and in the cartoons and covers. Known for his calm disposition and his flamboyant wardrobe, Irvin, the old man of the group in his early fifties, had the placid face of a character he himself had drawn.

As the editors approved drawings for purchase, suggested ideas, edited the roughs for clarity and style—directing a knitting needle at the inauthentic-looking Addams printing press, the closed mouth in another artist's cartoon—and wrote or rewrote captions, Daise Terry, the magazine's dominating office manager, kept the minutes, took notes, and held up the art under consideration. Promising roughs were later returned to the artists with sometimes-lengthy suggestions for improvement.

The Addams rough under consideration on October 22, 1935, shows a missionary and a native sitting on a shore as another native walks on water. The caption reads, "Pombo learn things quick, doctor." Without being specific, the editors said they wanted something else. The finished version, published on August 8, 1936, features the native parting the water as the other native and the missionary watch from shore. The edited caption now reads "Pombo learn things fast, eh, doctor?"

Though *The New Yorker* famously overedited at times (and underedited occasionally, leaving the rare talking cartoon mouth closed), they had much to teach a young cartoonist. Harold Ross, for instance, who had no training in art but had true instincts, pushed for cartoons that told the story without text—the ultimate in cartoon storytelling, which Charles Addams came to prize in his own work. When Ross was asked why he didn't run color cartoons, he said, "What's so funny about red?"

"Covers Oct. 22, 1935," said the art conference notes. "ADDAMS: Scientist, astronomer in his observatory on Jan 1st. His assistant is standing behind him as he gazes through the telescope, blowing a horn and ringing a bell. Make it more authentic observatory, with dome; two or three professors." A week later, a revised rough was on the table. "ADDAMS: Astronomers in observatory celebrating the new year. [Put them] all in robes; one or two in civilian clothes; fix bulging eye; not all bald; suppressed merriment. Make clearer it's a bell the man has in hand. Roll of paper tighter in man's mouth, cheeks puffed as in blowing. Color of letters?"

Addams took it back to the drawing board. The powerfully subdued final version, rendered from a predominantly brown palette with just the right touches of blue—shows a solitary white-haired astronomer with a receding hairline. Dressed in a sober black suit, eyes downcast, he wipes his spectacles with a handkerchief before looking into a gigantic telescope. For his first *New Yorker* cover, Addams was paid $175. It was published in January 1938.

After *The New Yorker* bought an Addams cartoon featuring rats gathered around a Salvation Army band, Katharine White wanted it "redrawn and the plate remade because I have discovered that a person coming to it cold just does not recognize these little people spelling the word 'Repent' as Salvation Army people," she wrote Harold Ross in a long memo. "If Addams would redraw it I would have it drawn for a page and have it a captionless page. The onlookers in the foreground would register surprise and astonishment without saying anything. You could have a flighty girl pointing at them, etc. . . . It would be a funny page for the fall season and I truly believe worth the cost of throwing the plate away. . . ."

Addams would redraw it. He would do what the editors thought necessary—even if it seemed absurd. Years later, when he was well established, he submitted a drawing showing a python on a tropical porch after it had swallowed a man. "Oh, speak up, George! Stop mumbling!"

the wife of the unlucky man says over her shoulder as she looks up from her book. Behind her in this famous 1941 cartoon, a wicker chair has been overturned, and a drinking glass rolls on the wooden floor. Katharine White, "who was sort of the paragon of good taste on the

"Oh, speak up, George! Stop mumbling!"

magazine in those days," noted Addams, "objected to the bulge in the snake's body in the shape of the man and wanted it covered up a little bit." Addams added a token slash of palm in front of the snake's swollen belly. The revision didn't soften the impact of the cartoon, "but she made her point," said Addams.

Years before the infamous snake, during that start-up time when Addams was riding the train from Westfield to New York to peddle his drawings, he often found himself sitting next to Peggy Hall, a young brunette who worked as a model for Sabour, a "swish" Manhattan dress shop open by invitation only. "He would always show me his drawings and ask me what I thought of them, and of course I thought they were kind of ghoulish," remembered Peggy Hall Segur nearly seventy years later. "Sometimes we'd happen to meet on the ferry and go home together. He always seemed to be there. I think he kind of liked me."

"Satyr," Addams wrote in his notebook in neat black ink; "Repent," "Shark in Fountain," "Quicksand," said a few of the entries for 1936 and 1937. But his cartoons were not all dark. Many of them were simply funny, the product of a literary mind loitering in the worlds of history, fantasy, and myth—alternate worlds which were always close at hand. Hunters return from a shoot with a moose head tied to one automobile fender and an angry-looking Pan to the other; a man riding in an open car at a high altitude sprouts rabbit ears; Medusa visits the beauty parlor.

The New Yorker was granting more and more reprint rights on Addams cartoons in both British and American publications (including *Boys' Life* and *Literary Digest*), a welcome source of income Addams shared with the magazine. *The New Yorker* was also handling more requests to purchase the originals of Addams cartoons. This scattering of extra moneys—$3.40 from royalties on *The Seventh New Yorker Album* (which published one of Addams's early cartoons), $15 to $25 for the sales of originals, $15.92 on a reprint, $10 to $15 here and there for additional pay on *New Yorker* cartoons—added up. In his second year as a freelancer, Addams published thirty-five cartoons in *The New Yorker* alone, and earned $2,535.48 for "drawing only," he wrote in his notebook—$387.49 more than he'd earned the first year. Even when he paid out of pocket for a cartoon idea—typically $10 on a $50 cartoon—he did all right. That August, he took a three-week vacation, in Montana.

By the late thirties, Addams was paying for ideas out of pocket for about half of all the cartoons he sold, mostly to the prolific Richard McCallister, whose apparently bottomless imagination furnished cartoon subjects for such different talents as Richard Decker, Richard Taylor,

George Price, and Peter Arno—ultimately resulting in some five thousand *New Yorker* drawings.

To what extent Addams's invisible collaborators influenced his development, or his productivity, is impossible to say. The best of the gag writers had a chameleon-like gift for adapting themselves to the cartoonist they were writing for. Though Addams himself apparently dreamed up the gag for "Goalie's Spider Web," a captionless 1940 cartoon in which a bored ice hockey goalie rests against the goal overtaken by an enormous spiderweb, Richard McCallister provided the idea for the cartoon Addams listed in his notebook as "black widow." It showed a limp little man with his hat in his hand addressing a nurse in a crowded waiting room— "Are there many ahead of me? I've been bitten by the black widow spider." McCallister often matched the Addams wit so seamlessly that even Addams couldn't tell who was talking.

Chapter Six.

Just My Idea of a
Pretty Girl

A SKED IF MORTICIA WAS MODELED ON ANYONE, ADDAMS claimed she was "more or less something from my own head"—"just my idea of a pretty girl"—though he did concede that "there might be a little Gloria Swanson in her." As he talked about his unlikely dream girl—"eyes slightly up-centered, and dank, snake-like hair," his voice trailed off in a tender drawl. Morticia had always been "sort of an ideal for me," he said. "It was a kind of good looks that I appreciated at that time, and still do, really," he said.

The dark lady of the Addams cartoons made her debut on page nine of *The New Yorker* on August 6, 1938. She had a painted, pointed face, black hair pulled back into a tight chignon, and a curvaceous figure that seemed poured into her full-length, cleavage-revealing black dress. Odd tendrils fan out from her hem and drip from her sleeves like Spanish moss. A big, bearded retainer stands next to her in the foyer of her dilapidated Victorian house as she listens, incredulously, to a vacuum cleaner salesman giving his pitch: "Vibrationless, noiseless, and a great time and back saver," says the dapper little man in the white summer suit. "No well-appointed home should be without it." Cobwebs stretch across the empty spaces in the neglected mansion, connecting a broken second-floor baluster to a fringed newel lamp and forming a net between the arms of an antique chair. A bat drifts up the wide, bare staircase. From the second floor, a strange character peers down on the people below, gripping the wooden balusters like bars.

"Vibrationless, noiseless, and a great time and back saver. No well-appointed home should be without it." The first Addams Family cartoon.

In this wonderfully layered performance, Addams achieves the effect of a little painting, a story interrupted. Diffused light enters through both the opened front door and a window on the stair landing; one can almost feel the silky cobwebs that would stick to the hand brushing them away. In this place that time has forgotten, a life seems to be unfolding. Who are these people? one wonders. Who is clutching the stair railing above?

The cartoonist himself had no idea. With this first Addams Family cartoon, as it would be known, he had ventured into new territory with the same uncomprehending innocence as his polished little salesman. Though he had drawn the elaborate picture with great attention to detail, it was all in service of the gag. (And what a gag. The cartoon was the most ambitious use to date of what cartoonists called "the Switch," a twist on a slogan or cliché.) To be sure, the woman in black was alluring—a cross between Gloria Swanson as she had looked in the silent films of Addams's adolescence, and the startling Elsa Lanchester in 1935's *Bride of Frankenstein*. In her carefully made-up face, long, willowy silhouette, and deep décolletage, she owed something to 1930s fashion as well, which stressed fantasy over reality. But the mysterious woman was not the point. Addams recorded the $85 cartoon sale in his earnings notebook not as "Witch-Woman," but as "Vacuum Cleaner." He had no thought of doing anything more with the house and characters.

Though nothing like the Addams vacuum cleaner salesman cartoon had ever appeared in *The New Yorker*, Addams may have gotten the idea for a haunted house drawing from a heavy-handed, unfunny cartoon by his *New Yorker* colleague Richard Taylor. It concerned a couple who have just arrived at a spooky place where they are greeted by a sinister-looking man holding a candle. "You'll be surprised [by] the kind of service we give you at Wyvern Manor," he tells them, as a spider and various creepy characters lurk in the background. Taylor cartoons often featured odd-looking people with the same enormous fish eyes—and in this haunted house, the gag got lost in the creepy style.

The Taylor misstep was one of several dark *New Yorker* cartoons by talented artists that had failed during the years since Addams began finding his niche. Though Addams himself sometimes went overboard, his style generally worked with his macabre subject matter.

By now, Addams had not only mastered the wash technique, he owned it. For the previous three years, he had been moving back and forth between pen-line drawings and washes of varying complexity, as if he couldn't quite make up his mind about style. His recent *New Yorker* cartoons had included one of a woman in mink arriving at "Dr. Thompson's Rest Farm," where a pair of interested vultures perch at the front gate, and a drawing of two lovers sitting by a romantic, moonlit fountain pool suddenly disrupted by a shark's fin. With talent and patience, he had learned how to manipulate the unpredictable medium of ink and water—how to tease and tame it to achieve the richness of color using a wide scale of black and white. He knew how to shade with the antique-like sepia—the pigment made from the inky secretions of the cuttlefish when in danger—and with lampblack, the almost pure carbon soot left from burning gas and oil resins. He learned how to get the whitest whites, and how much to wet the rag board to find varying shades of gray. He also discovered the right canvas for his technique: the high-quality English-made Whatman board, an expensive but rugged material. He could wet it repeatedly, and it wouldn't curl.

And yet for all the artistry and technical mastery that had gone into this novel drawing technique, for Addams the real work of cartooning went into the rough. Using a soft carbon pencil called a Wolff's pencil, and a paper stump, he did his roughs on bond paper, typically spending half an hour or so on each, filling in enough detail so that one could see what the finished cartoon would look like. But the typical half hour could stretch into several hours if he had to do research, as he had presumably done for this cartoon, with its authentic architectural period details and streamlined upright vacuum cleaner, which closely resembled the stylish Hoover Model 825 (made in England from 1936 to 1938). Once the rough was "okayed as an idea" by *The New Yorker*, he would "just blacken the other side of the paper and trace it down and then refine it," he said with characteristic understatement. With the image now on Whatman board, he began the finished drawing. He tried not to be too careful in the final version, so as not to lose the spontaneity of the rough.

HAVING SUBMITTED THE vacuum cleaner cartoon with no idea of developing it into a series, Addams found himself encouraged to do just that by Harold Ross, who thought there should be more characters in the delicious house. But Addams was stumped for material. He continued to turn out enough quality work to keep him in *The New Yorker* two or three times a month, but it was a year before he sold another Addams Family drawing.

In the second Family cartoon, Addams refined his still-unnamed characters. He loosened Morticia's black hair from its controlled chignon, letting it fall to her shoulders in ragged tendrils echoing the fabric dripping from her sleeves and hem. Just this once he put her in a pale dressing gown that clung to her breasts. For the now clean-shaven butler, he borrowed from Boris Karloff's Frankenstein monster, giving him one opaque eye and "scanty hair . . . damply clinging to his narrow flat head," as Addams later described it. On his perfectly constructed set, he lavished the same care as he had given the first cartoon. He cracked the glass lamp shade on the pedestal table, peeled the wallpaper, pulled up a few floorboards, and broke a slat or two in the high, shuttered bay windows where spiders had been working. But he did not move beyond the sexy witch-woman and her butler to create new characters. Looking up from her book, Morticia addresses Lurch, who has just surprised her with a tea tray. "Oh, it's *you!*" she cries as one of her sharp-nailed hands reaches protectively upward. "For a moment you gave me quite a start." Addams was paid $110 for the full-page cartoon, which ran in *The New Yorker* on November 25, 1939.

October 1939: While the third Family cartoon percolated, Addams drew a diaphanous man standing below the QUIET sign in a glossy hospital corridor. He seems to have floated in. His black suit swells below his collar as though it is filled with air. His balloon head—made of skin so translucent you could almost see through it—is gathered in a fold at his collar. He wears rimless glasses on his needle nose, and an anxious expression as he regards the nurse, hat in hand. "Congratulations! It's a baby," she says as she pokes her head around the maternity room door.

Published on November 9, 1940, the latest Addams triumph was as original as any cartoon that had appeared in *The New Yorker* in its fifteen-year history. But Addams had no more plans for the benign little man he had created with such delicacy and sweetness. He pocketed the $60 he earned from *The New Yorker,* sold the original cartoon to Katharine White for a collegial $15, and moved on.

Before Addams arrived at his next mutant, he drew the ski-tree drawing, as cartoonist Ted Key later called it. "The Skier" followed a number of skiing cartoons by various *New Yorker* artists, though none of them had pulled off the magical feat of the skier who has left a single track around each side of a tree after whizzing past another skier. This second figure brings the act "into reality," Addams explained later. Without the witness, "you're not sure that it really happened and I think [he] gives it a logic that it would not have otherwise."

"Congratulations! It's a baby!"

Hailed by *Time* magazine in 1942 as "that haunting simile of the mind's disintegration," the cartoon published in the January 12, 1940, issue of *The New Yorker*, shortly after Addams turned twenty-eight, brought the cartoonist more mail than he had ever received for a single drawing, and made him world famous. *The New Yorker* itself got more reprint and purchase requests for "The Skier" than for any other cartoon they published that year. In years to come the little drawing was inter-preted and plagiarized countless times, with and without apologies, even by Abbott and Costello in their 1943 film, *Hit the Ice*.

Addams was "surprised" by the public reaction to the cartoon, which had started out as so many *New Yorker* cartoons did. Someone had pitched the idea to him (Addams did not enter a name in his notebook, which suggests that the gag was dreamed up by a *New Yorker* staff member), and he had drawn it. He was paid $45 for it.

"The Skier" was a simple drawing by his standards. Before he realized the full impact of the cartoon, he sold it to the president of Packard for $35, and soon regretted it. In later years, he made at least one copy of the drawing for a friend, and another for himself that was virtually indistin-guishable from the original.

More rewarding for Addams than worldwide attention—including "a long treatise" in German by a doctor who analyzed the cartoon and fi-nally suggested "that maybe it was supposed to be funny"—was its inclu-sion on the Binet scale, a test used to measure intelligence. Two months after publication of "The Skier," Addams received a typed letter directed to *The New Yorker* from a psychologist named Harriet Ray, who worked at the state school for the feebleminded in Lincoln, Illinois.

As she explained, the Binet scale included pictures that lent themselves to the query "What's funny about this?" After seeing the Addams cartoon in *The New Yorker*—perfect from the tester's standpoint because of its "simple construction" and lack of a caption—she began including it on the test. "My hunch was right," she wrote Addams. Most adults with a mental age of nine or more understood that the picture was absurd; below that level, wrote Ray, patients were "stymied. Some of the failed responses . . . were as follows: The limbs of the tree are downward instead of upward. This man is [skiing] looking backwards, going forwards. Branches don't grow that way on a pole. . . . That tree in the way, only thing I can see—I don't know what's foolish about it. They're going in opposite directions. The tree is cut off at the top." Even the patients who understood that the drawing was a joke failed to laugh at it—all of which Harriet Ray found "rather fascinating to think about."

So did Addams. Though he was mostly bored by psychological interpretations of his work, which he preferred not to analyze, this was a treat. He loved the image of feeble minds digesting his work and puzzling over it; he took a genuine clinical interest in it. He answered Ray's letter with a charming letter of his own, and asked her for "an absurdity picture for a mental age higher than ten."

WHILE ADDAMS TRIED to think himself back into the house where the witch lived with her manservant, a shark's fin pierced the surface alongside a water skier in one of his 1940 cartoons. Occasionally a cartoon offers a hint of Family drawings to come: As Christmas carolers sing outside a house, the wall safe inside stands open and empty, the butler lies unconscious, and the wealthy homeowners writhe on the floor, bound and gagged. There is something of Morticia in the glamorous brunette in mink saying good night to her top-hatted escort—at the opening of a manhole. Little Wednesday Addams, who had yet to be invented, is present in the wretched girl skipping rope on a dark sidewalk: "Twenty-three thousand and one, twenty-three thousand and two, twenty-three thousand and three. . . ." These last two cartoons were based on gags by Richard McCallister.

Back in November 1940, as "The Skier" was about to make Addams famous, he had again found himself drawing someone round and hairless, a sinister man with a bulbous nose and shadowed eyes who kept his hat on indoors. He stands at a railway ticket counter a couple of feet from his unsuspecting wife. "A round trip and a one way to Ausable Chasm," he tells the clerk.

Two months later Addams worked another variation on a cliché: The gaunt young witch steps next door to borrow a cup of cyanide from a smiling, walleyed hag, another new character, inspired by Grandma Spear. Almost unnoticed is the fat man in the long black coat running up the stairs behind the hag, who might have been taken for the man who sent his wife into a gorge near Lake Champlain.

"People always want to know more about them," Addams told a reporter after a less-inspired fourth Family drawing involving a squeaky trapdoor, "but I've never been able to figure out what they are doing. Maybe they are at a gathering with some hobby in common. I've become quite attached to them. I think maybe I'm in love with the young looking witch."

What Addams didn't tell the reporter was that he had fallen in love with a girl who resembled his bewitching cartoon goddess.

Chapter Seven

One of the Great Comic Artists
of All Time

BARBARA JEAN DAY WAS A WESTFIELD GIRL. SHE WAS seven years Addams's junior, a graduate of Butler University: small and slender and feminine, about five foot six. She had melting brown eyes, pale skin described as having "the pallor of angel cake," and black hair worn in a softly curled bob above her shoulders. Though much would be made of her resemblance to Morticia—so much that "I think she lived to be plagued by that," said Addams—she was soft where the witch-woman was hard.

"She was very, very lovely—warm, like an invention of his," said painter Hedda Sterne, who was married to Saul Steinberg and did an oil portrait of Barbara during the 1940s. Beyond her stark beauty was the woman herself, who was far more than an Addams set decoration. Described by Addams friends as sharp-minded and intelligent, Barbara, who was nicknamed Bobby, inspired much the same affection in people that Addams did. Friends emphasized her beautiful manners, her sweet nature, her gentleness and kindness, the pleasure of her company. "She had a lovely little giggle," said Lyda Hall. And "she was a real flame thrower," said *New Yorker* editor Gardner Botsford. "She would do anything on a dare."

There was a hint of Barbara in a cartoon Addams sold *The New Yorker* in December 1942. "Do you have one in which a wife murders her husband in a *very* ingenious manner?" asks the cartoon brunette in the book-shop. But whatever Addams was feeling for Barbara Day, he had any number of other distractions to think about, beginning with the army. "*Drafted*," he wrote in his earnings notebook.

For thirty-year-old Charles Addams, the draft had arrived at a moment when he had everything going for him. Footloose and well connected, he was a much-admired cartoonist who might be found having dinner with Boris Karloff at publisher Bennett Cerf's Manhattan townhouse, or riding in a car down Third Avenue with James Thurber and Wolcott Gibbs, "Gilbert Seldes hanging on the running board," as they made the rounds from "21" to Costello's. In those young New York days when there were still "two-way streets and not much traffic," Addams had some fun. "His mother [had] a fit about everything he was doing," said Guy Fullerton. "And he was loving it."

It was during this time that Addams, who was always making new friends—he "had more friends than anybody I've ever known," said the sociable Jay Rutherford—began two of his major art friendships. The deepest was with James Geraghty, *The New Yorker*'s talented and tactful first art editor, a great nurturer of artists, who had been a radio scriptwriter and sold *The New Yorker* written ideas for Arno at $50 a pop before being hired himself in 1939. And there was the Romanian-born Saul Steinberg, who immigrated to New York from Italy on a "slightly fake" passport and sold his first drawing to *The New Yorker*—a "reverse centaur . . . with a man's rear end and a horse's head"—in 1941. Addams never forgot his first sight of the artist: He saw "a hollow-eyed man sitting in [*The New Yorker*'s] reception room, and knew instantly it was Steinberg." For the chilly Steinberg, it was friendship at first sight—"a quiet friendship," as he put it later, which would endure.

Addams's career was soaring. He had been hailed in a 1942 book as one of four "zanies" of *The New Yorker* "who have nothing in common except the mad propensity to abolish the law of gravitation, to change the highest mammal into a paramecium, and to murder their fellow creatures by the most casual methods of torture"—the others being Thurber, Richard Taylor, and George Price. The year before Addams was drafted, he had published thirty-eight cartoons in *The New Yorker* alone, a personal record. That fall of 1942 the magazine had published its fourth Addams cover—an ingenious illustration depicting the Chinese-Japanese conflict raging in a porcelain plate. The cover had so excited the Shenango Pottery Company in New Castle, Pennsylvania, that they asked to incorporate the design in their own Blue Willow china pattern. Addams had drawn the lighthearted illustrations for the 1940 comic novel *But Who Wakes the Bugler?*—the first by Peter DeVries. And his own first book—a cartoon collection called *Drawn and Quartered*—was published by Random House. Priced at $2.50, with an introduction by Boris Karloff and an original dust jacket illustration by Addams, it got a favorable notice in *Time*. Of the 115 cartoons, all but four were from *The New Yorker*. *Look* magazine ran a sampling of Addams cartoons from the book and observed that the "high priest in horror" was in person "not at all frightening—being gentle, low-voiced, extremely tall and attractive."

As Addams prepared to enter the army, he seemed to be having the time of his life. There were stories about his heavy drinking, and his reputation as a "woman lover," as one anonymous source put it, was well established. An older tale involved an affair with another man's wife; newer stories concerned his affair with an older woman, which was considered "quite risqué" then. So charged was the subject of Addams's love life, at least in provincial Westfield, that even decades later one of his hometown girls would not talk about it.

IT WAS DURING the last months of 1942, the year Addams apparently met Barbara Day, that another story, which had been unfolding in ink wash in the pages of *The New Yorker*, took a decisive turn. After reigning alone for four years, on November 14, 1942, the black queen later known as Morticia found her mate. Addams pictured her in the embrace of an ugly, flaccid man whose suit jacket strained at the buttons. Like Morticia, the new character had black hair ("parted in the middle, so it could easily be a toupee," explained Addams); but unlike her, he had a big head. "Are you unhappy, darling?" asks the hideous paramour. "Oh, yes, *yes*! Completely," Morticia sighs, snuggling closer. Addams, a Democrat, had based the young witch's lover on a reasonably attractive man, Republican Thomas E. Dewey—but Dewey crossed with a pig. Whether intentionally or not, the character also resembled actor Peter Lorre.

Though Addams watchers later linked Barbara Day to the cartoon—for surely Addams had been drawing his own romance into the series—it was in fact based on an idea by cartoonist John Ruge, who had also provided Addams with the gag for the fourth Family cartoon involving the squeaky trapdoor (and had once acquired an original Addams cartoon in exchange for an unidentified "Nazi item"). This new gag cost Addams $25, leaving him with $105 from his *New Yorker* sale. He recorded the drawing in his notebook as "Completely Unhappy."

HE WASN'T UNHAPPY in the army, he wrote Daise Terry from the army base at Sea Girt on the New Jersey coast on January 16, 1943, eleven days after he'd gone in—"just exhausted." (Though he was not too exhausted to see a girl there, who was not Barbara Day.) He remained in constant touch with his mother, whom Barbara saw as possessive and dominating, and who now handled *New Yorker* queries from Daise Terry concerning the purchase of Addams originals.

As the army turned the cartoonist into a soldier, another soldier, named Lou Marcus, noticed Addams at the rifle range. He was "a good shot," said Marcus, "big and strong."

From nearby Fort Monmouth in February came another image of Addams, courtesy of Al Hirschfeld, whose peerless caricatures of theater people had been running in *The New York Times* for fifteen years. As Hirschfeld explained later, he was at Fort Monmouth to do something for the enlisted man. Having been "too young for World War I," and now, at thirty-eight, "too old for World War II," he conceived the idea of drawing portraits as gifts to the soldiers. He and artist Don Freeman turned up at the USO; they ran off copies of the drawings on the mimeograph machine, ten or fifteen at a time.

Hirschfeld asked the private now sitting for him what he did for a living. "I'm an artist," said the soldier, whose big elastic nose, thick eyebrows, and thin lips—a mere line—were made for caricature. It was the "glandular" type of face Hirschfeld liked best, a clown's face. He drew it resting on top of a long stalk that made the private's collar look low, and slightly disreputable.

As Addams told it, the army had been "about to make a telephone

Al Hirschfeld caricature of Chas Addams. It was the "glandular" type of face Hirschfeld liked to draw.

lineman out of him when word got around that he could draw." One day a colonel appeared at Sea Girt and selected three soldiers for noncombat duty in the Signal Corps; Addams and Lou Marcus were among them.

In February 1943, the month after Addams entered the army, his mother suddenly died following gallbladder surgery. She was sixty-six. He took it hard.

Three months later, on Memorial Day weekend, May 29, Private Addams was given a few days' leave to marry Barbara Day in a traditional ceremony at St. Paul's Episcopal Church in Westfield, at four o'clock in the afternoon. Bobby wore a dress of white tulle and carried a bouquet of white orchids. Her sister served as matron of honor, a friend from Westfield was Addams's best man, and the bride's father gave her away. The *New York Herald* ran a photograph of the lovely young Mrs. Addams under the heading "Cartoonist's Bride." After a small reception at the Day home in Westfield, the couple took a short honeymoon at the Pierre Hotel on Fifth Avenue. Then Addams returned alone across the Triborough Bridge to the Signal Corps' base in Astoria, the old immigrant neighborhood in the northwest corner of Queens.

With a war on, even married soldiers were required to sleep in the barracks, though it was easy for both married and single soldiers to slip out. While Addams spent his nights at the barracks in Astoria—or didn't—Barbara lived in their new apartment in Manhattan, a fifth-floor studio next to a steakhouse in a "shadowy, ornate Georgian structure" with a Mad-Hatterish half number: 36½ East Seventy-fifth Street. The self-service elevator reminded Addams of a coffin ("If I get stuck in it some day, I won't know whether to send for a doctor or a plumber," he said), and the windows were obscured by "a massive balustrade," noted a delighted reporter. Though Bobby thought the studio was ugly, and the claustrophobic elevator challenged Charlie's equilibrium, the couple turned the place into a semblance of home. They filled it with a couple of cats, a dog named Shortie, a stuffed hawk Addams claimed to have shot, and various artifacts. On one wall Charlie painted a fantasy mural starring a hermaphrodite in green underwear.

Because Charlie liked her hair long, Barbara gamely grew out her bob; because he liked her in black, she often indulged him in her wardrobe choices. Even with her contemporary short bangs, she resembled the cartoon woman, and everyone from Charlie's dazzled teenaged cousin, Dudley Smith, to Lou Marcus and his wife noticed. Addams drew large valentines for her. A sketch he did for a soldier who had forgotten to get his own girl a valentine offers a hint of what they might have looked like: Encircled by a lacy heart and flowers are a boy centaur and his love, shy in her nakedness, with long black hair.

If one had to be drafted, the Signal Corps was the place to end up. In 1943, *The New Yorker*'s Gardner Botsford requested a transfer from infantry training at Camp Croft, in South Carolina, "to the Signal Corps, to the Coast Artillery, to the Norman Luboff Choir, to anywhere at all that was not the infantry." He was refused. *New Yorker* writer John Cheever, who got transferred to Astoria from the 22nd Infantry Regiment at Fort Dix, was luckier. Addams credited the timely publication of *Drawn and Quartered* with his own assignment to the Corps.

In the Signal Corps—"where SKILL and COURAGE count," said the 1942 poster showing a soldier in wartime—one needed mostly skill. Only the elite combat photographers and cameramen got close to the action in Europe. While these foot soldiers slogged through the mud, water, and rubble of foreign battlefields, risking life and limb to send back pictures and newsreel footage, the majority of the Corps spent the war stateside, drilling in the streets of New York, "where we were ticketed by the police for obstructing traffic," remembered playwright and screenwriter Arthur Laurents.

Here in Astoria, home of the Signal Corps Photographic Center, the land of make-believe was taking shape on sheets of cellulose acetate. For the Signal Corps—which had begun in 1861 at Fort Monroe, Virginia, where Union soldiers first used the new visual alphabet spelled out by hands, flags, lanterns, and torches—was in the movie business now.

World War II had caught the nation badly underprepared. In its haste to turn millions of civilians into soldiers and to rally the home front, the army settled on motion pictures as a training and propaganda tool. They turned to a Who's Who from both the enlisted and civilian populations—writers, artists, musicians, animators, photographers, and filmmakers.

Behind the movies and training films that began replacing the old, crude films and dull training manuals of yesteryear were such movie directors as John Huston, Darryl Zanuck, and Frank Capra. Capra worked on the "Why We Fight" series, which explained the reasons for going to war to both Americans and their British allies, and was later considered among the war's most influential film productions. The aging George Cukor was there as Private Cukor, directing a short with Ingrid Bergman. A young production assistant named Stanley Kramer—whose *High Noon* and *Judgment at Nuremberg* lay in the future—was also in the Corps. Among the scriptwriters was Ring Lardner, Jr., who turned up in Astoria fresh from his first smash hit, *Woman of the Year,* starring Katharine Hepburn and Spencer Tracy.

The Army's Signal Corps Photographic Center—the SCPC—was housed in the midst of a densely populated area, in the old Paramount studio at Thirty-fifth Avenue and Thirty-fifth Street in Astoria—a tall, white-columned building where for twenty years everything from silent movies to talkies, musicals, shorts, and the "eyes and ears of the world" Paramount newsreels had been made. Here the Marx Brothers had filmed *Animal Crackers* and *The Cocoanuts;* John Barrymore had starred in *Dr. Jekyll and Mr. Hyde;* and parts of *The Sheik,* starring Rudolph

Valentino, had been filmed. The ghosts of Gloria Swanson and W. C. Fields, whose looks and screen personas found their way into the Addams Family's Morticia, Pugsley, and Uncle Fester, lurked about the six soundstages.

Morning after morning, Addams and his unit lined up behind the barracks on the back lot where the Battle of Paris had been staged for a movie. After roll call, the army gave each soldier a nickel for the subway. Then they set off for a building on Thirty-second Street in Manhattan, where a group of writers and artists were soon housed with the Army Air Force's art department. Upon arrival, they lined up again in front of the building, and from there they marched to the East River Drive for training and exercise. They were trudging along the Lower East Side one day, singing a rousing chorus of "Tipperary," when a tenement bum mistook them for infantry about to be shipped out. "Go get 'em, boys!" he hollered from a window.

Addams was assigned to Unit A, which included several World War I artists, paid as civilians. Among the regular soldiers were Clarence John Laughlin, a well-known New Orleans photographer who became a good friend; Gerry Davis, who later produced *The Odd Couple* on television; the boyish Stan Lee, who would become a writer and co-creator of *The Amazing Spider-Man*, *The Incredible Hulk*, and other Marvel Comics superheroes; and two former Disney animators who had worked on the world's first animated feature film, *Snow White and the Seven Dwarfs*.

The atmosphere had its rewards. There was soldier Frank Napoleon, always joking about his name; and six-foot-four Abe Levikov, whose favorite gag was to enter the room holding hands with Herman Cohen, who stood about five feet tall. "See? This is the way they grow them in California," he'd say.

But for Addams, the Signal Corps was cartoonist Sam Cobean, "one of the great comic artists of all time." A dark, strikingly handsome man, he looked like Tyrone Power—"on a good day," joked Cobean. He was slightly younger than Addams and significantly shorter—a detail he wildly exaggerated in a series of private comic sketches he drew to relieve the boredom of army assignments. Like Addams, Cobean was prankish and kind, full of life and enthusiasm, and well liked; also like Addams, he loved sordid newspaper stories, parties, New York City bars, long automobile trips, archery, animals, antique furniture, anything "bizarre," and practical jokes. He was "a great foil for Charlie," said Jay Rutherford. And Cobean too was a newlywed; he had married his college sweetheart, Anne McCool—a lovely blue-eyed blonde who nevertheless looked Indian, thought Hedda Sterne, paintbrush in hand—almost exactly a year before Charlie married Barbara. Soon Addams and Cobean were working side by side and having dinner together, with their wives, at a steakhouse next to the Addams apartment almost every night.

While Addams attended Animation Artist School and illustrated training films, "about syphilis, or prosthetic devices" and "a manual instructing the troops in the art of barbershop harmony," Cobean illustrated a pamphlet on "the treacherous tactics of Japanese soldiers," among other assignments. "What talent you had would never really be used," said Addams. He himself would be asked to draw "congratulatory posters for a second lieutenant," that sort of thing—"just amateur stuff," he said. ("I mean, that was during the Second World War. Of course, I was doing it in the Civil War, too. I was just a drummer boy, then.") When Addams wasn't drawing for the army, he posed with a group of soldiers for a big allegorical mural featuring a plane named the *Matthew Brady*, which temporarily hung in the cafeteria; and he appeared in one of the training films, which often used SCPC soldiers. Cobean drew the result. "Now he can't get it out of his blood," says cartoon Bobby to tiny Cobean in a Cobean sketch of Addams as film star. Meanwhile, the cartoon Addams in beret and sunglasses, with a cigarette holder in his mouth and a copy of *Screen Secrets* under his arm, admires himself in a mirror.

Not everyone was resigned to throwing away his genius on the Signal Corps, even if it did mean avoiding the infantry. While Addams and Cobean drew cartoons on the side, and John Cheever and Irwin Shaw (who was part of the literary group of Addams friends) quietly worked on *New Yorker* stories at their army desks, William Saroyan refused to play the game. Saroyan, who had been averaging two books a year since his big 1934 debut, *The Daring Young Man on the Flying Trapeze*, had made him a literary star, quickly established himself as the Corps rebel. Assigned to do a booklet on logistics, he wrote, simply, "You fill the car up with stuff"—and came close to getting court-martialed, said Lou Marcus. And he wasn't about to sleep in the barracks. He paid a kid real money—$10 a day—to make his bed in the barracks appear that he'd been sleeping in it, while he spent his nights at his Sutton Place penthouse on the other side of the East River.

While Saroyan went his own way and didn't fit in, Addams, with his big smile, got along with everyone. He was "always good natured and

The SCPC soldiers. Addams (to the right of the woman) "got along with everyone."

happy-go-lucky," said Lou Marcus, who would have a lasting image of Addams crouching at the bottom of a human pyramid of three or four Signal Corps soldiers, grinning. Asked to sign a copy of *Drawn and Quartered* for Marcus's soldier brother overseas, Addams did more than sign it: He drew an army version of "The Skier" showing a hesitant soldier who has just skied through his stunned commanding officer on a snowy slope. He was so pleased with a second book inscription he did for Marcus's brother, featuring a defiant Pacific island native tattooed with emblems of the Rising Sun—one for each enemy plane or ship he had picked off—that he copied it and submitted it to *The New Yorker,* where it ran as a large spot drawing in the January 1, 1944, issue.

And Addams could drink with the best of them. The night Marcus's father-in-law plied a group of soldiers with alcohol over dinner, Clarence John Laughlin got so drunk he left the house wearing his hat backward, but Addams kept his head.

If nothing else came of Addams's three-year stint in the army, his

Army version of "The Skier."

friendship with Sam Cobean, and Cobean's private history of the SCPC—starring Addams in a series of absurd and sometimes porno-graphic situations—went far to make up for the loss of freedom.

Ultimately amounting to about a hundred sketches, some of which Addams framed and some of which he put in a scrapbook, Cobean's drawings preserved "the screwball days," as another staff artist called them, of the SCPC. Here are the cartoonists' sex fantasies and hangovers, the USO dances short on female partners, Cobean's rendition of the moments spent spying on colleagues with binoculars, and the boredom of army life, that would otherwise have been lost. Here is Addams in his curious new life—"half-civilian, half-soldier," as he put it. Cobean drew him with a fierce head, oversized hairy hands, dog tags, jockstrap, and scowl:

AN INTERESTING STUDY OF THE CHEMICAL AND ORGANIC CHANGES IN A MAN WHO HAS CHANGED FROM SEDENTARY TO MANUAL LABOR. THIS PATIENT, A NATIVE OF WESTFIELD, NEW JERSEY, IS SHOWN AFTER SIX WEEKS OF ARMY DETAIL.

Here also are the revenge fantasies. When James Geraghty rejected an Addams cover idea, Cobean drew Addams forcing the editor to eat the drawing; in another, particularly masterful sketch, Geraghty is reduced to puzzle pieces in a wastebasket. Yet another Cobean depicts Franklin and Eleanor Roosevelt and their dog, Fala, so diverted by an Addams cartoon that the president brings out the service medals. An "alternative storyboard" Addams and Cobean "developed for a particularly hair-raising lecture on the perils of venereal disease" shows Addams as Frankenstein's monster being serviced by a prostitute. A Cobean version of Morticia greeting her butler stars a naked Addams in dog tags. "Oh! It's only you—" she cries. Addams gets nose-stuck on a tree during training exercises. "There was something about me, namely my nose, that amused, even amazed, Cobean, and he drew it endlessly," remembered Addams. "He was carried to great heights by my nose."

Though Cobean's talent was widely appreciated at the SCPC, it was in Addams that Cobean found his greatest champion. "His drawings were beautiful—he drew more easily than anyone I ever knew," said Addams, who immediately appreciated Cobean's fluid and supremely assured line. In Addams's opinion, no one drew a funnier dog, bum, or peacock; no one depicted "the helpless but noncommittal men, the predatory chippies," as Cobean did. But Cobean, who had worked briefly for the Hollywood company Screen Gems after leaving Disney, had yet to break into the major magazine market. At the time Cobean entered the Signal Corps, Anne Cobean was shopping his cartoons around New York during her lunch hours as a secretary for *McCall's,* and getting nowhere.

Addams sent a batch of Cobean's drawings to James Geraghty, and took Cobean over to the *New Yorker* offices on Forty-third Street to introduce him to people. Geraghty enthusiastically passed the sketches on to Harold Ross. "Tell him to clean these up, and we'll print them," said Ross.

Sam Cobean drawing showing James Geraghty reduced to puzzle pieces in the wastebasket as Cobean and Addams look on.

On April 8, 1944, *The New Yorker* published the first of many Cobeans, a sketch showing a naked woman breezily posing in a 15-cent photo booth. Cobean was soon turning out wonderful panel drawings, including the "dream cartoon" he invented—a captionless drawing showing a character's thoughts or dreams in a bubble over his head. (A man looks at a woman on the street and mentally undresses her; a woman visits her psychiatrist and then revises her fantasies.) He impressed everyone—from the cartoonists who quickly tried to imitate his line, to writers such as Philip Hamburger, who considered Cobean "remarkable . . . fantastic . . . a genius."

Cobean was soon outstripping his friend in productivity. And yet there was no competition between them. They were so close that each preferred to talk about the other's work. Their drawings even briefly reflected each other's—less in imitation than salute. For a 1944 caricature of Cobean for *Mademoiselle,* Addams assumed a streamlined, jazzy style that could have passed for the work of his friend. And in two *New Yorker* cartoons concerning monstrous children, Cobean suggested Addams. But it was in a sly tribute done in wash, not Cobean's typical style, that he most tenderly evoked his friend. As a monk lies ill on his straw pallet, an aging monk with a very large nose takes his pulse, keeping his eyes on the small hourglass in his free hand. There is no mistaking the model for this cenobite who tenderly watches over his figurative brother.

THOUGH ADDAMS'S *New Yorker* output dropped by more than half during his first two years in the army, such was the prominence of his work that he seemed only slightly less present in the magazine. While rising "at the crack of dawn" for roll call, and squandering his talent on posters, manuals, and secret and regular training films for the army, he did some of his best work for *The New Yorker.* Harold Ross was so taken with a Valentine's Day cover drawing Addams produced in late 1943 that he predicted Addams's "fame should increase with its appearance." It shows two lonely souls in a rooming house; the bachelor has just slipped a valentine under the door of the apprehensive old maid. "That is one of the funniest cover drawings ever to come in here, and touching, too," wrote Ross. Addams, by then a corporal, was paid a whopping $350—big money at a time when the nation's per capita annual income was $1,223. The Addams valentine cover appeared on *The New Yorker's* February 12, 1944, issue.

During the 1940s, *The New Yorker* adopted a contract system for its favored artists, which gave the magazine first option on their work and guaranteed a basic fee upon acceptance. Productive artists earned a quantity bonus as well. But not all favored artists were equal. In Harold Ross's pri-

*Cobean's three profiles:
girls, girls, girls.*

*Cobean's private version
of Addams as monk.*

vate ranking, Addams was a triple-A artist; the only other was Mary Petty. This category, explained Ross biographer Thomas Kunkel, was trumped only by the golden three who remained above ranking: Peter Arno, Helen Hokinson, and Gluyas Williams. Even James Thurber, Whitney Darrow, Jr., and George Price—all AA artists—were rated below Addams. Cobean, who was greatly admired and imitated at *The New Yorker*, was in the A group along with Carl Rose, Otto Soglow, and others.

While other artists filled the wartime *New Yorker* with air-raid drills and plane spotters, soldiers and WACs, planes, bombs, Hitler, and drawings about such homefront shortages as gas, tires, cigarettes, and housing—often to marvelous effect—Addams remained Addams. He drew bad boys and cannibals, murderous spouses and enchanted woods. Hansel and Gretel discover a candy house with a sign below a frosted window: "Contains glucose, dry skimmed milk, oil of peppermint . . ."

Addams bought his first crossbow the day after the Japanese bombed Pearl Harbor. But his work remained largely untouched by the war. He made a conscious effort to stick to the themes that would outlive current events. And yet in being Addams, in tapping into the American "fascination with violence," as Dwight Macdonald would write some years later, he became "the characteristic *New Yorker* cartoonist of the war and postwar period."

In the years leading up to the war, Addams had contributed a few topical cartoons; then came Pearl Harbor, and *The New Yorker* sent telegrams to Addams and other "preferred artists and idea men" requesting "war pictures, comic or commentary particularly Japanese angle." Addams had immediately responded with a good captionless cartoon, but he had little more to say about the war.

Of the seventeen known Addams cartoons relating to World War II, including an ad and a cartoon for *Collier's,* the best of them fit his inclinations naturally. A sinister-looking character cackles over the automobile tires he has hoarded in a locked room; a giant-sized goon-faced drill sergeant greets his new recruits: "You men will hear all sorts of stories about me—one, that I was suckled by a werewolf."

The war seemed tailor-made for the work of certain artists. Hokinson ladies took advantage of the male shortage by trying to get into the Yale Club; they devoted club meetings to appeals for blood and shoes, and made more personal sacrifices as well—parting with one's butler, encouraging one's maid to cook with weeds, even offering one's dog—a dachshund—to the army. "I thought perhaps he'd be good for crawling under things!" the matron explains. The wife of a hungover Arno man told his doctor, "It's just a simple case of too much aid to Britain last night." And a fluttery Mary Petty maid dons a gas mask, to be transformed into a billowy winged insect.

But in the ramshackle Victorian mansion where time stood still, there was no talk of building an air-raid shelter, or of sacrificing the silent, broad-shouldered butler to active duty. The closest Addams came to turning his "weird Family" into patriots was an unsold cartoon rough based on an outside idea. As wholesome boys fly their toy airplanes on long strings, the unnamed little menace later known as Pugsley approaches from behind with an enemy bomber.

"Poison," Addams had written in his notebook in late 1943, noting a sale to *The New Yorker* for $125. After they waited in the cartoon bank for a year, on August 26, 1944, Morticia officially acquired two children. One day a few months after Addams's marriage, they had simply appeared in an upstairs hallway: a plump blond boy wearing shorts and a malevolent expression, emerging from a room with a glass in hand, and a thin, anxious, anemic-looking girl with black braids and an austere black dress and stockings that suggest the Amish. With her mother's black-and-white coloring, but not a hint of her sexiness, the little girl later christened Wednesday is decidedly not pretty. Her small round eyes look like birdseeds; her lifeless braids hang from her porcelain doll's head like a wig. "Well, don't come whining to me," Morticia tells her. "Go tell him you'll poison him right back."

In blessing his witch-woman with issue, Addams followed his conviction that "children are all kind of sadistic." The boy who would be called Pugsley in the television series was "an angry little W. C. Fields," Addams's idea of "the universal little boy—nasty." He was "the kid next door," the bitter fruit of a "completely unhappy" couple Addams later said he "couldn't bear to think of as married." Addams drew him tenderly, to the roots of his hair, which grew in a whorl from the back of his head.

The boy had come first. Blond and wearing a striped shirt since a June 1943 cartoon showing him constructing a coffin in shop class amid the wastebaskets and birdhouses of the other boys, he evolved from a line of small monsters who had begun creeping into Addams's cartoons during the early forties. Often cherubic-looking and pudgy, the boy builds an Erector-set guillotine; he buries his father in sand at the beach, then proceeds to tunnel through him. He plays a deadly game of Indian, returning home with a bloody dagger and an array of small scalps fastened to his summer shorts, and proudly displays the fish he caught. "This is nothing," he tells his horrified mother with a broad smile. "You should have seen the one that got Pop." He is in the crowd of New York City spectators in a well-known 1941 cartoon, watching as an octopus rises from a manhole to catch a man. While the other scouts and the troop

"Well, don't come whining to me. Go tell him you'll poison him right back."

leader fumble with their loop knots in one of Addams's numerous Boy Scout cartoons, the little menace expertly fashions a hangman's noose. In a famous cartoon, he opens a bedroom door to find his father standing on a stack of books on a chair with a note pinned to his trousers. As the wretched man reaches for a noose dangling from the light fixture, the chubby, smiling scout in the October 25, 1941, *New Yorker* says, "Hey, Pop, that's not a hangman's knot."

Reprinted not only in *Drawn and Quartered* but in Joseph Goebbels's *Berliner Illustrierte Zeitung,* this last cartoon earned Addams something more satisfying than money. Nazi editors sniffed that "jokes of this sort often appear in magazines which are convinced of their mission in the American Century."

With the arrival of the children, it was only natural that Addams should include a grandma, as he had one in his own household. A month after Pugsley poisoned his sister, the family gathers for home movies: Gomez, Morticia, the two children, and the lumpish, benevolent old hag next door from 1941's "cup of cyanide" cartoon. Lurch operates the projector. "It's a lovely spot—so unspoiled," observes Morticia of the cave dripping stalactites where the family was filmed picnicking. As they all enjoy the movie, the mysterious peeker seen in the first Family cartoon watches too, from a trapdoor in the ceiling. Addams came to think of this being as "The Thing," a term that would be applied in the television show to an altogether different creature, who had not yet been invented. "We don't know who or what he is," Addams explained many years later, "but whatever, he's the soul of good nature—at least he grins perpetually and may occasionally whimper."

Harold Ross wrote Addams a congratulatory letter on his "tasty little household," saying he considered the cartoon "probably a masterpiece." And he asked for even more characters, though he realized that the ideas for them weren't easy to come by.

THREE YEARS AFTER ENTERING the army and getting married, Addams seemed to be living out his cartoon life, or a glamorous semblance of it. With Bobby at his side, his army hitch over, he was seen driving swell sports cars. The couple posed for *Harper's Bazaar* in a 1929 Mercedes—a "souped-up 220 Merk" Addams had received in dilapidated condition from the playwright Philip Barry and had restored. Their toy poodle, Tulip, sat next to the picnic hamper in back. In the midst of tire and gasoline shortages, they had also acquired a rare 1933 Aston Martin roadster (one of 130 built in 1932 and 1933) and a prized 1926 35C

Bugatti, a supercharged version of the original racing car introduced at the 1924 French Grand Prix.

They gave wonderful parties and dinners, where one might see anyone who was anyone in the literary and cartoon worlds—John O'Hara, Dorothy Parker, Mary Petty, Alan Dunn. They had moved from the gloomy studio with its amusing half-number to a roomier apartment at 20 East Thirty-fifth, taking over the lease from Barbara's parents. (Addams was crushed to learn that the new tenants in the old apartment had painted over his hermaphrodite in green undies.) And in 1945, they purchased a forty-eight-acre farm in historic Bucks County, Pennsylvania, reportedly covered with hex signs, where they spent weekends with the Cobeans and the John O'Haras.

Photographed by Irving Penn for a series on couples, they seemed in perfect harmony—Bobby wearing a long black dress and a funereal expression, Addams in a crew cut that made him look older. (He hated his crew cut.) The couple added the appropriate Addams touches to their homes: a gilded skull; a dubious sample of Abe Lincoln's hair; the papier-mâché anatomical model, "complete down to the last intestine"; a nineteenth-century "fly intimidator," which threw "wonderfully weird shadows" across the room; a thirty-seven-and-a-half-pound antique sea-diving helmet, which claustrophobic Charlie gradually learned to wear. (One day when he was home alone, he put on the helmet and leaned out the window—about four stories up—to see if the people milling on the sidewalk would look up. No one did, and he finally gave up. But as he withdrew his head, he saw that people in the executive offices across the way were at their windows, staring intently at him.) They kept their gin and scotch in druggists' bottles labeled Carbol, Crud, and Arsenate, and a once-live stuffed bear presided over the hallway, an umbrella hooked over his extended arm.

People expected Charles Addams to live among crossbows, skulls, and fly intimidators (Hedda Sterne remembered something "sinister-looking in the car to kill flies"), and the cartoonist was happy to accommodate them. Once while visiting Jim and Eva Geraghty at their farm in Craryville, New York, with Sam and Anne Cobean, he had wandered through an ancient churchyard desecrated by bulldozers, where he found a tombstone reading "Little Sarah, Aged Three." A mechanic later en-

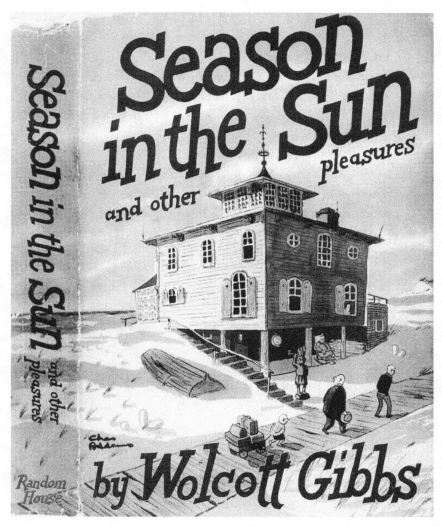

Dust jacket illustration by Addams.

countered it in the trunk of one of the Addams cars. "It's all right," Charlie told him. "It wasn't attached to anybody." He used the stone as a cocktail table in the apartment. As Geraghty explained later, "Charlie felt that little Sarah's spirit was happier hovering over his cocktail table than she had ever been on her cold New England hillside."

With fame and success had come an increase in his income—from $8,292 in 1943 to more than $21,000 in 1946. Of this, $1,000 or so a year was from his mother's estate, which included the sale of the Westfield home. But most of Addams's money came from his art. Along with his *New Yorker* cartoons, he was selling drawings to *Cosmopolitan*, *True*, and *Wish*, and doing the occasional ad and special illustration. In 1946, the summer after he mustered out of the army, he earned $100 for the dust jacket illustration for Wolcott Gibbs's *Season in the Sun and Other Pleasures*, and $400 for a picture for *Mademoiselle* to run with a Ray Bradbury story called "Homecoming." Flush, Addams and Barbara spent the months of July and August on Fire Island.

It happened that as Addams drew and redrew Victorian structures, he divested himself of the only real estate he had ever owned. About a year after purchasing the farm, he and Bobby began to find the long drive back to Manhattan on the weekends burdensome. They were coming home one Sunday when Bobby turned to Charlie in the car and said, "You know what?"

"Yeah, I know," he said.

They sold the place for $4,000.

Another house, dipped in sepia and lampblack, loomed in its place.

Chapter Eight

Boiling Oil

A S ADDAMS WAS LIVING THE ROOTLESS ARMY LIFE, MOVING his home base with Barbara from one temporary quarters to another, the Addams house, as it would be known, first came fully into view. Based on an idea by Herbert Gochros, a professional gag writer, the drawing in the November 10, 1945, *New Yorker* showed a Victorian pile behind a leafless tree and a chained drive giddy with weeds. A sign warned, "BEWARE OF THE THING."

The old place was elaborately detailed, with garrets and roof cresting, numerous chimneys and sloping dormers, oculus windows and shuttered bays with broken slats like missing teeth—all rendered with an intricate laying-on of inks and water applied with a tender brush. Addams drew what he loved.

Though it was not the first architecturally serious cartoon house, it was the first memorable one. In the twenty years since *The New Yorker*'s founding, only a few cartoons, by Alan Dunn, Carl Rose, and others, had featured authentic-looking houses. But such was the individuality and presence of the deserted Addams mansion, which virtually became another character in the Family series, it seemed like a cartooning first.

Though Addams never drew it exactly the same way twice, people began to see it as one house. They insisted that its model stood at Westfield, Colgate, Penn. "Rhinebeck has a house that's almost exactly the same," Addams told a reporter many years later, adding to the confusion.

But "the Addams house," as it were, was an amalgam of period features and flourishes the artist had seen and sometimes photographed—"really a style developed by Mansart and others," he explained. "The constructions come from my imagination, but I enjoy studying photographs of these houses." Into the ever-changing design went the nineteenth-century façades that had hidden sordid private intrigues during the cartoonist's Westfield childhood, and the mansard-roofed halls and fraternities from his daydreaming college years. There was an echo, perhaps intentional, of Edward Hopper's 1925 masterpiece, *House by the Railroad*. The lonely sun-washed blue Victorian by the train rails suggested the Addams homestead both as it was first sketched and as Addams later pictured it for a Schmid Brothers decorative plate featuring the Addams Family, in which he placed the house above a railroad track.

In one thing only, Addams remained consistent: The wooden structure was always Victorian, a style he thought looked "better for haunts. I can't picture a castle musty and cracked, with peeling paint," he said.

DURING THE FALL of 1946, James Geraghty realized that he was without a cover drawing for *The New Yorker*'s Christmas issue, and he summoned the brilliant Peter DeVries to the Geraghty home in Connecticut. DeVries, who was then writing casuals for *The New Yorker*, was one of its best cartoon doctors and gag writers. Geraghty and DeVries now spent an afternoon on the lawn at Geraghty's home, brainstorming ideas until they had it. The result of this session, as famously drawn by Charles Addams, showed four of the "weirdos," as Geraghty called them—Morticia, Lurch, Gomez, and Thing (the latter lying so flat, fingers gripping a cornice, one almost misses him)—gathered outside the attic story of the family mansion. On this snowy moonlit night, as a cluster of unsuspecting Christmas carolers sing their hearts out at the front door far below, the ghouls are about to answer them with a pot of boiling oil. As in the Greek tragedies from which Addams took his cue, the violence is implied; not a drop of oil (or lead, as Harold Ross thought of it) spills from the tipped cauldron.

Addams's feeling for his subject and his mastery of technique reached sublime new heights: in the steam rising at an angle from the bubbling pot; in the shawl Morticia clutches against the winter night; in the bars of indoor light filtered through a shuttered window onto the snow; in the

"half circle of light which is mirrored by a circle of molten lead" and "the footprints in the snow . . . a wonderful touch," noted his fellow *New Yorker* cartoonist Ed Koren in later years. "No one is aware of what [the fiends] are doing, so it isn't scary," he added. "There's a wonder, an inno-cence, about the characters."

The fabulously detailed and executed black-and-white cartoon, which had the effect, but not the overwhelming realism, of a color paint-ing, took Addams just over a day to complete.

Feeling confident and excited about the drawing, Geraghty took it to Harold Ross for approval. "You mean you'd use that as a Christmas cover?" Ross said incredulously, effectively putting a lid on the thing. "In matters of taste, as they say, there should be no argument," explained Geraghty later, but though he gave in about the cover, he could not let the Addams masterpiece die. After some persuading, Ross finally agreed to publish it on the inside of the magazine. *The New Yorker* purchased the cartoon known thereafter as "Boiling Oil" in December, and ran it as a full page in the December 21 issue. (On the cover by Edna Eike, holiday guests arrive with presents at a tidy Colonial house all decked out for Christmas.)

With the classic "Boiling Oil," which earned Addams $268.71 and an even greater reputation, the house he had been working out in cartoons and dust jacket illustrations achieved its iconic status. It also became one of Addams's personal favorites, not least because of the hundreds of re-quests he received from readers thereafter, who wanted to use it on their Christmas cards. And he had no intention of parting with the original. When John Mason Brown singled out the cartoon for praise in a *Satur-day Review* tribute to Addams's work a few years later, Addams replied, "I don't think anyone . . . could ask for more, no matter how grasping he might be." But he was also uncharacteristically deceitful, writing that he would "be glad to send [the cartoon] to you—but unhappily, it was given away a while back." And he sent Brown another Family drawing in its place. As for the public's desire to reproduce it on their holiday cards, as long as people weren't planning to mass-produce it, Addams always said yes, though he was giving away income. He empathized with their feel-ings about the cartoon. "It expresses their exact feeling about Christmas," he said approvingly. And his exact feeling about Christmas carolers.

AFTER YEARS OF drawing his favorite monsters, Addams still didn't know their backstory. They were wealthy, to be sure. "Money is no problem—they are quite well off," Addams wrote in his production notes for the television show years later. "Some ancestor made a real killing." And by the time Addams mustered out of the army, the Family had also revealed itself to be close-knit, polite, domestic, and civilized enough to take tea on a silver tray. They were undeniably sociable in their way, if not on Friday the thirteenth.

At some point he realized that the shuffling grandma was Gomez's mother, not Morticia's; that Gomez was "the only one who smokes—though Pugsley can be allowed an occasional cigar." He saw Pugsley's hair as "blondish red," and heard his voice as "hoarse." He had "popped blue eyes." As for the "solemn" and "delicate" Wednesday, who had her mother's coloring (but not her beauty), had "six toes on one foot," and was "given occasionally to tantrums," Addams found her "secretive and imaginative, poetic." "Seems underprivileged," he wrote in the television notes, and "on the whole pretty lost." He added: "Gomez is wild about her." He considered the grandma "foolishly good-natured" and "easily led. Many of the troubles they have as a family are due to her fumbling weak character," he wrote. As for the devoted butler, Lurch, a "towering mute" who had "been shambling around the house forever," Addams was sure that he was "the object of good-natured ridicule from the family."

He found it harder to come up with material for the Family than for anything else he drew. But he kept at it, sketching all kinds of gags. With the Wolff's pencil that he sharpened with a knife, he drew Pugsley flying a coffin-shaped kite; Gomez offering a departing guest "one for the road" as Lurch pours a drink from a bottle of poison; Morticia and Gomez presiding over the construction of a new wing of the Victorian mansion—a tumbledown structure which looked exactly like the old part of the house. Apparently rejected by *The New Yorker*, these roughs were never worked into finishes.

Readers and would-be cartoonists sent in ideas. To "Charles Addams, c/o *The New Yorker*" came vampires at the blood bank, cyanide cocktail parties, a crucifixion pageant, Morticia holding a laundry basket filled with bloody hands. Sometimes people even sent him their own drawings, "for possible re-rendering in your inimitable style": the Addams Family and other happy mourners sprinkling quicklime into an open grave; a sketch of Morticia—fat and droopy-breasted, as Addams had never drawn her—standing in a big black cookpot. "My God! They forgot the onions!" she cries. Over the years, people wrote Addams from Burbank, California; Wilmington, Delaware; Chicago; Fort Lee, New Jersey; San Antonio; Sewanee, Tennessee; Johannesburg; Switzerland; the Pentagon. They cornered him at cocktail parties. "That's really not the sort of thing we do at *The New Yorker*," he'd say, and extricate himself as soon as possible.

Sometimes Addams himself got carried away; irritation with the little monsters—or something—trumped subtlety and wit. "Why can't you spank us like other mommies?" asks a voice from within a locked trunk as Morticia walks away, key in hand. (Addams wrote both the name and the address of the person responsible for the idea on the rough.) An astonishing unpublished rough depicts an enraged Gomez wielding a crude club as he drags Pugsley, who is dressed in a YMCA sweatshirt, by the ear to the woodshed.

Addams resisted the idea sent by William Saroyan: "This legend for a picture emerged out of comic sleep last night: 'Well, what do you know? Here I am home, drugged and dismembered.' This picture to go with the legend is not clear to me, but maybe the legend will suggest an appropriate picture to you," Saroyan wrote in 1947. He resisted a gag from Arthur Laurents: "a woman coming out of a French Hand Laundry holding several hands." ("Too ghoulish," said Addams.) As Gomez observed while Lurch passed around a tray to their strange-looking guests one day, "I've heard it said that there isn't one of us who doesn't have a novel in him somewhere."

IT WAS BY CHANCE that the year that ended with a pot of boiling oil produced the last Family member.

At first the relationship wasn't clear, even to Addams. But he kept coming back to the character, following where the loathsome man was leading him. After years of out-of-town tryouts, as it were—in cartoons where the old bugaboo was seen feeding vultures in a public park or waiting for an optometrist to fit him with a single eyeglass, made for a Cyclops—Uncle Fester finally came to rotted fruition in a captionless and popular drawing Addams called "Movie Audience."

Published by *The New Yorker* in February of 1946, it showed a movie theater filled with weeping people—and one fat little ghoul, laughing at the tearjerker on the screen with openmouthed abandon. Addams gave the character the same color scheme he used for Morticia and little Wednesday—"dead white skin" set against funereal black, along with

some of his own features, grotesquely reimagined. In Fester the Addams nose was longer, the crinkly eyes "pig-like and deeply embedded, circled unhealthily in black," wrote Addams. The funny mouth that never showed the cartoonist's teeth was transformed into "no teeth"; the slicked-back hair was now an unnaturally white skull. Fester, noted Addams, was "absolutely hairless." For this most irreverent of souls, whom Dwight Macdonald called "the moral monster," Addams settled on an austere, monklike garment. "His one costume is a black great coat with an enormous collar—summer and winter," wrote the cartoonist. He has "pudgy little hands and feet."

Fester shared many of his creator's own attitudes and tendencies, such as laughing during funerals and other solemn occasions. Fester was a kindly uncle figure to other people's children—and your basic bad influence. They both drove fast, Fester blasting through the tollbooth in his old-fashioned car without paying. But the eminently civilized Addams never actually harmed anyone; Fester was the executioner who liked his work—sometimes literally. (A dungeon scene shows two poor souls shackled to the wall. Enter the guard, with a smiling Uncle Fester, hands folded, wearing a medieval costume. The guard speaks: "Fellows, I'd like you to meet the gentleman who will be in charge while I'm on vacation.")

"Uncle Fester is incorrigible and except for the good nature of the family and the ignorance of the police, would ordinarily be under lock and key," Addams explained.

In future cartoons, Fester would be seen cheerfully signaling the couple in the car behind him on a sharp mountain curve to pass him—into the path of an oncoming truck; happily skippering his small yacht— a slave ship; and driving an old-fashioned car carrying torpedoes and pulling a small submarine toward North Haven Marina on Long Island.

Though Fester would come to be associated with the Family as much as any other character, he was "not just a Family man," said Addams. Living with the happy immunity of the unmarried, this bamboozler remained largely on the periphery of the family circle. Apart from a sly cameo turn as a smiling head in the mansion's portrait gallery of monsters, where he was pictured in a suit of armor and an Elizabethan collar, he appeared in only one other *New Yorker* cartoon with other Family members. There was no sign of Fester when the family gathered to watch television or home movies. His rotund body—observed sitting alone at a table and shocking a waiter with his whispered off-the-menu order—was absent from the family's holiday table, where Lurch served a two-headed pig with apples in both mouths. Fester, it seemed, had his own plans for the holidays. During one Thanksgiving week, he was sighted in a liquor store gripping a bag of cement under a thick arm. "A cask of Amontillado, please," he says in the 1946 cartoon.

DESPITE SO MUCH LABOR on the part of their creator, the Family cartoons appeared less often than a full moon. During all of the 1940s,

The New Yorker published only thirty of them (out of Addams's entire output of 244 cartoons and three covers). A particular favorite of Addams fans and colleagues starred Pugsley. During the worst drought in New York City history, when citizens were being asked to go unwashed and unshaven, Addams placed the evil-faced boy out on the street, uncapping a fire hydrant.

And yet, like film stars, they attracted a devoted and eager following. Even the children of *New Yorker* readers, who would not otherwise have picked up the magazine, had come to watch for the cartoons that made scary things funny and celebrated breaking the rules.

Like all great humorists, Addams shaped his comedy seriously. He gave it a heart, and a solid foundation. He built his sets to last. The Family mansion, into which you felt you could step, was constructed of splintery wood worn to the softness of velvet. Bent over his drawing table hour after hour, Wolff's pencil (then brush) in hand, Addams drew every wooden shutter, every carved baluster and warped floorboard, every silky strand of web, creating a fully realized world. Wednesday's room was decorated with a wallpaper border showing a scaly prehistoric creature in happy pursuit of a bat-child.

The children who loved Addams's cartoons understood that there was nothing really scary going on in them. The house was not a Grimm's fairy-tale cottage where children were left orphaned and alone. One could see quite clearly that it was made of glucose, dry skimmed milk, and oil of peppermint, and that the witch peering over the Dutch door looked just like Grandma.

John O'Hara was proud that his little daughter, Wylie, recognized an Addams cartoon at a glance. Addams happened to be visiting the John O'Haras the week of August 14, 1948, when Morticia told Pugsley to "kick Daddy good night and run along to bed." There came a moment during the evening when O'Hara's wife, the dark-haired, exotic-looking Belle O'Hara, turned to Wylie, who had known Charles Addams for as long as she could remember. "Now kick Daddy good night and run along to bed," Belle told her daughter, just as they had rehearsed it.

The Family's popularity led to the 1947 publication of *Addams and Evil,* the cartoonist's second collection, which included seventeen cartoons featuring the haunted house and ghouls. The dust jacket was covered with a series of Rorschach ink blots. "I firmly believe that this is the best damn cartoon book to hit the market in years, and the advance sale is most encouraging," wrote Bennett Cerf from Random House. "Incidentally, the New Yorker Magazine itself is buying 3500 copies to distribute to advertisers and supposed well-wishers. That is more than some cartoon books have sold altogether, and calls for an inter-family drink, I believe, as soon as you and your bride return to New York."

Ten years after the series began, Morticia, the slithery silhouette in unvarying black, whom Addams saw as "the strength of the whole Family," remained a siren—even after childbirth. There would be no sagging muscles, no matronly housedress for her. Gomez, referred to as "Daddy" in the cartoons, would never be called her "husband."

Addams remained captivated by his cartoon queen—"an unsavory creature," he told John Kobler in an interview, "but I have always been in love with her."

Chapter Nine

And Then the Dragon Gobbled Up
the Handsome Young Prince

AFTER NEARLY SEVEN YEARS OF MARRIAGE, CHARLIE and Barbara Addams seemed "the most in love people," thought Carol Marcus, the ex-wife of William Saroyan, who spent a number of weekends under their rented roof on Long Island, in Quogue. To John Kobler, Bobby also seemed "healthy and cheerful," with "a well-developed wifely tolerance for her husband's foibles."

After renting a number of houses on the eastern end of Long Island, Charlie and Bobby bought a Victorian carriage house on the ocean side of Dune Road in Westhampton Beach. The human part of the dwelling had been spirited away in a hurricane, leaving only the stable block with its fireplace and forty-five-foot-long wassail hall, where carriages had once been stored, the horses' stalls, and a gated center courtyard. Both Charlie and Bobby loved it. They set about furnishing the place with crossbows and bric-a-brac and turned the stalls into bedrooms, leaving the heavy sliding doors intact. The wooden gate to the courtyard of the pale yellow block was always open; inside one found puppies in the shower. "There was always someone having a drink out there, and cars in the driveway," remembered a friend. In the morning, Charlie sat out in the courtyard in his pajamas, taking the sun and reading. Afternoon visitors found Bobby sitting in a chair surrounded by black poodles.

If friends tended to romanticize the Addams marriage, letting their affection for two charming, attractive, hospitable individuals guide their perceptions of the couple, they were also aware that Charlie and Bobby had different feelings about the kind of life they wanted. Though fun-loving like Charlie, Bobby longed to settle down and have a baby; Charlie was reluctant. He had never craved children. "I am my own child," he said later.

Barbara Addams on a trip to Europe in 1949.
Addams "always spoke so beautifully of her."

He didn't dislike children so much as "the idea of children," as a friend put it—though he did "find very young ones annoying." In his cartoons he pictured children behind bars, behind a brick wall, in little animal carriers—"Kids in Boxes," he called the outrageous Family drawing he had sold to *The New Yorker* in 1946 after he and Bobby visited a noisy family on Fire Island.

In the midst of all the noise and commotion, made worse by an Addams hangover, their hostess said, "You know, the other two children are coming back from camp today." And Addams heard himself say, "You mean in those little animal carriers?"

Gomez peers down apprehensively from the stair landing; the watchful Thing clutches the balustrade above the cobwebby stairwell; Lurch pauses with his feather duster—everyone except the self-possessed Mor-

"It's the children, darling, back from camp."

ticia coming to an abrupt halt, as in a Victorian tableau. "It's the children, darling, back from camp," she says. (Addams heard her voice as low, "never raised but has great range.") At the door stands a deliveryman holding an animal carrier in each hand.

The problem with children was the way they interfered with things, disrupting conversation and dinner, upsetting travel plans. Addams enjoyed the unencumbered life: restaurant dining and boozy late-night parties; stylish two-seater cars; travel; quiet time in which to work. There was the matter of auto racing—the Indy 500, "a sacred event" he attended in person when he could, and the amateur car races he watched and participated in as a member of the Sports Car Club of America (the SCCA). He delighted in taking Bobby and various friends such as James Jones and John O'Hara for "begoggled rides" in his Bugatti. (O'Hara, himself a classic-car man, pretended to enjoy himself when Addams took him for a spin in his Bugatti. "He was, in fact, absolutely terrified," remembered Wylie O'Hara.) Cars alone took up a fair amount of his time. As Addams put it later, "you must exercise them occasionally, or they will get cranky."

During the summer of 1949, he and Barbara had sailed with the Cobeans to Europe, where on one stop they lingered in Monte Carlo for some ten days, an indulgence they might not have been able to manage if they'd had children.

Marriage itself was confining—perhaps another reason for his reluctance to start a family. "Monte Carlo is thick with heavily muscled girls in Bikini suits on water skis," Addams had written Jim Geraghty. "Somehow I find I can look at them without tiring." Over the years, he had done more than look. There was Daphne Hellman, the wealthy wife of *New Yorker* writer Geoffrey Hellman, whom Addams seems to have slept with as early as 1945. There was Audrey Cosden, a redhead he met under a tree while sitting out a charity tournament at the Shinnecock Golf Club in Southampton in 1946, and drove off with. Later, when they found themselves sitting outside a bathhouse, Charlie said, "I'm so hungry I could eat a chocolate-covered fish"—endearing himself to Audrey. Thus began a long affair. (To Audrey, Addams complained that his wife "insisted on taking that wretched little dog to bed," which bothered him a great deal. What if a baby came along? he might have wondered.) Though Barbara didn't find out about the redhead, she did hear about others.

And yet for all his reservations about having a family, Addams was wonderful with children. Like Bobby, who would sit down next to the

Geraghtys' shy fourteen-year-old daughter, Sarah, drawing her out with questions about her life, Addams was one of those unusual adults who went out of their way to take an interest in other people's children. And he was especially good with difficult kids who didn't get along with adults. ("Charlie likes the monster in children," noted Wolcott Gibbs. "When it's not there, he invents it.") Always "Charlie," never "Mr. Addams," he was funny and kind. He entered into their play and drew pictures for them. He once flew to Maryland with a friend to pick up an angry thirteen-year-old girl at boarding school to attend her grandfather's funeral in South Carolina—enduring en route a clothes shopping trip and rude behavior to the stewardess. The girl, to whom Addams remained close, heard only a sigh and saw only a subtle shifting of dark brows. "Oh, come on," he said. And he was an inspired gift-giver who always seemed to know what a kid wanted. He gave the troublesome thirteen-year-old a silver and amethyst poison ring. He gave ten-year-old Tony Gibbs "a gleaming human skull," varnished yellow and covered with medical school signatures, and a pair of antique military pistols, about sixty caliber. Wylie O'Hara got any number of great presents, including an authentic gaucho doll from Argentina. From Charlie and Barbara came Wylie's first dog, which she had wanted badly. Since her father didn't want her to have a puppy, Charlie gave her his and Barbara's own four-year-old black toy poodle, Abraham, companion of Straus, who was presented in a shoebox with a bag of Cheetos.

And Addams himself had the most fantastic, expensive toys. Young Tony's reputation at boarding school was sealed the day Charlie drove Wolcott and Elinor Gibbs out to Lawrence, New Jersey, to visit him in a car Tony remembered as a replica of a German general's staff car (it was probably a Packard touring car)—a spectacular, "incredibly uncomfortable" machine with a supercharger, which would go 120 miles per hour. Afterward, Tony was known around the Lawrenceville School as (1) the kid who knew Charles Addams, or (2) the kid who knew the man who drove the car with the supercharger.

But Barbara wanted a baby of her own, and, however reluctantly, Addams agreed to have a child. When Barbara didn't become pregnant, she wanted to adopt, and Addams hesitated. Though he "wouldn't have minded" if Barbara had become pregnant, he said later, he had reservations about adoption. In the end, he compromised: He would not adopt an infant, but he agreed to an older child. He and Barbara contacted The Cradle, the famous agency in Evanston, Illinois, known for its celebrity adoptions by such entertainers as George Burns, Bob Hope, and Al Jolson, which tried to match children to adoptive parents of similar background, physical characteristics, and talent. Having gone through the paperwork, the Addamses waited.

In the meantime, Sam and Anne Cobean had adopted a little boy from The Cradle, whom they named Scottie. Dark in coloring like Sam, and adorable, Scottie Cobean might have been taken for Sam's biological child.

Things were going well for the Cobeans. In the years since the war, Sam's career had soared. Not only was *The New Yorker* "printing all the Cobeans it could get," noted Addams, but Cobean cartoons were also appearing in *Collier's, Harper's,* and *The Saturday Evening Post.* He had published his first cartoon collection, had been featured in *Life,* and was in demand for advertising work, to which he brought "taste and understatement in a field not generally noted for either," said Addams. Success had bought him a home in Connecticut with a greenhouse, and an antique farmhouse overlooking Seneca Lake, near the picture-postcard village of Watkins Glen, New York. Cobean was driving a Jaguar—a choice Addams facetiously attributed to Sam's love of animals. He was seen tooling around Watkins Glen in the red Jaguar with his Afghan hound—who wore a scarf, so that he occasionally "was mistaken for someone's grandmother." And with success had come another property, for which talent alone was the only currency: an office on the fifteenth floor of *The New Yorker,* which he shared with Addams.

But there was a smudge in the idyllic picture, which Cobean glossed over with attentiveness and charm: Anne had a serious drinking problem. As their Watkins Glen friends Cameron and Jean Argetsinger later explained it, "Sam could drink all night and be fine." But Anne couldn't handle it. "Sam protected her," said the Argetsingers, "and covered it up."

Charlie and Barbara visited Watkins Glen often enough to talk to the Argetsingers, the parents of a large brood, about their efforts to adopt a child.

Addams had first met Cameron Argetsinger at a Sports Car Club

Anne Cobean (subject of a portrait by Hedda Sterne) and Sam,
who looked like Tyrone Power "on a good day," sailing to Europe in 1949.

get-together at the Indy 500 in 1948. Argetsinger credited Addams, a
club member, with helping to change the club's policies, which had denied membership to Jews. Addams had gone about things in his low-key
way, by making a point of introducing Argetsinger to Erwin Goldschmidt,
and having him ride with Goldschmidt in his car so he could see him
drive. After that, Goldschmidt was allowed to drive in the SCC races,
and won the Grand Prix in 1950.

When, at a cocktail party, Argetsinger had raised the idea of a race at
Watkins Glen, Addams's hand was the first to go up. That first year of the
amateur road race, in October 1948, Addams—wearing his trademark
tweed fore-and-aft cap, which afterward became all the rage at the famous annual race—had driven the 6.6 miles "at a 53.6 clip" in his 1928
Mercedes with Bobby by his side. (Though earnest about racing, Addams was less interested in winning than in "animate scenery," he said.)
Cobean, who loved the beauty of cars but wasn't inclined to race, worked
on the pit crew.

After adopting Scottie, Sam and Anne decided to spend their first summer with the baby near Charlie and Bobby—in Westhampton Beach. Charlie found them a rental house, and the summer of 1950 the Argetsingers helped the little family move to Long Island in two cars, theirs and the Jaguar. The night they arrived, about eight of them, including John O'Hara, sat down to dinner at the Addams carriage house on the dunes. Charlie made faces at the baby.

There came a day when an older child was eligible for adoption, and Charlie could not go through with it. Barbara, who was now thirty-one and had invested eight years in the marriage, was heartbroken.

The end seemed to catch most of the couple's friends by surprise. "All right, children, a nice big sneer now," said Morticia on June 12, 1951, as the wretched children posed for a photograph against an outside wall of the shabby mansion. Three days later, Addams made a terse entry in ink in his pocket-sized datebook. "B.A. leaves," he wrote in the formal manner of someone trying to distance himself from something painful. He wrote it again in his earnings notebook: "B.A. leaves 12." He did not note that Bobby had left with another man—their next-door neighbor at Westhampton Beach, Joe Kaufman, a wealthy man of leisure, possibly an alcoholic, and "a very funny, witty fellow," who was also married. Kaufman had lost both of his ears in the war, reportedly at the Battle of the Bulge, and yet "women were always falling for him," reported a baffled Gardner Botsford.

Apart from telling Cobean, Addams said little or nothing about Bobby and Kaufman, even to his closest friends. Most remembered hearing the details of the separation from Barbara, not Charlie.

As the Addams marriage was breaking up, an Addams cartoon husband imagines his wife falling into a wishing well. In another cartoon, "the dragon gobbled up the handsome young prince and his lovely young bride and lived happily ever after," says the smiling grandma, as the pale little girl with the limp braids happily grips the crazy quilt on her bed. (Through the wood grain on the footboard, the painted octopus looks startled.) That year, Addams's *New Yorker* output dropped to fifteen cartoons, from his previous annual average of twenty-five.

Three weeks after Barbara left, Cobean called from Watkins Glen with a scheme to arrange a "marriage" between his poodle and Charlie's for the following weekend. It was the first time he and Charlie had spoken since Bobby left. They hung up, and Sam left home to mail some cartoons to *The New Yorker*.

Cobean was on his way home when he saw Cameron Argetsinger at the local garage, where he was leaving his Cadillac for repair. Cobean offered him a ride home, and they set off for the lake, stopping at Seneca Lodge en route so Sam could telephone Anne.

During the five-mile drive from the village to the Argetsinger house on the west shore of the lake, Sam told Cameron about Charlie's separation from Bobby, and about Kaufman, the butt of private jokes between Charlie and Sam, who called him "No Ears."

As the car headed north on Route 14, Cobean drove fairly fast, though not recklessly, on the straightaway. Suddenly, without signaling, another car turned left in front of the Jaguar into a driveway. Cobean swerved, but there was nowhere to go, and he hit a tree. Thirty-year-old Cameron Argetsinger was hurled through the windshield, breaking it; he suffered a concussion and facial lacerations requiring about twenty-four stitches. Cobean wasn't as lucky. Pinned behind the steering wheel, whose bullet-shaped horn button pierced his heart, he was killed almost instantly. He was thirty-eight.

"Sam killed," Addams wrote in his little datebook for July 2. He used a pencil, as if the entry might be a mistake he would later erase.

Anne herself had called him with the news. "I didn't believe it," Addams wrote later, "nor will I ever, quite." He told Frank Modell he felt responsible for Sam's death. It was *his* interest in cars that had got Sam started, he said, and led to the purchase of the Jaguar—a machine Addams described as "very sleek, and terribly fast." As if to remind himself of his role in the death of his closest friend, he saved a copy of the gruesome newspaper photograph in the *Elmira Star-Gazette*, which showed Sam's body lying facedown in the grass alongside the Jaguar, his feet hooked inside the car.

Addams and Barbara—always a class act—went to the funeral in Watkins Glen together. It was well attended by *New Yorker* colleagues as well as other friends. After the service, and after lingering at the Cobeans' farmhouse for a while, Charlie and Barbara drove to the Argetsingers', where Cameron remained in bed, recovering from his injuries. They stayed for about an hour to visit and talk with the children, which meant a great deal to Cameron and Jean. Even during this terrible time, Bobby looked "great," thought Jean, though she must have been deeply affected by Sam's death.

"What a remarkably fine friendship existed between you and Sam," Anne Cobean wrote Addams in a friendly, slightly formal note that betrayed nothing of what she herself had lost.

After Cobean's death, the Unitarian minister in Watkins Glen became close to Anne. It was his opinion that she should return Scottie to the orphanage. With Sam gone and Anne an alcoholic, the boy would be better off elsewhere, he argued.

Anne was not easily persuaded; it took the minister a full year to convince her. Finally, against the advice of The Cradle, Anne returned three-year-old Scottie Cobean to the orphanage. And then she moved back to her hometown of Norman, Oklahoma, where she thought people would understand her. Addams kept in touch with her, but she essentially disappeared.

ONCE BARBARA DECIDED to leave Charlie, she left completely. She cut her hair short—"she looked like a Japanese boy," said Lyda Hall—got a St. Thomas divorce, and married Joe Kaufman, whom she also soon divorced.

She had left Westhampton Beach in an apparent hurry, without stopping to pack many personal effects—not her yearbook and family photograph albums, her correspondence, or the full-sized valentines Charlie had made for her every year since their marriage—all things she could pick up later. She asked nothing of Charlie, no support; she didn't take "a nickel" from him, he said in admiration. Afterward, "he always spoke so beautifully of her," said Odette Terrel des Chenes, a statement with which all of Addams's friends agreed.

Years later, Barbara married another man Addams knew casually, the handsome Pulitzer Prize–winning author John Hersey, whose *Hiroshima* had been published in a single groundbreaking issue of *The New Yorker* in November 1946, the month before "Boiling Oil." With Hersey—"Mr. Straight Arrow," as Gardner Botsford called him—Barbara got her baby, a daughter, and a long-lasting union. Botsford ran into her when Hersey was Master of Pierson College at Yale during the years 1965–70, and found her "completely changed." The fun-loving young woman with the lush black hair and girlish puffy sleeves, who had jitterbugged the night away with a uniformed Addams in Cobean's cartoon portrait, who called Addams "Chooch" and laughingly posed in an Addams sports car filled with beer bottles and friends, who would "do anything on a dare," was now demure, said Botsford. The perfect academic's wife, she referred to the students as "our boys."

—

Chapter Ten

Everything Happens to *Me*

AFTER CHARLIE'S MARRIAGE ENDED, OBSERVED ELINOR Gibbs, he seemed to go through a period of dating girls who resembled Bobby: tall, with dark hair. There was Gillis MacGil, a very dark-haired Bergdorf's model whom Addams took out a few times, and brunette actress Rosemary Pettit, who had a role in the 1952 FBI movie *Walk East on Beacon!,* filmed partly in New York City. Addams began a long and very public romance with the actress the summer Barbara left. And there were others. "Veronica Lake," he wrote in his 1951 datebook about two weeks after Cobean was killed, "1770 Inn"—though the actress who had caused a craze during the 1940s with her famous peekaboo hair was tiny and blond. Doris Lilly—the tall, blond, leggy author of the 1951 book *How to Marry a Millionaire* also made the Addams datebook. A glamorous former starlet and dedicated party girl, Lilly, like Carol Marcus, was one of Truman Capote's models for Holly Golightly in *Breakfast at Tiffany's.* Addams was observed in a French restaurant sketching Lilly on the tablecloth as a witch riding a broom.

Along with women and drawing, he had any number of other distractions. When Addams wasn't officially racing, he "organize[d] his own," reported *Current Biography:* "Addams vs. all the cars on the road from New York City to Long Island." He worked on a short film with his close friend the actor Burgess Meredith—a send-up of art films. "We'll use some of my cartoons, and a lot of sincere music," said Addams. His third cartoon collection, the 1950 *Monster Rally*, was followed by *Homebodies* in 1954. There was a new line of merchandise adorned with his cartoons: crockery and Richard Farrar silk scarves, modeled by Rosemary Pettit and Kaja Meredith, Burgess's wife, at the beach. The Dune Deck Hotel in Westhampton Beach commissioned Addams to paint a mural—his first—on the wall of its popular bar.

Perhaps of most consequence to Addams, he had expanded his property holdings with the purchase of an odd little clapboard structure. Built as a children's playhouse by a wealthy resident of the old summer colony in Westhampton Beach, it consisted of two small rooms, top and bottom, connected by outside stairs, each floor with its own porch. Addams was enchanted. It looked to him like "a little tower with one room over the other." Addams had it moved from its original location on the dunes, and now it stood across the street from the carriage house, which Addams rented out to Burgess Meredith during the summer of 1952. In time he would add old-fashioned touches—an octagonal stained glass Victorian rose window, a garage and cupola ("I'm the only two-cupola man on Long Island," he later bragged), and a dock, where Gardner Botsford would often see him sitting alone, dangling his feet in the water.

Life in the little house, said Addams, was "like being on a houseboat." The upstairs balcony led out from Addams's new bedroom, which had a small fireplace and water views; the room where the ghosts of children held puppet shows began to fill with crossbows. The only disadvantage was that you had to go up the outside stairs to get from one floor to the other. After a drenching rain one night, in which Addams had to come down the stairs from his bedroom to close the living room windows, he simply cut a hole through the bedroom floor and drove pegs into the kitchen wall below.

In the midst of his romance with Rosemary Pettit, Addams also began an affair with thirty-five-year-old Maeve Brennan, *The New Yorker*'s resident Circe—though with Maeve, writing always came before men. Witty and exquisite-looking, Maeve Brennan was a dainty five feet tall, with upswept brown hair, porcelain-doll features, and an "entrancing Irish brogue." Wearing black and high heels, with a singular touch of color in the form of a red rose or carnation pinned to her dress, she swept through the magazine's dreary offices like a seductive breeze. "Brendan

Gill was the first to topple," remembered Gardner Botsford. "He was followed by Joseph Mitchell, and Mitchell by Charles Addams." Brennan was with Addams the night of March 1, 1952, when *The New Yorker*'s first couple, Katharine and E. B. White, threw a big party for William Shawn at their Turtle Bay Garden duplex to celebrate Shawn's appointment as editor following the sudden death of Harold Ross. As Shawn played hot jazz on the piano, followed by the dashingly handsome Peter Arno, people danced and drank into the wee hours. Seemingly everyone who worked for *The New Yorker* was there, crowding the Whites' stylish beige book-filled rooms looking out onto the tree-shaded garden.

At some point Maeve's brogue began to rise above the party sounds. First she got into an argument with critic Anthony West. The shy E. B. White, known by his friends as "Andy," caught the word "bastard," and fled into the kitchen. The party continued. Again Maeve's voice transcended the noise. "Charlie Addams, you're a pig!" she cried. Gardner Botsford caught something about her having let Charlie into her bed; he gathered the affair was now over.

The formidable Katharine White, whose graying chignon was held in place with old-fashioned bone pins and tortoiseshell combs, appeared at Botsford's side.

"Maeve is misbehaving," she said, and asked if he would take her home.

All the way down Fifth Avenue in the taxi with Gardner and Tess Botsford, Maeve shouted her lament out the window. "Charlie Addams is a pig! Charlie Addams is a pig!"

And so went the known part of the private life of one of New York's most sought-after men. Addams "was quite a catch," stressed Anna Hamburger, wife of Philip Hamburger. At the Westhampton Beach carriage house, where people gathered for impromptu visits and cocktail parties, "there was always a very attractive woman in attendance, waiting for his arm," said Arthur Laurents. Laurents happened to witness the moment when a courtyard bench filled with guests collapsed. "Because of Charles, I think, it was neither embarrassing nor hurtful, just funny," remembered Laurents, who had turned to his host and asked "if he knew the bench would collapse. He laughed."

At the St. Regis Maisonette, Constance Moore dedicated her show to

Addams—"a honey and a scream." Offers came in the mail: "YOU SHOULD BE HEARING FROM MANY WOMEN ABOUT NOW, SINCE THE FACT YOU ARE SINGLE AGAIN," wrote a woman from Binghamton in a rambling 1953 letter addressed to "Mr. Charles Samuel Addams, Fifth Ave. (Upper Part), New York Town, N.Y." Addams did not reply to the woman in Binghamton. When, however, he was invited to pick "Miss Sewanee" (Tennessee) from a group of photographs submitted by the student body of the University of the South, he said yes.

And yet for all the gaiety and girls, Charlie hadn't seemed as happy since his divorce, thought Carol Marcus, who would run into him at parties and talk about whom they were dating. Though Carol later stressed that this was just her impression, Gillis MacGil told an Addams story that suggests that the loss of Barbara had left Addams more vulnerable than usual, though this too is speculation.

Having met the brunette model at the Duke Box, the Southampton bachelor pad of Angier Biddle Duke of the Duke tobacco and philanthropy family, Addams took Gillis MacGil out at a time when she was getting over her own divorce. He never made a pass. As Gillis talked, he would listen "with that sweet slow smile"; she made him laugh, he told her.

And yet when Gillis unintentionally hurt him, he could not get past it. Following an early morning booking on the *Today* show, she had returned home and fallen into a deep sleep, never waking until the next morning. "Why didn't you answer the phone?" Addams asked when she tried to explain. In his quiet way, he was "really, really p-o'd," said Gillis; he simply could not understand how anyone could sleep through a ringing telephone. They remained friends, but he never asked her out again.

By the spring of 1953, Addams had been dating Rosemary Pettit for nearly two years. As he was overseeing some improvements to his Westhampton Beach property, "The Voice of Broadway" wondered in print whether he was making "orange blossomish plans" with the actress. ("Is it warm in here, or is it me," Addams wrote in the notes section of his datebook, evidently for a cartoon idea.) The couple were photographed together for *Look* magazine, Rosemary wearing a fluttery white dress and shading her eyes from the sun as the toned, forty-one-year-old cartoonist, dressed in a short-sleeved black shirt and belted gabardines, shot his longbow at the beach. The following month, Rosemary wore another white dress as she stood alongside Addams, also in summer white, while he signed his autograph for the beaming blond socialite Carrie Munn.

The occasion was the premiere marking the unveiling of the fifteen-by-five-foot black-and-white mural Addams had painted for the Dune Deck Hotel, which starred the Addams Family enjoying an unconventional outing at the beach. The hotel turned the well-publicized June 29, 1952, bash into an all-Addams celebration. The rooms were festooned with spiders, skeletons, and bats; caviar sandwiches shaped like vampires and bats were served on cocktail plates decorated with Addams drawings. Against the backdrop of the Addams Family's picnic preparations, with Grandma plucking a wishbone from a picnic hamper, drinks were served from bottles marked "Formaldehyde," "Cyanide," "Arsenium," "Poison," "Paris Green," "Carbolic Acid," and "Chloral Hydrate."

"Aren't they carrying this too far?" asked Rosemary Pettit.

As guests milled about the room talking and drinking and eating, a prominent local lawyer stood regarding the Addams painting. "I'm sure I defended that guy in 1936," he said, perhaps referring to Gomez, whose suit pants are rolled up as he reels in something monstrous that is causing beachgoers to flee in terror, while Uncle Fester waits with a net and a club and Lurch holds the silver martini shaker. "I got him off with eighty to life."

WHILE THE DUNE DECK enjoyed a surge in business attributed to the Addams mural, the cartoonist entered another bar in New York, and his life was never the same again.

Shipwreck Kelly was there with a date. John "Shipwreck" Kelly was the ex–football star for the University of Kentucky who later played for the Giants and the old Brooklyn Dodgers football team, and who married Brenda Frazier, the world's most famous debutante. A couple of years older than Addams, "Ship" was big and handsome, with the heavy, lantern-jawed face of a comic superhero. Like Addams, he was a man-about-town. The two covered some of the same romantic territory. Kelly dated Joan Fontaine, with whom Addams later became involved; Addams had once slept with Brenda Frazier, a rail-thin, stark brunette with shoulder-length ink-black hair, death-white skin, and red lipstick who had made her spectacular society debut at the end of 1938, four months after Morticia was introduced to the world in the pages of *The New Yorker* puzzling over a vacuum cleaner. By now, Kelly and Brenda were separated.

In the bar with Kelly was another brunette. This one favored the Veronica Lake look: shoulder-length hair pinned back behind one ear and falling in a glossy tumble down the other side of her face.

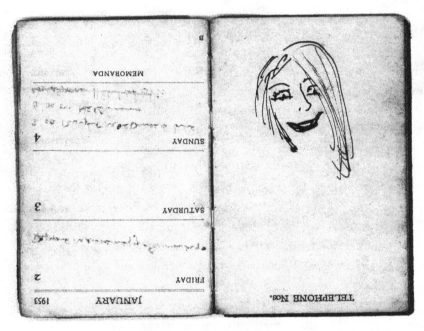

Addams sketched a dead-ringer portrait of Barbara Barb in his datebook.

Soon after her introduction to Charles Addams, she turned up uninvited at his apartment naked under a mink coat. By September 1953 she was dominating his datebook. Addams sketched a dead-ringer pen-and-ink portrait of her on a blank page—all eyes, smile, and Veronica Lake hair. There were no more entries in the little book for the long-running Rosemary Pettit. And judging by that confident, smiling face surrounded by white space on the page intended for telephone numbers, there wouldn't be.

—

LIKE HER FICTIONAL-SOUNDING name, Barbara Barb was flashy and sharp, with a penchant for Hollywood glamour: black matador pants worn with gold-braided black slippers; one-sleeved evening dresses. She had "a woman's body—built for action," said Nancy Holmes, herself a beauty. And she knew how to make an entrance. Shortly after Arthur Laurents built a house on the dunes at Quogue, Addams brought Barbara for a visit. Many years later, Laurents would remember the occasion: "I could see the ocean literally sparkling in the early summer sun; through the other [window] I could see the bay sparkling across the wetlands. But what really caught my eye was the woman coming up the long walk to the house with Charles Addams. She looked like what was called in the mid-Fifties a bimbo: long long tanned legs in very high heels and ending in very short shorts, a tight blouse knotted at the exposed mid-riff (yes, even back then), a striking face partly hidden by hair hanging exactly like one of the Addams Family Vampires."

By the fall of 1953 they were an item. Draped on Addams's arm at a party at the apartment of violinist Nathan Milstein and his wife, Thérèse, Barbara wore a stunning black dress she had had designed, described by Thérèse as indecent. "She was very spectacular-looking," said Jane Gunther, one of New York's loveliest women, adding that there was "an excitement in her" which was quite dazzling and winning. She looked "like a beautiful showgirl," thought Hedda Sterne.

Addams's friends were immediately struck by her resemblance to the first Barbara, by which they meant to Morticia. But though both Barbaras had long dark hair, it was Barbara Barb who more suggested the cartoon woman—a likeness she enjoyed playing up with the scandalous black dress. Though she lacked Bobby's black-and-white coloring, she was composed, like Morticia, of hard angles. Her severely bobbed nose, which had strangely elongated nostrils, had completely altered her face, making it look somewhat asymmetrical, her eyes slightly up-centered. (Thérèse Milstein even thought Barbara had had her nose done to look more like the Addams witch.) Addams's delighted datebook sketch perfectly captured her fascinating smile.

Not everyone was charmed. Carol Marcus deplored the one-sleeved evening dresses. The elegant Gardner Botsford dismissed Charlie's new woman as "a big, brassy number"; he could not understand how any man could be attracted to her. Neither could Botsford's former stepfather, Raoul Fleischmann, *The New Yorker*'s attractive and well-heeled publisher and moneybags. One day, the two men ran into Barbara in Quogue.

"What's the real name of the whore of Babylon we just met?" Fleischmann asked Botsford.

People were astonished to learn that this woman with the movie-star hair, tiny waist, and long black gloves was a practicing lawyer. Poured into a tight skirt and an expensive, low-cut blouse with French cuffs, Barbara Barb suggested Hollywood's idea of a woman lawyer—more Barbara Stanwyck than Katharine Hepburn. She lived in a swanky apartment at 4 East Eighty-eighth Street, with miles of white rugs and dark walls and a Louis XVI desk. Her Manhattan office was reportedly staffed with three male lawyers.

Specializing in international law—an unusual choice for private practice in those days, noted Nancy Wechsler, then a young attorney with Greenbaum, Wolff & Ernst, who represented *The New Yorker*—Barb handled clients discreetly identified as "titled or wealthy persons living in various countries." When she wasn't jetting off to Europe on business, she spent her time swimming, riding, playing tennis, drawing skillful courtroom sketches she called "legal satire," and writing a prospective book titled "Murder In Law," an apparent reference to her own youthful victories in the criminal courts. The dazzling Miss Barb also seemed to possess an impressive academic pedigree—Columbia University, followed by St. Lawrence University School of Law, from which she had received a master of laws magna cum laude. The sultry-looking lady lawyer gave her age as thirty-three.

The true story of Barbara Barb, who was thirty-eight when she shaved five years off her age for an impressionable reporter, was considerably more provocative than the *Photoplay* version. Like all good actresses, Barbara had borrowed from life to create her fictional persona, using enough of her own experiences and secondary knowledge to convince intelligent people that she was far more accomplished than she was. Born Estelle B. Barb to Polish-speaking Jewish immigrants Sane and Regina Barb of Brooklyn ten years after they arrived in Ellis Island from

Austria, she was the youngest of six children. By the time she was four, her father had died, but the family had prospered. Regina Barb owned her own home and a trucking company. One son, Max, had served as overseer of that company; another, Jacob, had graduated from both Columbia and its College of Physicians and Surgeons and was a surgeon at the Jewish Hospital in Brooklyn. They were, in short, an American success story—just not the story Barbara wanted for herself. Estelle graduated from Brooklyn College and its law school—which only later joined forces with the WASPy St. Lawrence to offer a one-year graduate course leading to a degree of LLM or JSD. After graduation she set up a solo practice at 675 Gates Avenue in Brooklyn at her mother's residence, where she had grown up.

A year later—in 1939, at the tender age of twenty-three—Estelle B. Barb seemed poised to fly. She got her big break when—apparently through her Brooklyn or brotherly connections—she came to represent a man charged with first-degree murder. Marching into court in "a black ensemble topped off by a tiny sombrero" she called "my lucky court hat," she impressed both the judge and the court reporters with her youth and confidence, and won an acquittal. She enjoyed a little burst of publicity when both the *Herald Tribune* and *The New York Times* ran small items with photographs about the "girl lawyer" who had represented a black man with winning pluck. The photographs showed a lot of dark hair billowing around a pretty, heavily made up, smiling face that bore no resemblance to the cool revision Charles Addams met fourteen years later.

During her quick journey from Brooklyn to Manhattan, she dropped the "Estelle," the big hair and heavy eye makeup, the old nose, the college known for its immigrant students (which she replaced with her brother's Ivy League university), and more. She told Addams she had no family. How she got from the one-woman law practice in her mother's home in Brooklyn to the Fifth Avenue office that she said included three male lawyers is a blank page. As Nancy Holmes heard it from their common circle of friends, Barbara had made her money not from a brilliant legal career, but as the mistress of a shipping magnate. By now, Barbara's lovers, past and present, included a Japanese man; a British MP named Henry Colyton, whose wife died in 1953, the year Barbara met Addams; and the novelist and columnist Robert Ruark, who called Barbara "a tort with tits"—a line that made Addams laugh. There were whispers about her relationship with an accomplished, witty, and beautiful woman who would soon become the wife of a famous man. (Though one of those doing the whispering—English director Peter Glenville, who was overheard talking to Irene Selznick at a Selznick party—could be malicious, the woman in question also made a point of implying that she was having a lesbian relationship with Barbara.) Somewhere along the line there had also been a husband from whom Barbara was divorced—identity unknown.

More troubling stories concerned Barbara's manipulation of people. Nancy Holmes knew a very malleable woman Barbara had completely taken over and pushed into a loveless marriage. Both husband and wife had ended up committing suicide. "There was a lot of evil around her," said Nancy. Though she had liked Barbara at first, she became a little afraid of her when she realized she couldn't trust her, and distanced herself. "Spooky, that woman," was Lyda Hall's terse assessment of the new Barbara.

If Addams heard any of this chatter from the flock of pretty girls Barbara posed with on his porch at Westhampton Beach—all smiles and summer shorts—it seemed to have no effect on him. He was utterly captivated. "Charlie just absolutely adored her," said Thérèse Milstein, a perception echoed by Jane Gunther. He squired Barbara to parties at the Nathan Milsteins', where the guests were named Balanchine, Horowitz, Toscanini, and Rachmaninoff. He kept track of her comings and goings—"BB sails England," he wrote in his 1954 datebook—and blocked off two or three days at a time to see her, while continuing to see other women. He was impressed that Barbara was a lawyer. He was fascinated by her thick glasses, which she removed for photographs; without them, he told Buddy Davie, she couldn't see more than five feet. She had half a dozen pairs for different distances. When Hedda Sterne and Saul Steinberg arrived at Barbara's glossy apartment for a party one evening, Barbara mistook Steinberg, in his white dinner jacket, for one of the waiters, and began giving him instructions.

Addams was soon confiding in a number of his friends about violent arguments during which Barbara would assault him. "Evidently, they didn't get along too well," remembered Frank Modell, who was himself seeing an actress he described as "a madwoman, hysterical." He and Addams would get together and commiserate.

In the midst of this reckless affair, Barbara told Addams she was pregnant. He confided in his lawyer, Harriet Pilpel, that he and Barbara planned to get married. But nothing came of it. There was no wedding—and no pregnancy. Then Barbara again said she was pregnant, and they

Nancy Holmes adjusts Barbara Barb's hair at Westhampton Beach.

renewed their plans to marry. Addams's 1954 datebook shows that something significant happened, or was scheduled to happen, on Saturday, September 25:

BB

*

he drew. But still there was no wedding.

For months, while continuing to fight, they kept trying to get married, and failing. They made at least two trips to South Carolina in 1954 for the purpose of marrying, but did not.

Though there is no record of what they argued about or why the marriage plans kept falling through, Barbara's well-documented temper and her subsequent behavior suggest that she was making certain demands on Addams—possibly insisting that he add her name to the deeds of his Westhampton Beach properties before they get married—and he was refusing.

Buddy Davie heard a marriage rumor and asked Addams whether it was true.

"I really think I've had enough," said Addams.

"Charles Addams is now mixed up with a woman lawyer who bites him and is said to be handy with a knife when she's mad," James Thurber wrote his daughter, Rosemary, on October 4, 1954.

That October or November, about a year after the affair began, Addams moved out of his apartment at 20 East Thirty-fifth Street and into Barbara's fashionable place with the white rugs and dark walls on East Eighty-eighth. On the tenth of November, the month after Thurber's gossipy letter to his daughter about Addams and the knife-wielding woman lawyer, Addams and Barbara took out a marriage license in the county of Charleston, South Carolina. Finally, on December 1, after untold miles of driving from north to south and back again, they had a "gin wedding," in the common vernacular for marriages taking place without a religious ceremony, in Florence, South Carolina. It was twelve days before Barbara's fortieth birthday; on the license, she gave her age as thirty-five. Though a few friends knew about it, the marriage was to remain a secret for a while, most likely because Barbara wanted to keep it from someone. "Oh, my God, I'm married to a lawyer," Addams joked to Carol Marcus. "I think I'm in trouble."

"Addams called and said he prefers to get his bill so he can pay it in '54," wrote Harriet Pilpel in an office memorandum on December 31. "He also said that things were fairly peaceful with his wife, although there had been one more episode of violence in which she attacked him with an African spear."

Sometime between the gin wedding and the African spear, the Addamses slipped away for a honeymoon in that hot spot of pagan attractions and unsettled souls, Haiti. They checked into the enchanting Hotel Oloffson in Port-au-Prince—a white Victorian refuge set down in a tropical garden trimmed with voodoo sculptures, Haitian artifacts, and carvings of such deities as the spirit god of the dead and Erzulie Freda, the goddess of love and melancholic seduction. If Barbara's version of the honeymoon can be trusted—Addams himself left no record aside from a few photographs—it was a happy idyll. The nightmare images were confined to the Haitian dead in their shrouds.

As Barbara later told it with girlish pleasure, their first Haitian adventure might well have been their last. Before leaving New York, Barbara had fallen while rushing to her office and badly scraped her knee. Now in the tropical heat it became infected, and she "could barely walk." The owner of the Hotel Oloffson told Addams about a good doctor several villages away, and he took his bride to see him. The good doctor turned out to be "Papa Doc" Duvalier, "the doctor who was killing all those people!" Barbara recalled with a laugh. They found him to be "a very nice little man, who took good care of my knee."

From the hotel terrace where Addams sat reminiscing about W. C. Fields movies with the hotel's owner and repeating favorite lines, the newlyweds watched the natives come down from the mountains singing and dancing in their masks and costumes. They watched voodoo rituals, visited old Haitian graveyards, and made a pilgrimage to see a native painter who lived near the border of the Dominican Republic, where a Haitian ruler had reportedly been shot and killed with a golden bullet. There they found the artist, a "charming little man" with "bright blue eyes" in a black face, wearing a straw boater. He took the visitors into his studio to see his extraordinary primitive paintings. Another day they drove up a steep mountain peak in search of a restaurant serving marvelous food—only to find that they had been misinformed about the location. Unable to turn the car around, Addams was forced to back all the way down the ribbony narrow road, which abutted a huge precipice, as in one of his cartoons—Barbara in terror, his superb driving notwithstanding. Having finally asked some villagers carrying baskets on their heads for directions, they arrived at this Brigadoon to find Noël Coward having lunch with Claudette Colbert.

SOON AFTER THEIR MARRIAGE, Barbara telephoned Addams in tears, apparently at his *New Yorker* office. He rushed home to find her sitting up in bed, crying. "I've lost our baby," she told him.

Confronted, apparently, with his questions, Barbara went to the hospital with "a false miscarriage," as Addams gently put it later to Jane Gunther. And he added that Barbara had never been pregnant, and was not able to have a baby.

Once the lie about the pregnancy was exposed, other lies surfaced too. "She told him she had no family, and it now appears that she has brothers and sisters and all the usual," noted Harriet Pilpel in an interoffice memo. Still Barbara insisted on hiding her background. Addams, the least pretentious of men, who could not have cared less about a person's lineage except as it made him interesting, was baffled by Barbara's attitude toward her family. "They're very nice people," he told Jane Gunther. And Barbara would not utter the word "Brooklyn" in the house. "I'm going to see my family in B," she would say.

"I may even need your help on this," an exasperated Harriet Pilpel wrote a colleague on June 29, 1955. "Mr. Addams has been having relations with a female lawyer for some time," she explained with barely disguised contempt. And she briefly recounted the two alleged pregnancies, and the marriage in South Carolina. The two-page typed memorandum told a wild tale of infidelity, jealousy, physical violence, and a grab for Addams's Westhampton Beach properties, most of which was later echoed by several close friends in whom Addams also confided.

> *All during their marriage [wrote Pilpel of Barbara Barb six months after the wedding], she has maintained a highly loving correspondence with a British M.P. whom she is apparently holding in reserve and whom she is visiting in London at the moment. Mr. Addams brought in some letters from him yesterday written since the marriage which I have put in the safe and which make very good reading indeed.*

The Englishman was Lord Colyton, Henry Lennox D'Aubigne Hopkinson, Minister of State for Colonial Affairs. An impressive, attractive, likable man of great charm and "exquisite manners," Henry Colyton was in his early fifties, well educated—Eton, followed by Trinity College at Cambridge—and an accomplished diplomat and politician. Widowed for two years following a twenty-six-year marriage, he was the father of an adult son and master of Netherton Hall, between Honiton and Colyton in Devonshire.

Barbara had been in England for two weeks, ostensibly on business as she had often been before, and was due back in three days when Addams brought Colyton's love letters to Pilpel's office in the summer of 1955. He told his lawyer that he intended to watch Barbara closely after her return "and perhaps get evidence of adultery." He added that he also suspected her of having men at the apartment when he was away, and that he and Barbara had not had sexual relations in months.

Adultery was the least of it; living with Barbara was the hard part. "Barbara Barb appears to be, to say the least, a highly emotional woman," allowed Harriet Pilpel. "They have had many altercations in which, at least two, she has come close to seriously injuring him." Addams told Pilpel and others of uncontrollable rages when Barbara had set about mutilating things that he loved—shattering the mirrors and headlights of his 1928 Mercedes with a hammer, smashing his antique papier-mâché anatomical model. While he lay in bed watching, she cut all the left sleeves off his jackets. Worst of all, at the carriage house where traces of the beautiful first Barbara lingered, she destroyed every reminder she could get her hands on: Hedda Sterne's portrait of Bobby; the big valentines Charlie had made for his first wife every year of their marriage, along with his letters to her—even Bobby's own yearbooks and her irreplaceable family albums and mementos.

Then there were the physical assaults on Addams himself. In addition to the African spear incident, Barbara had hit him over the head with a stiletto heel, sending him to the hospital with a deep triangular gash he said he'd gotten walking into a door. She pressed lighted cigarettes against his arm while he was driving. During one of her fits, she was flailing about and hitting him so much that he had to wrestle her to the floor and pin her down; the police were called. "Also, she constantly goes through his papers and when she is angry, attempts to get even with him by trying to get other people with whom he had relationships in the past in trouble with their husbands, families, etc.," noted Pilpel. The gorgeous travel writer Leila Hadley, an Addams friend who had never been romantically involved with him or met his second wife, had been happily married to her second husband, Yvor Smitter, just two years, and was now living in Johannesburg, when she heard about some telephone calls Barbara had made to both her husband and her mother-in-law. Smitter happened to be in Pasadena, California, on business at the time; his mother, psychologist Dr. Faith Smitter, lived and practiced there. Though neither Smitter had paid much attention to the strange accusations from a Mrs. Barbara Addams informing them that Leila was carrying on an adulterous relationship with Charles Addams, Leila was furious.

Harriet Pilpel was particularly concerned about the contracts Addams had made or otherwise bound himself to, against her advice. "In a weak moment" four months after the marriage, he admitted, he had put his Westhampton Beach houses in their joint names—"although I have specifically warned against his doing this," noted Pilpel. Now, six months into a disastrous marriage based on fraud, with no sexual relations for months, he had agreed to sign a contract with a corporation named Barbare Artists that Barbara had formed in order to market Addams cartoons rejected by *The New Yorker*, which had first refusal rights. Barbara herself was president and treasurer of the corporation, whose only client was Charles Addams. As Addams understood it, Barbara was about to make a deal with a syndicate to market the cartoons. "He knows nothing about it," wrote Pilpel, "although, as I explained to him, he may be bound because she or her corporation have apparent authority and he has talked to the syndicate about the mechanics."

In fact, Barbara had already drawn up a letter of agreement with the McClure Syndicate for a one-year period beginning July 15. Under the terms of the letter dated July 1, 1955, Barbara Barb, acting as agent for Charles Addams, would receive "fifty per cent (50%) of the gross income from the sale of these cartoons to the newspapers throughout the world," and be paid a minimum of "two hundred dollars ($200.00) a week net." Addams owned the copyrights and all other rights, as well as the originals of his own cartoons. But neither he nor Harriet Pilpel knew the details. "I urged him not to sign anything until we had seen it and to give as an excuse that THE NEW YORKER insisted on seeing it. He agreed," wrote Pilpel. Barbara was also demanding that Addams "pay her at least $1,000 per month, although she herself makes good money," added Pilpel, without mentioning exactly what Barbara was earning.

"Although he was in some doubt for a while, he is now pretty convinced that the marriage should terminate and does not wish to pay alimony," wrote Pilpel in conclusion.

"B Idlewild," Addams wrote in his datebook for July 1. By July 22, exactly a week after the deal with the McClure Syndicate was to begin, Harriet Pilpel had the signed agreement in hand. It was a "particularly bad contract," she wrote in a memorandum. "Since Mr. Addams is (confidentially) not getting along with his wife (incidentally, no one knows they are married) the statement at the beginning of the next to the last paragraph: 'It is understood the copyright and all other rights in these cartoons belong to you as Mr. Addams' agent' is not good." She added, "the contract is obviously insufficient on so many grounds that I shall simply advise Addams to this effect." And yet there wasn't much to be done about it. Word got around that Addams's new wife had incorporated him.

And so went the *danse macabre* of Addams's second marriage. Harriet Pilpel was its third, secret partner. Again and again Addams sought her advice, only to capitulate to Barbara.

How to explain such madness? In the years ahead, Addams's friends—some half-dozen of the people who knew him best, including his other wives—would struggle to make sense of his second marriage. How to understand that a man such as Charles Addams—successful and self-possessed, so normal himself, and so attractive to women—would put up with Barbara and give in to her? How could he have followed his marriage to "the sweetest girl in the world" with one to this pretender Barbara? The future third Mrs. Addams later expressed the feelings of many of Addams's friends when she dubbed the two wives "Good Barbara" and "Bad Barbara."

Affection, perhaps, had something to do with it, for there were good times, too—picnics and barbecues, baseball games at the beach, "al fresco lunches," shared jokes—excitement. Though other women who knew

Addams intimately found him to be a healthy lover who was not attracted to violent sex, there seemed to be a "terrible dark passion" between him and Barbara. And there is no question that Addams was afraid of Barbara. She had proved herself to be not only psychologically unstable but dangerous, willing to do anything to get what she wanted. By giving in, he thought he could appease her and eventually extricate himself from

"George! George! Drop the keys!"

the marriage with less damage to his personal property and to the people he cared for. After Barbara had savaged every reminder she could find of the first Barbara—a woman Charlie had really loved, she realized—he recovered a few scraps, put them into an album, and sent it to Bobby. (He held on to a torn photograph of his first wife in a black bathing suit, her pretty legs stretched out in the sun as she smiled her bemused smile.) As he maneuvered under the watchful eyes of Barbara, he confided in friends. Nancy Holmes, who knew a lot about Barbara, had heard about the so-called pregnancy, which she hadn't believed "for a minute"; so had Bobby, who was silent on the subject. Even Westfield friends heard "funny stories" about his second marriage—and yet he was careful to

"Everything happens to me."

cover his tracks. He did not write his Pilpel appointments in his datebook; he either paid his lawyer's bills in person or had them sent to his *New Yorker* office.

For all her pretensions and efforts to reinvent herself, Barbara Barb could claim one true triumph: She had a kind of genius for sensing human weakness. She knew where Addams was most vulnerable, and she knew how to play him. Essentially a gentleman who had married the woman he thought he had made pregnant—against reason, because it assuaged his vanity—Addams was a truly gentle man. In the talons of such a woman, such a force, he didn't have a chance. Like the man carried off by an enormous bird of prey while his wife runs after him on the beach calling for him to drop the keys in the famous 1948 Addams cartoon, Addams himself was entrapped, and finally helpless.

But he did have one advantage. For all her strength, Barbara was also a narcissist of the first rank, and her self-absorption could blind her to the goings-on around her. (Addams had drawn such a character in a cartoon about a two-headed woman, wearing identical hats and a single stone marten around her necks, in a movie audience. As she watches the movie, the man sitting behind her complains to his wife, "Everything happens to *me*.")

As Barbara hurtled through life, making contracts and secret plans, she never realized that Henry Colyton's love letters were missing, let alone tucked away in her husband's lawyer's safe.

—

Chapter Eleven

I Am So Lucky

IN THE LIFE RENDERED IN INK WASH, THE WAR BETWEEN men and women proceeded with deadly intent. But though people always remembered Addams for his dark cartoons, much of his work continued to be informed by a sense of wonder at the magic in everyday life. An old tramper riding a donkey in the American southwest finds a unicorn's skull; an archaeologist discovers a gigantic sea turtle bearing a heart-shaped legend: CLEOPATRÆ A MARC ANTONIO.

After eight months of secret wedlock and secret meetings between the groom and his lawyer, in August 1955 the new Mr. and Mrs. Charles Addams finally stepped into public view. Posing for the cameras at the Brown Derby in Hollywood during a trip to California—she smiling happily in a lovely pale beaded dress that showed off her figure and carrying a scarf and a straw handbag appliquéd with a pickaninny, he smiling in a sports jacket and tie—they made an attractive couple.

Addams had come to Hollywood to narrate one of Roald Dahl's gruesome little tales, "The Man from the South," for NBC-TV's *Cameo Theatre*, "an ordeal" because of his shyness, said Barbara, who seemed to relish the spotlight herself. When he was reluctant to go on a live television show with Lena Horne and Harry Belafonte following the Cameo Theatre performance, Barbara took his place—at his urging, or so she told it years later.

For her part, Barbara had come to California to be seen, and to make money. Looking as stylish as a film star, she seemed to relish her public role as the cartoonist's wife, which included posing for photographers and socializing with Hollywood royalty, including the Alfred Hitchcocks.

In Barbara's telling, her marriage to Charles Addams—"Charles," she called him, not "Charlie"—was full of domesticity, great fun, and loving wifely gestures. On poker nights at her apartment, she made the sandwiches; she baked a cake Addams loved, done a special way because of his diabetes, which had been diagnosed after his marriage to Bobby ended. On her dining room table she kept a plant whose tendrils would reach out and catch flies; Addams loved it.

In Addams's version, Barbara was "impossible."

Together at parties and social occasions, the couple seemed fine—or so some of Addams's friends would remember many years later. Patricia Neal was one of several people who found Barbara "gay and good"; she could be a charming hostess, said others, and fun to be with. But Patricia Neal also perceived something black in Barbara; she "had that sense of her," said the actress after learning about Barbara's violent temper and the problems in the marriage. Charlie, on the other hand, was a good man; she adored him, and never heard of anyone who didn't.

As the new Barbara Addams was being officially introduced to the public in California—beaming for the cameras, posing with Addams—she kept Lord Colyton very much on the line and interested in faraway England. On her black cocktail dress she wore a sparkling hint of her titled British lover, perhaps a gift: a diamond pin in the shape of a royal crown.

WHEN ADDAMS DID NOT get the money due on his Barbare Artists contract after he returned home from California, he quietly informed his lawyer. Pilpel queried a colleague. "Is the contract void by reason of Charles A. not getting the minimum amount?" she wrote on September 6. "If so—we ought to send a letter of termination?"

Summer became fall; still the marriage continued. "I like working in any sort of mild catastrophe," Addams told a *Newsday* reporter. "I love cooking," said Barbara, "and of course, we entertain a lot." The reporter noted that the couple were thinking about adding some guest rooms to the unfinished left wing of their unusual house.

As husband and wife sat for the interview on Long Island, they appeared as solid and snug as the converted carriage house hugging the Westhampton Beach dunes, impervious to sea winds and invading armies. She chatted amiably about "their" collection of medieval crossbows, armor, and such objects as a Victorian birdcage inhabited by a toy parrot. ("Vultures are too hard to keep," Addams apologized.)

"When we're touring," she said, "he is fascinated by old architectural styles. The first things he looks for are old Victorian or early American furniture he can bring back." Addams talked about his crossbows and cartoons. "Who knows," he mused. "I might be in Alcatraz now if I didn't express myself in my work." During the interview he fingered a small white Victorian pocket flask painted with an eye and the legend "Eye opener."

"Addams called to say that things were pretty rocky with his wife who is now insisting that he take out a life insurance policy in the amount of $100,000 naming her as irrevocable beneficiary," wrote Harriet Pilpel on October 25, three weeks after that cozy interview. "I told him the last time I had word of such a move was in a picture called DOUBLE INDEMNITY starring Barbara Stanwyck which I called to his attention. It looks as if the situation will not improve there and he wishes us to be posted as he goes along." Barbara's latest scheme had made Addams livid; he accused her of wanting him dead. And then he gave in, and agreed to the $100,000 policy on his life.

Though the marriage remained stormy, a part of Addams resisted another divorce. He persuaded Barbara to see a marriage counselor. "His doctor is going to recommend one and [Addams] is to let me know who it is," wrote Pilpel. "Obviously, I cannot be the source of the referral since he is not supposed to be talking to me."

But he did talk, and talk.

This third, imperceptible player in the Addams marriage considered it her duty to listen to her client's problems. It was part of the job that lawyers too often shirked, she wrote in a *Harper's Monthly* essay several years later. The attorney, she argued, had a human responsibility to his client, and legal guidance and advice required psychological insight. Pilpel also emphasized that the lawyer needs the ability to recognize when he himself "is beyond his own depth in the troubled waters of human tensions and complexities." When she felt herself drifting into uncharted territory in the Addams marriage, she did not hesitate to reach out to a colleague.

Though clearly frustrated at times by Addams's tendency to capitulate to his wife's demands, Harriet Pilpel reserved all her disgust for the "female lawyer" he had married. And her disgust was well warranted. A graduate of Vassar and Columbia Law School, from which she also held a master's degree, Harriet Fleischl Pilpel had the legal luster that Barbara Barb, in her retouched portrait, only pretended to have. Hired right out of law school by the great civil liberties lawyer Morris Ernst, who made Pilpel his protégée, Pilpel was now managing partner at Greenbaum, Wolff & Ernst, at a time when women lawyers in law firms were rare. She was Addams's age, forty-three in 1955. Conspicuously brainy and attractive—brunette, and alabaster-skinned, said one admirer—she was charming, amusing, dynamic, and utterly loyal. Whatever her faults, Harriet Pilpel never "dissembled or misled" her clients; and "the client's interest always came first." Possessed of boundless energy, and passionate about her causes, she was a civil libertarian, a leader in the contraception movement, and an expert in many areas of the law, including family law, entertainment law, and intellectual property rights. While trying to disentangle Charles Addams from the contracts and deeds of his messy marriage, she was also working tirelessly on behalf of writer Erich Maria Remarque, who had his own problems with contracts and women.

Like Remarque, Addams was more than a client to Pilpel; he was also a friend. She often invited him to dinners and cocktail parties at her apartment. Her son, Robert Pilpel, would remember the "great affection, admiration, and personal pride" with which his mother always spoke of Charles Addams. She kept a compendium of large-format Addams cartoons in her apartment, and she delighted in introducing the charismatic cartoonist to her less sparkling guests. Robert and his sister Judith, who were in elementary school during the 1950s, saw Addams as a tall, debonair man—"a cross between Noël Coward and Abraham Lincoln," with kindly, craggy features, a rueful smile, and the time to draw a kid a picture. He drew young Bobby Pilpel a sketch of Pugsley chasing a two-headed cat with a hatchet.

IN THE SPRING OF 1956, Addams decided to hire a British detective agency to follow Barbara during her next trip abroad. Harriet Pilpel handled the arrangements through Greenbaum's London liaison, Rubenstein, Nash & Co. Addams now had a bank address in England where Barbara could be reached, though no telephone number. Notwithstanding an uninspiring start to the investigation—in which Pilpel, in her letter to the London law firm, referred to Lord Colyton as "Lord Collington"—Joan Rubenstein figured it out, and the cloak-and-dagger game began in earnest.

That summer, Barbara traveled to England at Henry Colyton's expense—"apparently to see whether she wanted to take him on or not," wrote Harriet Pilpel.

She returned from England trying out a British accent—an odd, decidedly personal patois that was more Brooklyn than Britain. The new accent startled Gardner Botsford when he ran into Barbara one day on a visit to Addams in Westhampton Beach.

Though husband and wife continued to live together and maintain a public façade of marital harmony, the situation was, to say the least, uncomfortable. Addams told Irwin Shaw he thought Barbara was trying to kill him. He claimed she was putting glass in his food, and trying to poison him. Shaw realized that Addams was serious, and he repeated the allegation to George Abbott's ex-wife, Mary Sinclair, who told Barbara.

When, exactly, Addams asked for a divorce is unknown. But Barbara agreed. "I am so lucky," Addams told Thérèse Milstein. "She doesn't want any alimony; she doesn't want any settlement. She just wants the rights to my cartoons." But in fact the cartoons—which translated as the rights to the Addams Family—were only the beginning of what Barbara wanted.

On August 28, she insisted that Addams sign a paper increasing her half ownership to full ownership of the Westhampton Beach properties. As an excuse she said that the change to her name alone would be best for tax purposes. She argued that he could go on using the canal house; they would rent out the carriage house to pay for the property taxes. She promised to leave the houses to him exclusively in her will, but for now, she said she would not actually record the document. He signed the paper.

In the next document, dated October 2, Addams gave Barbara fifty cartoons of her choice, including "Boiling Oil." In addition, she would

". . . and now, George Pembrook, here is the wife you haven't seen in fifteen years."

also remain the irrevocable beneficiary of his $100,000 life insurance policy. But she was still not quite satisfied. She now put some extra insurance into safekeeping, against the day when the marriage might come into question.

The first of these items was a letter dated September 28, 1956. It was written in Addams's hand on *New Yorker* stationery:

> *Barbara darling—*
> *I am utterly destroyed by what has happened and am overcome by the horrors you surely have undergone as the result of the slanderous lies I told about you.*
> *Please believe me that I made them up because I was insanely jealous and vindictive.*
> *I cannot bear the thought of losing you and if you will not see me to let me attempt an explanation of my actions, I can only say that there is no point in my continuing to live—and I promise you to see to it that I don't.*
> *I always have and always will love you with all my heart and soul.*
>
> > *Devotedly—your*
> > *Charles*

It "*isn't* Charlie," said Audrey Cosden Chickering when the document came to light long years later. Axie Whitney called the letter "bullshit"; Leila Hadley described it as "coercion . . . a ransom letter." To Frank Modell, it read "like TV drama"; he added that it did not "sound like the kind of letter you write when your heart is breaking. It's not coming from his heart, or his balls." Even if one could picture Addams writing the letter under extreme duress, particularly if he was "totally high," said Odette Terrel des Chenes, it was still easier to believe that Barbara had drugged him or held a gun to his head. Not one of a half-dozen people who knew Addams intimately could believe he had written it of his own free will.

And yet he had written it. The handwriting belonged to Charles Addams—but the language and sentiments did not. The pitiful letter writer bore no resemblance to the man who had been happy all his life until Barbara Barb got hold of him, who was never known to have harbored a suicidal thought, behaved vindictively, or perpetuated a "slanderous lie" about anyone.

This was the fearful Addams, the Addams who knew what he had to say to appease Barbara, thereby smoothing the way to divorce. "Lovers lie, too," noted Nancy Holmes. It was one more desperate act from the man who had signed any number of bad documents against his lawyer's advice. Audrey Cosden, who ultimately knew Addams for decades, thought the word "afraid" was the whole key to Addams; for him, everything was "both terrible and funny." The same man who drove a Bugatti around a racetrack at a hundred miles an hour could freeze when confronted with anything unexpected—such as a goose stuck in the chimney at the Westhampton Beach canal house. (On that occasion it was Audrey who cleaned up the mess while Addams followed orders and handed her a drink through the trapdoor in the bedroom floor. "Charlie was always being protected by women saying 'if you don't do it, I'll do it,' " said Leila Hadley.) In later years, noted Axie Whitney, Addams had a fear of being carjacked and stuffed into the trunk. Against that day, he kept a dagger and one of his smaller crossbows in the trunk of his Bentley.

Without specifically referring to the document in question, Addams later said that he would have "done anything," "signed anything" to get out of the marriage. He had "desperately" wanted out, he repeatedly told friends.

And yet if the letter can be explained as the jottings of a frightened, abused man, there remains the riddle of the hackneyed phrasing. Frank Modell, who knew Addams for forty-six years, never heard his articulate friend use such "vocabulary, syntax, or language"—none of his friends had. But Barbara Barb did write and speak in maudlin, clichéd, self-dramatizing prose. "My heart is so broken," "You know I love you with all my heart," "from the bottom of my heart," "from the depths of my heart," she would write Addams. Was he communicating with her in her own language, the better to reach her—or did she dictate the letter?

The letter was in fact Barbara's picture of Addams, the portrait of the man she herself tried to peddle in later years, mostly to people who did not know better. She insisted that he "was *not* a *happy* man," but "a *lonely* man," who had lied about her because he was "jealous." Though he was "always unfailingly devoted" to her, she said, he had made everything up. It was all the "fancies" of a creative mind.

Six days after Addams wrote the letter, Barbara went through the motions of returning the houses to him. A deed dated October 4, 1956, was drawn up, and signed by both Barbara Estella Addams and a notary. But it was neither witnessed nor recorded. Along with the damaging "Barbara darling" letter, this second deceptive document—created as evidence of Barbara's good intentions, perhaps to use as a bargaining tool with Addams—was tucked away for the day of reckoning.

Suddenly, after all the wrangling of the previous two years, and all the paper accrued—cartoons created and signed away, rights and properties relinquished, love letters written and confiscated, investigators' reports commissioned and paid for, lawyers' memoranda typed and filed—the divorce itself came and went like a passing mood. Even in the annals of "speedy decrees," the Addams divorce was newsworthy.

On October 9, 1956, Barbara boarded a plane for Alabama. She arrived in Huntsville in the early morning hours, checked in to a hotel where her lawyer had reserved a room for her, and registered under her maiden name. Hours later, in an Athens courthouse, Judge D. L. Rosenau granted the divorce. The entire proceeding took forty-five minutes. Barbara climbed into a waiting taxi and headed back to the airport. The woman who had sworn she was "a bona fide resident of the State of Alabama" had been in the state less than nine hours.

The next day, she left New York for Henry Colyton and a new life in England.

Like a retreating army outrunning the enemy, she was out of town before the press broke what they knew of the story. Given Addams's celebrity, the divorce was of particular interest to the New York papers: "BARE HALF-HOUR DIVORCE MILL: N.Y. CELEBS PART IN ALABAMA." Even *Time* couldn't resist an item, in which Barbara was described as a "slinky, lank-haired Lawyer." While the press focused on the time it had taken

Barbara to get her divorce, only the well-connected Dorothy Kilgallen challenged the grounds, abandonment: "Residents of the Hamptons were amused at newspaper stories reporting that a year's 'desertion' had been charged in the recent quickie divorce of cartoonist Charles Addams and his Barbara Barb," she wrote. "Throughout this past summer Mr. and Mrs. Addams were seen everywhere in the elegant Long Island area, not only together but appearing happy and affectionate. One August instance: they duetted at the Boys' Harbor Carnival."

How, the chorus wondered, was a forty-five-minute divorce possible in the United States? Though in recent years hundreds of New Yorkers had been slipping down to Alabama for quickie divorces, returning with their decrees after only a weekend, Barbara Barb had "set what must be a record in elapsed time for shedding a husband," noted the *Sunday News.*

The key to Barbara's dizzyingly fast decree turned on the state's residency requirement. Though residency was defined as one year, the law required no actual proof. Some Alabama courts insisted upon witnesses or other proof of domicile; the more casual court over which Judge Rosenau presided in Limestone County did not.

The Alabama courts winced at the publicity. The Addams divorce was the second in recent months that had brought unwelcome press to the state, which had hitherto been quietly operating as a divorce mill. Now Judge Rosenau declared "that in the future he would require some corroborative evidence that a plaintiff actually lives in Alabama and isn't just between planes."

Though Alabama was in fact only part of the problem of "migratory divorce"—a practice that bred "disrespect for the law . . . confusion and uncertainty as to marital status, legitimacy of children, and property rights," Harriet Pilpel and her co-author had warned in a 1952 book on marriage and family law—it was a particularly risky place for divorce. The state's highest court had "cast considerable doubt on the validity" of its speedy decrees. "Since even the judges themselves are not in agreement as to what recent decisions mean, it is only the very desperate and very foolhardy who will rely on" such a divorce, wrote the authors.

Addams had indeed been desperate to get out of the marriage. Knowing that the fastest way out was to let Barbara divorce him on her terms, he had taken her poisoned apple, but not without permitting himself an angry glance: "Respondent denies each and every allegation contained in his said bill of complaint," he had replied in his own answer and waiver to Barbara's deposition, though only Barbara's charge of desertion got into the papers.

ONCE AGAIN, A WIFE named Barbara had left Addams surrounded by reminders of her. In an act she considered generous, Barbara Barb allowed him to borrow her furniture, bedding, kitchenware, gramophones, air-conditioning unit, animal skins, decorative objects—virtually everything in the apartment, including his own fifty drawings given her in the divorce deal—with the understanding that all would be returned "in the same condition" or replaced. Addams was permitted to remain in Barbara's residence until he found another place.

Barbara left a few unintentional remembrances as well. In the attic of the carriage house were a handful of forgotten 1954 Christmas cards from male admirers in London. "Darling Black Sheep," wrote a man named Jack, "Please let me know when you'll be here again. Can't have you knowing only Ministers of State!!" "As usual always ready to rescue you," wrote another.

In the address section of his 1956 datebook, Addams began a curious list for a book he was contemplating:

In pic coll.
Suicides
death masks
(photo of violent
death
Abels—torture books
[word unclear]—death
      (allegorical)

get etiquette books
at beach—re burial
   customs—funerals etc.
morning
Polyvinyl Acetate
Emulsion
   (Copolymer) permanent
         pigments

Chapter Twelve

The Tunnel of Love

I N DECEMBER 1956, TWO MONTHS AFTER HIS DIVORCE, Addams found himself in Nashville, Tennessee, beginning an affair with the pregnant wife of an old friend. Attentive readers of the *Nashville Banner* might have detected something between the socially prominent hostess and her guest in the photograph that ran in the paper on Christmas Eve. Something about them drew the eye, diminishing everyone else in the picture.

Taken at the home of Mr. and Mrs. E. T. Bedford Davie in Belle Meade the night before, it showed Tee Davie in a pale maternity blouse and skirt standing between her husband, Buddy, and their guest for the holidays, "Charles Addams of New York." Smiling radiantly, she faced Charlie's right shoulder, with her back to Buddy; Buddy looked stiff and out of place. Charlie inclined his head slightly down and toward her, away from the attractive, smiling blonde on his left. It was Tee's thirtieth birthday, and she and her husband of nine years were expecting their second child.

She first met Charlie in about 1947, shortly after her marriage to Buddy Davie. As Tee remembered it, she had been carrying water around a Daytona racetrack for one of Buddy's cousins, an amateur racer and member of the Sports Car Club, when Buddy introduced her to Charlie.

Born Marilyn Morris Matthews on Christmas Eve 1926, she had been called Tee since childhood. When Tee's baby brother came along and couldn't pronounce her name, she was called "Sister," which some-how turned into Tee; and it stuck. Tee so preferred her nickname to Mar-ilyn, which she hated, that she considered legally changing her name.

The name "Tee" suited her diminutive size, her delicate features, and her playfulness—the tee-hee of her, the anything-but-a-teetotaler of her. As the middle child and second daughter of Robert Morris Matthews and Alice Lucile Robertson, she had led a larking life—riding her pony bareback through the orange grove her father had bought in Winter-haven, Florida, even after losing a lot of money in the crash of 1929; water skiing; playing tennis. After a brief marriage at eighteen to a young fighter pilot named Jimmy Webb ("It was lousy sexually," said Tee, and "we were too young"), she had left Florida for New York. Jimmy moved on to the battlefields of Europe; Tee moved on to the Barbizon for Women, and became a Powers model.

In those days Powers models were in a class by themselves. To begin with, they were known for a certain look that made them hard to tell apart. "The first thing that causes a columnist, man about town, or ordi-nary citizen to look with interest at a Powers model is her face," wrote E. J. Kahn. Tee's face was composed of almond-shaped brown eyes, a dainty nose, a bowed mouth with a slight overbite, and high cheekbones that gave her an American Indian look. Powers models, Kahn had writ-ten, were also known to follow their modeling careers with successes as actresses—Barbara Stanwyck, Norma Shearer, Joan Bennett, Anita Louise, Joan Blondell—or as the wife of Mr. Somebody: Winthrop Gar-diner, Marshall Hemingway, Woolworth Donahue. Tee became Mrs. E. T. Bedford Davie, the wife of a good-looking heir to the Standard Oil fortune.

As Tee saw it, her first marriage had hardly counted; she and Jimmy Webb had merely played house. Her second marriage was grown-up, real. She was in love. And at twenty-three, she became the mother of a little girl named Deirdre, whom they called Bunki. But housekeeping de-pressed Tee, and her own child made her "nervous." She and Buddy had different "habits and interests." She was drinking and smoking too much. She and Buddy quarreled; they argued about her "sloppiness," her lack of interest in her child.

Even in the first years of motherhood, Tee had been strangely uninvolved with her baby. One day some years before Addams came to Nashville, she and Buddy had gathered up little Bunki for an Austrian skiing holiday in Kitzbühel. They liked it so much there, and found they could live so cheaply, they decided to stay. When they returned to New

Tee Davie. "The first thing that causes a columnist, man about town, or ordinary citizen to look with interest at a Powers model is her face."

York several years later, four-year-old Bunki understood English, but spoke only German. Tee was reduced to communicating with her own child through Fräulein, Bunki's German governess.

Now, with another baby on the way, the marriage was in trouble. Tee blamed Buddy. He was "a wonderful lover, but a lousy husband," she said later. He was always out playing golf. He was too critical of her, too un-involved at home. As for her, "I can and will give up the drinking and smoking entirely (it seems to be one of the major irritants for you)," Tee would write in a letter that told the story that was wearing down both husband and wife in 1956.

Buddy wasn't buying any of it. "It wasn't me, it was your father who said you were your own worst enemy," he reminded her.

Into this picture Charles Addams had lightly stepped. A trusted friend of husband and wife (both Buddy and Tee ultimately regarded Addams as their best friend), he apparently set off no alarms in the cuckolded husband. Even Buddy's wealthy mother, whom the family called Muds, adored Charlie.

The affair wasn't serious. Tee, hugely pregnant, was still in love with Buddy; Charlie was still smarting from his second marriage and divorce.

Whatever Addams was feeling that Christmas, he found life in Tennessee sufficiently congenial to linger until sometime in January. Buddy having announced that he would be away during New Year's, Tee persuaded Charlie to stay on and keep her company. Thus began a love that neither one of them could have anticipated.

While Tee tried to sort things out in her marriage, Charlie drifted along in her domestic idyll. He accompanied Tee to the supermarket, where he was fascinated to discover Green Stamps, which he had never seen before. He sketched Tee in her maternity smock and her foul morning mood, distorting her lovely face as she threatens him with a lamp base. "Miz Davie ain't had her mawnin' coffee yet," Tee's old black maid, Amanda, is saying to the person on the phone, as the dog cowers under the table and wide-eyed Bunki peers around Amanda's skirt.

He took Tee to the psychiatrist she was seeing about her marital problems, and picked her up an hour later. "Here's your lover, and your dog," he said. He was wonderful with Bunki. He showed the child his teeth, and helped her put on a funeral worthy of her hamster. Tee watched from a window in her house as Charlie marched up and down the driveway with the little girl, chanting a song to the dead pet.

Tee emerged as the ultimate good-time girl. Even pregnant, she was game for travel and adventure. When she and Charlie weren't visiting friends, they explored the local architecture—Charlie in a sweater and sunglasses, Tee clutching a mink coat over her big belly—and took in the cemetery ("Weather was Ghoulish—Addams Visits Cemetery," noted the *Nashville Tennessean*). They drifted as far as Monticello and New Orleans, where they found a cemetery ravaged by vandals. Skeleton hands reached up from the ground; kids played with a human skull. Charlie picked up a femur, turned it over, and found it swarming with maggots—which was too much even for him. Tee shrieked. "I don't think you should have your wife in this place," a stranger told him. "Oh, it's all right," said Addams, "she's not my wife."

Finally Charlie said he had to be getting back to New York to work. Tee persuaded him that he could work just as well in Tennessee. So he got some art supplies, and Tee shut him up in a room in her house. He emerged two days later with a captionless cartoon showing a city mortuary, the sign reading "E. T. Bedford—Mortician." Against a potted plant in the window a placard said WE GIVE GREEN STAMPS. *The New Yorker* bought the drawing for $237.50, and published it in the February 9, 1957, issue. "It's too bad he had to use Father's name," sighed Muds.

Addams had not been back in New York long when Tee followed him; she claimed that she simply wanted to have her baby in New York. In April, about six weeks before her due date, her water broke, and she went into the hospital.

"Tee—boy," Addams wrote in his datebook on April 26. His was the first face Tee saw when she opened her eyes after the delivery. Charlie visited her in her private room every day. The room had a small refrigerator Muds had thoughtfully stocked with champagne and caviar.

Addams was in Tee's room when the doctor came in to discuss the baby's circumcision, and he was duly alarmed. He responded to the scheduled procedure with a sketch showing himself looking grumpy behind the wheel of an antique car, his jaw set against the ignominy of his circumstances. A boot trailed from the sign on the back fender, which read, "Just Circumcised."

Tee and Buddy returned to Nashville with baby Bedford. Soon after, Muds bought them a big house on Forrest Drive in Palm Beach, filled with servants and leaded glass doors opening out onto terraces. There was a lawn with a waterfall, and a saltwater pool. It was a showplace, but "not a cheerful place," thought Odette Benjamin (the future Odette Terrel des Chenes), who also lived in Palm Beach with her husband and four children.

While Tee and Buddy continued to struggle with their marriage, the family friend from New York made an impression on Bunki, who wrote a list for school of the ten most famous men in the world:

"Tee—boy," Addams wrote in his datebook.

Chareles Adam
Maharasa
W. Churchill
Fearless Fosdid
Napolean
Mussilini
Vincent van Goch
Dari
Leaanardo
De Gaulle

That Thanksgiving, the most famous man in the world was back in Nashville enjoying a surprise birthday present from Tee—a private viewing of a red-haired mummy named Hazel, which the owner had refused to sell—when a letter began making its way to him across the Indian Ocean.

From Kuala Lumpur, Malaya, came a letter from someone longing to share the holidays with Addams. "And in three days it would have been our anniversary," noted the sad woman who called Addams "Dearest Porker Bell."

Now known as Lady Colyton following her quiet marriage to Lord Henry Colyton almost a year earlier, Barbara had blown in and out of New York at least twice since the divorce. On one of these occasions, she had dropped in on Hedda Sterne, who had always liked her, and told her all about Henry's engagement present: a Rolls-Royce with leopard-skin upholstery, a liquor cabinet, and a makeup compartment. Barbara had put her best effort into becoming thoroughly Anglicized. She filled her personal letters with British spellings and odd capitals on common nouns. But she had not relinquished her old claim. She had no sooner married Lord Colyton than Cholly Knickerbocker and Leonard Lyons reported her intention of maintaining a law office in New York. It was noted that "the glamorous barrister" would "continue to represent her ex-husband, cartoonist Charles Addams."

Writing in her typical motherly style, Barbara urged Addams to take care of himself and watch his drinking. While claiming to rejoice in his happiness as a popular bachelor, she missed him, she said. He was still her "Porker Bell," her "Zoe Porker"; she was still his "Monstre." On the crossing back to England in October, "I wished you were with me." She pressed him to write her—not at her home, but in care of her London bank. On her next visit to New York, she said, she was determined to find an apartment. She could not survive without a home in the United States. She did not mention her new husband.

And so it was that a year after his headline-making divorce, Addams again began noting Barbara's airline arrivals and departures in his date-book. He saw her when she was in New York, wrote her, and telephoned as he was told. He recorded her birthday in his datebook, just as he had done when they were married, and sent her a present. At her request, he even promised to dedicate his next cartoon collection to her. She planned to look at it in secret when she was missing him most.

The dedication for the 1960 *Black Maria*—"To Estella"—appeared in a corner of a page showing a sketch of little Wednesday Addams watering her garden of poison ivy, deadly nightshade, poison oak, and Venus fly trap.

In the wreckage of a dead garden choked with weeds, an odd friendship began to bloom. To one who knew nothing about Barbara or her history with Charles Addams, the letters would have sounded harmless, if clinging—the sentimental longings of a lost love who has had to settle for something else, but can't bring herself to let go.

Given Barbara's need to control her lovers, and Addams's need for tranquillity, going along with her was perhaps the best course. But he also wanted his houses back, and he may have reasoned that if he gave Barbara what she wanted, he would in time get what he wanted. And besides, a note from him made her so happy. Kuala Lumpur, she wrote cheerfully, was just as he suspected—infested with a variety of snakes. Why, just last week she had been chased by a snake charmer's cobra. She imagined her Porker, in faraway Nashville, hearing her scream.

—

Chapter Thirteen

Dear Dead Days

"YOUR PICTURE OF THE FAMILY PLANTATION WAS WONDER-ful, if infuriating—it has been notably dismal around here this winter," Addams wrote his friend Leila Hadley in March of 1959. (Leila and Yvor Smitter were living with their children in Jamaica, West Indies, though not on a plantation.) "I did escape for the holidays and then some to Mexico, followed by a short study of gas wells in Texas."

As the 1950s ended, Addams's career continued "in an ever-rising, unbroken curve," as Irwin Shaw had put it, adding "we can say that, unhappily, about none of the rest of us." Addams's fifth cartoon collection, *Nightcrawlers,* had been published in 1957. Addams was photographed for *Good Housekeeping,* where his picture ran alongside a photograph of a bell-skirted Amy Vanderbilt lolling in a hammock with her three children; he was snapped by Cecil Beaton. "Charles Addams has introduced a gothic element into daily life," Beaton had written in *The Face of the World,* adding that "at many parties, even an undiscerning eye can spot at least one lady with [a] green, drowned-looking face, weirdly scissored hair, tight black dress. . . ." Beaton's 1958 book placed a photograph of Charles Addams among the "famous names with little-known faces," which included James Thurber, Carson McCullers, Alistair Cooke, and Saul Steinberg. Unlike Steinberg—a man who looked "suspiciously like one of his own wiry drawings," wrote Beaton—Addams "proved to be the complete negation of the macabre in his own cartoons." The Beaton camera recorded a man "in a smart blue alpaca suit" who suggested the "handsome, tough gangster-hero of some Hollywood film."

Addams seemed to be everywhere. *Paris Match* ran a cartoon. Addams was mentioned in Cholly Knickerbocker's column in the *Journal-American* and in "The Lyons Den" in the *New York Post,* whose reporter had observed the cartoonist at the Bolshoi Ballet's *Romeo and Juliet.* After the final curtain, when the troupe's stars were presented with a bouquet, Addams had said, "Those flowers came too late."

Everyone, it seemed, was courting him. "I revisited your old apartment last week to see Pat and Roald—along with three model friends, calculated to fascinate me," Addams continued in his letter to Leila Hadley, who had once rented the Dahls' apartment. "The conversation, under Roald's supervision, was entirely obscene."

With everyone wanting to meet him and so much going for him, Addams found himself working on an album of sorts—"a Treasury of the Macabre (I'm supposed to be the editor!)," he wrote Leila, adding that he wished he'd "never said yes" to it. At a time when he was earning $38,000 a year and doing the occasional assignment for *Holiday* and other magazines along with ads for such products as Camel cigarettes, Remington typewriters, and Lee tires, he had accepted a $1,500 advance from Putnam, and had "two slaves digging up material—it's all quite shapeless—and I predict a pretty lame offering."

The result was *Dear Dead Days,* a prolonged stare at the freak show, the grisly traffic accident, life's exit wounds and exits—the strangest work Addams ever produced. Here were photographs of dwarfs and Siamese twins both human and animal ("Mouton à deux Corps"), an albino family, a pig-nosed woman, a bearded lady; here was the gun-toting corpse of outlaw Rube Burrow following his last train robbery, and an anonymous, bespectacled dead man preserved like a Popsicle in a block of ice. Here was a nauseating close-up of the unfortunate Robert McGee, "scalped by Chief Little Turtle, 1864." A curiously self-indulgent chapter titled "Remains to be Seen" devoted no less than thirteen pages to corpses, funerals, and their accoutrements: antique casket wagons, specially fitted train cars, morticians' tools and supplies such as embalming fluid, razorless post-mortem shaving powder, and "the Davis Never-Slip Chin Support."

But to look at the dust jacket of this 1959 work, who would guess its contents? It featured the Addams Family innocently examining an X-ray, a shrunken skull that looked like Gomez, and a picture whose contents one could only guess at, as they lounged, inexplicably, in a gazebo in the snow. Billed as "the treasured memories of Charles Addams' famous cartoon family," *Dear Dead Days* was subtitled *A Family Album.*

Addams had been thinking about such a book for years. The ghastly list he'd made in his datebook for 1956—the year of his second divorce—reminding himself to research books on torture, suicides, and death masks, had been a beginning of sorts. For years people had been sending him shocking newspaper articles, grotesque photographs, tasteless cartoon ideas, and ghoulish trinkets. "I have gotten a lot of letters about my work, most of them from criminals and subhumans who want to sell ideas," he told James Thurber. "Some of the worst come from a minister in Georgia." The minister's ideas, which "were all unprintable," left Addams "horror struck." From the National Press Club in Washington came a letter from Homer Joseph Dodge. "I have heard of an undertaker's child who, for Christmas, wanted a toy cemetery with old leaning tombstones and with a horse-drawn hearse, the horses, of course, draped in black net and plumed and all the other appurtenances. I wish you would do something about it." ("Under Xmas tree," Addams scribbled at the bottom of the letter.) E. B. White had passed on a photograph of a large, ramshackle Victorian house in Brookline, Massachusetts. "I like the little top floor with the balcony—save it for me when I visit," he joked. Another admirer contributed an old picture of a Boston shop advertising "shoes for the entire family"—which meant "shoes for the lame and the halt and the club-footed and nothing else," noted Addams, who used the photograph to close *Dear Dead Days.* To his way of thinking, the shoe store display "wouldn't be funny in a drawing. It needed the realism of a photograph, I think, to make it funny."

But funny was not entirely the point of the book, which mostly offered a free fall into "some of [Addams's] sources of inspiration," as the flap copy put it. Though Addams had told Bennett Cerf he was considering "eliminating people with two heads" from his cartoons ("too many angry letters from the two-headed set"), the present assignment relieved him of that constraint.

In making his selections from such sources as the 1957 *Practical*

Forensic Medicine, the *Naughty 90's Joke Book & Dyspeptics Guide to the Grave,* and a funeral register called *The Western Undertaker,* Addams was following his own interests, which had always led him to the nearest churchyard and antiques store, to the circus, and to mental institutions, where the inmates, he said, "have a refreshing conversational approach." He was not posturing. He was fascinated by any sort of abnormality: by the cross-eyed child of an acquaintance, who wore a funny high collar; by a six-foot-six-inch man who could not get into a suit. He loved Johnny Nicholson's restaurant on East Fifty-seventh Street, not only for its good food, but because it had been a mortuary in the nineteenth century. When Buddy Davie asked Addams about the gutters affixed to the restaurant's interior, he happily explained that "that was where the blood used to run down when they cleaned the floor." Addams also treasured a particular Nicholson waitress: a floaty woman who mumbled to herself and whose round, blue-eyed face was completely free of lines. It was the kind of face he frequently drew.

"Saw 3 mutes, 2 dwarfs; the rest of the population is legless or blind," Addams once wrote to Leila Hadley after a visit to Madrid. "Saw 1 crossbow and numerous fakes." A clipping Addams saved about an astonishing medical procedure found its way into *Witch's Milk.*

He could wax eloquent on horror movies, bizarre medical history, cockroaches, pinheads, coneheads, and "fistheads," as he called them— the limbless wonders of the circus sideshow who were sewn up into a bag, giving them the appearance of a fist. His recall of "the good old days" of the electric chair was impressive. Kids passing through the horror movie stage could ask Addams "anything weird, freaky, bizarre" they wanted to know about—something not in the encyclopedia—and they were always rewarded with an answer. He considered horror movies "a healthy escape from an almost hopeless tangle of psychoanalysts and freckle champs," but thought the genre "perhaps leaned a little too heavily on hirsuteness and unclipped fingernails to achieve their effects." (He himself favored "the hairless, no fingernail school, with burbling giggles.") Along with Lon Chaney's *Phantom of the Opera* he particularly valued Werner Krauss in *The Cabinet of Dr. Caligari.*

This, then, was the human carnival. Freaks, death, and torture were part of it. Addams embraced it all. "One screwball is worth a room full of squares," he said. As a storyteller who loved the fantastical, he offered no analysis of the attraction except to say that a part of him had never really grown up. ("It's hard to figure whether you're eccentric or not. An eccentric is really a very practical person," Addams would say. "They're just trying to make their fantasies work.") Though he talked about his own fear of snakes, he preferred simply to draw them, again and again.

An Addams datebook sketch: two versions of a strange-looking man.

One of his personal favorites was a 1941 cartoon showing a crowd gathered on a city street before the spectacle of an octopus rising from a manhole to snatch a man. "It doesn't take much to collect a crowd in New York," says one blasé businessman to another as they proceed down the sidewalk. Later, the cartoonist who disliked introspection would explain the cartoon simply: It was the expression of a "morbid suspicion." He'd long imagined that the New York City drainage system was harboring an octopus or two. He just liked "the idea of knowing there's an octopus there all the time," he said, echoing similar comments about his fondness for drawing little people. But then one notices the way he drew the scene, in a relatively unthreatening way, the octopus looking almost innocently up at the little man coiled in his sucker-bearing arm—a "doll-like" figure, noted Lee Lorenz, who added that even as the man is about to be swallowed, "he's not screaming bloody murder; his shoes aren't flying off." Though the Addams restraint was an artistic decision, it perhaps offered a certain reassurance to the artist himself: After all, the idea of an octopus under the city streets needn't be that upsetting.

Some years after *Dear Dead Days*, Addams was asked about his somewhat "romantic, nostalgic" takes on such mythological figures as the Minotaur in the labyrinth. Addams drew the Minotaur not as the fearsome creature of mythology, drawn on a shattered cliff by Gustave Doré,

"It doesn't take much to collect a crowd in New York."

but as a two-legged beast leaning dreamily against the wall of a modern art gallery or a rat's maze, or lurking in an information booth, his face more reflective than menacing. "Well, I find him sweet and human and the way everyone wants his own particular Minotaur to be," Addams told Philip French. In the Minotaur, he found "the monster that is in all of us."

If there was anything particularly significant about the subject matter of *Dear Dead Days*, it may have been that the loss of two close friends during the 1950s, as well as two wives—one of whom was violent—had contributed to the Addams preoccupation with death. Seven years after

Sam Cobean was killed, Addams was visiting Wolcott and Elinor Gibbs on Fire Island and enjoying a drink on the porch with some other people before lunch while Gibbs read proofs in his room. It was a familiar scene. During the last ten years or so, when Gibbs had been working at home and writing theater reviews for *The New Yorker*, Addams had been "a presence" in the Gibbs family, as well as one of Wolcott's closest friends.

On this pleasant day, August 16, 1958, Elinor kept calling to Gibbs to come down. Finally, having failed to get a response, she sent the maid. The maid returned and asked Addams to go up. He found Wolcott dead in his chair. "He had his feet up on the windowsill," said Addams, "and the proofs of his book *More in Sorrow*," whose dust jacket illustration Addams had drawn, "were in his lap. He had a cigarette in his hand, and it had burned right down to his fingers."

Nonetheless, the Addams view of death remained irreverent and obsessive. He liked to show guests his stereopticon picture of dead World War I soldiers. And though he had been deeply touched by the death of Sam Cobean, a loss he continued to feel, he saw nothing strange in showing people the newspaper photograph of Cobean's dead body hanging from the crumpled Jaguar. After all, death was a natural part of life. It was something to be faced. If you looked at the crumpled Jaguar hard enough, you also saw one of the great comic artists, a man who looked like Tyrone Power on a good day. At the end of *Dear Dead Days*, Addams drew a sketch of a smiling Iron Maiden whose shadow is that of a shapely girl.

Pocket datebook in hand, he jotted down scraps of overheard conversation, and the ideas that came to him. He seemed to record his own experience in the shower when he wrote "hot cold scalding"—an idea that would result in a 1961 cartoon of Uncle Fester in the shower. He sketched the man on the street with the black barbed-wire eyebrows, a runaway line for his chin. His surreptitious Kodak caught the backsides of both the toned bathing beauty and the cartoonish pair of waddling fat ladies whose knee-length dresses reveal four almost identical V-shaped calves. (Addams later drew those calves for Jack Sprat's wife in his own rendering of Mother Goose rhymes.) His curiosity seemed limitless. When Buddy Davie told him that it had taken Henry VIII three whacks to cut off the head of Anne Boleyn, Addams sent away to England for an authentic executioner's axe. Standing next to Tee at the private mummy viewing in Nashville, he had wondered, "Was she a *true* redhead?" And when the owner wasn't looking, Addams had lifted the period skirt, and smiled.

"How great to see a freak," he later commented. The day he discovered a shoeshine man at Fifty-sixth Street and Sixth Avenue who was wonderfully disfigured by warts was a banner day. There was a wart on his finger "the size of Doris Duke's engagement ring," warts on his nose that looked "like nipples" and that wagged as he shined Addams's shoes. And as if all this wasn't reward enough, the man also gave a beautiful shine. "If you just see a person on the street—you just see him—you can't study him," explained Addams. "That's what's so great about having your shoes shined."

As Addams regaled Steven Aronson with the shoeshine man story while they ate at a Japanese restaurant one day during the 1970s or '80s, a lone diner listened. "Charlie looked very respectable—burgher-like," stressed Aronson. "And while he was describing this to me in this restaurant, the person at the table next to us was absolutely horrified." Out on the street afterward, Addams said, "Did you notice that he was, in fact, freaking out?"

Dear Dead Days never quite found its audience, and earned only $5,000 in royalties from all editions. Addams liked the finished book. But William Shawn refused to advertise it in *The New Yorker;* "Shawn felt—said—it was maybe a little too far out and probably in bad taste," remembered Addams. "I don't agree with that but what can you do?" Fans were disappointed. "I can't imagine why anyone would want to see the book," wrote a man from Roselle, New Jersey. "I must say that I thought *Dear Dead Days* a piece of morbid trash. After all, one does not enjoy seeing *too* many burial devices." But it was a fourteen-year-old kid from Lakewood, Ohio, who best expressed what was wrong with the book. "One word about *Dear Dead Days,*" he wrote in a meticulously typed letter, which Addams answered. "It was a very interesting collection, but it seemed to lack the Charles Addams touch."

But what, exactly, was the Addams touch? the cartoonist seemed to wonder. That fall, through Barbara Colyton, he had sent an original cartoon to Evelyn Waugh, whom he had never met, though Waugh's brother, Alec, was a friend—and now also an acquaintance of Barbara's. Based on an idea by Peter DeVries, the 1948 captionless cartoon depicts a barbershop, an empty chair surrounded by feathers, and several men, including a black man sweeping up the feathers, staring after the unseen customer who has just left. "Barbara (in a bizarre hat) brought it," Waugh wrote from his home, Combe Florey House, near Taunton, England, on All Souls' Day. But Waugh, an Addams fan, didn't understand the cartoon; "it has proved a damnosa veritas," he wrote. "I can't even do the crossword puzzle, still less write for worrying. Why did he not attract attention when he came into the barber's shop? I can well understand the consternation and speculation with which they watch his departure. How did he get to the chair? He has lost feathers but he now seems from the angle of the nigger's eyes to have flown out. I have a severely literal mind and I am gravely disturbed." Unbeknownst to Addams, Waugh asked Barbara if the cartoon could be exchanged for another.

As for the dreadful *Dear Dead Days,* Addams never saw it as a mistake. He remained somewhat baffled by the criticism of *Dear Dead Days,* and yet matter-of-fact. "I think probably that it was maybe a little ahead of its time," he said.

Chapter Fourteen

Mr. and Mrs. and Mrs. Addams

"THIS IS THE KIND OF MAN CHARLIE WAS," SAID CAROL
Matthau (the former Carol Marcus, who married Walter Matthau in
1959). "If he called, and you sounded low, he'd say, 'You don't sound
happy. Is there something wrong?'

" 'Oh, *yes,* things are awful,' you'd say, launching into a self-pitying list
of complaints.

" 'Have dinner with me,' he'd say."

And he listened, "always listened, interested in what you said," recalled another friend, Barbara Gross, who, along with her husband, knew
Addams through the classic car group—just one of Addams's many
groups of friends. George Plimpton described the experience of spending
an evening talking to Addams. You'd "come away feeling that you'd had
the most marvelous time—and realize that *you* had done all the talking."
Any number of people thought that they had a special relationship with
Addams.

Barbara Gross was one of several female Addams friends who added
that she was "not on his level." Still, Addams focused on his companion
as though she was the only person in the room, making her feel like his
"co-conspirator," said Jessie Wood, wife of the writer Clement Wood.

Here, then, was the essence of the Addams appeal to women: "He
took an interest in what you were doing and thinking and in one's chil-

dren, to whom he was also kind," said Axie Whitney. "And of course he was lots of fun to be with."

Just walking down the street with him was fun. "Are you limping, Charlie?" Axie asked him during a walk one day. "What? Me limp?" he said, and began dragging himself along the sidewalk in an exaggerated hobble. In the midst of Charlie's routine, a man approached. But instead of resuming a normal walk, Charlie kept it up, staying in character until the stranger had passed. As he explained to Axie, he didn't want the man to see him limping and then not limping.

As one of New York's most amiable men—and for long periods a bachelor—Addams was a sought-after party guest. "Spirits always soared when he entered the room," said Arthur Schlesinger, Jr. And yet he "didn't perform, ever," said Philip Hamburger. While he listened to the talk going on around him, his narrow eyes twinkling, a smile beginning to tug at the corners of the mouth that never showed his teeth, his whole face seemed to reflect what he was feeling—it "reminded you of a summer meadow lightened and dimmed by fast-moving overhead cumulus," wrote Roger Angell. When Addams talked in "his mumbly, rumbly voice," as Drue Heinz described it, people would lean in to hear the unexpected, often witty remarks he made half to himself. ("It was almost like eavesdropping," said Budd Schulberg.) One day as Addams was driving with a companion through the Bowery, a man swaddled in filthy rags crossed the street. "Going skiing, no doubt," observed Addams. You never knew what he would say. Sliding over to Carol Matthau at a Matthau party attended by an Indian writer, he said, "Don't trust Indians."

As a conversationalist Addams was not only unpredictable but "funny as hell," said Philip Hamburger. In Addams-speak, you didn't get drunk, but "stewed"; you were "overserved." And his wide interests and knowledge enabled him to talk intelligently about anything from robin's eggs to photography, jazz—New Orleans jazz, Chicago jazz—to train whistles. He once brought a record of train whistles to the home of one of his car friends, Bobs Harrison, and played it for everyone. He could argue the merits of the crossbow versus the longbow. "Any antique would fascinate him," said Budd Schulberg, and "he would ask lots of interested questions" about it. He was, for instance, absorbed by an antique phonograph of Schulberg's, and advised him to take better care of it. When he discovered that Schulberg had been trying to feed the vicious swans in Westhampton Beach, he warned him about their powerful wings, which could kill you. In fact, they had killed his handyman, he maintained, straight-faced.

Though he read everything, from Shakespeare to Steinbeck, Hemingway to John O'Hara, his real interest was in people. Addams "had very true instincts about things—a reliable eye for phonies and pompous people," said Arthur Schlesinger, Jr. And yet he tended to be more intrigued than offended by difficult people. While others were put off by John O'Hara's social pretensions, Addams was "fascinated by O'Hara's eccentricities, that O'Hara saw things in a social hierarchy," said Sidney Offit. And while a less assured man would have felt threatened by a homosexual overture, Addams was amused when a gay black man made a pass at him. When Addams rebuffed him, the man said, "Oh, you're only doing that because you're prejudiced against blacks."

Once, at a party, someone said to Addams, "How could you talk to such an uninteresting little man?" "There is no such thing as a little man," he replied. "Everyone has something to tell you if you'll listen."

He listened to Lyda Hall's young daughter when she telephoned him at home at night with cartoon ideas. He listened to the diamond man peddling gems on the street, and to the doomsday sayer loudly proclaiming the end of the world. "Let's go tell Frank!" said a delighted Addams, referring to Modell, and he hurried back to *The New Yorker*. He was once bedazed by a man who constantly used "you" in conversation. "You take your Washington, D.C.," he'd begin. Everything was "you." "It took me five minutes to figure out what the hell he was talking about," said Addams. Once he listened so long to an elderly man describe a route he had driven from Florida to New York that he literally lost consciousness. "You're Charlie Addams, aren't you?" the man had said as he approached Addams's table at Bleeck's on West Fortieth Street. "I come from the same town in New Jersey. I just drove in to New York from Florida. It was a very interesting trip. We left the house at nine o'clock, backed the car out, turned left, went up the street. The firehouse was on the left, the church was on the right. We stopped for the traffic light. When the light turned green, we turned onto route . . ." He went on in this vein until Addams staggered out the restaurant door and, he said, fainted on the sidewalk.

Oh, the human comedy! his attitude said. "A fully clothed English nanny dropped overboard yesterday," Addams wrote Nancy Holmes in Gstaad. "Sank like a stone. With bubbles. Came up subsequently quite pissed off."

Another time he telephoned Steven Aronson to report on part of a conversation he'd had with Patricia Kennedy Lawford. She had asked him, "Do you go to every party you're invited to?"

"Certainly not," he said.

"I do," she said—a remark in which Charlie "found unaccountable depths of hilarity," recalled Aronson.

He had never outgrown his love of mimicry. "Mr. O'Hala," he had written in 1953, "Johnny Nokura—depresting Japonese television. We like to make your play Appt in Samalla with all Japonese cast. Pay plenty money up to 300 dolla Japonese. Take place in geisha house—world biggest glass Saki." There was "the acquaintance who sucked his teeth." There was Truman Capote, whom Addams ran into one day in 1963 as Capote was leaving a movie theater where the four-hour Elizabeth Taylor extravaganza *Cleopatra* was playing. "I came to see the *asp*," Addams later said, imitating Capote's funny high-pitched whine.

The courtesies, and kindness, defined him. At a cocktail party, Addams once caught the increasingly annoyed look on his hostess's face as she watched one guest monopolize a more desirable guest. And he slipped beside her and began to talk, charming her until she forgot she had been angry. Instead of the conventional host or hostess gift, he would arrive at a party with something unpredictable, such as a metal alligator with a back that opened up into little compartments, which George Plimpton's children loved to play with. After he broke a plate at Jane Gunther's house, he turned up with his 1953 cartoon of two men approaching a beautiful mermaid on a beach ("Now remember, act casual," one says), and a note to the effect of "A drawing instead of a plate." When Axie Whitney's cat died, Charlie arrived with his 1961 cartoon showing two salesmen regarding a "Beware of the Cat" sign as they enter a wooded path leading to a house. "There's a silly sign if I ever saw one," says one of them. Way up in the treetops lurks the Cheshire cat.

He faithfully recorded Daphne Hellman's gigs around New York, where she played a mean jazz harp with her trio, Hellman's Angels, and went to her yearly party at the Village Gate. He attended funerals, though he hated them. He even endured the occasional children's party, bringing something that was sure to beguile the birthday boy or girl, such as a stuffed owl with eyes that glowed in the dark. He appeared at sickbeds, not with flowers, but with his attention, which was better. When Lyda Hall was in the hospital, Charlie visited her so often that she thought the doctors took him for her brother. (Lyda would turn her head and see him: a nose protruding from behind the screen as he yakked it up with the men in white coats, wanting to know all the clinical details.) On the night the painter and Jazz Age icon Gerald Murphy died, Charlie turned up at the Murphys' home in East Hampton to offer practical support to Murphys' widow, Sara. "We went into a sort of stupor, and it would have been absolutely impossible to have talked on the telephone to the newspapers," wrote the Murphys' daughter, Honoria, in a thank-you note. "You really saved our lives."

When Jane Gunther's dog died, Charlie wanted to see the ashes. And so Jane stopped by his apartment after having Josephine cremated. Charlie told her that she should scatter some of the ashes in New York, where she lived most of the time, and some in Vermont, where she spent the summers at her girlhood home, as the dog had lived in both places. And he and Jane proceeded to release the New York Josephine from Charlie's balcony overlooking the Museum of Modern Art sculpture garden.

"He was a *great* friend," stressed Carol Matthau. "He had a sweetness that someone who was less of a man would be afraid to show." Carol found Addams "shy, so sweet and darling." Unlike most men, he confided his own intimate secrets to women.

During the years when Carol was still single, Lillian Ross found herself out somewhere one night sitting with Charlie and Carol, who were engrossed in conversation. As they talked "a certain kind of sophisticated talk," Lillian sensed that Charlie "was crazy about Carol"—a witty, luminous blonde then in her early thirties, whom both James Agee and Kenneth Tynan had loved—and wanted her all to himself. "I *wish*," sighed Carol Matthau when she heard Lillian Ross's memory many years later. But she and Charlie were just friends.

"Charlie had a true interest in women as friends," explained Tee. "Where another man would be wondering, 'Can I get her into bed?'

Charlie would be thinking, 'Now here's an attractive person. I wonder what her story is.' "

The beautiful Gwladys Hopkins Whitney, known as Gee, was the ex-wife of Cornelius "Sonny" Vanderbilt Whitney, and was between her second and third marriages when Addams met her. She was a great horsewoman, trained German shepherds, and drove a Duesenberg. Charlie "flipped" after Gee's niece, Gerta Connor, introduced him to her; "he had never met anyone like her," said Gerta. Gee was likewise taken with Charlie, and she loved being with him. He took her to a restaurant and nightclub on Sixth Avenue; she invited him to her house in Villanova, where he chased her and cornered her in her bedroom one evening.

"Don't you ever need a man?" he said finally.

But Gee Whitney was not attracted to Addams physically, she told Gerta. She later married a renowned British neurologist, Dr. Frank A. Elliott, whose research concerned the criminal mind.

Then there was Greta Garbo. Soon after they were introduced by John and Jane Gunther, sometime around 1960, the dapper man-about-town was spotted at various places in New York with "the hermit about town." Off they would go in the Bentley for an Addams tour of New York. They visited the historic Trinity Church and chapel in lower Manhattan—a Gothic Revival oasis with a bell tower and an ancient graveyard, surrounded by the skyscrapers of the financial district. They explored the big Sunday market on Allen Street, on the eastern border of Chinatown, where Garbo bought "a set of red woolen underwear for two bucks." He took her to a bar on City Island, the quaint seaside village in the Bronx, and to an out-of-the-way restaurant where they knew Garbo but respected her privacy. They went window-shopping and antiquing, Garbo camouflaged in her "face concealing hat" and dark clothing. He called her "Miss G," as all her friends did; she called him "Mr. Addams."

Seven years older than Addams, Garbo was in her mid-fifties when they met, and past the peak of her matchless beauty—none of which mattered to him. He liked her big feet, and "he liked that her face was very immobile—it never changed." And she was funny. She talked about her health, for instance, with inelegant frankness. "I am not feeling good. I'm having trouble with my bladder," she said when Addams invited her to dinner one night. And she had a curious habit of referring to herself as a male. Sitting out on Addams's terrace, Garbo once said, "I am a lonely man circling the earth."

"What do you mean by that?" asked Addams.

Garbo "took a sip of Vodka. 'Someday I will tell you how it is with me,' she said." And then she smiled her fleeting smile, "and changed the subject."

Addams described the beginning of a typical outing with Garbo. It was a Sunday. He telephoned and offered to take her for a ride.

"Oh, Mr. Addams," she said in her husky Swedish accent, "do you think I should do it?"

"Absolutely," he told her. "It'll do you good."

"All right," she said, "I will walk past your apartment in half an hour."

"The unlikeliest twosome of the season is Greta Garbo and Charles Addams," chirped Sheilah Graham in the *Daily Mirror*. "They've been dining and driving!"

In Charles Addams the hunted Garbo found another little zone of safety. He "reached people very easily—people who were not always easy," said Jane Gunther. And "he was absolutely genuine, and so a person like Greta Garbo, who was terrified of being exploited, would trust him." At parties, to which Garbo often came alone, she would gravitate toward him, happy to see him. But when Addams offered to take her home, she always declined. "She always says, 'Oh, thank you so much. I can manage,' " Addams noted. "You often wonder how she gets home."

Once, he and Miss G talked about taking a drive across country, as she had done years earlier through Austria (with Baron Erich Goldschmidt-Rothschild). But somehow it was "the wrong time," and they never did. Years later, Addams thought of the missed opportunity with regret: "What a mistake," he told himself. And he reminded Garbo of the plan.

"Mr. Addams, I was serious," she said.

WOMEN CRAMMED HIS DATEBOOKS, competing for space and attention. "Don't Forget I Love You to Utter Distraction. Indeed I do!" wrote one in the little book, consuming six days of the week. "I AM MORE MAD FOR YOU THAN EVER DEAREST LOVE!" went another entry. On and on went the ecstatic scrawl, twining around the social engagements with friends, dental appointments, and a solo Addams visit to California like a noose. "Are you behaving yourself??" the unidentified woman wrote in his book before leaving for a trip of her own. "Only 11 More Days! I Love You With All My Heart Charlie."

The Addams harem included a woman with a lot of teeth, who spoke of herself in the third person ("Marsha wants a drink!"), and the now-divorced Leila Hadley, the great-great-great-great-granddaughter of James Boswell, who, at twenty-five, had sailed around the world on a three-masted schooner with her five-year-old son and four unknown men—an adventure she had chronicled in a wonderful 1958 book, *Give Me the World.* Leila was altogether dazzling: big doe eyes suggesting Audrey Hepburn, a pert nose, and a soft mouth exaggerated in a sexy caricature by Al Hirschfeld. There was also Leila's "adorable, frisky" Cousin Ronnie, Veronica Eliot Mosby, who conveniently lived in Sarasota, the winter home of the Ringling Bros.; sculptor Axie Whitney, who met Charlie at a party sometime around 1964; the Russian-French trompe l'oeil artist Odette Benjamin, whom Tee and Buddy Davie had introduced to Addams during the late fifties; and bad girl Sloan Simpson, "suffering from a post Addams depression" after he left Acapulco, where she was residing. There was Daphne Hellman ("She had eight million dollars in 1954," Addams told Steven Aronson); Jim Geraghty's secretary, *The New Yorker*'s Kay Draper—"very statuesque, absolutely beautiful," said Frank Modell—who later married Paul Leperq; the exotic-looking Mimi Neshimi, who would marry Prince Alexander Romanov, thereby becoming "the first Jewish Italian American princess," said Addams; the brilliant, stylish, never-married Dona Guimares, a former reporter and executive editor of *Mademoiselle,* who later became editor of the Home section of *The New York Times.* A collector who shared Addams's love of the offbeat and of Victorian style when it wasn't fashionable, Dona renovated a nineteenth-century barn and a 1924 worker's cottage in Quogue, and gave wonderful parties; she lectured on fashion and design at the Smithsonian and the Cooper-Hewitt Museum in New York, among others, and usually traveled with a tape measure. Her fine, somewhat large features were partly obscured by oversized tinted glasses worn to protect her eyes, which had been damaged in a birth injury. There was actress

Leueen MacGrath, the much younger wife of George S. Kaufman. At Kaufman's behest, Addams escorted Leueen, who was just two years his junior, to the theater and other places Kaufman was no longer up to going. Addams continued to see Leueen after her divorce from Kaufman. A small, pretty, brown-eyed blonde, Leueen talked in a soft, refined British

Leila Hadley, the great-great-great-great-granddaughter of James Boswell, and the author of Give Me the World.

accent, and spoke excellent French. Years after she had driven a London ambulance during the Blitz, she would "visibly" shake at the mention of the Nazis and "wartime London."

Even *The New Yorker*'s Maeve Brennan, who had eventually forgiven Addams his piggery, was a recurring name in his little datebooks during the early sixties.

"There was Charles Addams—still a bachelor although many have tried—looking quite dashing always with his cigar and dry smile," reported *The Daily News Record* in 1964 in an account of a Braque exhibition. There Addams stood in a glossy eight-by-twelve photograph apparently shot for a print ad in the summer of 1963: a debonair man in black tie and very shiny shoes, gesturing with his hands in mock conversation with a beautiful, receptive girl. Young enough to be his daughter, she wears a simple long black dress with a ruffle at the bottom, a sixties version of the Morticia look. This girl with the flawless mannequin face is obviously a model, posing. But the polished, mature man with the thirties-style backcombed hair and crinkly, smiling eyes focused on her with such happy interest is simply playing himself. And yet Addams never let an affair completely overtake him; "nothing interfered with his work," said Odette.

A dinner with one woman often followed lunch with another, and perhaps had been preceded by a trip to Gettysburg with yet another. An ideal date involved an excursion to Pennsylvania, Addams-style: a visit to the battlefield, or perhaps to Pennsylvania Dutch country, where Charlie would point out the hex signs and map a route taking you past the signs reading "Intercourse," "Blue Ball," "Paradise," "Bareville," "Sporting Hills," and "Bird-in-Hand," followed by dinner at a good restaurant.

As the 1960s got under way, Addams's datebooks recorded the juggling act: dinner with Maeve at Delmonico's; a drink with Maeve and Dawn Powell at the Fifth Avenue Hotel. A date with actress Joan Fontaine, then a weekend at Westhampton Beach with the British writer Barbara Skelton, after which he spent another two days with Fontaine. Tee, who was now divorced from Buddy Davie and married to a rather staid corporation lawyer named Dudley Miller, recalled her new husband's stunned expression the night Charlie switched beautiful women over cocktails. Tee and Dudley had met Charlie and Joan Fontaine for a drink. "Joan looked divine," remembered Tee. But she had another engagement, and left early. She had been gone only minutes when another of Charlie's girlfriends swept in to take her place. The timing had been so close, it seemed that the women must have passed each other in the elevator. Charlie was a picture of grace throughout.

Though Dudley Miller liked Charlie—who didn't like Charlie?—he was "very jealous" of him, said Tee. She therefore did not always tell her husband that while he was out of town on business she had had lunch with Charlie, though they were just friends at the time. Once, she made a plan to go off to Amish country with Charlie and Nancy Holmes. They all set off in the Bentley, Charlie wearing a chauffeur's cap, the two women riding in back. After lunch at Colligan's, at the historic Stockton Inn in New Jersey, it was on to Pennsylvania, where they posed for pictures at the First National Bank in Intercourse. Nancy snapped Charlie and Tee as they entered the building under the sign with the word "Intercourse"; Tee took the picture of Charlie and Nancy as they exited. On the spur of the moment, they all decided to stay overnight in Pennsylvania. "How shall I register?" Charlie said at the hotel. "I know," he answered himself: "as Mr. and Mrs. and Mrs. Addams."

"Mr. and Mrs. and Mrs. Addams." Left, Addams and Tee Miller;
right, Addams and Nancy Holmes.

It had all been very proper. The two women shared a room, staying up late and talking about Charlie, who was in his own room. Tee had not yet returned to her apartment at the U.N. Plaza when Dudley Miller arrived home from Japan, and checked his wife's appointment book to see where she could be. "Intercourse with Charlie and Nancy," he read.

AFTER HIS SECOND DIVORCE from a woman named Barbara, Addams had told a reporter, "Now I'm careful to go out with women named Clarisse or something." Which was not strictly true. There was the married Barbara with a child with whom he had an affair.

And there was the married but separated Barbara Skelton, over whom he got into a naked fistfight. One glance at the English beauty explained the recourse to physical violence: green eyes set above high cheekbones; dark, curling, chin-length hair; an hourglass figure described as "the envy of London," which had inspired Schiaparelli. And she was absolutely wild, said Leila Hadley, bright and terrific. She loved to drive fast; she had a "silvery laugh." She had also published both a novel and a story collection. Upon meeting Barbara Skelton at a small luncheon at Le Bistro

Addams's little house at Westhampton Beach, the "floating palace of pleasure."

arranged by Elaine Tynan, Charlie invited her to lunch at the Rainbow Room in the Waldorf the next day. Afterward, they sped off to Westhampton Beach in his Bentley.

When Addams met her in 1960, the new Barbara was already, at thirty, a femme fatale of the first rank. Her lovers had included King Farouk, who had once whipped her with the cord of a dressing gown on the steps of his palace in Cairo. "I would have preferred a splayed cane," was her sassy reply. Her husbands to date had both been Englishmen: the essayist, critic, and enfant terrible Cyril Connolly, and publisher George Weidenfeld, whom Barbara called "Weedenfelt." Barbara Skelton, reflected Connolly, had done "much to redeem the London literary world from the taint of homosexuality."

In keeping with the best and worst Barbaras, she was witty, moody, adventurous, animal-loving, regretful about her lack of children, nasty, and fun to be with. She was also capable of tough self-appraisal. After too many Addams martinis on her first visit to the canal house, she "became very aggressive and accused him of being 'mean,' 'a rotten lecher,' 'vain,' and 'selfish.'" "The following day," she noted, "we drove at full speed back to New York, where I was dropped off on the kerb with a serpenty kiss and the words, 'Call you next week.' I spent that Sunday alone with a drainpipe for company." The next tryst on Long Island resulted in more name-calling: "an 'American Blimp' and a 'tin hoarder.' When we returned to New York, it was no longer 'I'll call you' but 'Call me.'"

But Addams did call, and he kept calling. He took her to parties, and to "21"; he introduced her to Thurber. During a European holiday that summer, somewhere between a dinner with the café society hostess Elsa Maxwell in France and a dinner with someone else in Verona, he slipped off to Sardinia with Barbara and did not return for four days. "Charlie just thought she was great," said Leila Hadley, who added that he came close to marriage with this third Barbara.

Writing from London in October, Barbara warned him about a friend of Cyril Connolly's who would soon be staying with Drue Heinz: Lady Rosie d'Avigdor Goldsmid. She "seems to be very curious and one doesn't want any gossip. Also, she has been rather malicious," Barbara explained in a typed "Oh dear! It's me again" letter. "If, by any chance, Sardinia crops up in the conversation, please don't let on that I was there, do what comes naturally to you, look enigmatic!" Just the night before, she added, she had had a close call with "Weedenfelt," to whom she was still married. "He said Mrs. Heinz had made a point of dragging him across a dance floor to meet you, saying 'Your wife's lover' and was it a nice thing to do? I said that probably would be her idea of fun, and it was quite harmless."

A few years later, Addams was involved in a more literal collision over Barbara Skelton. She was having an affair with a younger man, Alastair Hamilton, the handsome son of Addams's English publisher, Hamish Hamilton. With Hamilton away for the weekend, Addams had spent the night with Barbara in New York. Just "as Charlie was scurrying naked into the shower," Barbara recounted, Alastair returned unexpectedly. Fists flew. To Barbara's surprise, her older lover prevailed. Hamilton got to his feet and solemnly addressed the naked middle-aged cartoonist. "How do you like the colour process my father has just done on your book?" he asked.

IF ADDAMS DID NOT make lovers of all his friends, he made friends of all his lovers. "Charlie was, on the whole, a passive man, with immense charm and a most appealing way of moving," wrote Barbara Skelton. He had a captivating way of talking, too. Driving past a crammed Long Island cemetery one day, he observed, "They must be standing up in there." Another time, when Barbara reacted with surprise as he praised a particular book—"But I've never seen you reading," she said—he replied, "Do you expect me to sit here and read in front of you?"

He was "a wonderful beau," said Leila Hadley—and woman after woman agreed. At the canal house that Audrey called "a floating palace of pleasure," certain images lingered in his lovers' minds: "crossing the road, clutching our clothes, eager for the privacy of conversation"; "the *New York Times* early in the morning—the 'Whistling Swans'—Albert and Josephine, the barbecues, the antique shops . . . the Hamburgers à la Addams . . . the cozy fire, the view from the top balcony, the sunset. . . ." Above the white-iron-and-brass bed, which was flanked by a pair of pretty wall-mounted lamps, Charlie had placed his captionless 1951 cartoon showing an ornery man in an old-fashioned nightshirt standing on a footstool and thumping his cane on the ceiling to protest the racket in the apartment above—where a bound and gagged man thrashes on the floor amid his overturned furniture.

Only Charlie always woke up in the morning with a funny story, and turned the water spots on the ceiling into cartoons. If other men were sexually adventurous—"I've got something wonderful; we've got to try them," Charlie said as he drove his Bentley toward a motel during the sixties, referring to those amyl nitrate wonders known as "poppers"—only Charlie innocently went through a whole box with you during a single evening, and lived to tell about it. If other men also laughed with you for a half hour after the bed fell, only Charlie said he wished he had a microdot on the end of his cock, so that when he got an erection, you could read the Lord's Prayer. (Then again, he said, it would be an identifying mark if he was caught shoplifting.) There he stood under the outdoor shower at the little house, which was only partly concealed by overgrown hedges, happily washing off—in the nude. There he was in his swimming attire—an antique striped bathing suit that left nothing to the imagination. The elegant man whose casual dress ran to cashmere and gray flannels had no qualms about wearing the unlined wool suit when he went to meet Budd Schulberg for the first time after the screenwriter moved to Westhampton Beach; nor did he think twice about wearing it to a bar on Fire Island. On both occasions, Charlie and his girl had traveled by boat—his skiff, named the *Polyp*. This man Leila Hadley described as "a sophisticated innocent" could still recite Longfellow's *Song of Hiawatha* ("By the shore of Gitchee Gumee") and the Boy Scout Oath: "A scout is Trustworthy, Loyal, Helpful, Friendly, Courteous, Kind, Obedient, Cheerful, Thrifty, Brave, Clean, and Reverent," he said. "He knew all the funny words for things—such as the terms in the *Kama Sutra*," said Leila. And he had surprisingly soft skin, like a baby's, noted Odette.

If Addams wasn't the only man who ever gave a woman a black velvet Gucci handbag, he was the only man who made her a present of his *New Yorker* cover painting showing a sizzling red Manhattan melting like crayons under a fiery sun—complemented by another hot summer sun in ink and watercolor, hovering above his own laughing, melting, puddling face. He was the only jazz-loving man who sat with her and her mother through an opera—Wagner's heavily religious *Parsifal*, no less—"absolutely rigid with boredom." And if other men were also sensitive, no one could repair a broken ego quite the way Charlie could. When Audrey Cosden's estranged husband announced over the telephone from his hospital bed that he was going to marry Zsa Zsa Gabor, Charlie understood the look on Audrey's face. "I think he had the wrong operation," he said. "He should have had a lobotomy."

And who else would you call after meeting Sean Connery on the ship from Europe and learning that what he most wanted to see on his first visit to New York was the docks? "My father was a long-distance lorry driver," Connery told Nancy Holmes in 1965 as she was returning to the States. "I have just the person for you," said Nancy. Upon landing in New York, she telephoned Charlie. "Get out the Bentley," she announced.

Even men who were fathers didn't reach one's children as easily as

Addams did. Of course Charlie himself was a big kid, chortling about the woman on the street someone had addressed as "Mrs. Butterinsky," or laughing at Daphne Merkin's name, "merkin" signifying only one thing. On a trip to Saratoga, Nancy Holmes found Charlie hunched over a tabloid with her fourteen-year-old daughter, Brooke, laughing. The newspaper heading read, "My Husband Has Cancer and Is Loving It."

An Addams self-portrait for Odette Benjamin.

After Leila's abandonment by her second husband, Yvor Smitter, who went overseas to work for a month and returned four years later, Charlie began spending a lot of time at the apartment she shared with her three children. There was more than one "lovely unexpected weekend" when he brought Leila and her brood out to Westhampton Beach—an experience Leila worried "might have convinced you to be a cenobite," she wrote Charlie in a thank-you note. But if Addams had felt imposed on by the children, he never let on. And for the children, the visits were magical.

Leila's Caroline was between the ages of four and six when she skipped down the long, winding wooden boardwalk connecting the garage to the house on the canal that looked like a two-tiered cake, the poison ivy Addams allowed to flourish in the yard where a sign said KEEP OFF THE GRASS reaching up and licking her bare legs. Inside the house the children found a miniature guillotine and a hatchway. Matthew particularly "loved to climb up the trap door," he wrote Addams after his joyous escape from the city. "In New York it is just like living in a garbage pan."

An Addams rough.

Leila soon found herself having The Talk. Asked what sex was, she dived in with a graphic explanation. "Oh, no, Mummy," objected one of her brood, "Mr. Addams would never do a dirty thing like that."

There was simply no one like him. Who else went to the Metropolitan Museum to have the strings of his crossbows replaced, and turned up for a costume party in an actual medieval suit of armor, oiled by his handyman? Who else would pay a housekeeper who, as Charlie himself put it, "made everything a little dirtier"? Known only as Katie, the ancient, "lumpish" black woman Addams paid to sew things and clean his apartment in New York shuffled about the place in carpet slippers and wore a dirty yellow rag around her head, which she occasionally removed to dust something or wipe a glass. She broke things; the kitchen was filthy. Tee would wash a glass before drinking anything at Charlie's apartment. "Why don't you fire her?" she finally asked. "I can't fire her," he said. "She's old; she'll never work again."

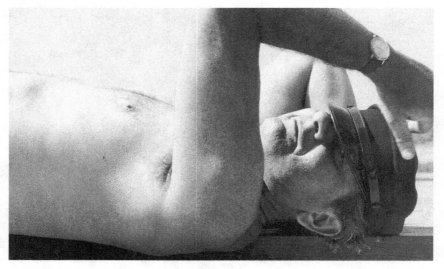

Addams on the dock at Westhampton Beach: "There was no one like him."

And this man, to whom the Indy 500 was "a sacred event," was a remarkably calming presence. "My dock seems to be on fire," he said casually when his flaming hibachi plunged through the boards at Westhampton Beach. No one else had his joie de vivre, his "child-like experience" of the world, his "weird sense of things." And "only babies have that little toothless smile," said Leila. Leila gave him a stuffed raven, a Tibetan sorcerer's tray, a rare Tibetan exorcist book, a "blotted Victorian love poem . . . punctuated only with tears" from her great-grandmother, and a seven-inch black wrought iron dragon. Odette gave him a fuzzy boa constrictor from Neiman Marcus. From London, Barbara Colyton sent a leather pig, and a picture of a boa constrictor eating a baby elephant.

Though Charlie was not excessively prone to flower sending or door holding—he considered women his equals, after all—he was reassuring as only he could be. When Audrey awoke in a Vermont inn during the middle of a snowy night and heard a strange scratching sound, she asked Charlie what it was. "It's the little people, trying to get out," he said. And Audrey went back to sleep.

As for his endless philandering, "that was one of his charms," said Audrey. He didn't mean any harm, and "he couldn't lie," said Leila. He talked to the women in his life about one another, chatting fondly late into the night about Odette to Leila, to Barbara Skelton about Joan Fontaine. ("She had the map of the U.S. on her face," he said about another woman he'd slept with.) And since being with Charlie was "a joyous escape," with never a harsh word, said Odette, she assumed the attitude, "If I had him for a length of time, I had him for that length of time." Said Leila, "Charlie was the only man I've ever known who women never got jealous about—except for that dreadful Joan Fontaine."

Chapter Fifteen

Remarkably Well Preserved

I
N 1961, WHILE SEEING AT LEAST FOUR OTHER WOMEN, Addams plunged into a very public affair with Joan Fontaine. The eye-catching couple were seen everywhere together—at parties and pre-mieres, such as that of the 1962 film *The Wonderful World of the Brothers Grimm,* Fontaine clutching Addams's tuxedoed arm with the simpering look that old movie audiences knew so well; at restaurants such as Elaine's, the St. Regis, and the historic White Horse Tavern in Green-wich Village, where Fontaine gave Addams a black-tie fiftieth birthday party.

They were seen smiling into the desert sun atop camels in Cairo, Addams in caftan and kaffiyeh, Fontaine in a pale gray cashmere sweater, matching scarf, and pedal pushers. They were spotted at a fall fashion show, Fontaine looking attentive as she leaned close to Addams, Addams looking domesticated and bored as he discreetly checked his watch. They were observed picnicking at car races, and at a Sports Car Club meeting, where Fontaine looked bored. And surely it was Joan Fontaine, thought one dazzled Addams friend, whose scarf trailed behind her in Addams's Bugatti as it soared along the Dune Road in Westhampton Beach.

By now Fontaine was long past the height of her film career, yet she remained every inch the star. At forty-four, she was still beautiful—a tiny, impeccable blonde, with the same sweet face that had charmed movie au-diences during the 1940s, when her honeyed performances in two Hitchcock classics had won her an Academy Award nomination for *Rebecca* and the Oscar for Best Actress for *Suspicion*. Always camera-ready, she was perfectly coiffed, and a vision in her movie-star wardrobe: strapless brocade with matching stole; winter velvet; a floor-length satin coat with mink cuffs. And she was a woman of many talents—a canny business-woman, a licensed interior decorator, and a Cordon Bleu cook.

Though she had continued to act in the occasional movie and on the stage, her most memorable performances were currently off the set. Leila Hadley remembered her introduction to Fontaine. Charlie had tele-phoned and invited her to Joan's apartment for a drink. Leila had just ar-rived and had not yet removed her coat or been formally introduced to the actress when Joan said, "How do you spell cunnilingus?"

Leila fairly spit out the letters.

Though Fontaine could be "hearty, easy, a lot of fun—like Tee," said Jane Gunther ("witty, funny, mean," in Drue Heinz's tougher appraisal), she could also be stunningly cruel. She "had all the characteristics of women in 1930s movies," said Gillis Addison (formerly MacGil and then Stearns), including that of "wench."

After their divorce, Gillis and her ex-husband, photographer Philip Stearns, had remained friendly. Years before Addams became involved with Fontaine, Stearns had had an affair with her. And he had once taken Gillis to a party at Joan's apartment, where she watched the actress delib-erately humiliate her guests of honor. Now, seeing Fontaine with the wonderful Charlie Addams got to be too much for Gillis. After becom-ing a little intoxicated at a celebrity-packed New Year's Eve party Char-lie was attending with Fontaine, Gillis told him he must stop seeing Joan. And she spilled the story about Joan's cruelty to her party guests.

Addams listened with a bemused expression, and said he'd take it under consideration. Later in the evening, Gillis saw him again. "Gillis, Joan disagrees with you," he told her.

Gillis was horrified that he had repeated her remarks to Joan. Addams explained that Joan had wanted to know why he was talking to Gillis. "Well, Gillis, I just thought Joan should know how you felt about her," he kidded. It turned out that he hadn't told Joan a thing.

During the time he was caught in Fontaine's footlights, Addams, who got plenty of his own fan mail, began getting letters from *her* adoring fans, too, who confused the woman with the characters she had played. A woman who had admired Fontaine since her 1943 performance as a teenage gamine in *The Constant Nymph* implored Addams to take "the best possible care of the star" and to "protect her from any and all who would *USE* her."

For a long time, it seemed to his friends, Charlie was smitten—"passionately attached" to Fontaine, observed Barbara Skelton. He took the actress to the Roger Angells' annual Christmas party; to the Gunthers'; to Daphne Hellman's musical evenings at her East Sixty-first Street townhouse; to the cemetery. Smoking a cigar in Joan's elegant pied-à-terre on Central Park South, Addams looked at home among the painted Italian furniture, green velvet, and crystal chandeliers. If he was bothered by Fontaine's actressy affectations, crude language, and pretensions at domesticity, he seems not to have let on. But then came the marriage talk. Alistair Cooke sat down for a drink with Addams on Long Island one evening when Fontaine was not with him.

"So, Charlie, how's your love life?" he asked.

As Addams sipped his drink, he "slowly shook his head."

"You know, Alistair, the trouble with women is they always want a [permanent] relationship."

And yet the marriage rumors, fanned by the actress herself in a coy disclaimer to Louella Parsons, persisted. Speaking of her soon-to-be-third ex-husband, Fontaine said, "We get our divorce any minute, and then I'll be free." And she added that she was "not going to marry again."

The truth was that Addams had considered it, "but no—too difficult," he decided. Meaning that Joan was too difficult.

To begin with, she was impossibly vain. Addams imitated her to Leila: "I am *remarkably* well preserved," he said in his distinctive drawl, all six-foot-one of him preening in front of the mirror. Worse, her constant craving for the spotlight led to tantrums and rudeness. The moment Fontaine was no longer the center of everyone's attention, she would "get the vapors."

Lyda and her husband, Randy Hall, were in the real estate business when Addams brought Joan to an open house. Everything was pleasant until the attention shifted away from Joan. Abruptly announcing that she was not feeling well, she went upstairs to lie down on a bed. As the open house continued, prospective buyers drifted through the rooms, peeking in. "There's a woman lying down upstairs who looks like Joan Fontaine," they kept saying.

On another occasion, Addams and Joan met the Halls at a restaurant. Again the conversation turned from Joan to another subject. Charlie and Lyda began to talk to each other, leaving Joan to talk only to Randy.

"Look at him!" cried Joan. "He doesn't care, and I have cancer!" And she said that she was feeling ill.

This time Addams became visibly angry. "C'mon, Joan," he said roughly, and left the restaurant with her.

"I popped her one on the jaw," he later told Lyda. Lyda wasn't sure whether he was kidding.

Before Addams realized what he had gotten himself into, Fontaine had moved in on him with her wardrobe and maid and stack of Victrola records. She complained about his little boat; she wanted him to get something grander than the *Polyp*. She disliked his poison ivy yard; she wanted him to grow tomatoes in Westhampton Beach and sell them. In fact, she wanted to uproot him altogether and move him to California.

And when she heard that Odette Benjamin was in Westhampton Beach, her caterwauling reached the ears of Cholly Knickerbocker.

"Charlie Addams, the famed cartoonist, is the point of contention between two beautiful women," reported the columnist in the *Journal-American*. "They are actress Joan Fontaine and socialite Odette Benjamin."

In January 1962, the month Addams turned fifty, he accompanied Fontaine on a forty-two-day, eighteen-port Mediterranean cruise with a shipload of celebrities including Gloria Swanson, Paul Newman, Joanne Woodward, Jacqueline de Ribes, and Gore Vidal, to promote the Italian liner *Leonardo da Vinci*. They had no sooner set off down the Hudson River in twenty-degree weather than Addams found the romantic climate equally cold. As the ship moved from one exotic port to another— Las Palmas in the Canary Islands to Morocco, and on to Italy—they fought. They fought their way around the world, said Addams—from Athens to Istanbul, from Istanbul to the island of Rhodes to Egypt, Beirut, Geneva, Italy again, Cannes, and finally Lisbon. Decades later, Lyda Hall tried to remember the words Charlie had repeated to her: "I don't like you, piss face," Fontaine had said—or something to that effect.

Addams and Joan Fontaine. They fought all around the world.

Though the marriage rumors continued, after the rough crossing Fontaine began to preserve her dignity. "It's such a wonderful friendship that it would be a shame to spoil it with marriage," she told the press.

By Labor Day weekend 1963, when Addams and Fontaine's mother helped Joan move into a luxurious apartment she had bought on East Seventy-second Street, Addams himself was moving toward the exit. "I was afraid *I* was going to be the last antique moved in," he told Nancy Holmes. "J—finis," he wrote in his datebook on September 27. Soon Joan departed for Sweden to make a movie. "The relief was almost like getting a divorce," said Addams.

Months later, Fontaine married Alfred Wright, Jr., the editor of *Sports Illustrated.* She kept a favorite hooded chair of Charlie's—his "whispering chair," in which he liked to draw, which he had not given her—and a classic Family cartoon, which he apparently had given her, the 1947 "It's the children, darling, back from camp." Addams was left with a series of oil paintings that Joan had done at Westhampton Beach showing the canal house in morning, afternoon, and evening light—an oeuvre that suggested less Monet than a paint-by-numbers kit, though Charlie was "never cruel about the lack of talent." He stored the works in his garage.

In her memoir, Fontaine reduced Addams to a pleasant weekend companion. She remembered cocktail cruises in Charlie's boat at the beach; painting in oils during the day "while he tinkered with his ancient Bugatti." And she allowed a few thorns to poke up through the bouquet. "I knew a sick lady was not his idea of an enjoyable companion, that our romance was finished," she wrote. "I'd always joked with him that he would spawn with anything that twitched. He frankly agreed."

Outside the pages of the memoir, the woman who had haggled over the price of tomatoes said that Addams had been "a bad investment"— a remark that made Charlie really furious when it got back to him.

In a letter from England, Barbara Colyton could not resist comparing the actress to herself, who had done so much for Charles. "As for La Fontaine—*she will never give you anything*," she wrote. And she advised him to "*get* yr. property back. But in any event—get *my* property back," she wrote, apparently in reference to an Addams cartoon now in Fontaine's possession. "I really mean this."

Chapter Sixteen

The Addams Family

"I WANTED TO CALL HIM PUBERT," ADDAMS SAID OF THE bad boy in the Family drawings, "but a guy who was making dolls of the characters thought that sounded dirty. I thought that wasn't a bad name for a kid."

As he talked in his unique drawl, his narrow eyes twinkled; the hint of a smile tugged at the corners of his narrow mouth.

"Then I thought, 'Let's call him Irving.' But one of the salesmen said, 'What's so funny about Irving? That's my name.'"

The year was 1963. Along with the marriage rumors about Addams and Fontaine came a set of large cloth Addams Family dolls made by Aboriginals, Ltd. A television show based on the cartoons was also in the works, and Addams was to name the dolls so that they could be tied to the series. Addams, who had earned a royalty of $769 the first year and $1,756.66 the second, helped promote the dolls by posing with them for publicity shots—cradling the wan little girl in black on the knee that had never cradled children while her bad blond brother leered over the back of the wing chair in Addams's apartment, and pointing out the Manhattan skyline to their impassive mother in plunging black. One of the dolls turned up in *House Beautiful,* which ran a picture of Addams's Manhattan living room featuring "smart black-and-white print fabrics, black felt table-skirts, black lamps posed against stark white walls," a Maximilian suit of armor, crossbows, and a small statue of a raven. "He enjoys to the full the myths that have grown up around him and his sinister creatures," the magazine said of Addams.

With the exception of "Wednesday" for the daughter full of woe, which Aboriginals chose, Addams named each character. There were three dolls representing the mother and her children; the other family members would apparently follow. Priced at $7.98, Wednesday had wool hair and black empty eyes, the image of the cartoon girl. Addams came up with "Morticia" while looking in the phone book under "morticians." The Morticia doll was four feet tall, yours for $19.95. After "Pubert" was rejected for the delinquent in stripes, Addams settled on "Pugsley," the name of a stream in the Bronx he saw on a map. ("Dear Mr. Addams," wrote Joan A. Pugsley from New Jersey, "Would you be kind enough to tell me how you [or why you] decided upon the name 'Pugsley' for the cartoon character after which a doll has been designed. In the Manhattan directory there is only one Pugsley—a lawyer from White Plains. Actually there are two in New York—our aunt has an unlisted number.")

The other names emerged as the television show took shape. For Morticia's repulsive consort, Addams offered two, Repelli or Gomez (the name of an old family friend), and allowed the actor John Astin, who was cast in the role, to choose. Astin liked "Gomez," so Gomez it was. The shuffling grandmother based on Grandma Spear was called Granny Frump; "Lurch" was suggested by the Frankensteinian butler's halting walk. Uncle Fester was likewise named for obvious reasons. "I just thought that up as befitting a rotten guy," said Addams.

Various concepts for television and stage versions of the Addams characters had been tossed around for years. Wolcott Gibbs had seen the dramatic possibilities in the cartoons as early as 1947, after a mere seventeen Family drawings had appeared in *The New Yorker*. "Something really ought to be done about that haunted house bunch," he had written Addams. And he suggested that he and Charlie try collaborating on a play. The trick, as he and Addams had already discussed, was to "avoid that old, foolish scream and trap door note, and the problem is to get a sound plot to offset too much fantasy, but I think it can be done," Gibbs wrote Addams.

But the Addams-Gibbs collaboration never materialized. Other proposals, suggesting less of Gibbs's wit and more of the scream-and-trapdoor variety of humor, had befallen Addams at regular intervals. In 1961, a script based on *Addams and Evil* turned up. The playwright, named Richie Pew, had written a bad play reeking of banal, obvious, vampire-at-the-blood-bank humor, which he sent to Addams with a letter. ("Rack" and "Ruin" for the kids' names; "Monster" for the family's surname. And the spooky mansion would have a distinctly 1960s touch: a marijuana wreath on the front door at Christmas.) Addams replied to Pew's letter, scribbled "Save in case of blackmail" across the top of it, and moved on.

A couple in Forest Hills proposed a television series. They had already written scripts and outlines for thirteen episodes and taken them to certain "powers that be in television," they said. Nothing came of that, either. A New York writer named Jo Coudert presented a musical comedy based on his cartoons, particularly his 1954 collection, *Homebodies*. Addams had turned that one down, too, in part because he thought the Family came across as "unsympathetic."

Once in a while a good idea blew in the door. Though there had not been another Wolcott Gibbs, there were other interpreters who seemed to understand Addams's work and to possess the taste to adapt it in a way that would not embarrass him. One was Myra Kinch, who wanted to do a ballet or stage production; though Addams licensed his characters to her and even designed some animal costumes, apparently nothing came of it. Another possibility came from Imperial Records, which wanted to produce some music inspired by his drawings; Addams entered into a 1960 agreement with them, results unknown.

The irony was that at the moment of their big break, the Family had all but disappeared from the pages of *The New Yorker*. Almost all the Family cartoons were published during the 1940s and '50s—fifty-eight of them altogether, not including a few drawings of Pugsley and Uncle Fester solo. The first years of the 1960s had seen only a trickling of cartoons featuring the Family characters, and one true Family drawing in which the parents and children appeared together. "Suddenly, I have a dreadful urge to be merry," the hideous Gomez tells his mystified wife and children as he sits in the window seat before a snow-covered holiday scene. In October 1963, Addams had introduced a new character, though it was not clear that this creature was a member of the haunted household. Seen from behind as he answers the telephone in a wallpapered corner of the house, this squat hairball says, "This is it speaking." (Addams had been paid $174 for this addition to the Addams Family, who became the endearing and incomprehensible Cousin Itt.)

By the time Addams was approached for the television series, the work of two other cartoonists had been successfully translated into pop-

"Suddenly, I have a dreadful urge to be merry."

ular shows. Hank Ketchum's *Dennis the Menace,* which began as a cartoon strip in 1950, inspired a show by the same name, which ran on CBS from 1959 to 1963, and *Hazel,* based on Ted Key's long-running cartoon in *The Saturday Evening Post,* had begun on NBC in 1961, and was still going. Though Addams's work was wildly different, his cartoons had by now been used in ads for such shows as *The Bat* and NBC's *Dow Hour of Great Mysteries,* and Columbia Pictures had tastefully reprinted some Addams drawings on the title cards for their movie *The Old Dark House*— an arrangement requiring little work on Addams's part, but which paid him more than six thousand dollars. All that remained was for someone to convince him that television would not corrupt his characters.

David Levy was an independent television producer, and the former vice president of programming at NBC. Don Saltzman had been David Levy's manager of program services at NBC, and had left the network when Levy did.

It was Levy who approached Addams. Addams was initially hesitant. He told Levy he was concerned that television would destroy the family concept of his cartoons and reduce his characters to a bunch of strange people. But Levy was entirely respectful, and he began to win him over.

During 1963, producer and cartoonist met several times. They lunched at the Oak Room on May 9, five days after Barbara Colyton arrived for one of her visits from London. As the idea for a show took shape, Levy communicated with Addams "step by step," said Saltzman. The producer and the cartoonist soon formed a good relationship, and Addams decided to trust him. He even began to want the show, though he had his doubts about whether it would work. He would have no veto power over the scripts, but he would have a vote regarding the casting, and he would have Levy's ear. He agreed to write some notes about his characters.

By September 1, they had a draft of a written agreement for a show with Filmways TV Productions. Negotiated by Greenbaum, Wolff & Ernst, the contract called for a minimum of thirteen television programs. Addams was to be paid $1,000 for each half-hour episode, and $1,900 for any hour-long episodes; these amounts would double if the show went into a sixth season. He would get an advance payment of $3,000 for the first option period, which gave Filmways the exclusive right to make the show, and $5,000 for a second. If the option was exercised—and there was no guarantee that the episodes would be picked up by a network— and the television show actually aired, Addams's $3,000 advance would be in addition to his future earnings rather than an advance against them, as is standard. He was to receive 50 percent of the producer's net proceeds from merchandising and commercial tie-ins, or 30 percent of the gross, whichever was greater. And if David Levy left the show as working producer, Addams was to be consulted about his replacement.

It was a good deal. Then Barbara found out about it, and all hell broke loose. Barbara fired off warnings to Filmways, ABC, and others stating that she owned the rights to the cartoons and characters and they could not proceed with the show. (As Harriet Pilpel reported, she " 'sounds a little remote and strange' and kept reiterating, 'I have an open and shut case.' ") Addams assured his lawyer that he himself owned all the rights to his cartoons, a statement he clearly believed. Awash in ink, confused by the paper stranglehold in which Barbara had been wrapping him for the past decade, he had simply failed to understand what he had given her—that she, not he, did in fact own the dramatic rights to his creations, which he had signed over to her in 1960. He broke the bad news to Levy.

Thus began another rescue operation. Harriet Pilpel threw Addams a rope, which Addams reluctantly grabbed. "I finally caught up with Addams last night although unfortunately his ex-wife got to him before I did," wrote Pilpel on February 25. "In any event, the situation appears to be somewhat under control. I gather he was furious but somehow feels sorry for her and is willing to give her some cut. He asked me to call her last night which I said I would not do but I did agree to meet with them this morning at 11 A.M.," she concluded.

The next day, having "spent two and a half hours . . . trying to disentangle Barbara Bard [*sic*]" from Addams, Pilpel won a small victory when she got Addams and Barbara to sign an agreement she thought sufficient to save the television deal.

So there they were in February of 1964: Barbara raging about her ownership of the Addams rights, Addams and Pilpel scrambling to save the television show. Faced with the threat of litigation, Barbara had finally settled for 10 percent "of all sums due Owner," and at last the show could go on. (Addams ended up giving her another 10 percent out of pocket.) Barbara saved her greatest hostility for David Levy, who had succeeded in realizing the big-money dream she had been vainly chasing for years. "She was interested in the money," said Don Saltzman; "Charlie was interested in not screwing up the characters."

Barbara's fury about the Filmways contract followed a flurry of affectionate, anxious letters to "Porker Bell," "Angel Porkerish," "dearest Apple Cheek Zo Porker." Seven years, untold miles of wandering, and another husband to whom she had been married three times as long as she had been married to Addams had not diminished her appetite for him. "I get so nervous if I don't hear from you, darling Porkerish," she had written. Her connection to him, and to her native country, which she still called "home," remained essential to her, and she took every occasion to remind Addams of it. Once, having failed to reach him after four days of telephoning, she had felt that "now my Christmas will be spoiled," though he had not forgotten to send her a birthday card.

Written in a hasty, spidery scrawl, Barbara's letters conveyed a maternal solicitude and possessiveness lightly spiked with eros. "You know I love you with all my heart and you are my baby & there's nothing I wouldn't do for you," she wrote. A most welcome letter from him "made me say Porker Bell, Porker Bell, Porker Bell—about 100 times, & you know what that means," she told him in another letter. Though the dominant tone was more maternal than erotic, Barbara could not resist sending Addams the occasional frail reminder of old, hot times. Once, she mentioned running into an admirer. After her marriage to Addams, she added, the man had written her, saying that Addams was the luckiest man in the world.

In the years since the divorce, Barbara had steadily tightened her hold over Addams's affairs. At the same time, Harriet Pilpel was serving as Greek chorus, telling Addams "that he *must* extricate himself from the house and insurance policy," and advising him of "the foolishness of continuing the foregoing arrangements" with his former wife—who remained co-owner, as Pilpel understood it, of Addams's properties, and the sole beneficiary of his life insurance policy. (Pilpel knew nothing of the document Addams had signed in 1956 giving Barbara full ownership of his Westhampton Beach properties.)

Though she had remained ignorant of Harriet Pilpel's efforts, which Addams was always careful to hide from her, Barbara was very much aware of romantic threats working against her. In 1962, as marriage rumors about Addams and Fontaine circulated through the gossip columns, Barbara had written letter after anxious letter urging him to confide in her about his problems.

She worried aloud about darling Porker's health and happiness, about his fast driving and drinking; she played on his sympathies with her own health problems. The tenderhearted Addams could only have been touched by Barbara's mysterious, crippling set of symptoms, which included a pervasive rash, anemia, and high temperatures that sent her to the hospital. Added to this, Barbara claimed that she and Henry were "having great financial difficulties because his son has all the money." In London a year before the battle over the Filmways contract, Barbara had even charged medication and books to Addams, then reminded him that he had given her permission to do so.

She used possessions as another bargaining tool. As Harriet Pilpel was counseling Addams that he was "in a seriously exposed position since [Barbara] is now in the hospital," Barbara was promising to leave the Westhampton Beach houses to Addams exclusively in her will. Then, at almost the very moment he was meeting with Pilpel to discuss his will and estate, Barbara presented him with another document to sign, a letter acknowledging her kindness for the loan of all the furniture and goods from her former East Eighty-eighth Street apartment. In signing this letter, Addams not only renewed his promise to re-cover Barbara's furniture before returning it, so that each piece was "in the same condition" and color it had been in when she left New York for London, but he gave her the right to enter his apartment at will and remove her personal effects. He also gave her a set of keys.

Addams would avoid making dates when Barbara came to town, and would rush to pick her up at the airport. "He was suddenly frozen in his tracks," said Odette. His whole personality changed, she said; he'd announce Barbara's impending visit "in a dreading way."

Once the television matter was settled, Addams managed an escape to Barbados with a party of friends, including Garbo. "Sea shell situation bearish," he wrote Leila Hadley on a postcard showing native children at play; "have managed to find seven parts of human anatomy including diseased lung. Life saved by Bain de Soleil. . . . Happy celibate group here, and a small colony of bull dikes nearby. . . ."

IN THE MIDST OF the *Addams Family* contract drama, while seeing Leila and various other women, Addams was privately enjoying the company of the world's most famous widow. Like others in the Addams harem, this new woman wrote playful messages in his pocket datebook. "Jean Smith's birthday—send present," she wrote on February 20. "Did you send present?" asked the entry on the twenty-first. "She loved present," teased the note on the twenty-second. "Why did you spend so much on Jean Smith?" asked the twenty-third. "Pay for present to Jean Smith."

Garbo and Addams in Barbados, 1964. "Happy celibate group here, and a small colony of bull dikes nearby."

Two months after her husband's assassination, thirty-four-year-old Jacqueline Kennedy had begun going out a little. At first she attended small dinners at the homes of Washington friends. Then, as her streetside brick Colonial house lay under siege by reporters and tourists, she began escaping to New York on the weekends, where she saw Addams and other mutual friends including Irwin Shaw, Truman Capote, and Pamela Hayward. She was soon living at the Hotel Carlyle while her new fifteen-room apartment at 1040 Fifth Avenue was being remodeled.

He was "a big friend of the Kennedys," Addams said by way of explaining his relationship with Jackie, whom he had met earlier. He often socialized with the Stephen Smiths and the Peter Lawfords. At least once during "one of those very overcrowded Kennedy weekends," as Arthur Schlesinger, Jr., described it, Addams was a guest at the Kennedy compound at Hyannisport, where he shared a room with Schlesinger, who found Addams "a very jolly roommate." Now he was one of several discreet men who were taking Jackie out, and he was clearly captivated by her.

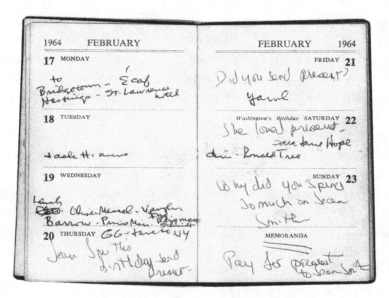

Addams's datebook, with Jackie Kennedy's handwriting.

He was "stunned by, enchanted by Jackie," said Nancy Holmes, whom Addams was also seeing during this time. "He was really quite in awe of her," echoed Odette, another Addams love interest during the Jackie period. At about this time, he went with Jackie to Hammersmith Farm, the twenty-eight-room "summer White House" overlooking Narragansett Bay in Rhode Island, which had been the scene of Jackie's wedding reception ten years earlier. On this day it had been raining without letup, and Jackie was suffering from cabin fever. "I can't stand it any more," she said finally. "I'm going to go out and take a run." And while Addams remained inside, Jackie left the house and ran through the rain like a girl. She returned wet but radiant. "You look wonderful," Addams told her.

And of course she did look wonderful, with her slinky thinness, very dark hair, and widely spaced dark eyes. Along with her physical allure she was "astute and low-key," said Odette, who had known Jackie in Palm Beach when Senator Kennedy was running for president. And she had that sense of mystery. "She did tell me how she felt during the assassination," Addams later said, without elaborating. ("Do you know, she had his *brains* in her lap?" he said to someone else.) And Jackie adored Addams and his work. "I love Pugsley and Lurch, but my favorite is Morticia. She and I have a lot more in common than you might think," she teased. Nevertheless, it was a Fester-like character that Addams drew for Jackie in an ink-and-gouache picture of a tricolored Victorian house with a little dog and a horse by the sea—"like Newport," Addams inscribed it. And the man standing before the house with one elbow resting on the fencepost has a decidedly proprietary air.

Jackie delighted in his crossbows and his grisly decorating scheme; she was playful and "very energetic," said Addams. "I drove her down to Pennsylvania at 110 mph in my Bentley."

It was perhaps at the end of such a day that he and Jackie stopped for dinner at the Stockton Inn, which had inspired the Lorenz Hart song "There's a Small Hotel with a Wishing Well." Jackie had just slipped off to the ladies' room when their waiter said to Addams, "Your friend looks just like Jackie Kennedy." "That's right," Addams said casually. "A lot of people tell her that." He and Jackie laughed about it later.

While Jackie went out with other men and Addams juggled other women, they saw a lot of each other—enough so that the adult Caroline Kennedy would remember Charles Addams visiting in New York. He took Jackie to the movies and antiquing, to dinner parties and house parties, to "21" and the other better restaurants. He attended John-John's birthday party and accompanied Jackie to Hyannisport, dropping off six-year-old Caroline in Westfield, Massachusetts, en route. There were dinners à deux at the Addams apartment, for which he picked up restaurant food. The dinners were served on Leila Hadley's best Crown Derby, Minton, and Waterford crystal, which Leila wrapped in tissue paper and carried over to the apartment ahead of time along with damask napkins, pepper pot salt and pepper shakers, and special soaps and hand towels for the bathroom. The next day she would return to collect it all before clumsy Katie got hold of it with her greasy cloth.

It was at the suggestion of Stephen Smith or Jean Kennedy Smith, Addams later thought, that he had a small dinner for Jackie at his apartment, and invited Greta Garbo. Though she was a great admirer of the Kennedys, Garbo had never met Jackie. Leila helped Charlie plan the menu, which he ordered from a local restaurant, and brought over her china and crystal. Charlie hired a maid to serve.

Jackie and Garbo sat next to each other on the couch, under the hovering crossbows. Jackie liked Miss G, and the food was "pretty good." But Garbo was drinking vodka.

"Mr. Addams," she kept saying in her formal way, "I must leave. I am intoxicated."

"Is she kind of stewed?" Jackie asked Charlie in her whispery voice.

"Well, she was, and so she left before dinner," remembered Addams.

BY APRIL 14, Addams had signed the Filmways contract, to which were attached his witty handwritten notes on the Family members, complemented with little sketches. The indemnity clause included a reference "to any claims by or on behalf of Barbara E. Barb." A Greenbaum, Wolff & Ernst attorney sent Barbara a check for $300, and Addams received the remaining $2,700. "Should Miss Barb decide to forego her claim, I would guess she would communicate the good news directly to you," he wrote. "But naturally if we hear from her, we shall let you know at once."

While Harriet Pilpel handled the remaining work on the television deal, Barbara fussed about the name on her $300 check, insisting that it be made out to her agency, Barbare Artists, Inc., and not to her. When the name was not properly changed through Filmways and appeared on the income tax form, Barbara telephoned Pilpel "in high dudgeon." Pilpel tried to explain to Barbara the disadvantage of getting Addams into a "fuss with Filmways"; Barbara "threatened to write Filmways herself and she also said she would speak to Charles about this," wrote Pilpel in a memo. "I think I may finally have succeeded in calming her down a little but as you know better than I, I do not imagine that she will stay for long in a calm state." Then Barbara objected to the foreign rights clause in Addams's contract, which she insisted was "shameful."

After Addams approved Levy's concept for the show, Levy, his brother, David Lee, and Don Saltzman went to work on a script for a television pilot. When the script was rejected by ABC, the three men put up their own money to have another one written. This one was accepted, and the show hurried into production.

Even before Addams saw the pilot for the half-hour show, he had begun to have his doubts about *The Addams Family*. The television executives had set up a private screening in an NBC studio projection room at Rockefeller Center; Addams arrived accompanied by three lawyers. From the opening title sequence, which included a shot of pinstriped Gomez happily filing the iron fence spikes outside the mansion as Uncle Fester had done in a 1950 cartoon, the lawyers had laughed. "They almost fell off their chairs," claimed Levy, adding that Addams sat there "stone-faced." When the lights came on again, "one of the attorneys turned to Charlie and said: 'Levy has made the Addams family more real than you have, Charlie.' Addams smiled."

As the show's debut loomed, Addams sent postcard bulletins to Leila, who was staying at the Hotel Rif in Tangier that summer. "Now faced with doing introduction to AFA creep show," he wrote of the plan for an Addams introduction of the maiden show. "Just be easy—desinvolte— and ratty," Leila advised him in a long letter. "You have, God knows, far more charm than Hitchcock. Don't grind your teeth." But Addams was nervous about it, and he apparently backed out.

"Having terribly checkered summer," he wrote in August. "Running Bugatti, redrawing book jackets & going to funerals. Nancy H. coming here next wk & will discuss [a possible vacation in] Spain." He was finding the publicity for the TV show "overwhelming"; he thought he "may have to run and hide. Is there an abandoned Riff tomb in Morocco?"

Finally, amid much fanfare, including a photograph in *Life* magazine, *The Addams Family* came to television on Friday, September 18, 1964, at 8:30 P.M. Addams noted the event in his datebook:

TV show
bring champagne

He apparently shared the champagne with Leueen MacGrath, a widow since George S. Kaufman's death in 1961.

Though Addams liked the show, he was disappointed to find his creation translated into "almost a typical suburban family. Not half as evil as my original characters," he said.

The problems began with the set. The television mansion was grand in scale, but it was brightly lit and cheerful. Gone were the cobwebby corners, cracked walls, and missing floorboards of the Addams cartoons. The center staircase was tidily fitted with an Oriental runner; civilized white lace curtains graced the windows. Situated at 001 Cemetery Lane, next to a graveyard, the house was crammed with sight gags: a mounted swordfish clutching a man's leg, a white bearskin rug that growled when stepped on. But other touches better suggested Charles Addams: a chaise longue made from a bed of nails; a children's playroom situated in an old torture chamber; an Iron Maiden; and an unrestrained live vulture, who emitted sudden screeches on the set.

The fine cast came closer to the Addams drawings, though they too were better looking. Hollywood in 1965 was simply not ready to accept a fat male fiend as the lover of a haggard young witch. The leading couple had to be attractive, and they were. Addams thought Carolyn Jones was "enchanting" as his "ruined beauty." Blessed with big eyes set in the high-planed face of her Comanche Indian ancestors, Jones had Morticia's thin, pale sexiness and silky presence. She evoked the "contemptuous and original" woman who "never uses a cliché except to be funny," whose "voice is never raised but has great range," as Addams understood her—the creature "given to low-keyed rhapsodies about her garden of deadly nightshade, henbane and dwarf's hair." John Astin—who had wisely declined the role of Lurch in an early concept that was to be built around the butler's adventures and called *Lurch*—was a tall, handsome version of Morticia's rather squat, nasty-looking cartoon mate—the "crafty schemer," Addams called him. But with his considerable charm, wonderfully oversized eyes, and lopsided grin, which gave him a rakish look, he was the "jolly man in his own way" that Addams had described, devoted to Morticia and the family.

Both Astin and Jones were longtime fans of the Addams cartoons, and their appreciation for the originals entered into their performances. Astin suggested to the producers that the couple's "romance be unceasing and in the grand manner," and together he and Jones conjured enough sexual heat to prompt one wag to observe that they were the only married couple on television that one could imagine having a sex life. Here, then, was the couple Addams could not bear to think of as married.

The cast was filled out by two more veteran actors: Blossom Rock as Grandma, a run-of-the-mill hag, and Jackie Coogan as a more clownish than sinister Uncle Fester, who was nevertheless memorably funny in the part. An extremely pretty six-year-old model named Lisa Loring played Wednesday, looking anything but woeful; chubby Ken Weatherwax, who was almost nine (the age Addams had envisioned the "dedicated trouble maker" of his cartoons) and had done some television commercials, made an appealing and slightly creepy Pugsley. Newcomer Ted Cassidy played Lurch, effectively rumbling rather than speaking his responses—though the cartoon Lurch was mute.

David Levy had worked with Addams to create two more family members who had been only briefly introduced in the cartoons: Thing, a character based not on the peeker, who was left out of the show, but on the mysterious hand that had been seen changing a phonograph record in a 1954 cartoon; and the hairball, Cousin Itt. Played by an Italian midget named Felix Silla, Itt wore a two-piece costume made of real hair, which was soon replaced with a fire-resistant synthetic version—a safeguard against all the cigarettes on the set. Sound effects engineer Tony Magro created Itt's rapid-fire, unintelligible speech.

Though the television family was a considerably softened version of the Addams originals, the show did make an attempt to honor the cartoons. This family was also fond of moonbathing and electric trains; as in the cartoons, Morticia was observed knitting three-armed garments, snipping rosebuds from their thorny stems, and lovingly tending her garden of poison hemlock and deadly nightshade. And though a scene involving Pugsley in a Boy Scout uniform would have been better served by Addams's wit—"Well, he certainly doesn't take after *my* side of the family," Morticia had said in the 1945 cartoon—the new tagline was in the right spirit: "After all," says Gomez in all seriousness, "this isn't some boyish prank, like setting the house on fire."

In a production for which much of the dialogue was run through the typewriter of executive producer Nat Perrin, who had written for the Marx Brothers, the Addams poison was watered down and accompanied by a laugh track. Instead of Grandma delighting her pale granddaughter with a tale about a dragon gobbling up a handsome young prince and his bride and living happily ever after, viewers got a show about school and the truant officer. (Outraged by the conventional fairy tales read to the children at school, Morticia and Gomez kept them home.) In place of Uncle Fester dynamiting boaters was a jolly bald man fond of putting lightbulbs in his mouth. To be sure, the butler's bellpull was a noose (a television invention), but no one was in danger of being hanged there—except by the ankle after a pratfall. This family didn't mean it.

And yet kids loved it. " 'The Addams Family' is, in my opinion, the best show ever on television," wrote a fan named Brian Shane. "The cast chosen is perfect, except for Grandmama, because her voice sounds too cheap." As the cartoons had done before it, the show spoke to the monster in all children, "in an age when non-conformity was beginning to be regarded as an asset, not a liability," noted a critic. "We almost had to do it," said Addams. Though "it was only a children's show," he also thought it was funny and fresh. And he was delighted with the catchy theme music by Vic Mizzy—a rich harpsichord-and-bass "da-da-da-dum" refrain, which he thought captured the family's spirit—and soon seemed to be on everyone's fingers.

Along with the show and the dolls came Addams Family merchandise, including five-cent bubble gum, a set of collectible picture cards from the series, board games, and puzzles. Ringling Bros. made a set of masks based on the Addams drawings rather than on the actors who portrayed the characters. *Life* proclaimed 1964 "TV's Year of the Monster."

An unrelated show called *The Munsters* had already been sold when the *Addams Family* pilot was bought, and it debuted at virtually the same time on another network. But "there wasn't too much of a clash," said Addams. Derived from such stock Hollywood monster types as Frankenstein's monster, Dracula, and the Werewolf, it was considered a "poor [relation]" to *The Addams Family*. And yet it enjoyed much the same popular success, and drew a larger audience. During the shows' first six months on the air, *The Munsters* was ranked eighteen with viewers, falling just below *Lassie* and just above *Gilligan's Island*. *The Addams Family* landed at twenty-three, sandwiched between the wholesome Western *The Virginian* and *My Favorite Martian*.

The Addams Family brought Addams fame on a popular level he had not known before; a welcome leap in his income, which rose from $30,000 in 1963 to $79,000 in 1964; and a certain ambivalent pleasure. Suddenly everyone seemed to know that the funny little house facing the canal on Dune Road in Westhampton Beach, which was wrapped in poison ivy and poison sumac and "invidious briars," belonged to Charles Addams. Addams would be outside barbecuing or having a drink, and people would start waving and calling out, sometimes singing and snapping their fingers. *Da-da-da-dum,* snap, snap, *da-da-da-dum,* snap, snap . . . Any man sitting outside would be mistaken for Addams: Frank Modell, to whom Addams lent the house; handyman Frank Corwin, whom Addams allowed to fish off the dock. The two Franks waved back, playing along. As for Addams, who wore his fame lightly, he didn't mind the kids—he'd smile and wave; but when the adults pointed him out like a sideshow freak—"There's Charles Addams and some of his strange friends"—he became angry and scurried inside.

Though he had wished for a more faithful rendering of his work, he remained loyal to the show, and publicly supportive. He watched it when he could—"It's on at an awkward time for me," he explained. He visited the set in Los Angeles, posed for pictures with the cast, and watched a show being taped. At Christmas, he sent each cast member a sketch of his or her character. And he made a surprise guest-of-honor appearance at a party given by Carolyn Jones, who had transformed the entrance hall of the white California home she shared with husband Aaron Spelling into a funeral parlor, and covered the tables with spider mums on black cloths.

After dinner with Barbara Nicholls one Friday night, Addams brought her to his apartment to watch the show. She had never seen it before, and he asked what she thought. "Pretty awful," she said. "You're right," he said.

Addams was happier with John O'Hara's handling of the Family. "I guess he cut her up and ate her, like a Charles Addams character," said the woman in O'Hara's latest novel, *Elizabeth Appleton.* Addams appreciated the plug—"one correction, though," he wrote O'Hara. "My people don't cut them up into small pieces. They eat them whole—like a python."

But he was not resentful of the television show. Along with the money from the series, he had earned $1,000 from *TV Guide* for two original drawings on a cover showing Carolyn Jones and John Astin dancing with their cartoon selves. "Look," he seemed to say with a shrug. He had done

Frank Modell on the dock behind the little house at Westhampton Beach.

the best he could in the cartoons; he had even written character sketches for the producers. Having worked his magic, he now assumed a necessary detachment. Like any self-respecting magician, he disappeared.

AS THE FILMWAYS checks rolled in at a steady clip, Addams found the cartoon ideas coming more arduously than usual. Though his seventh cartoon collection, *The Groaning Board,* was published in 1964, he went from twenty-two published cartoons in *The New Yorker* that year to thirteen in 1965 and six in 1966. Of more concern, he soon realized that the nicer television family was replacing his own "disreputable children."

In 1966, after almost two years on the air, both *The Addams Family* and *The Munsters* were abruptly canceled. Though the shows had remained popular with kids, neither one had been a ratings success, or even remained in the top twenty-five after the first six months.

In the end, Addams's biggest complaint was not about the television show, which ultimately earned him $141,276 from episodes, reruns, merchandise, royalties, and foreign rights, and which he came to think "was quite good." He recognized that *The Addams Family* had "reached a lot of people" who would never have discovered his cartoons through *The New Yorker*. The real damage had come from the magazine itself. Not only was the producer of *The Addams Family* not allowed to use *The New Yorker*'s name in connection with the show: Once *The Addams Family* appeared on television, William Shawn would no longer publish Family drawings in *The New Yorker*. As Shawn seemed to see it, vulgar Hollywood had compromised Addams's evils. "I don't think we want to revive them," he told Addams in his mild way after Addams submitted a Family cartoon. And so the Family's twenty-six-year run in *The New Yorker* abruptly ended. Shawn even returned the rights to Addams.

Addams was bitter about it. Over the next seven years, he rebelled a little, managing to slip a few pale echoes of the Family past the magazine's Praetorian guards. In November 1966, Pugsley turned up on a city sidewalk driving a kid-sized car towing away another tiny car. Benignly drawn versions of Uncle Fester's round, hairless head appear in a panel drawing of a caped man tossing a coin into a wishing well and exploding it, and again on an Orient Express–like train filled with exotic characters and one normal-looking misfit ("No, this is not the 12:38 to Bridgeport," the conductor tells him). A witty 1971 homage to the Family showed a hairy creature on skinny bird legs standing in a bookstore reading *The Sensuous Thing*. Addams couldn't resist chortling about sneaking in a Family reference unbeknownst to *The New Yorker*'s editors.

But mostly he kept his orphaned cartoon children alive through advertising work and special commissions, such as a delicious 1972 Mother's Day plate for Schmid Brothers, Inc., featuring Gomez tying Grandma to the train tracks as the rest of the family looks on approvingly. "It wouldn't have happened with a *Cole*, Gramma," says Pugsley to the old lady wearing a loose-fitting dripping black bathing garment (which is not a Cole) from which she pulls a baby octopus. An Addams idea for a company called Moonglow, which required the use of the slogan "It must have been Moonglow," showed the Family sitting around a wet bar in the Victorian mansion. "Lurch is the bartender," recalled Addams. "Gomez has turned into a really handsome old fashioned type, hair parted in the middle; and Morticia's leaning over the old lady, and saying, 'It must've been Moonglow.' "

But Addams missed doing the cartoons, and a feeling of resentment toward Shawn and *The New Yorker* lingered.

ANOTHER LOSS COINCIDED with the demise of the television show and the Family cartoons. Addams later put it this way: Yes, he said, he had taken Jackie Kennedy out—"but then the income from my television serial started falling off."

Though it was true that Addams wasn't rich enough for Jackie Kennedy, he had also apparently "made an indiscreet comment" about her to a reporter while he was still seeing her. Though he and Jackie remained friendly, he was cast out of her inner circle. In later years, he was sufficiently forgiven to be chosen for the select guest list of eighteen at a dinner given by Jackie and Aristotle Onassis at their upper Fifth Avenue apartment. (The other guests included Mayor and Mrs. John V. Lindsay, Frank Sinatra, the Peter Duchins, and Babe and Bill Paley.)

Though Jackie was clearly fond of Addams, she never regarded him as husband material. "Well, I couldn't get married to you," she told him. "What would we talk about at the end of the day—*cartoons*?" The putdown, which Addams repeated to both Leila and Odette, crushed him.

Leila remembered other patronizing remarks Charlie told her about. "*You* wouldn't know anything about that," Jackie would say in reference to something concerning diplomacy or politics. And when Addams referred to the late president as "Jack," she corrected him. "Don't call him 'Jack.' Call him 'the President,' " she said. Once, when the two of them were houseguests at Bunny Mellon's in Virginia, where they had been given separate rooms, someone accidentally walked in on them. Charlie was in his robe, sitting on Jackie's bed talking. After the door closed again, Jackie said, "Well, I'll be invited back again, but you won't."

And she could be a tease. He said to her, "Let's go to bed." "You should have brought that up before," she said, and went into her own room.

"One minute she is very sweet and tender," said Addams, "and the next minute she is an iceberg. She may be the moodiest woman I've ever met. Don't ask me what the real Jackie Kennedy is like because I really haven't the faintest idea."

And so the world's most famous widow essentially dropped out of the picture. Addams recalled the way she had always complained about people craning their necks to get a look at her; how the paparazzi had become impossible. But he also remembered the amusing moments with Jackie, such as the time she was showing him around Hammersmith Farm with her mother, Janet Auchincloss, tagging along. It was one of those small exchanges in which Addams found untold depths of humor. After Jackie was called away to the phone, Mrs. Auchincloss had turned to him and asked, "Why was Jackie whispering?"

"She always whispers," he said.

"I must ask her why," said Mrs. Auchincloss.

Chapter Seventeen

Whatever the Gods Are,
They Aren't Angry

Gomez is stretched out on the couch, talking, talking—about what dreadful plots or unmentionable schemes, one can scarcely imagine. His terrified psychiatrist flees the room, hat in hand.

Or Woody Allen by way of Chas Addams: A psychiatrist says, "Who are you trying to kid? You lifted that last dream straight out of Dostoyevski."

It was the mid-1960s, and Charles Addams was expected to "think neurotic." Or so he thought. *The New Yorker*'s editors were encouraging him "to move from the macabre to humor in a psychological vein," such as he had done in his 1961 magic carpet cartoon. "Now this one was owned by an elderly gentleman with acrophobia," says the Indian salesman as the stunned client regards the airborne rug. That cartoon had also been drawn in pen-line, a switch in technique that Jim Geraghty had prompted Addams to try—which is not to say that anyone at *The New Yorker* wanted Addams to be anything other than Addams, but that changing times required that *New Yorker* art evolve.

Though the magazine continued to publish cartoons about such favorite *New Yorker* subjects as the Tunnel of Love, aliens and spaceships, census takers, desert islands—"Every man is an island, I suppose, at *The New Yorker*," said Addams—modern art, hippies, protesters, and the Vietnam War were pushing their way in. Peter Arno had virtually abandoned his voluptuous dames and lecherous gents for aging couples whooping it up, bank robbers, and Western themes, though he also offered a number of cartoons about drunks, another old standard. *The New Yorker* had killed all the African drawings, now considered racist—an attitude Addams did not understand. "Cannibals still exist and are a fact of life," he said. Addams's last cartoon with native characters, published in 1963, showing a tiny white pole-vaulter running toward the low limbo bar as a calypso band plays in the jungle, had been rendered in an inoffensive style, without the stereotype that had always been the cartoon norm. An Addams rough of a psychiatrist pacing the floor in a witch doctor's mask as an African patient lies on the couch talking would remain consigned to the "unsold" shelf at home.

Psychiatrists had been a cartoon staple at *The New Yorker* since the early fifties; the psychiatrist gags had been preceded by cartoons exploring the effect of therapy on modern young couples and on child-rearing, which dated to about 1930. But Addams had never gotten far with psychiatry as a subject—perhaps because it seemed to him that his work itself was "sort of in a state of arrested intellectual development."

In a hippie culture where Wonderland was reached by the pill that made you smaller, and altered states owed more to Grace Slick than to Lewis Carroll, Addams continued to answer the literary sirens that had shaped him. There was something of Jack's magic beans in the 1963 cartoon in which a family is stunned to see giant stalks of asparagus poking up out of their garden. "You telephone 'Better Homes & Gardens,' " says the wife; "I'll start making the hollandaise."

One of his favorite themes was the little people, a subject that had begun appearing in *New Yorker* cartoons by Richard Decker, Alan Dunn, and Robert Day as early as 1936. In the original premise, the old windup toys that had become popular before Addams's own boyhood had been given their freedom and taken on a life of their own—veering off the pavement and into a jewelry shop in a 1936 cartoon by Alan Dunn, for instance, while the other female toys remained with the street vendor.

Addams had taken the idea further. In his hands, the toys shed the keys in their backs and became an Addams version of the Lilliputians—a concept that resulted in a marvelous 1958 *New Yorker* cover in which a helpless astronaut is tied to the ground of an orange-red planet while tiny moon men swarm around him. In the Addams cartoons, the little people go about their business in happy harmony with the real world, where they are part of the order of things: mugging one another on the sidewalk; revenging themselves on the toymaker; gathering on benches in a city oasis called "Vest Pocket Park"—and ultimately in a man's briefcase, where they are seen conducting a miniature board meeting. ("You often wonder if there aren't more of them in other people's briefcases," Addams quipped.) And the theme lent itself to variations in which Addams substituted mice, ants, and a tiny storm cloud hovering over a window box.

In a world that was becoming increasingly mechanized, Addams maintained an inherent distrust of mechanical objects, which he felt "really had it in for him." He had long sensed that the intrusions of the scientific age were taking over: "Sometimes I ask myself, 'Where will it ever end?'" the scientist tells the visitor to the robot factory as they proceed down the seemingly endless line of tin men making tin men in a 1946 cartoon. (The first "electronic brain" had appeared in the United States in 1942.)

And yet his was an ultimately hopeful view. The little woman with tightly curled hair and heavy glasses who sits all alone at the controls in the enveloping green room, computers rising from floor to ceiling, in *The New Yorker*'s February 11, 1961, cover drawing (which Addams listed in his notebook as "IBM Valentine Cover") is startled when the machine spits out a card imprinted with a big red heart. The man bending down to service a room-sized computer in a 1965 cartoon is himself a machine—but the old-fashioned windup kind, dressed in overalls, with a large key in the center of his back. The queue of people waiting patiently along a trail leading to a mountaintop, where the oracle sits framed by an enormous computer, suggests a mind ringed less by IBM or est than by the mists of Mount Olympus.

While remaining faithful to his own gods, in his work Addams became more surreal, his version of "thinking neurotic." The driver of a truck filled with crated turkeys is, one sees in the sideview mirror, himself

a turkey. The views from an office window offer both a look at the Washington Monument and a glimpse of Moscow. A makeshift window cut into a construction-site fence reveals something more sinister: a bare-chested slave driver cracking a bullwhip over a crew pulling a gigantic stone slab.

In a bitter aside, Addams also offered a cartoon that would have been funnier and more effective as a Family drawing. It showed a goon-faced man proposing to a pale blond walleyed girl sitting in a hooded chair resembling the whispering chair Joan Fontaine had kept: "There's enough hate in my heart for both of us," says the suitor. But, as a rule, Addams did not draw out of anger; the wellspring of his comic art was a gentle ac-

"Whatever the gods are, they aren't angry."

ceptance of, and reverence for, what Tennessee Williams called "that sense of the Awful."

"Whatever the gods are, they aren't angry," says the happy South Sea Islander of the brilliantly erupting volcano in Addams's popular 1964 cartoon.

Working with the stubby Wolff's pencil, shading with a paper stump, Addams sat in his drab corner office on *The New Yorker*'s eighteenth floor—a room that looked like "an unsuccessful private eye's office"— covering his drawing paper with tiny pictures: crude stick figures, airplanes, dwarfs, anything to get him going. He sat there for hours if necessary, doodling "till an idea occurred to him," noted Mischa Richter, who observed Addams's silver-threaded dark head bent over the paper.

Ideas might come from the work of another cartoonist, directly or indirectly. Perhaps unconsciously, in his "gods aren't angry" cartoon Addams reworked an old drawing by Garrett Price, but to better effect. The Price cartoon from 1945 had also presented a group of natives regarding a volcano. "Frankly, I don't take much stock in this business of the gods being angry," said one of the men. And there followed an overly long technical explanation of how he had gotten "doped out" by the volcanic gases. Decades after the Addams version, the premise would be used again in a Leo Cullum cartoon for a pharmaceutical company.

Often he ran dry. "Let's give Charlie the gray box," said Jim Geraghty's assistant, Barbara Nicholls, referring to the slush pile. Peter DeVries, who worked for *The New Yorker* on Wednesdays and Fridays, would also sift through the box for ideas for Addams.

When he wasn't stuck, he could work anywhere—in the tiny Westhampton Beach kitchen, where there was barely room for two people; at the home of a friend. He could even work with a bird sitting on his shoulder, chattering nonsense into his ear. Mumble, mumble, mumble, mumble—"Bedford!" said Tee's Tweetie Bird with sudden clarity, in his low budgie's voice. Which, at that moment during the early sixties, sounded exactly like Tee's voice.

Addams had had his doubts about taking care of the bird while Tee was away, but had ended up loving it, and in the end Tee let him keep it. Tweetie would perch on the rim of Addams's drink, dip his beak in, then "fly all around the room, blabbing everything it ever knew," marveled Addams. It would sway on the lampshade, nap for about fifteen minutes, then come to attention again. Addams got so used to having the bird attached to him at home that he would forget it was there. Once, he was out on the street on his way to work when he heard the familiar drone and saw Tweetie on his shoulder. He turned around very carefully and walked back to the apartment.

AS ADDAMS'S INCOME was falling after the cancellation of *The Addams Family*—dropping from a then record high of $79,763 in 1964 to $60,993 in 1966—two new opportunities came along in the forms of an article for *Playboy* and a children's book.

He had not been looking for a change. If you had asked Addams why he didn't write (he was a natural, as anyone lucky enough to receive a postcard from him could attest), or expand himself as an artist in some other fresh way to make money, he would have protested. He objected when Frank Modell mentioned an opportunity to produce a set of lithographs that would be sold as prints. "No, no," he said, sounding annoyed by the very idea that he would want to do anything other than what he was doing. ("He loved being a cartoonist," said Modell. "He never wanted to do anything else.") But in 1967, when *Playboy* invited Addams to write a piece on cars, he pocketed the $300 advance and began a promising draft with a sexy touch: "Almost never do I have the urge to take an automobile to bed with me," he wrote by hand on lined paper, "but the exception is my 35C Bugatti. So rather than give in to autoeroticism I have settled for keeping it in my living room during the winter months; and it is by far the most splendid furnishing in the room. It smells good, too." He tried to capture the thrill of ownership, which he likened to "being a foster father to a beautiful but misunderstood child." But he pitched about in the heavily interlined piece, tentatively titled "Bugatti Lover," sputtered, and ultimately abandoned it after two promising pages.

At about the same time, *New Yorker* artist Robert Kraus founded an imprint for children's literature called Windmill Books, and conceived the idea of launching his first list with work by *New Yorker* cartoonists—beginning with Addams illustrating his own selection of Mother Goose. Addams accepted.

And so it was that in 1967, the year of Ira Levin's *Rosemary's Baby*, and of *Bonnie and Clyde*, *The Charles Addams Mother Goose* was hatched. Addams again found himself depositing Filmways-sized checks in the bank: a $7,500 advance from Harper Windmill in March, followed by the same amount in June, along with another $9,000 from *The Saturday Evening Post* for first serial rights—but not before the usual shoot-out between his lawyers and Barbara.

"Your friend Barbara Barb, Lady something or other, ex-wife of Charles Addams, is constantly sniping at our negotiations," a Greenbaum, Wolff & Ernst lawyer wrote to Harriet Pilpel on December 21, 1966. Having agreed to the book contract and told Greenbaum's Nancy Wechsler that he didn't want any problem about it, Addams then sent the contract to Barbara, who had no percentage of it but marked it up with corrections she insisted were "absolutely essential," adding in a note to Addams that his lawyers were "dangerously incompetent as negotiators." The contract, she said, was riddled with loopholes. He had lost "millions" in the past by not heeding her advice, and now he was about to lose more. Given a single day, she herself could get Addams "a perfect contract." She next "raised holy hell" with Nancy Wechsler in a foul letter telling her she was not representing Addams properly. Addams himself expressed the feeling that his lawyers had been "dilatory"—a remark that prompted a long, respectful letter from Harriet Pilpel. Now, at the eleventh hour, Addams was saying he wanted "to retain the English rights (no doubt so that Barbara can busy herself handling them)," and Greenbaum had another situation on their hands.

In the end, though Greenbaum continued to handle the book contract, Barbara came to the United States to act as his agent on first serial rights. Leila Hadley, who was then working as an assistant editor at the *Post*, would remember it as the highest advance they had ever paid for a book excerpt. Barbara Colyton came to the *Post* to negotiate the deal. "Pay her anything—just get her out of here!" cried editor Bill Emerson.

In the familiar and strangely violent verses and stories dating to early editions of Mother Goose, notably Charles Perrault's witty 1697 *Contes de ma mère l'Oye*, later illustrated by Gustave Doré, Addams found a new outlet for his own talents and inclinations. He saw Humpty Dumpty as a painted egg—Fabergé by way of Addams, with fair hair and a striped shirt; his broken shell reveals a tiny dinosaur. The three blind mice are albinos wearing tiny sunglasses—the small round kind associated with the blind. They are presided over by a Grant Wood–like farmer and his wife, who holds an electric carving knife above their bloodlessly severed tails. In another verse, the old woman who lives under a hill sits happily knitting a sweater for her cat in the midst of an apparent nuclear holocaust that has left the world outside in charred skeletal ruins. In another, a medieval character leans over a battlement to aim his crossbow at an escaping blackbird. Many of the characters resembled the Addams Family, their colorless faces suggesting articulated bones.

The result was a Mother Goose that captured the inherent creepiness of the tales—and injected further creepiness where it was missing. If Wee Willie Winkie had not previously seemed sinister as he ran through the town in his nightgown, he did now, with his Lon Chaney–like Phantom face illuminated by a candle at the window of the murky green bedroom shared by the Addams Family children. And only in the Addams Mother Goose, on the "misty, moisty morning" when the unnamed narrator "met an old man / Clothed all in leather," does a girl who looks like Wednesday happily take the hand of the smiling Grim Reaper–like figure to walk down a delicately rendered snuff-brown cemetery lane.

Addams had put some time into the research, setting about his assignment with obvious pleasure. He selected verses that served his purposes: For a winning illustration unaccountably cut from the finished book, he chose a verse about a shepherd in place of the more common version using a sailor: "A red sky at night is a shepherd's delight. / A red sky in the morning is a shepherd's warning," Addams wrote in his sunny handwriting beneath the ink-and-watercolor drawing. Working in watercolor, or ink and wash, he approached the verses not as a tapestry, but as individual stories. His worried shepherd stands in a bulkhead cut into a hillside in a brown-and-white landscape, receiving his flock as an ominous tomato-red twister moves in.

For all of its fresh take on the time-honored verses, the collection also showed some signs of creative fatigue. The Addams Family was pressed into service for many characters, arguably too many; and the illustrations themselves echoed a few previously published Addams cartoons. And yet it all worked. The thirty-one drawings published as *The Charles Addams Mother Goose* had wings.

Not everyone was entranced by the book. Writing in *The New York*

Times in November 1967, Eliot Fremont-Smith gave the revered cartoonist a rare snide review. The critic found fault with Addams for delivering "purely a joke; the gruesomeness is familiar, safe and temporary—Addams at Halloween." Nevertheless *The New York Times Magazine* selected the Addams book as one of the nine outstanding illustrated books for children that year.

Though Addams ultimately earned back his $15,000 advance, the royalties were scant. However, he got an additional advance of $1,500 for the paperback version.

"A red sky at night is a shepherd's delight.
A red sky in the morning is a shepherd's warning." Mother Goose drawing.

To fourteen-year-old David Hogan, who had written Addams so intelligently about *Dear Dead Days*, the children's book was an unqualified success. "We all know that all of [the Mother Goose stories] are not exactly kiddie bedtime fare anyway," he wrote. His own favorite drawing was the droopy-eyed, wilting Mistress Mary, who waters her creepy garden of silver bells and cockle shells—their stems topped with the smiling heads of pretty maids all in a row—in a brown basement garden drearily lit by a single bare bulb. "Beautifully done," wrote the adolescent.

AND SO ADDAMS sat in the *New Yorker* office he had once shared with Sam Cobean, drawing the world as he saw it. It was a world where a strong wind could bring the Mad Hatter's hat sailing into the concrete path of a contemporary Manhattan woman as she held on to her own hat; where a sleeping giant lay under the rolling farmland that looked just like a patchwork quilt.

Once he did a very good drawing for an automobile rental company, which wanted him to redo it. "Why? What's wrong with it?" asked Herb Valen, an idea man who served as Addams's agent on advertising assignments. "He's doing this terrible-looking person who looks just like the client," said the executive. Addams did not redo it.

AS COBEAN FASHIONED his dogs, bums, peacocks, and sexy girls, he had stood "oddly erect before the drawing board," remembered Addams, working "quickly, the pictures moving from his hand to the paper." A while back, Addams had had a letter from Jean Argetsinger, a reminder of the old racing days at Watkins Glen, of days with Sam. Jean and Cameron had named one of their children after Sam—a tribute that would have made Sam happy, said Addams, and also "terribly embarrassed." "Dear Jean," he'd written in reply to her most recent letter. "It can't be that long ago—to think that I have progressed since then from childhood to early puberty."

ADDAMS SAT BY the shuttered windows of his Manhattan apartment, with the lower shutters open to admit the light, doodling, drawing. He had long amused himself by putting the names of relatives and friends in his cartoons—Dudley, the name of his Smith cousin, had served in more than one cartoon and rough; his handyman, Frank Corwin, supplied the name for the genial heavy figure in overalls replenishing the icing on the gingerbread house: "Another quality roofing job by the F. Corwin Co.," says the lawn sign.

For every idea that worked and ended up as a finish, scores of them didn't. Or they did, but they were rejected. ("I see the cartoon as labored

humor," he would tell Dick Cavett, meaning the statement quite literally.) Or he wasn't sure of them, and he put them aside to be submitted later, like the one in which a woman sits at one café table and a big spider at another, and a wall sign says SPECIAL TODAY CURDS & WHEY.

Addams did not work fast, as Cobean had, but he did work diligently—"maniacally, like a rug-maker," said James Geraghty, and "with absolutely no anxiety," said Lee Lorenz. "I never met an artist who had less anxiety about what he was doing. Everybody does." He tried always for an economy of concept, his ideal drawing remaining the single, captionless cartoon that made one "search a little bit" for the joke.

Unlike some of the other *New Yorker* artists, who would "throw a fit" if someone interrupted them at their work, Addams took the knocks on his office door in stride. He was at ease, said Lee Lorenz, even if he was in the middle of something. But it was also true that at the office he continued to work only on roughs; he always did the finishes at home, where he might have to deal only with a bird muttering on his shoulder.

In the studio where an old-fashioned smocked artist from a lost era has been painting a sleeping woman as an angel hovers nearby, the angel-muse says, "Very good—a little rest now."

—

Chapter Eighteen

A Medium-Sized Dog

ADDAMS WAS TALKING TO THE STRIKING NANCY HOLMES, a former Powers model with prematurely white hair, about Alice. "She has a sweet face and an obscene body," he said with satisfaction. Though he liked Alice for more than her physical assets, her decidedly old-fashioned look particularly appealed to him. You could call it an aesthetic appreciation, born of a feeling for the aerodynamic lines of a Bugatti, the figures on the carved walnut tiller of an eighteenth-century Italian stone-bow, or the friezes, stained glass, and sloping dormers of a Victorian house. During the early seventies, by which time Addams had been living alone some fifteen years, he was sufficiently smitten to have Alice's portrait taken, and it, too, was old-fashioned. A photograph in profile, it showcased Alice's aristocratic nose and dark hair, which stood out in dramatic relief against a white background.

He had paid eight dollars for her, "including her collar," he noted, after Thanksgiving dinner in 1970. He had just hosted his traditional feast in the old wassail hall of the carriage house, where each year he invited a group of familyless people like himself. On these occasions, Addams liked to dress as a country squire, in a long brownish-gold suede coat he had bought at a thrift shop. He wore it with a vest and tapered pants, cutting a natty figure. Over the wassail bowl that year, the subject of dogs had come up. Modell asked Charlie why he didn't get a dog. After all, he said, Charlie was very fond of Frank's dog, Tuli. And it had been years since he'd had a dog of his own—almost twenty years since the little black poodles had milled around Bobby's feet in the same sunny courtyard where Charlie, Frank, Dona Guimares, Kay Leperq, and other holiday revelers had posed for a group photograph with a sign saying CLOSED THURSDAY.

"Oh, I'm not ready for another dog," Addams told Modell. "But there is one I look at."

It turned out that Addams had been making private visits to an orphan at the Bide-A-Wee shelter in Westhampton. He found himself drawn to a scruffy white mongrel with a sprinkle of black spots and "a black-and-white Victorian face," as he put it. When he entered the kennel, this dog jumped higher in her pen than all the others.

"You mean you go to the pound and make *friends* with a dog?" asked a startled Modell. "Will you introduce me to your dog?"

And so that Thanksgiving, warmed by the wassail bowl, Addams set off with Modell to see the dog. Frank was immediately struck by the relationship Charlie had formed with the animal. The woman at the shelter opened the cage, and the dog gave Charlie her paw and licked him.

"How can you leave this dog who obviously loves you—and who you seem to like a lot—in this cage, this cold place?" scolded Modell.

Charlie insisted that he wasn't ready for a dog; it wasn't the right time. Just then, the shelter matron called out, "I'll tell ya one thing about that dog: it doesn't like children."

"I'll take it!" said Addams.

She was the dog Addams might have invented for himself: not a boy's dog, but an Addams boy's dog. He loved her outcast status and her "uncertain ancestry," which hinted at beagle and springer spaniel, though you could never be sure. "Nobody knows what she is," Addams drawled with a smile. "Alice, the medium-sized dog," he called her. No amount of bathing and grooming at Dapper Dog softened the wiry coat, likened to "something haphazardly fabricated by a committee of small children being creative with Brillo and cotton wool." He named her Alice B. Curr, "with two Rs," he noted, after another inelegant companion, Alice B. Toklas.

Though Addams relished telling interviewers that Alice detested children ("also old ladies who goo-goo at her,") he became seriously nervous the day she mistook a little man for a child and menaced Hervé Vil-lechaize, the actor best known for his role on the popular television show *Fantasy Island*. Addams finally put her upstairs in his bedroom. Another time, when he hired a midget to paint his apartment, he remembered to lock Alice up.

Here was a character full of fears and eccentricities—"When he took a step, she took a step," said an acquaintance—and unsettlingly human. Or just unsettling. When Addams took her to Ann Hall's office at *The New Yorker*, Alice approached Ann's chair, stood up and put both paws on her shoulder, and looked into her eyes in a curiously penetrating way. When he brought her to Dona's house in Quogue, she would watch as Dona's friend Robert Levering approached the house, following each of his steps with her wary eyes. Then she would break into a gallop around the house.

She was afraid of Jane Gunther's cat, a small white fluffy creature with one yellow eye and one blue eye; she hid under furniture, trembling and shaking, sometimes with good reason. And Alice "would eat anything— green pork chops," said Tee. "Nothing fazed her." Once she ate a pet rabbit.

People made allowances: She was Addams's dog, after all, and she had been abused in her pre-adoptive life. But when Alice began humping the bare leg of a woman in Bermuda shorts while she and Charlie were at Walker McKinney's house in Quoque, Charlie turned to McKinney with a sigh: "Where have I gone wrong?" he said.

And yet she was "a sweet dog," said Addams, and his friends, who lavished gifts on her, unanimously agreed. He would scoop her up in his arms and she would go limp as a rag doll, her eyes rolling back in her head. She did tricks, dancing on her hind legs like a circus dog, guessing which one of his hands held the biscuit. She "breathed hard" into the telephone when he called her at home, he said.

People began saying, "If you invite Charlie Addams to a cocktail party and he can't go, he'll send Alice." And Addams was in fact known to pencil the name "Miss Alice B. Curr" on the guest line of the invitations addressed to Mr. Charles Addams. She was seen emerging from under the dash of his Aston Martin after he had run his time trials. He took her on motor trips with his girlfriends. (Audrey, who didn't really like dogs, wasn't sure this was going to work. "Well, let's wait and see," said Charlie. And when Audrey insisted that Alice sleep *under* the bed, Charlie "was wonderful about it.")

"Hope you are acting decently at Frank's and not trying to have awkward relations with Tuli," Addams wrote on a postcard to her from London the spring after he adopted her. "Driving to a priory today where they're keeping me in an oubliette—you would hate it."

"It's just me and Alice against the world," Addams told a reporter. Alice began turning up in Addams cartoons as the RCA Victor dog, and the classic faithful companion. She was the dog bringing her master the paper (the *Dog News*) in a 1979 cartoon, the dog curled up on the floor beside the naked man reading the newspaper in another cartoon. ("You know something?" asks the man's lumpish wife in winter coat and unfashionably short boots in the 1981 drawing. "You're very tough to shop for.")

"Is Alice still shedding & eating?" Tee asked in a letter from her temporary residence in Paris in the summer of 1972. "Does the Bugatti still boil over—R U still smoking—How does the new basin look in the little house?" she wanted to know. "Who R U screwing (don't tell me). . . ."

Tee was by then a widow. Two years earlier, in 1969, Dudley Miller had had a heart attack and died at the age of forty-seven. Tee sold the Japanese-style house Dudley had built in East Hampton and purchased a summer cottage in Water Mill with a lawn sloping down to an ocean inlet called Burdett's Creek. Then, some twenty-five years after first meeting at a Daytona racetrack, Charlie and Tee began a serious affair. They fell in love. Tee's name began appearing so frequently in Addams's datebook, he soon abbreviated "Tee" to "T."

In their letters that summer of 1972, they sounded like an old married couple who had just discovered, deliriously and conveniently, that they were in love. Here was passion with none of the usual deception and struggle. "I am your girl—and it's the best thing that ever happened to me," Tee wrote in her lightly tender way. "Goats are not very good when it comes to putting things down on paper—unless it's their feet—but you know what I mean—as I understand you, too."

From Paris, where she had taken twenty-two-year-old Bunki and a girlfriend for the summer, Tee filled page after page with her hasty, girlish scrawl, the words half printed, half cursive, as though she were stuck somewhere between girlhood and womanhood, which in a way she was. At forty-five, Tee still looked young. Her dark brown hair was caught carelessly in a ponytail; her figure remained slender. From a slight distance, and in photographs, she might have passed for Bunki's older sister. Though she was not a disciplined person (in fact, she had trouble following through on anything), she planned to write Charlie often, "as it's heaven just knowing I belong to you." For his part, Addams was a less diligent correspondent, but Tee didn't complain. Calling him "Sam" for his middle name, or by his boyhood camp name, "Running Fox," she teased about the cute clerk at the neighborhood post office. She wanted to use up the air mail "blueys" she had bought so she could see the clerk again—though "he is not you—nor is anyone else." And she signed off as "Yr. Seminole Squaw."

The clerk got the Fox's attention. "Dear Red People," he replied, "Don't think that *I* don't know that cutie in the P.O. is just a cover up for Jean Pierre Cohen. Who do you think you're scroon, I mean kiddin'."

Well, she knew exactly who she was kidding. "All right, 'Mr. Smartie,' " she answered,

> *I dreamed last night I found you in a large hole in a hillside—! Before you pulled the bushes around, I saw that beautiful blonde with the furry pointed ears crouching behind you—Woke up at 6 AM . . . furious! (As matter of fact, still a touch annoyed)—Please, no Scrooda Foks—or vice versa—till I get home—Besides—Jean Pierre Cohen has greasy hair—the P.O. clerk, Bad teeth and Corner Gendarme, Bad Breath. I guess you are the only one for me—you have all three & I adore you—*
>
> *Walking Vixon*

Having made her point, Tee let the matter of Addams's fidelity drop. She was too smart to be possessive. Her letters—filled with the little details and playful banter that interested Addams—were calculated to entertain. She described her walk-up apartment, the Paris shops—"so marvelously old-fashioned you'd be in heaven"—and the produce, which included "fresh peas that make our L.I. ones taste like straw." "The apartment sounds most interesting especially the kitchen bathroom and the climb up as bad as mine," wrote Addams. "Also I'm jealous of your fresh peas. . . . I do miss you and it is a long time (Alice has been a brick) and I love you madly and wish I were there—Running Fox." And he drew a Fester-nosed Fox with an unmistakable gleam in his eye.

End of Addams letter to Tee, with Running Fox sketch.

Shopping for meat was a challenge, wrote Tee, "as it's all hanging up and I don't recognize a thing," but the street was so friendly she was "planning to get a woolen wrapper and carpet slippers for my morning croissant run"—an image Charlie found irresistible. He responded with a sketch on *New Yorker* stationery showing Tee in a frumpy robe and shaggy slippers, looking doubtful and aggrieved as she spots something she *does* recognize dangling from the meat hooks: a naked Addams. Titled "Le Boucher," it sent Tee into a laughing jag so hysterical and teary that the girls were "terrified 'till I handed it over," she wrote.

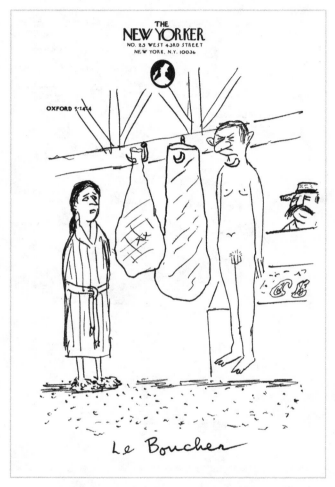

"Shopping for meat in Paris was tough," wrote Tee,
"as it's all hanging up and I don't recognize a thing."

While Tee collected the morning croissants in her bathrobe, took in the drunken Bastille Day festivities, and followed a man through a Paris bookstall who looked just like Charlie from behind, her pen pal labored to little effect in New York during a heat wave ("Alice has collapsed here in office with me," he observed).

His financial notebooks told a story of dismal productivity. Apart from a single cartoon sale to *The New Yorker* in June 1972 for $336, he came up with nothing new all summer. But thanks to *The New Yorker*'s cartoon bank, he had two good covers published, and Dan Silverberg, an old Wall Street man and philanthropist, bought one of them for $500. He collected money on reprints, and $1,500 from Hanna-Barbera for an upcoming cartoon series.

Two years earlier, in 1970—the year a fat new Addams cartoon collection called *My Crowd* was published—Filmways had approached Greenbaum, Wolff & Ernst about renewing the *Addams Family* contract. But by then Barbara was talking to Addams about doing a cartoon series based on the Family, and she was not about to lose out on another lucrative deal. (The Filmways agreement prohibited Addams from using his characters in another dramatic work.) Before the lawyers at Greenbaum learned of it, Addams had signed away the cartoon rights to her—their earlier agreement having expired. They were not at all pleased. To begin with, they felt that they "had a continuing interest in this property," and also that they "had been made to look foolish if not worse in the eyes of Filmways." They were also concerned about a contract Barbara had accepted, the terms of which they had already rejected as insufficient. Meetings ensued, and the familiar pattern began—Addams feeling torn between his old law firm and Barbara, and between Barbara and David Levy, to whom he felt indebted for the first television show. In the end, the talks with Filmways fell through. Barbara came to town and Addams clammed up, even with Harriet Pilpel. By 1972, there was a cartoon deal with Hanna-Barbera.

But money did not solve the problem of idea block, which sometimes lasted three or four months at a time.

"Can't work. But love you," he wrote Tee in haste on July 19. He attended a party at Tee's house in Water Mill, which was occupied by a friend for the summer. A mutual friend "was there with a girl . . . a reasonably dim blonde. I think they had a lousy time. But anyway the manse looked great with torchlight & cozy little wicker chair gathering spots in the bushes. It all seemed so familiar and horny," he wrote. He took a week to drive up the Maine coast and back down to Plymouth, Massachusetts, and Newport, Rhode Island. He drove over to Cutchogue, wine country on the north fork of Long Island, with Dona Guimares, "and looked over a cemetery but left intact. Did find a beautiful little old church which looked a little abandoned," he wrote on July 20. He had been roped into serving as a judge in a kids' arts and crafts show in Westhampton Beach. "Am hoping for some pornographic or truly embarrassing entries," he wrote.

In the absence of cartoon ideas, he did another naked self-portrait for Tee. Inspired by an article she had sent about a man whose big toe had been transplanted onto his hand to replace a missing thumb, he offered her Addams looking down at a big toe where his member should have been. His right foot was tied with a perky knot, and Alice was sitting up in the begging position. He titled it "The Transplant."

In one of Tee's letters, written a month or so after she had left New York for Paris, she had casually mentioned being five days late with her period. "When those anti-abortionists start marching up 5th you'd better be on your terrace with the crossbows," she wrote, and skipped on to an amusing description of her clothes. Then came another letter. "By the way, you can unwind those crossbows." She had celebrated the happy event with a shopping spree on the Rue St.-Honoré in Paris during which she bought Alice a carrying case and a custom-made leash and collar, and "also a jock strap for you—all matching of course." Then she left Paris for Venice.

Here was a woman who could take care of herself. A pregnancy scare merited no more than a passing aside in a letter. Even the presence in Addams's life of other women—including the independent and remarkable Dona Guimares, who shared so many of Charlie's tastes and interests, and the also worldly and talented Odette Benjamin, Tee's old friend—did not seem to ruffle her. When Charlie's letters began falling off, she simply decided that he was "either dead, married, trapped under the Bugatti, or being held prisoner." At first she considered telephoning him from her new hotel in Venice. But she feared intruding on him and Odette, and she refrained. She knew Charlie well enough to realize that he would not be faithful to her for long, even in the heat wave he claimed had "made a hermit" out of him—"non smoking & non drinking & non screwing, too hot," he had written on July 20 after a jolly salutation suggesting that it was Tee who was out playing around. "Dearest Redskin," he had begun, "Had hoped those old Parisian nights would stop the screwing but I hear they don't even slow you up!" he wrote, referring to a 1953 cartoon. ("Death ray, fiddlesticks! Why it doesn't even slow them up," says the patent attorney aiming a gun out the window of his office building as the inventor stands nearby.)

He sent her an ad for Relaxation Plus health spas showing a picture of a wrinkled man with a towel around his neck next to one of a sexy blonde with big breasts and cleavage. "If we give you as good a massage as Sammy—would you switch?" asked the ad. "I'm sticking with Sammy till you return," Addams scribbled. Tee knew which Sammy he meant. But she also knew that she was his "Creature," his "Dearest T-bird." "I do miss you and nibble the pillows at night and wish I were with you so I could say I love you," he had written.

Finally Tee was sufficiently worried about his silence to telephone. When Charlie refused the long-distance call, she was actually relieved. "I felt much better as I know you aren't sick, hurt or dead—just screwing around as usual (do hope my timing was exactamento)" she added from Venice in August. "Anyway, not terribly worried as she can't be nearly as difficult as I or make you laugh."

She wasn't difficult, but she was perhaps a threat. While declaring his love for Tee in every surviving letter he wrote her that summer, Addams was indeed spending time with the lovely Odette Benjamin, whom he had been seeing off and on for some ten years. Sexy, warm-hearted, intelligent, fluent in four languages, Odette was an elegant and yet adventurous woman who did not let the burn she'd sustained on a Bugatti ride with Addams prevent her from climbing into the car for another spin around the racetrack. And she made no demands. In the usual way of Addams romances, theirs was "light-hearted," but it was also something more. It was "bliss," Odette said simply.

Odette could hardly wait for her ex-husband to say that he was taking the children for a holiday so that she could get away with Charlie. And judging from the numerous photographs Addams took of the brunette with the soulful dark eyes directed right at him, he found bliss with her, too. He lent her the Bentley, also called the Black Maria—or the "Benchley," since the day in Intercourse with Nancy and Tee. ("What is she?" the old guy at the gas station in Pennsylvania had asked. "It's a Bentley," said Charlie. "A Benchley, eh?")

If it hadn't been for the money, and the demands of Odette's big family—four talented and attractive children with whom she was preoccupied, and two aging, squabbling sisters in the form of Odette's mother and maternal aunt, whom Charlie privately called "Mummy and Zsa Zsa," Addams might have married Odette. But marriage would have cost Odette her alimony, and neither she nor Charlie could afford it. (By 1971, his income had dropped to $30,000 a year, less than half what it had been in 1964, at the height of his *Addams Family* earnings.) Though Addams earned a very good living by the standards of most Americans at that time, it was not good enough for two in the privileged world he and Odette moved in. And anyway, he was not prepared to take on a large brood. Not that Odette's children ever sensed it.

"He was like the Dial-A-Dad: totally inappropriate under most circumstances, perfect for us," added Odette's son Christopher. "Let's go get some explosive devices!" Charlie would say. And off they'd go in the Bentley, soaring down the back roads of South Carolina, no seat belts required. At the fireworks store they would fan out, Charlie navigating the aisles to make his own selections, cackling and holding the cigar that was later used to light the firecrackers. While Charlie zoomed down the road home, the kids tossed depth charges out the car window. Because it was Charlie leading the pack, Odette and her mother sanctioned it. Christopher would see "Grandma having a heart attack from the house as she watched" while Charlie, Odette's younger stepbrother, Gordon Gale, and the other kids staged bottle rocket wars on the plantation road, which was surrounded by marsh grass.

"You have someone in your life who shows up in a black extended Bentley," said Christopher Benjamin. Someone clowning in your grandmother's satin bathrobe. "All right, I'll show you my teeth," said Charlie, after enduring their relentless efforts to determine whether he actually had any. Wearing an old straw hat and a red bathing suit over his "New York body," he served them cheese sandwiches Addams-style—at the end of a machete. (This during a family holiday in Jamaica following the death of Odette's stepfather, Daddy Gale.) Charlie had even talked to

Moon Dog, the frightening New York street character, a "Viking-type" with a huge beard and an enormous coat, who haunted midtown at about two in the morning. He would walk right up to him. "What are your hours?" he'd ask. William Benjamin was shocked. Charlie had a very "unadult" house on the water in Long Island, a kind of glorified tree house decorated with crossbows and lithographs of poisonous mushrooms; an equally fantastic and more sinister apartment in New York; and, by 1970, a dog with "attitude . . . built like a mini-hyena," said Christopher.

The Benjamin children would have been happy if Charlie had married their mother, but it was not to be. Years later, when Beatrice went to Mills College out in California, she found a large black balloon and sent it to Charlie with a newsy letter and an invitation to visit. She did not have to wait long for a reply. He came in a two-headed bird basket trimmed with festive bunting and propelled by a magnificent black balloon. Wearing a pith helmet and clenching a cigar between his teeth, he peered into a telescope, his squinty eyes trained on his destination. In the distance, a tiny flag saying "Mills" fluttered from a spire.

> *Dear Beatle [wrote the determined traveler],*
>
> *Thank you—thank you—for the lovely balloon! I have found some helium and have done my best to make a practical traveling conveyance. I've been wondering how I'd ever get out there to see you—so I have taken your hint. Just take a look in the sky around Halloween, that's all.*
>
> *Hope you survived the Pop Festival and that the feelings about school have become unmixed.*
>
> > *Love*
> > *Charlie*

While Tee and the girls summered in Paris in 1972, wandering to Florence and Venice, Charlie charted their movements in his datebook, noting where to write in care of American Express. In his letters he played down the other women he was seeing. "Our friend O is in the neighborhood visiting relatives & am going to the ballet tonight with Mummy & Zsa Zsa too. She is pissed off at you for never calling." He neglected to mention that O would also be spending the weekend with him at Westhampton Beach. "Off to try to do some funnies but mostly thinking of you," he ended. "Love you crazily, RF."

Tee responded in kind. Home from her summer wanderings, she dated other men—a halfhearted reaction to Charlie's other women, but

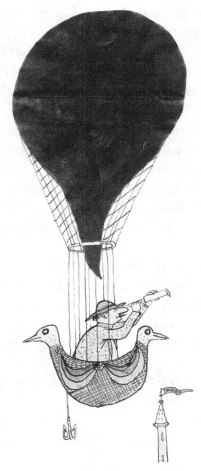

Self-portrait for Beatrice Benjamin.

other men were not Charlie. And at some point, almost imperceptibly, Charlie's black dirigible slipped its mooring mast at the Benjamins', and he drifted into a part-time living arrangement with Tee that encompassed her teenaged son, Bedford Davie. As for the Benjamins, there were no hard feelings. The Benjamin children all knew Tee and were fond of her; and after all, Odette and Tee were old friends. Beatrice and Bunki had been best friends in girlhood. "If I couldn't have him, I wanted Tee to have him," said Odette, meaning it. Tee was "a wonderful, wonderful person," she added, and she and Charlie "were meant to be."

Addams spent weekdays in New York, as he always had; on the weekends he and Alice drove out to Long Island, where Tee might join him at

Tee (left) and Odette. "If I couldn't have him,
I wanted Tee to have him," said Odette. Palm Beach, late 1950s.

the little house. On Sunday mornings he would rev up the Bugatti, which made a sound "worse than jackhammers," said Tee. "You couldn't hear yourself think." Fumes drifted over to the house next door, where the "very stuffy and formal" neighbor would be having a little luncheon party outside, and soon the phone would begin to ring. Charlie wouldn't hear it. Finally, the neighbor would run outside and thunder through the hedges. "You bastard, Addams!"

By now, the funky Addams house on the canal—known to the local kids as "the haunted house"—was *the* tourist attraction of celebrity-filled Westhampton Beach, surpassing even the house of President Nixon's in-laws, the Howard Coxes. Years after *The Addams Family* went off the air, people would pass the place in their boats, talking audibly about Addams, who had told a reporter he kept a Toledo blade at the house for protection. Smoked out by a reporter one summer, Addams posed alongside his Bugatti dressed in khakis, a short-sleeved checked shirt, and the Ringling Bros. Lurch mask. In that Long Island community, Addams was said to be "so popular he could get the Hamptons to secede from the Union, set up a monarchy, and appoint himself king—just because he's a real person." They could hear him coming miles away in his Bugatti. "Oh, here comes Charlie Addams," they'd say. Though his attachment remained strong to the little house he had furnished with weaponry and articulated bones, a drawing table and an ornately carved antique chair, an 1890 gas chandelier, and a "Home Sweet Home" sampler, he found himself spending less and less time there and more and more time at Tee's house in Water Mill, until he was a fixture there.

Bedford Davie had been about fourteen when Charlie began staying over at the house. Since he was not allowed to have girlfriends sleep in his room, his mother and Charlie tried to maintain a sense of propriety as well. At first, Charlie had slept in Bedford's room, each occupying a twin bed. Then one night when the three of them were watching TV, Charlie withdrew to Tee's bedroom to take a nap. Later in the evening, Tee said casually, "Well, you know what? I'll just leave him in here with me." And there Charlie remained, to Bedford's private amusement.

To Amy Wehle, a shy girl who dated Bedford Davie during the early 1970s, the living arrangements at Tee's house seemed quite natural, though different from those in her own household. Called Toad Hall since the day Charlie had driven up in his motorcar wearing a *Wind in the Willows* T-shirt, Tee's house was a fun, kid-friendly place with frog wallpaper in the bathroom and a sign reading USE THE KNOBS YOU SLOBS. On hot summer nights, everyone except Tee slept out on the porch *en famille*.

They cooked mussels at Charlie's little house on the canal, Amy and Bedford having cleaned them while the adults had a drink and a cigarette with Budd Schulberg. Tee made a special effort to draw out her young houseguest; Charlie entered with interest into Amy's scheme of making a chain-mail breastplate for Alice out of the aluminum pop-tops on soda cans.

After Amy returned home, she continued to hoard the silver crescents. When she had collected enough, she sent them to Charlie. In due time she received a Toad Hall postcard featuring a drawing of noble Alice dressed in chain mail and wielding a sword against an unseen enemy.

Alice in chain mail.

"No kids," Charlie had said of the life he wanted with Tee, "but Bedford's okay." And Charles Addams was "the *one*" of his mother's husbands that Bedford really liked to be around, though of course Tee and Charlie were not married. He had always remembered a mural Charlie painted on the kitchen wall of the fancy new duplex apartment Tee and Dudley Miller had bought in the U.N. Plaza after they were married. On a visit to see the new digs, Charlie had picked up a brush left by the painters and sketched a naked LBJ and Lady Bird Johnson. Tee herself had been so delighted with the portrait that she left a sign for the painters telling them not to paint over the drawing. Unfortunately they didn't see it, and an Addams treasure was lost.

Charlie didn't act like a father. Fathers didn't break up laughing when your mother was lecturing you to be on your best behavior. "Now, he's kind of slow," Tee once explained about the child of a family they were going to visit, "but very advanced for his age. . . ." Bedford caught Charlie's squinty eyes in the rearview mirror, getting smaller and smaller with his silent laughter; then he started to squeak. Fathers didn't drive Bugattis. In the mornings, while Tee was still sleeping, the men of the house would go out and get the paper. Charlie would warm up the Bugatti outside, rather than in the garage, but inevitably the house would begin to shake. Up went Tee's window. "God damn it!" she cried. And fathers didn't advise with humor. "What do you think about marrying for money?" Bedford asked him. "You know, somehow there's never enough money," Charlie said in his offhand way.

Or if Bedford was admiring an expensive car, Charlie would quietly observe, "It's beautiful, but you can have just as much fun with less." And he not only let the kid drive his expensive cars, he gave him his own helmet, fitted with a cloth to keep the bugs out. Charlie himself wore a beige linen helmet Tee had bought him during her summer abroad, his "sperm helmet," Bedford called it, after the Woody Allen character in the 1972 movie *Everything You Always Wanted to Know About Sex (But Were Afraid to Ask)*, accessorized with tiny goggles.

On the crisp spring day that Charlie and Tee and Bedford set off for a road race at Lime Rock, Charlie was dressed for driving. The fellows were to ride together in the Aston Martin, Tee following in a backup car. But Bedford began making a fuss about wearing the funny-looking glasses Charlie had given him. People would look at him, he complained. "They will never see you!" Tee cried. "They will be looking at that apparition sitting next to you!"

And so, without actually planning to, Addams was living with Tee—his "girl," he called her. Instead of cooking up "little messes" by himself, he enjoyed Tee's cooking. He and Alice had become part of a family, which included Tee's shifting assortment of foundling animals. He accepted Bedford, and Tee welcomed Alice. And Alice—well, Addams was slightly hurt that she would climb willingly into Tee's car and go right to sleep, but resisted riding with him. Ever since the day Alice had been thrown from the Bentley (unharmed) as he took a sharp turn, she had not trusted his driving. Now he had to chase her around the house and pull her out from under a table to get her into the car. Then she'd sit bolt upright on the seat behind him, never again beside him, her miserable eyes boring a hole in the back of his head. "Alice looks just like me when I have to get in your car," said Drue Heinz.

In 1974, at the age of sixty-two, Addams made a new will, leaving half of his estate to Tee—"Mrs. Dudley L. Miller"—and all his property to "Barbara Estella Barb," whom he also appointed executrix. In the pocket datebooks he received from Odette inscribed "F.R.W.L."—From Russia with Love—he listed the husbandly gifts he was assembling for Tee's Christmas: a dog basket, a swivel chair, white shell earrings with a gold rim, a wooden spoon, a knife sharpener, and *The Joy of Cooking*. He inscribed the book with another naked self-portrait, showing his worried-looking self slowly turning on the spit in a large brick oven.

—

Chapter Nineteen

Real Estate

Guard towers stand at either end of the stone cellblock, but this is not a penal institution. Positioned under Romanesque arches like figures in a frieze are *The New Yorker*'s staunch guardians, watchful but unarmed: Harold Ross, William Shawn, Wolcott Gibbs, William Maxwell, Katharine and E. B. White, and other pillars of the magazine. The writers include Truman Capote, Philip Hamburger, and John O'Hara, who had died in 1970. The cartoonists are represented by Steinberg and George Price (flanking James Geraghty), Arno, Thurber, Whitney Darrow, Jr., and Addams himself—squeezed in to the right of J. D. Salinger and partly cut off. He included "two unidentified wretches (put in to avoid hurting the feelings of people there wasn't room for)"—or so Addams explained of his droll dust jacket illustration for Brendan Gill's 1975 memoir, *Here at The New Yorker*.

The architectural restraint reflected Addams's view of the magazine's cloistered atmosphere. He thought of the *New Yorker* offices at 25 West Forty-third Street as "a little bit like visiting a monastery." The offices themselves were "a series of rabbit warrens or cells, and the people aren't what you would ordinarily call gregarious. . . . They wander silently up and down the hall, sometimes speaking, sometimes not." His picture showed the magazine's representatives in monks' robes with cowls and cinctures, looking as though they'd taken a vow of silence.

Though he could earn more for a *New Yorker* cover—by 1975 he was getting up to $1,650 for his cover illustrations—it was a profitable assignment. Addams was paid $1,000 for the Gill jacket, plus another $250 for the English edition, and he later sold the original for $350. But he was privately disgruntled about the book itself, which was published to coincide with *The New Yorker*'s fiftieth anniversary.

Like many longtime contributors and staff members, including Katharine and E. B. White, Addams was offended by Brendan Gill's depiction of Harold Ross as a cartoon hayseed—a characterization that was both false and undeserved. But he was more riled by what Gill wrote about *him*.

In this gossipy, entertaining, charming, and malicious book, the portrait of Addams was fond but trivializing. This A-list cartoonist—*the* cartoonist in the eyes of many *New Yorker* artists and contributors, though he had diminished himself in the Gill illustration to the point that he was barely noticeable—was reduced to a playful character with macabre tastes and a love of classic cars, a man with a comical, "boneless" nose and a funny face he used to wondrous effect before the looking glass in order to draw his ghouls—as if Charles Addams couldn't draw without a mirror. Calling Addams "my closest friend" among the magazine's artists, Gill served up the old apocryphal tales about the cartoonist's mental breakdowns, when he would draw "The Skier" again and be carted off to the loony bin, as well as the grisly maternity room cartoon Addams had never drawn. (Gill had at least noted that the second story was false, but Addams remained irritated.)

"A lot of people took their raps in Brendan's book, I think," Addams told Heywood Hale Broun during a radio interview. He pointed out Gill's focus on physical defects—such as Addams's "boneless nose." He thought he might tell Gill, "I really like your book, Brendan, but there are a lot of boneless noses, thickening waists. . . ." And yet the tired rumors offended him less than the lack of any critical appraisal of his work. Though *Here at The New Yorker* reprinted several classic Addams cartoons, Gill said nothing about Addams's contribution to the magazine— as he did of Steinberg's, for instance. "He said what people wanted to hear," Addams grumbled to a reporter. In a private conversation, he even took an uncharacteristic personal swipe. "Have you ever been to a party where Brendan was not present?" he asked. "He turned up at Johnny Nicholson's the other night, making a speech. He's great at that."

In the dust jacket illustration, Addams placed Gill to the left of John O'Hara, who had never forgiven Gill or *The New Yorker* for a bad review of his 1949 novel, *A Rage to Live*. The Addams O'Hara looked aggrieved; Gill—an attractive man in the flesh—appeared subtly cadaverous and swarthy, with an open book in his hands.

ADDAMS BEGAN 1975, the year of *The New Yorker*'s fiftieth anniversary, on a celebratory jag. He took a trip to Gettysburg with Dona, his favorite antiquing buddy, and attended a round of golden anniversary celebrations for *The New Yorker:* a bash at the Plaza, an "enormous party at Ben Sonnenberg's that was so crowded I don't think anyone had a very good time," and a screening party at the Rizzoli Bookstore, which showed a film called *Letter from Paris* narrated by the lifelong writer of that *New Yorker* column, Janet Flanner—"eighty-three years old and a fine actress," said Addams. Mayor Beame proclaimed February 15 "*New Yorker* day." Addams did his part to toast the magazine, giving interviews and loyally defending *The New Yorker* against complaints of dullness— which, after all, were not new. People had always complained, Addams noted. Though he himself had bemoaned the changes in the magazine— "If only *The New Yorker* would start trying to be like *The New Yorker* again, and stop being so serious," he told a reporter in 1972—he rallied for the occasion. "I think the spirit of excellence—or something—is still there. The spirit of Gibbs and White . . . is still there, and they're still editing by the standards they set."

Addams himself had recently received a big salute in a place where it counted. Writing in *The New York Times,* John Russell had designated Addams "an American landmark, one of the few by which one and all have learned to steer." Though the encomium must have gratified him, Addams would never have thought of himself in such lofty terms. "A good cartoonist" was enough for him. If he had drawn himself as a building, it would have been as the modest brownstone he later painted for a 1977 *New Yorker* cover: a good structure interestingly carved, holding its own among the Manhattan skyscrapers, which in Addams's modest cartoon beginnings had been represented by George Price, Gluyas Williams, and Peter Arno.

Forty years after finding his niche in *The New Yorker*'s cellblock, he regarded himself as lucky. "I came on at the right time—everything is more or less timing," he said in his self-effacing way. "Think of the things I used to do—they wouldn't be scary now." Given the magazine's more serious tone, he wondered whether "Thurber could sell a piece today."

For cartoonists, *The New Yorker* was by the 1970s virtually the only game in town. *The Saturday Evening Post* and *Collier's* had folded; other markets, such as *Playboy*, were limited as to subject matter. At *The New Yorker*, which might publish more than eighty cartoonists in a year, an artist could earn $500 for a cartoon, a price that jumped with bonuses, COLAs (Cost of Living Adjustments), and contractual payments, which were determined by an artist's gross average income over a three-year period. But many cartoonists managed to sell only one drawing to *The New Yorker*, making such extras irrelevant. Addams earned $2,700 for his contractual payment alone in 1974 and again in 1975.

He was now one of the few artists left from the early days, and one of the few who kept an office in those hallowed halls. Much to his pleasure, George Price, Whitney Darrow, Jr., Frank Modell, and Saul Steinberg were also still there, drawing as brilliantly as ever; Steinberg, arguably the last skyscraper to follow Addams, remained a towering presence. And William Steig, who had established himself at the magazine before any of them, had continued to evolve, becoming more and more abstract. But more of the old masters had gone. Thurber, Arno, and Al Freuh had died during the sixties. Alan Dunn—the magazine's most prolific artist, with 1,906 drawings to his credit since his work began appearing in *The New Yorker* in 1926—had died in 1974, at the age of seventy-three. Prized at the magazine for his push-button ability to read a news item and instantly transform it into a cartoon, he was also one of the first cartoonists to draw architecture seriously. (Like the Addams house, Dunn's tenderly drawn Victorians were enchanting. "Try to build a house like that for thirty thousand today and see how far you get!" said the real estate agent in a fine 1947 cartoon.) And just two months after *The New Yorker*'s anniversary blitz, Otto Soglow died at seventy-four, taking with him the deceptively simple-looking illustrations he had been drawing for "Notes and Comment" for forty years. The Romanesque arches would embrace no more little kings.

Quieter changes had taken place in the art department, resulting in a new direction for the cartoons, in the way Addams worked, and in his feelings about the place. First Jim Geraghty retired in 1973, after nearly thirty-five years as art editor. Addams missed him, both personally and professionally. "Things are much more static here," Addams wrote his longtime pal in Florida. "*I* don't see alligators murder pelicans on my own property—which I rarely see anyway. What with the [gas] crisis the old Bentley languishes here in the garage just hoping for an emergency. . . . My maid never arrives and I have taken up dusting and roller sweeping." Then, under pressure from William Shawn, the old system of buying cartoon ideas fell away.

For twenty years William Shawn had wanted to publish artists who drew exclusively from their own ideas—a 180-degree turnaround from Harold Ross's collaborative regime in which most of the magazine's important artists had flourished and been shaped. With gagmen now off *The New Yorker*'s payroll, the art editor had a problem: Since neither Shawn nor anyone else wanted to lose the magazine's great old talents—namely, Addams and Price—the talent had to be fed another way. Thus the new art editor, cartoonist Lee Lorenz, looked through the slush pile for roughs that might be cannibalized for Addams cartoons, as Geraghty had done before him. This method presented its own problems. Some cartoonists would sell their work for ideas; some would not.

Frank Modell estimated that *The New Yorker* bought "maybe three to five [unsolicited gags] a year." But Addams ideas were hard to come by. ("Dear Mr. Adams," read a typical letter, "The other day on a highway leading out of Syracuse I saw a girl holding up a sign reading: BINGHAMTON; I AM ON THE PILL. I wonder if you could replace the girl with one of your old hags.") "People send in little vultures and ideas for cartoons," as Addams had put it; "usually they've been suggested at least ten times before."

But occasionally something worth pursuing arrived unbidden in the mail. "Dear Mr. Ogilvy," Addams wrote in February 1975, "I'm trying to think of a suitable idea for your caption—as sick as you suggest." Modell, who had once handed Addams the idea for his galley slave cartoon, would later offer Addams the gag for his 1985 New Year's cover in which a solitary black Scottie watches, from the window of his dark apartment, a party in full swing across the way. For his own part, Addams kept Herb Valen on his private payroll. (Valen, who had done many ideas for Cobean as well as others, had provided Addams with some of his best cartoon gags, including the idea for the captionless 1956 drawing of two unicorns on a rain-swept bluff watching Noah's Ark recede.) Along with dreaming up material, Valen continued to act as Addams's agent for advertising assignments (Avis, Mobil, *TV Guide*)—a service he also provided to other cartoonists. But an important creative well had dried up. In the end, Addams had to rely mostly on himself.

Soon the loss was felt in the slush as well, as under the new system cartoonists who had gotten in the door of *The New Yorker* by selling their roughs as ideas finally got their own cartoons published. The first was Jack Ziegler, whose brash, comic book–inspired cartoons had been published in *National Lampoon*. Before Ziegler's work began appearing in *The New Yorker* in 1974, the magazine bought two of his roughs for Charles Addams. One showed a contemplative Edgar Allan Poe at his writing table, thinking of the word "Nevermore" spoken variously by a pig, a moose, and a turtle; this became a 1973 Addams cartoon. (Among Addams's roughs at home were some rejected or undeveloped Poe ideas: A raven wears a T-shirt saying "Nevermore"; a raven perched on a bust of Poe tells a parrot, "Watch it, buster. 'Nevermore' is *my* line.") The other Ziegler-Addams was instantly recognizable as an Addams subject: a tiny mail truck, letter-slot height, proceeding down a city sidewalk after a delivery.

Leo Cullum's first sale to *The New Yorker* resulted in a triple hit for Addams: Not only was it classic Addams in subject, it was captionless, and it required that the reader look for the joke. Published in 1975, it depicted an elderly couple drifting in a rowboat on a serene, wooded lake. As the dowdy, contented wife sits in the bow with her eyes closed and arms folded, the husband peacefully smokes his pipe and rows. But the reflection in the water tells the true story playing out in the man's head, as he reaches out with his oar to whack her. Cullum sold three other roughs to *The New Yorker* for Addams.

Seeing what Addams did with one's work could be either instructive or deflating. When P. L. Steiner sold a painting of a tabletop aquarium filled with exotic fish swimming against the Manhattan skyline as viewed from New Jersey (which became a 1980 *New Yorker* cover by Addams), he was gratified to see how the master had improved upon the original work, altering Steiner's dimensions and much else. "It's the opposite of when you see a bad copy of a great painting," he said later. Young Michael Maslin saw his own rough of a woman pushing a grocery cart through a store whose shelves are all empty beneath a sign reading "IF YOU DON'T SEE WHAT YOU WANT ASK FOR IT" similarly improved upon in a 1983 drawing. In his rendering, Addams had blown up the space, "giving the emptiness of the store more play," said Maslin, who liked the Addams version better than his own. But a Steiner cartoon rough showing mourners gathered around a deathbed to hear the dying man's final pronouncement—"To . . . hell . . . with . . . yogurt"—had merely been re-drawn. Addams hadn't changed much from Steiner's work. Even the position of the characters around the bed was the same.

One of the best of the new generation of artists was George Booth, whose character-driven world of misfits, proliferating cats, and flea-bitten dogs (always "dawgs" in a Booth cartoon) owed something to the other George, Price. Addams particularly admired Booth's auto mechan-ics—"quite good, rather seedy old time" characters with "sagging pants," he observed. Ed Koren had also changed the look of *New Yorker* art with a furry line that made his original species of man and beast funny even without the gags; William Hamilton provided another fresh take on car-toon art with his striking pen-and-ink drawings capturing overheard conversations and pronouncements. James Stevenson, who had first been hired as a gagman and fired when he insisted on drawing his own work, was now one of *The New Yorker*'s most versatile and productive artists.

But Addams said little for the record about the new artists. "The draw-ings are indeed different and one can only pray that the New Years cover does not indicate a trend," he wrote Geraghty in January of 1974. The in-nocuous cover by Charles E. Martin, rendered in mellow blues and browns, showed footprints in the snow under a bridge in Central Park.

This was the era of serene, framable *New Yorker* covers by such artists as Arthur Getz, Charles E. Martin, and Gretchen Dow Simpson, a look reflecting Shawn's own "delicate and subdued" tastes, noted Lee Lorenz. Into this tranquil pool of cover art dropped the most dreamy of Addams offerings: a bare brown hill dotted with grazing sheep melting into the fluffy clouds in a blue sky until they become the clouds. Addams was surprised by the enthusiastic response to this May 1975 cover. "It was a doodle that just hung around for a year or two, and I never thought it was worth turning in," he later told Dick Cavett. He not only got a lot of mail "from closet sheep lovers," but he was paid $1,650 for it and quickly sold the original for $1,000, making it one of his most lucrative doodles.

While Steinberg, George Booth, James Stevenson, William Hamilton, and Ed Koren (teaming up with Calvin Trillin on text for "The Inquiring Demographer") experimented with illustrated texts and cartoon strips, Addams confined his own artistic adventures to an occasional return to a shaggy pen-line style. "I was under the mistaken idea it was an improvement," he admitted later. Though many of *The New Yorker's* cartoons were topical, taking up such subjects as the energy crisis, junk language, and the intrusion of electronic devices into daily life, Addams went his own way. "I think of my people as timeless," he told a reporter. Topical cartoons, he observed, "last as long as yesterday's newspaper."

When he occasionally did something timely, he did it his way. His answer to the current fashion trend of sweatshirts labeled with famous names (such as Jane Austen) was an automobile showroom featuring a car called "The Thing," and a familiar hairy creature walking toward it. In another cartoon, an allusion to the gasoline shortages and inflated oil prices of the 1970s, he worked a variation on a 1950 cartoon of "that little bastard I draw," Pugsley, introducing a small submarine into the boat pond in Central Park. This time, the bad boy pushes a leaking oil tanker toward a fleet of happy sailboats.

By the seventies, Addams was only one of a handful of artists who had staked out their own territory at *The New Yorker* with work that was utterly distinctive in style and subject matter. No one but Charles Addams could have drawn the prostrate snowman staked through the heart with a broom. Though census takers remained a favorite subject of the magazine's artists, only one cartoonist could have produced the startled polltaker arriving at Apt. 26a to be greeted by Tweedledum and Tweedledee—Tenniel filtered through the gentler lens of Addams. Only at an Addams garage sale, taking place in a structure with a cupola not unlike the artist's own garage in Westhampton Beach, would you find a hangman's noose, an Iron Maiden, an executioner's ax, a rack, and various other torture devices. MORE UPSTAIRS, says a helpful sign.

As it happened, the garage sale cartoon was published at almost the same moment that Addams formally lost his only real estate. He had sold the drawing to *The New Yorker* in August of 1974, following a fight with Barbara. The offended tone of Barbara's summer letters suggested that Addams had been telling naughty tales out of school—not for the first time—which had duly made their way back to her. After a groveling telephone call from Addams, in which he apparently denied saying what he

was accused of, Barbara seemed appeased if still wary. Forsaking "Porker" for "Charles," she wrote him a short letter from Portugal, followed by a longer one. She emphasized her deep hurt, and warned him to keep his mouth shut in the future. Along with all her hard work on his behalf— "I've always tried to take care of you & look after you in every way"—she had always treated him "as someone dearer than any member of my family," even lending him her treasured belongings. And her health, she said, was precarious: "I have been very ill again and am just now trying to regain the use of my limbs—& I am walking again," she wrote.

Cowering in Barbara's handwritten lines was the Addams nobody else knew, the cringing figure of the suicide threat—upset, unhappy, as Barbara put it in a letter. Judging by the sound of her letter, Addams was in danger of harming himself. After all, she added, she knew him.

By late July, they had smoothed things over sufficiently to agree that when Barbara came to New York she would stay at his apartment if she needed to. She reminded him to sign the letter she was enclosing the moment he got it, she wrote in capitals, and mail it to the Ritz in Lisbon so

there would be no problem about her gaining access to the apartment while he was away.

In early September, Charlie and Tee flew to Paris for a two-week holiday. In their absence, on September 16, Charlie's garage sale cartoon appeared in *The New Yorker*. Three days later, a transfer of property was recorded for the town of Southampton, which included Westhampton Beach. In consideration of one dollar, the two parcels of land in the vil-

lage of Westhampton Beach jointly owned by Charles Addams and Barbara Estella Barb Addams, "his wife, residing at 4 East 88th Street," became the sole property of said Mrs. Addams. Without telling Addams,
Barbara had finally recorded the document she had insisted he sign eighteen years earlier.

Addams was unaware of the loss until sometime later—when, exactly,
is uncertain. He clearly did not know by October 7, when he signed the
new will, leaving the property to Barbara Estella Barb, "my friend." Nor,
one supposes, did he know by October 10, when he signed an obviously
dictated letter to Barbara acknowledging her ownership of forty-two of
his cartoons and *New Yorker* covers "that were part of the contents of her
former apartment at 4 East 88th St and which are presently in my possession"—including four of his Mother Goose illustrations, which he had
drawn in the decade after their divorce. And then something apparently
happened. Sometime between October 10 and November 7, he became
rattled enough to telephone Barbara long distance. "Porker dear," she
wrote from Monte Carlo on November 7, "I could never do anything that
was unfair to you, in any way."

Had he found out about the deeds? Tee later remembered a day when
she and Charlie were discussing the houses. Charlie had seemed confused about whether he owned them or not, and Tee asked why he didn't
just look it up and settle the matter. Finally he did. He returned to Toad
Hall shaken.

For eighteen years, he had endured it. Desperate to get out of his second marriage, he had signed away his properties, trusting that Barbara
would honor her promise to return the houses—in her will, perhaps sooner.

While speaking often and bitterly about the arrangement to friends
such as Jane Gunther, he had rented out the carriage house to pay the
taxes, had dealt with real estate agents, handymen, surveyors, and ac-
countants. He had paid for repairs and miscellaneous upkeep out of his
own pocket. In exchange Barbara had treated him "like a caretaker," said
Tee. She would telephone him and "give him hell."

In the end, he would have given up the carriage house without a fight.
"All he wanted was that little house," said Tee.

He titled his next cartoon collection, published in 1976, *Favorite
Haunts.*

Chapter Twenty

Mrs. Rupert Hutton

"DEAR ONE," HE SCRIBBLED TO TEE IN MARCH OF 1977, A week after she left for Africa on safari. And there followed a playful, telegraphic report on his activities, all Addams in content and form. In the days since Tee's departure he had done some traveling of his own, to Cape May with Dona, and to Chadds Ford, Pennsylvania. He had been to "many antique shops," he wrote. "Bought giant meat cleaver and a sword cane—can that be significant. Wonder how your diggings at Nairobi are working out. This is St. Patrick's, with skirling bag pipes & London taxis outside. Are you having an absolutely shattering safari? Please send a pygmy."

In Paris five years earlier, Tee had purchased a live fruit bat for him, but had had to leave it behind when it was not allowed through customs.

To read Addams's note to Tee and riffle through his datebook, you would never guess that ten months earlier he had had an alarming incident while he was out driving and had been told by his doctors not to drive alone anymore. (He hadn't been driving alone, he said. He'd had his dog with him.) Or that Tee, shaken by the mishap and her powerlessness to get Charlie transferred to a better hospital because she was "only the girlfriend," had insisted that they now get married. "You're so romantic!" Charlie had told her as he lay hooked up to the IV. Everything had changed, and yet, on the surface at least, everything remained the same.

Charlie and Tee still lived together on the weekends, enjoying a semblance of family life while maintaining their independence.

The incident had occurred on the Sunday evening of May 2, 1976. Addams had been driving in the vicinity of Westhampton Beach when he felt he was going to vomit. He managed to pull his car off the road and crawl out before losing consciousness. A passing motorist saw him and called the police. Addams landed in the emergency ward of the nearest hospital, in Patchogue, about fifteen miles west of Westhampton Beach, where he was diagnosed with a bleeding ulcer. While he lay unconscious, someone got hold of Tee, presumably through information in Addams's wallet. At the hospital, she was left pacing until a doctor in a blood-stained robe emerged from surgery and told her that if Charlie didn't regain consciousness in fifteen minutes, he was going to operate.

Though Addams came to in time to prevent the surgery, the experience had a sobering effect on him. It didn't "sway his atheism, but it did make him stop drinking," he announced. (Well, not entirely, though he did stick to wine.) There would be no more "fighting back to health with small dollops of booze," as he had once put it. No more sliding behind the wheel after an evening at a bar and saying, "Who's for a little drunken driving?" Now when interviewers turned up, Addams was more likely to offer a reporter a cup of tea—or a diet soda, though he himself never got used to it. "It has a wonderful poisonous cloudy look," Addams said after he was handed a glass of Tab. "What are you doing to me?"

Though friends and colleagues had sometimes seen Addams "loaded" at parties (Frank Modell once had to drive him home), many people who knew him well perceived him not as an alcoholic but as an in-control heavy drinker. In his various social worlds, where serious drinking was the norm, Addams might be drunk "by midnight," but never during the day. He would become talkative in bars; and unlike other, morbid drinkers, "Charlie drank cheerfully," said Budd Schulberg. And yet Addams had in fact gone on drunken benders with Tee and others, sometimes during lunch. He had been very upset on an occasion when John Cheever wasn't drinking at the Coffee House, a club frequented by *New Yorker* people. If Addams was, as Burgess Meredith claimed, "disciplined" compared to other boozers, it may have been that his tolerance for alcohol made him seem so—though drinking apparently never interfered with his work.

The bleeding ulcer incident did not sway his feelings about marriage, either, which he considered "a passé institution, unless there are children," but he did take note of Tee's continuing presence during the days after his attack. She had seen to everything, and almost never left his side. After he regained consciousness and she knew he was going to be all right, she rescued a growling, frantic Alice from his car—even the police hadn't been able to get near Alice—and took her home. And then she stayed close to him during his two days of treatment at Brookhaven before he could be moved. She rode in the ambulance with him to Lenox Hill, where she remained by his side until he was released from the hospital on May 8. Addams entered Tee's name in his datebook next to those of his attending physicians. And he made plans to write a new will—and guard it from Barbara. The new Addams will "is never to be mentioned in any letter to him," wrote Harriet Pilpel in a memo. "It is to be confidential information."

Even sixteen years earlier, before Tee's divorce from Buddy Davie was final, there had been speculations about Addams and Tee in the press. "Then there's pretty Tee Davie, estranged wife of rich and social E. T. Bedford Davie," said the "Society by Suzy" column. "Tee and Charles Addams, the macabre cartoonist, should not be cast aside lightly. I mean they're pretty thick and all. And if Tee *ever* gets things straightened out financially with E. T. Bedford, it might be thicker than that even." But the closest they had come to marriage was the fake "Mrs." that Tee had assumed when they slipped off to Bermuda in November 1961 on a celebrity junket, and were photographed by Jerry Zerbe. Tee knew Zerbe, and she begged him not to use her real name. Her divorce was pending, she explained. And when the photograph appeared in the paper, showing a smiling Charles Addams relaxing beside Tee as she leaned languidly against a doorjamb with her cigarette, the caption identified her as "Mrs. Rupert Hutton," a Zerbe invention.

Now, while Tee pressed for marriage, Charlie held back. By all accounts, he was crazy about Tee. He loved her; anyone could see it. They were so close that he noted *her* illnesses in his datebooks along with his own. But there were all those other names in the little books, the letters he still received addressed to "Darling" and "Dearest C." There were the women he hadn't met.

In that innocent time before his misadventure at Brookhaven, he had enjoyed the comforts of a weekend domesticity with an easygoing woman while reveling in his freedom. "Well, Charlie, what are we expecting tonight—blonde or brunette?" Jack Heinz would ask before a dinner party at his home.

Posing for *Single* magazine a year before his ulcer attack, Addams had sat in front of his Maximilian suit wearing a herringbone jacket and tie, and the medieval helmet from the suit—visor up, like a crested bird. He had crowed about the single life, and the women—not woman—in his life. "They are all old friends," he said, without mentioning the names of the women whom interviewer Patricia Coffin described as "bright young magazine editors, well-to-do divorcees with houses in the country and with-it intellectuals whose figures are as admirable as their brains." Only the names of Addams's ex-wives, and those of his most famous past dates—Onassis and Fontaine—were given. "I don't have to struggle with them anymore," he said of the current flock. "It is very comfortable. It's like having a harem away from home." And he added, "I wouldn't mind *living* with someone but somehow I never have." By his calculation, it seems, residing with Tee on the weekends and going their separate ways the other five days of the week did not constitute cohabiting.

And yet at the same time, he had left the door open for marriage. Admitting that he used to think that if he got sick, "friends will rally around," he conceded that he "might have to take it all back and get married." But now he had come through his crisis; he was doing fine, he might have reasoned as he put Tee off. He would cope with the bleeding ulcer as he had coped with his diabetes for the last twenty-five years: sensibly, but without becoming a fanatic. (He managed it with diet alone.) He would handle it as he had handled the large polyp he had had removed during a colonoscopy in 1974—casually. (His polyps looked like "little mushrooms," he had told Tee. But they were "not poisonous I don't think," he wrote Jim Geraghty.)

He faithfully recorded little *B*'s, *G*'s, and *T*'s in his datebooks to denote blood testing, glucose levels, and the Trental he was taking for his circulation, a problem related to the diabetes. He kept track of his colds, which would have pushed his sugar levels up, and wrote "YG" to remind himself that he had eaten yogurt, which would also have affected his sugar levels. He was "not ultra-serious about his condition," said his doctor, Stanley Mirsky, but he followed the diet Mirsky gave him well enough, and came in regularly for checkups.

As for formal exercise and other extreme measures, his attitude was best summed up by a March 1976 Addams cartoon showing a carving of a heavyset middle-aged jogger endlessly running on his tombstone. Perhaps it is no coincidence that a more recent cartoon, published the day after Addams's blackout, while he was still on the IV, featured a Fester-like gym instructor cracking a bullwhip over two columns of sweating men at the rowing machines.

"IF YOU COULD choose your end—how you'd die—what would it be?" came the query from George Plimpton, who was taking a poll among his artistic friends.

"I am hoping to break into a thousand tiny pieces while attending a theremin concert in Malone, N.Y., in mid-January," wrote Addams.

Plimpton was excited by the answer, but puzzled. He telephoned Addams for clarification, admitting that he didn't know the meaning of "theremin."

"A theremin is a musical instrument . . . a sort of electrical coil which gives off a humming sound," said Addams. "It works by the distance you hold your hand to it. The closer you put your hand," he explained, "the higher the tone, until right up close you can get a terrific vibrational shriek."

FOUR MONTHS AFTER his bleeding ulcer scare, Addams received a potentially lucrative proposition. Filmways was interested in bringing *The Addams Family* back to television. Having failed to reach Barbara Colyton at two different addresses in England, Walter Schier telephoned Harriet Pilpel.

After her unladylike eruption in 1964, when Barbara had nearly prevented *The Addams Family* from airing, there was no question about who would be representing Charles Addams on Addams Family rights. But while Addams waited to hear from Barbara, he asked Harriet Pilpel to telephone Schier in California to see what he had in mind.

Twenty years after Addams's second divorce, Pilpel was still trying to extricate him from the paper tangles and get him on solid legal ground that would protect his interests. Now, as another rematch with Barbara loomed, Pilpel proceeded cautiously. "Addams is obviously uncertain as to who he wants to handle this and is always afraid of Barbara in any event," she wrote on September 9.

Things moved quickly. David Levy was to produce the show. By January 1977, Addams was depositing money in the bank—how much was from the television deal is unclear. He recorded a $15,500 check from Barbare Artists, but that included his cut from a British book advance (most likely the English edition of his eleventh collection, *Favorite Haunts*, published by Simon & Schuster in 1976). Then came the usual hitches—Barbara, Barbara—and hair-pulling by Harriet Pilpel.

"There is absolutely no point in our trying to do anything about this," she advised a colleague after a call from the television people in California in May 1977. "Charles' former wife, Barbara, who was Lady something or other, and who lives in Monte Carlo, handles all his properties and is apparently negotiating for a 'possible spectacular' in the fall. Words fail me and there is no rational explanation of the hold she seems to have on him."

Less than three weeks before the show was to air as a pilot for a possible new series, Pilpel and her colleagues found themselves running interference on a Barbare Artists licensing agreement that put Addams at risk of a lawsuit. Just ten days before the television show, Pilpel was sounding worried. "I think you should keep a very careful record of your conversations with Charles Addams and Barbara Barb," she wrote her colleague. "She is a very dangerous lady and we will be blamed for whatever goes wrong here."

The result of all the fuss was a dismal reunion show hyped as an NBC-TV "big event": *Halloween with the New Addams Family*. It ran on October 30, 1977, and starred all the original cast with the exception of Blossom Rock as Grandma, who was ill and frail. Filmed on a cheap, inferior set, in color (an effect akin to colorizing the original Addams cartoons), with a bad script, the show got poor ratings and was panned by the critics. David Levy blamed "network bureaucratic interference" for the quality of the show. "The people who knew what 'the Addams Family' was all about did not have the right of final decision," he said. "Therefore, that show maybe reflected 40 percent of what it should have been." Addams himself thought the so-called reunion "really awful." But he deposited a consoling $22,593.75 check from Barbare Artists in the bank, bringing his total take for the television special to perhaps $30,000. And he dreamed about a musical version of the Family.

As Addams dreamed his dreams, Barbara Colyton dreamed hers. She always tripled or quadrupled any Addams offers that came her way; she handled his British book sales. And she sent Addams enough money to keep him happy, while keeping her own percentage from the various contracts to herself.

Another Barbara was also making money for Addams now, and sending checks in a steady, and honest, trickle. Barbara Nicholls had left *The New Yorker* and opened her own gallery at 1014 Madison Avenue. Along with work by other *New Yorker* artists, the Nicholls Gallery sold Addams originals and limited edition prints, and offered a fine showcase for the cartoonist's work. (It was after seeing a 1974 exhibit there that John Russell had declared Addams "an American landmark.") Since 1974, the gallery's sales had increased Addams's income by thousands of dollars a year—$2,310 at the low end, $14,770.50 at the high. (Barbara Colyton, who handled mostly Addams Family business, got no cut of this income.) Barbara Nicholls also acted as sometime agent for Addams, handling reproduction rights and advising him.

NEARLY THREE YEARS had passed since his brush with death on a highway. Though he continued to limit his drinking to wine, he had neither slowed down nor otherwise changed his ways. He raced his cars. He showed no signs of getting married. He had acquired a beard—"an early sign of total reclusion," he said—which emerged, like an Addams wash, in varying shades of gray and dusk and white below his dark mustache and silvery backcombed hair. "You look great in that beard," wrote Jim Geraghty from retirement in Weston, Connecticut. "Distinguished yet devilish." Wearing the French linen aviator hat Tee had given him, which "looked like a baby hat on him," he drove his Bugatti in the Bridgehampton races.

On the two-lane Montauk highway, which was lined with pitch pines and framed by the Atlantic, he drag-raced Steven Aronson—Aronson driving his sixties Maserati, Addams in the Bugatti—at about 100 mph.

Addams in beard—"an early sign of total reclusion"—
on The Dick Cavett Show *in 1978.*

"On the road one is deaf to all comments good or bad," he had written in the unpublished "Bugatti Lover." "The twin pipes really talk to you even at idle. When the revs go up there comes an organ tone played by a mad monk by candlelight." "An elderly friend of mine was found drooped over the bonnet of his type 35," Addams had written, "and I have often wondered if he succumbed to some final exasperation or whether his arteries were unable to cope with the excessive love I know he felt for this jewel of a car." He drew some sketches in the back of his datebook for a decal racing number, Bugatti No. 8. He was sixty-four years old.

On January 27, 1979, a Saturday, Addams was walking Alice on Sixth Avenue, trying to figure out why the press was swarming around his apartment building. He had asked one of the building staff, a man he generously tipped at Christmas, what was going on, but the man had suddenly clammed up. Ordinarily, Addams would have been in Water Mill with Tee, but dinner plans with Barbara and Henry Colyton and Jane Gunther had kept him in town.

The initial report in *The New York Times* said that seventy-year-old Nelson Rockefeller, vice president under Gerald Ford and four-time governor of New York, had died of a heart attack while working on a book about modern art in his office at 30 Rockefeller Center. An unnamed personal security aide had been with him at the time, said the paper, and attempted to revive the governor. Rockefeller had apparently been in good health, with "no history of serious illness."

As Rockefeller's longtime spokesman, Hugh Morrow, stumbled over his official statements, the papers printed contradictory accounts of the time of death, the location of the body, the governor's state of dress, who was present when he died, and the identity of the 911 caller who reported Rockefeller's collapse. There was a nagging question about why an hour had elapsed between the time Rockefeller was stricken and the time the paramedics were called. Then the story cracked open. Rockefeller had not died in his office, as first stated, but at a brownstone he owned at 13 West Fifty-fourth Street, which was linked by a private walkway to Addams's building at 25 West Fifty-fourth. And he had not been with his personal security aide, but with twenty-six-year-old Megan Marshack, his assistant on the art book and other projects. It was she who had tried to revive Rockefeller with mouth-to-mouth resuscitation. About a year earlier, the former governor had officially lent Marshack $45,000 to buy an apartment in Charlie's building, a debt forgiven in his will.

While the press was staking out his building, Addams was conducting his own investigation. Though he had met Megan in the elevator before Rockefeller's death, and had never taken her out, he told Leila Hadley he was in the sack with Megan the day after Rockefeller died. It was "fast work," a stunned Leila told him, "even for *you*, Charlie." Addams later delighted in telling friends how Megan had struggled to get the governor's shoes on after rigor mortis had set in. "Everything you've read—all the gossip—it's all true," he told Steven Aronson.

Now he began seeing Megan on certain weeknights when he was in

New York, taking her to dinner and the movies (*Dracula* at the Cinema Studio). Megan Marshack was a departure from the mature, sophisticated women of the Addams harem. She was all buttery lines—a young, plump, pretty version of a type Addams liked to draw. She wore big glasses, which gave her the incongruous look of a young girl playing dress-up. And she was both notorious and "child-like," said Frank Modell, who took Megan out himself once. Sometimes she would telephone

Tee and Charlie in Gretel Harrison's 1908 Columbia Electric.

to say, "I'm lying in bed, lusting after you," Addams told friends. And yet she didn't know what an orgasm felt like. She had never had one, she said.

"You must have—why not?" asked Addams. "She answered, 'Nelson Rockefeller having a heart attack and dying in my arms, that's why.' I realized that didn't explain it, but I let it go."

Addams described an orgasm to her: "It's like a flock of geese flying out of your ass."

"Oh," said Marshack.

If Addams had listened to his art, he might have stopped seeing Megan Marshack sooner than he did. The cartoons he sold to *The New Yorker* that fall and winter struck a common theme: In the first, a caption-less drawing, a robed and sandaled man resembling Charles Addams as-

"There's no cause for panic, Mrs. Munson, but, frankly, there are certain indicators that cannot be ignored."

sumes the defensive position as he confronts a banana peel on the floor. ("Karate banana," Addams labeled it.) In the second cartoon, a particularly fine one, later reprinted and anthologized, a matron consults her stockbroker in his city office. "There's no cause for panic, Mrs. Munson, but, frankly, there are certain indicators that cannot be ignored," says the broker. The view from his window shows a crisscrossing, partly shaded expanse of windows, and a number of strategically placed small figures poised to jump from office rooftops and ledges, which the reader's eye discovers gradually as it moves from left to right. The third cartoon shows a businessman in opaque glasses walking to the end of a barren corridor precipitously dropping off into thin air. PLEASE HOLD RAIL, says a wall sign.

But the Marshack entries in Addams's datebooks continued. Then gossip items and photographs began turning up in the press, and the tolerant Tee had finally had enough. "Marry me, or else," she told him—or so friends heard it. Tee herself later denied giving Charlie an ultimatum, though she did tell him to "cut it out," or something to that effect, she said. She even asked Lyda to help her persuade Charlie to marry her.

On January 16, 1980, about a year after the May-December affair had begun, Addams took Megan to the West Village to see the new Wallace Shawn play, *Marie and Bruce,* a talky, crude, sexy, uncomfortable one-act about a New York couple who take turns blasting each other in filthy language and assuming the role of victim. Frank Modell had a small part in the show, which perhaps explained Addams's attendance. "8 [P.M.] Frank show—Meg," he had written in his little book. Whether because of the play's bruising dialogue, which was delivered so authentically in a later performance that the entire first row of the audience walked out, or because Addams had finally seen himself clearly—as a sixty-eight-year-old man with a grandfatherly beard, a trench coat, and a baby-faced young thing in a fur coat on his arm—certain indicators could no longer be ignored.

"Beard off," Addams scribbled in his datebook the day after the show. "I got rid of the girl, got rid of the beard, and got rid of the trench coat," he told Kennedy Fraser.

Three months later, he married Tee.

—

Chapter Twenty-one

The Way It Was

T HEY WERE MARRIED IN THE PET CEMETERY AT TOAD HALL, under "appropriately gloomy skies," noted *The New York Times*, at five o'clock in the afternoon on the last day of May. The bride wore black. The groom wore dark glasses following eye surgery for a torn retina four days earlier. One day he was seeing spots—"eye flashes," as he elegantly put it in his datebook. The next, he was ambling along Tee's lawn toward a specially prepared place beneath a Japanese pine tree.

The tree stood next to the small graveyard, which was dressed up for the occasion with Bridal Veil hedges in pots rented from a local nursery. Tee had planted alyssum at the stone figures marking the graves of some of her dearest pets: five dogs, a cat, and a turtle. The couples' four beribboned dogs, in yellow, including Alice "and her dog, too—she has a dog," Addams explained to a reporter, served as indifferent attendants, crashing out the door of Tee's house ahead of the bride, then romping along Burdett's Creek with the guests' dogs during the ceremony. The human attendants—Dona Guimares and Lyda Hall—carried yellow and white bouquets, and wore long black dresses. Bedford Davie, now a senior at Vanderbilt University, and Charlie's godson since a late-life baptism, served as best man. No fewer than four judges presided, two from the state court, two from the civil court. Their long black robes fluttered under the ominous sky as they crossed the sloping lawn leading down from the house.

Tee made a memorable bride. "She looked lovely," said Addams with a smile. Her full-length black velvet Calvin Klein dress, borrowed from Dona, seemed designed for her sleek dark looks and high cheekbones. She held a small fan of peacock feathers and white stock, tied with a simple black ribbon. "You either camp it up—you go all the way—or don't," stylish Dona had advised when Tee said she was going to wear black.

"You either camp it up—you go all the way—or don't."
Dona Guimares, Charlie, Tee, and Lyda Hall, May 31, 1980.

They moved into place. As if on cue, it began to sprinkle. Some of the eighty-odd guests—including Irwin Shaw, Budd Schulberg, Joseph Heller, Cheryl Tiegs, Constantin Alajalov, and Daphne Hellman—most of whom thought they had been invited to celebrate the honorary doctorate of fine arts that Addams had just been awarded by the University of Pennsylvania—huddled beneath black umbrellas. Only about twenty people had been let in on the secret and told to wear black. "Don't forget to bring the dog with you," Addams had told Frank Corwin, referring to Corwin's dog, Wiz, of whom the other dogs were afraid. Each one of the four judges said something—"everyone wanted to get in on it," said Tee—though only one, Justice Richard W. Wallach of the New York State Supreme Court, performed the actual ceremony. Shirley Baty took informal photographs. Kay Leperq picked ticks off the dogs.

Once Charlie and Tee had decided to get married, they didn't remember how to do it—"in spite of having been married about eight times between them," cracked Shirley Baty. As Tee recalled years later, one of them, she or Charlie, said, "You take blood someplace." One said, "You get a license . . . Where do you go?" And so they consulted the never-married Dona, who suggested a justice of the peace. Shirley knew a married couple who were both judges, Ira Gammerman and Margaret Taylor, and offered to ask them. "They've got to wear their long black robes," said Tee. Though both judges wanted to come to Charles Addams's wedding, as civil court judges they could not actually officiate. And so they asked Justice Wallach, whom they knew, and somehow a fourth judge who wanted to come to Charles Addams's wedding invited himself. This hanger-on did a card trick in the middle of the ceremony, making Tee angry. Addams omitted him from the two color drawings he did to commemorate the event.

In both, Uncle Fester wears a blue suit and black tie and shades—not Addams's shades, but the kind Charlie had given the Three Blind Mice. He stands under a dripping black umbrella held aloft by a grinning skeletal figure hovering behind him; Morticia clutches his arm. In one rendition, the couple, attended by Alice B. Curr, face Judges Gammerman and Taylor. In the other version, with Justice Wallach, a wistful orange critter, Tee's New Dog, peers at them over a tombstone. "I'm not sure it's a dog at all," said Addams. In lieu of payment, Addams made the respective judges a surprise gift of the drawings. He captioned them "The Way It Was."

The new Mr. and Mrs. Addams thoroughly enjoyed the day. They posed for wedding pictures in front of the pet cemetery, and joked it up with the *Times* reporter Dona had perhaps arranged to have there, offering quotable remarks. The black dress, explained the bride, was in deference to her new husband. "He just likes black," she said. "He thought it would be nice and cheerful." Regarding the unconventional location, she explained, "It's my favorite place in the world. It's full of white flowers that I plant every year, and I hope that I will end up there myself. . . . Charles too," she added, sounding uncharacteristically formal.

"I know it's a bit impractical," said a chuckling Addams when he was asked whether he wanted to be buried in the pet cemetery, "but there are worse places."

The wedding gifts included a black bottle of champagne, a gimmicky foot-long bat with a push button that sent fake blood flowing through its clear veins, and a baboon skull with a red apple in its fangs. This last and best gift was from Jill and Roger Karas, local friends involved with ARF (the Animal Rescue Fund), who had been let in on the surprise nuptials, and who gave the couple a set of brass knuckles as well.

Asked about the honeymoon, Tee announced that she was traveling to Kenya to study hyenas in the wild. The groom would be staying home and working in his office at *The New Yorker*. But first, said Tee, "we're going to a motel in Garden City, Long Island."

Addams summed up the celebration. "I got to be a doctor," he said of his honorary Ph.D.; "I had an eye tear and I got married. Each was progressively worse." And then, noted the *New York Times* reporter, "he smiled."

"They were like kids—delighted with this new feeling about their wedding," said John Sparkman, whom Charlie and Tee met with to discuss a new will. On the morning of the wedding, they had sent off a giddy telegram to Odette, who was now living in San Francisco:

ONE GIANT STEP FOR MANKIND GETTING MARRIED
THIS AFTERNOON

ALL LOVE CHARLIE AND TEE

Amid the general merriment and well-wishing that came from such friends as Ralph Fields in London, who hailed "the beautiful and lucky ex–Mrs. Miller," there was a dissenter or two. Having heard about Addams's impending eye surgery, but not of the upcoming wedding, Barbara Colyton had telephoned the hospital early on the morning of the operation. Both of Addams's eyes had had to be bandaged the night before— an ordeal, given his claustrophobia. The sympathetic surgeon, Dr.

Jackson Coleman, had arranged for Tee to have a bed in the patient's room. Charlie and Tee had held hands all night. On the evening before the surgery, Tee had left instructions with the nurses that Mr. Addams was not to be disturbed. But whoever took the long-distance call was wowed by the Britishy voice identifying herself as Lady Colyton calling from London, and put the call through to Addams's room. Tee answered the phone. Mistaking her husky voice for Charlie's, Barbara cried, "Porker, darling!" and was greeted with a rude response such as she was not accustomed to hearing.

Had Bad Barbara known about the impending wedding, thought Tee, she might have persuaded Charlie not to go through with it.

"Love you madly," wrote Tee at the end of a typically lively letter from Nairobi in July, "—hope old Barbara not bugging you." But if Tee was seriously worried about untoward influences, she didn't let on. (Or scarcely: "Be careful of them geese," she added lightly.) She sounded like a bride on her second honeymoon, past blushing, serene. "It's wonderful belonging to you as Mrs. Addams. I am signing M. M. Addams constantly and being reminded of you," she wrote soon after her fifteen-hour flight.

The mission, which the animal-loving Tee undertook with the seriousness of an honors research student, and her usual pluck, was to study hyenas in the wild. Never one to write a soppy love letter, she crammed her missives to her new husband with funny and evocative prose snapshots of life in and out of the African bush: "Vultures nesting in tree near tent"; Masai "leaning on their spears when I came down to breakfast"; "hyena laughs and noises all night"; "leopard in the trees over my tent— thought I'd died and gone to heaven—the days would have been perfect for Running Fox," she wrote. After a face-to-face encounter with a lioness, even the intrepid Tee began relieving herself *inside* the tent, in a stainless-steel ice bucket swiped from the Hilton. And yet it had not made her fearful, or diminished her pleasure in being there. "Last night a sub-adult hyena dropped in for dinner—two huge shining green eyes on the other side of the fire," she wrote Charlie. "Impossible to tell males from females, except by feeling scrotum for balls."

As a member of Team III, Tee helped dig a five-foot-deep pit outside her tent to catch hyenas at night: "flickering firelite and flashlites—3 hyenas on their backs—Masai camp guards leaning on their spears & Daphne with her magnifying glass peering at their penis or whatever—God damn, I didn't bring the camera flash!" She helped tranquilize, measure, and catalog the creatures—the occasion for a breathless "lovely afternoon" drive across miles of open plain, where the team spotted "lion, zebras, antelope, gazelle, etc," and commenced a "mad chase" in pursuit of a tranquilized beast. Once they captured him, Tee held him in the back of the Land Rover, careful "to keep his head from bouncing as we hit the holes."

She pinned a "most welcome" photograph of Charlie over her "tin wash basin" and pressed on. "God, am so torn between missing you and wanting to be here," she wrote. "But know that I love you—even more than the varmint [*sic*] hyenas—the Wife."

The wife stayed away a month. She returned with rolls of film, two good vests with cloth-covered buttons she had found, after much searching for each of them, and a new contentment.

Though married life made no outward changes in their life together— Charlie and Alice still spent the weekdays in New York, while Tee remained in Water Mill—marriage worked a kind of magic on them both. During a sailing trip to the Virgin Islands with Constance Mellon, John Sargent, and others over the Christmas holidays, Charlie and Tee were noticeably happy. "T & Chas very cute together—he rather fussingly enjoying being fussed over by T," wrote Sargent in his diary. While Tee dived for conch with the other guests and the crew, Charlie remained on board "reading Capote's short pieces," noted Sargent. "The girls snorkel a bit and Addams and I recline trying to spot topless young ladies."

As Steven Aronson later observed, Tee had "had to work awfully hard to get [Charlie]." Even after Addams had agreed to the marriage, he had had his doubts. "Are you going to get married?" Buddy Davie had asked him. "I really don't think it's a good idea," said Addams.

And yet in rejoining the matrimonial ranks, Addams found himself surrendering few liberties. If he was not exactly free to swim off in lusty pursuit of Virgin Island mermaids, he was not quite hobbled, either. "Go ahead," Tee would say if he and Dona wanted to go antique hunting and stay overnight at a motel. Before the wedding Tee had said that she did not expect him and Dona to stop taking their antiquing trips, and she meant it. As long as he was discreet, she would not tie him to her. She got what she wanted, and she felt sure of what she and Charlie had together.

She also knew that Charlie was not in love with Dona. Though she was aware that they slept in the same room during their excursions, she privately assumed that the sex wasn't very good. (Dona was attractive, said Tee, but overweight, "with big piano legs.")

If Tee was a bit harsh in her judgments, she also knew Charlie. And she had a more selfish reason for taking a European attitude toward fidelity. Shortly after the wedding, she had lost interest in sex, and she was determined to keep her man. By all accounts, her strategy worked. Addams would say of Tee, "She's a great girl." As for the sex, said Leila Hadley, "he forgave her because he loved her."

The harem saw that Tee was good for Charlie at this time of his life. Even Barbara Hersey thought her first husband had gotten it right with Tee, whom she regarded as better suited to Charlie than she herself had been. Drue Heinz, who remembered Charlie in love with Barbara Skelton and in lust with any number of women, thought that he had always been in love with Tee but that the timing had not been right earlier. As far as she knew, Tee was the only woman he had ever wanted to marry, with the exception of the first Barbara.

And yet during the 1960s, Addams had asked Leila Hadley to marry him; but she was not yet divorced from Yvor Smitter, and she wasn't ready to think about getting married again. And according to *The New Yorker*'s Kay Leperq, just before Charlie married Tee, he had begged *her* to marry him—a claim that both Johnny Nicholson and Frank Modell found credible. Both men had witnessed Addams's long-standing desire for Kay. Nicholson had seen Charlie and Kay come into Café Nicholson all the time; they were "inseparable," he said. But Kay had been off men since her divorce, and she said she refused Charlie's proposal. (Kay also said that Charlie told her he had ten million dollars—probably a jest that she took seriously.)

If marrying Tee offered few surprises, Addams never voiced a regret about his decision. He settled happily into Toad Hall, a dwelling that helped compensate for the loss of his little house, now entirely Barbara's. He was at least still near the water, which he loved, in a place that had its own charms and pleasures. He liked to shoot rats with a rifle from an upper window of the house. And soon Tee bought him a beautifully renovated chicken coop, fitted with a door and windows that filled the room with light, so that he would have a quiet studio in which to work. It stood on the Burdett's Creek side of the house, where they had been married, and where there was a willow tree.

With Tee he found a home. Knowing how he loved to have people in, she gave him Derby Day, Super Bowl Day, and Christmas parties, serving plenty of good food.

And she was mad about his work. Playing E. B. White to Addams's Thurber, she scooped up the roughs for his *New Yorker* cover paintings that he was throwing away—fine watercolor miniatures that were sometimes quite different from the finished products—and had them ingeniously framed, with the small version in its own mat above the finish, forming a kind of window onto the artistic process. When she asked him to draw something as a raffle prize for her garden club and he presented her with a painting of Morticia watering a plant that sprouted from Uncle Fester's head, she couldn't bear to part with it. She hung it inside the bamboo armoire they used as a bar. On top sat the Ringling Bros. papier-mâché heads of the Addams Family, which grew progressively more sinister as evening shadows overtook the room. She photographed the Addams Family pumpkins Charlie made at Halloween, having carefully selected just the right shapes for his black ink faces at the Green Thumb nursery in Water Mill. When he painted the Family on a series of eggshells, she preserved them in a small glass case.

But Tee was no mere preservationist and helpmeet. She entered into Charlie's schemes with her own childlike glee, trimming the Christmas tree and painting and hiding Easter eggs, though there were no children on the premises to find them. Once, they spent two days making a two-story Victorian gingerbread house from scratch, which they meticulously trimmed with white icing, gumdrops, and peppermint candy. On their first married Halloween, Tee dressed the table in front of the fireplace in black velvet and set it with silver plate, matching cutlery and goblets, black candles, and the wedding baboon skull clenching the apple. The menu, Mr. and Mrs. Addams confided to a reporter for the *Bridgehampton Sun,* was funeral pie, stuffed beef heart, and bone marrow on toast, washed down with champagne. "It can be done with human bones," said Addams, "but that's less tasty."

The year before they were married, Tee had thrown herself into the decoration of the latest Addams conveyance, "the Heap," a seventeen-foot-long Dodge Sportsman van, bought on drunken impulse after lunch at Herb McCarthy's restaurant in Southampton. Charlie had picked up the advertising section of the paper, spied the seductive heading—

"Home Away From Home"—and off they had gone to see it, "half in the bag," remembered Tee.

They bought the van for $8,000 on credit and set about transforming it with Victorian oil lamps; an old green glass flower vase from an antique limousine; a small wine cellar; a stained glass panel separating the galley from the living quarters. There were two choice examples of the taxidermist's art: a wall-mounted partridge and a raven Leila Hadley had given Charlie, which rested on a brown velvet tablecloth as though it had just flown in. There was a dagger for show, and a handgun for protection, which Tee, who was the better shot, had no intention of entrusting to Charlie should the occasion arise. A naked baby picture of eighteen-month-old Charlie, grinning toothlessly as he stood in a basket "to protect my modesty," mingled with a photograph of General Winfield Scott and a panoramic shot of Teddy Roosevelt among the pup tents during the Spanish-American War, which Charlie placed above the driver's seat.

Talking to a 1981 interviewer, Addams was in his element. "Living in the Heap is like riding on a train in the great days of the first class Pullman cars," he said. "The Heap is the poor man's Lucius Beebe railroad car." So named because Addams regarded all American cars as heaps, the van boasted a tiny kitchen, a propane tank, a water closet, a stereo cassette player with four speakers for listening to Vivaldi, and a pullout sofa bed too small for Addams to sleep on, covered with needlepoint pillows. During their expeditions to Gettysburg and to "isolated campsites on barren ground with no trees," as Addams put it, they turned the bed over to the four dogs and slept outside in sleeping bags under a tent. "I'd love to take a trip to the Southwest," said Addams. "You know, Tombstone, Death Valley. We might pick up some nice mementoes there." Mr. and Mrs. Addams had driven the Heap as far south as Virginia, where Bunki was training horses for the Japanese Olympic team, and as far north as the Bay of Fundy. "Let's rev up the Heap," Charlie would say, and off they'd go, Charlie wearing his L. L. Bean hunting shoes—to Greensboro, Vermont, to visit Jane Gunther at her summer home, to the Sag Harbor cemetery for a picnic. Dinner plans with the renowned interior decorator Sister Parish? Charlie said, "I know, we'll give them a traveling cocktail party first." And off they went, roaring around the Hamptons. When Budd Schulberg got married, Charlie and Tee arrived in the Heap and had their own private cocktail party in the parking lot before the ceremony. Irwin Shaw got wind of it and came knocking at the back door, where a brass sign read:

BEWARE OF THE DOG
AS FROM 1ST MAY 1864,
SIR JOHN RUMBLELOW
WILL NOT BE RESPONSIBLE
FOR TRESPASSERS ATTACKED
BEYOND THIS POINT

And so the romance that had begun as a physical attraction in the late 1940s had turned all these years later into a life with children and pets. But the children were grown and gone, and there was no possibility of a baby—a state of affairs that pleased both husband and wife. Once when they were at a hotel in California with the car group, they found themselves in a room overlooking the pool, which was filled with the racket of kids in the morning. "I wish I had an alligator—I'd throw it in," grumbled Charlie, a sentiment with which Tee could agree, though she was a calming influence. "The invitation said nine o'clock," Tee reminded Charlie as he groused on the way over to Budd Schulberg's house in Westhampton Beach one night. "I'm sure the children will be in bed." But the young Schulberg children, who were always up late and running around at adult parties, had not been in bed. As one of them zoomed around the dining room table, Charlie stuck a foot out and tripped him.

Addams found that he liked being part of a family. When twenty-three-year-old Bedford got involved with a rich older woman married to a horse groom and stayed out all night, Charlie left him a warning in the form of a fake headline affixed to the *Daily News*.

HUSBAND SLAYS HEARST
HEIRESS, PLAYBOY LOVER
Stepson of Macabre Cartoonist Found by
Returning California Horse Groom

And instead of chastising Charlie for not being fatherly, Tee ran to get the camera.

In the end, whatever his private reservations might have been, life with the new Mrs. Addams agreed with her husband. During the week, he had all the excitement of New York. "Why, just the other day there were nine fire engines outside the University Club," Addams told a reporter. "I went down there, and immediately overheard a bag lady telling somebody '—— you' on a pay telephone. It appeared that a man had climbed 10 floors up the scaffolding of a building and was threatening to jump. A crowd had gathered, and some were coaxing him, of course. I saw a dreadful teenage boy drinking beer out of a paper bag, and then a policeman came over and threw him down on the sidewalk. . . . In the end, he didn't jump. I myself was not disappointed. Some others were."

And on the weekends there was Tee. "She matched his wit," said Drue Heinz. "It was lovely to hear them go backwards and forwards." Once painted as a female matador, Tee had actually tried her hand at bullfighting. She could ride a horse and herd cattle like a cowgirl, and still throw herself together with minimal makeup and fuss and look like a million.

Years earlier, when Charlie and Tee's friend Jay Rutherford had dropped in on Tee unannounced one too many times, she peeled off all her clothes before he reached the door of her glass-walled Japanese-style house in Easthampton and appeared to be casually going about her business when he saw her. He fled in embarrassment, forever cured of unannounced visits to Tee.

Addams drawing beneath a painting of Tee as a matador.

"We're having partridge for dinner!" she told Charlie on the phone one day. And when he came home, mouth watering at the good cooking smells, and asked where on earth she had managed to find a partridge this time of year, she said, "Roadkill." It turned out that she had been driving somewhere with a friend when the bird ran out in front of the car. It had been a clean kill, she explained. So she bagged the bird and brought it home. Charlie confined himself to the vegetables.

If Tee sometimes went too far, she was a great girl. Stepping on the accelerator to beat the red light, Addams called out, "Watch it! The old Heap's comin' through!" And he cackled.

Chapter Twenty-two

When It Stops Being Fun,
I'll Quit

"DEAR MR. ADDAMS: TODAY I WAS PLEASANTLY SURPRISED to learn that you are still alive," wrote the fan asking for an autograph on an enclosed copy of a cartoon. And it wasn't a recent letter, either. It had been lying around the Addams apartment for eight years.

It had amused him enough to keep it. "You look at George Price, who's eighty," Addams said by way of a reply in a 1981 interview with John Grossman for *TWA Ambassador*. "He's still going strong. So I'm just a kid of sixty-nine." But his age was starting to tell. He sometimes forgot things now, such as a birthday greeting he had been asked to write. Never mind. He would keep drawing "as long as I don't get arthritis of the hands," he said. Among the cartoon roughs he hadn't worked into a finish was a cheery executioner waiting on a scaffold surrounded by an impatient mob. "When it stops being fun, I'll quit," he tells the black-hooded priest.

At the brink of seventy, Addams felt very much alive, and looked it. He was big and lived-in, with a small potbelly and strong arms that could still pull his Bugatti by a rope and draw back the target bow of the seventeenth-century German crossbow he pointed out to a guest. He had the same sleek hair, now silvery, like a hood ornament, and in need of a trim. His kindly, drooping face still resembled Walter Matthau's. A cabdriver had been excited the day he dropped Addams off in New York, thinking he had been driving Matthau.

Nearly fifty years after his first sale to *The New Yorker*, he was still a freelancer, and making a living by his art alone. Not once since the Depression-era days when he had lightened the blood in crime scene photographs at *True Detective* had he ever had to do anything but draw

"When it stops being fun, I'll quit."

cartoons. He had begun the year with more than $20,000 in his checking account. And he could still make the gossip pages in New York. During a Long Island benefit for ARF, noted Page Six of the *New York Post*, Addams had stepped outside a restaurant in Bridgehampton to relieve himself and was caught by a cop. "What if my wife saw you doing that?" the policeman scolded. "Why, she'd be delighted," said Addams.

If he had not been completely tamed, his habits were regular enough. He rose "fairly early"—between eight and eight-thirty; "I read the paper and have breakfast. I take Alice out for a walk. It's usually about two hours before I really get going. The tough part is to make yourself sit down. Your time's your own, and in a way you're always retired," he said.

After a sluggish start to the new year—one *New Yorker* cover published, and no new sales in all of January—he averaged a few sales a month, including the Addams originals sold at the Nicholls Gallery. He was in fact having "a dry spell"; by year's end, his black leather spiral notebooks would record a total yearly income of $30,681.28, a plunge from a heady $112,655.05 just twelve months earlier, in 1980.

He dug around in the "idea box," as he called the *New Yorker* slush pile. He'd been trying to come up with a Valentine's cover one day when he found himself doodling valentines. "Then I happened to look across the room to where someone had placed a poster." It was a reprint of a 1979 captionless Addams cartoon: A bland little man in thick glasses is fastening the fourth of seven deadbolts to the door of his apartment—an arrangement that looked very much like the Addams fortress at 25 West Fifty-fourth—as a tiny saw cuts a circle around his feet on the floor. "I thought: A Valentine!" said Addams. In the new version, the man stands before his heavily locked door as a valentine slips underneath—a cover that "made me weep," wrote the former longtime publisher of the *New York Post*, Dorothy Schiff.

Yet another variation that remained in rough form showed a man in a seedy room aiming a machine gun at the door as a valentine slides underneath.

He enjoyed reworking a theme ("perhaps it becomes a mild obsession," he had told Philip French) and drawing the same figure repeatedly, such as the Santa Clauses in a 1980 rigged-court cartoon in which Scrooge stands trial before a Santa judge, Santa jury, and Santa prosecutor. (He admitted that "maybe Scrooge was the most fun of all.") He still aimed for the captionless cartoon—"a small victory." It was the highest he could go in cartoon art—which was not to say that cartoons were "great art, but they're not as low on the art ladder as some people think. I don't think what I do is any less good because it happens to be funny." He liked drawing sequences, "but not too many of them lend themselves to that and I find that economy is the best policy," he explained. As for his subject matter, he had never tired of tiny people, the Minotaur, English explorers, and those New York elevator operators who somehow looked "exactly alike." After decades of lavishing pencil and ink on intricate structures, the architect's son still relished the chance to draw "a complicated picture" such as the baronial house in a 1980 cartoon—a charmingly detailed rendering that had required some research and "a day and a half's work," though Addams completed many of his cartoons in "three and four hours." As the staff of fourteen assembles before the castlelike manor house, the butler

reads an announcement: "Inflationary pressures oblige us to reduce expenditures. Therefore, the following three staff members shall be dismissed." And the reader's appreciative eyes travel up the queue of uniformed figures, picking out the jester, the falconer—and, following two nondescript manservants, including one who bears a subtle resemblance to Charles Addams (but Addams in a toupee), the wizard.

Doodling—"the brooding of the hand," Steinberg called it—

accounted for "about 60 per cent" of Addams's ideas, by his own estimation. His brooding hand had produced hundreds of unpublished roughs lying around the apartment, covering everything from such classic Addams themes as hell and grim reapers, cemeteries and torture chambers, slave ships, and the war between men and women, to more timely subjects, including the intrusion of advertising into daily life: On the box of the Little Match Girl is imprinted "Matches—A Division of Amatco."

Though Addams maintained a high standard of professionalism at *The New Yorker,* in private he "was always terribly offended" when a rough was rejected, said Al Hirschfeld, who had long admired his friend's "wonderful, strange talent," which "defies analysis." Addams himself "was always enchanted with the things they turned down," added Hirschfeld.

Such as a castle scene surrounded by the peasant population. "And the wizard has come out dangling a frog and says, 'It's a boy.' " Addams had described the cartoon to Dick Cavett, who wondered who could possibly reject it. "Someone in a bad mood on Tuesdays," said Addams.

There was always something he could do to make money—an advertising assignment (Dewar's, Chivas Regal), or a cartoon collection, though there was "no money" in such books anymore beyond the publisher's advance. ("People seem to be buying 'how-to' books instead," Addams noted. Nevertheless, *Creature Comforts,* his tenth cartoon collection, came out that year.) Or he might do a special illustration, such as the *New York Times* drawing he'd done in 1976 to accompany a reprint of Ogden Nash's "Election Day Is a Holiday." (Addams had come up with Uncle Fester in a suit, sitting in a gentleman's home library holding a book as an angry mob of protesters outside his window floats his likeness on a pike.) He did drawings for ARF fund-raisers, which were printed on sweatshirts and invitations, and for Boys Harbor, a New York City educational organization for inner-city youths. Addams had long helped raise money by donating his own cartoons for auction—an act that had prompted local artists to do the same. He also served as a judge for the children's pet fair. One year when he and Budd Schulberg were both judging—Schulberg assigned to fowl because of his interest in swans, Addams to reptiles for obvious reasons—he said, "Budd is an expert on swans, but if they bring in any ravens or vultures, I'll judge them."

It was a measure of his youth and optimism that when Whatman board was discontinued by the English manufacturers, Addams bought all he could find and stored it under the bed in his apartment. "I think I have enough in my studio to last me the rest of my life," he commented.

Except for the weekends, when he went home to Tee in Water Mill, bringing along the roughs he was working on, his time was luxuriously his own. He read. "Unlike many cartoonists," commented Chip McGrath, "Charles Addams actually read the magazine." He liked humor writer Veronica Geng; he knew historical trivia. He apparently read an Anne Tyler novel. ("Dinner at the Homesick Restaurant—Tyler," he wrote in his 1982 datebook.) "I just do what I feel like, really. I'll sometimes go to a museum, the park, or look around antique shops to see if I can get any more crossbows," he said. He loved the Staten Island Zoo for its snakes, particularly "a very poisonous little green snake." Once he painted the Bugatti black. On the day George Booth and his wife came to visit, Addams explained that this particular car was always painted blue, but he thought black was better. "Yes, Charles, it's warmer," said Booth. Charlie's upper lip twitched.

He and Dona would set off in the Benchley for some arcane place, such as a streetcar museum, Dona holding a cigarette and wearing one of her pairs of enormous tinted glasses. She would climb into the car and promptly fall asleep, exhausted from her demanding job as editor of the Home section of the *Times*. But she was always game for something new that might be interesting. She wasn't fussy about motels, and she adored Alice. Their favorite pastime was rummaging around the Long Island dumps and rooting out treasures (an old tub, a small jacket).

He still spent untold hours investigating cemeteries and reading the tombstones. "I'm glad that it has become chic to do it," he had told an interviewer. He visited Sherman's statue in the Grand Army Plaza on the corner of Fifth Avenue, opposite the Plaza, where people accumulated on benches. "After five minutes of looking at people there, even my oddest drawings begin to look mild by comparison," he had told Thurber. Once, after cleaning out his bookcase, he took the books over to St. Patrick's Cathedral and left them on the ledge. Then he stood across the street in the rain, watching to see who picked up the books and carried them away.

Gillis Addison often ran into him on Fifth Avenue looking in the window of Bergdorf's. Gardner Botsford "was studying a display of miniature woodworking drills and scrapers in the window of a hardware store on Sixth Avenue—tiny little things, used by advanced cabinetmakers—when Addams, who had been passing by, moved in beside me. 'Planning to fill your own teeth?' he asked."

Sometimes he sauntered over to the New York Public Library to research something; he might "check a book on medievalism to get a window just right" before he turned in a rough. He once spent hours in an aquarium studying the difference between freshwater and saltwater fish.

Those close to him had long since learned to recognize when he was dreaming about his work, and to leave him alone. "I live in my imagination quite a bit," he admitted. "I imagine things and they become acted out in my mind, dialogue and all. Usually an argument of some sort which of course I always win." As Tee passed by the spare room at home, where Charlie was hunched over his drawing board working on a finish, she'd see his tongue inching out as he concentrated.

He had recently depicted himself as the pajama-clad husband in a cartoon. "More coffee, honey?" asks the dim-looking frump in a matching bathrobe. "Who *is* she?" thinks the man who looks like Addams, raising his eyes heavenward from his paper.

YOU ARE HERE says the sign in the tunnel dripping stalactites. The hamburger, fries, and soda look up from their canoe with anxious little faces, gripping the sides as the current swirls around them. The arrow on the sign points to an illustration of the stomach of an adolescent boy wearing a baseball cap.

During the health-conscious eighties, references to cooking with fresh vegetables and herbs found their way into *New Yorker* cartoons. "It's going to be great!" says the fat witch to her ugly sisters as she stirs the bubbling cauldron of snakes, frogs, and unmentionables. "All natural ingredients." (Addams listed the 1981 drawing in his earnings notebook as "Natural Brew.")

But timely subjects remained the exception in his work. As more cartoons reflected the culture's concern with celebrities and the trendy, the cartoonist who favored antiques, listened to classical music and Dixieland, and was delighted that no one recognized his face on the street, stuck to the old standards. Let other artists take on Phil Donahue, Michael Jackson, and Joan Rivers; Addams offered the Mona Lisa, Henry VIII,

Whistler's Mother, Rodin's Thinker, and Federico di Montefeltro gathered around the television set to watch *Masterpiece Theatre*. When other cartoonists drew "the great communicator," Ronald Reagan, Addams turned to that truly great talker, lexicographer, essayist, and poet, Dr. Johnson, "[getting] off a good one."

Addams's answer to the designer labels on clothing, which had turned people into walking billboards? "The T-Shirt of Dorian Gray."

In Hell a sparsely populated express lane appeared: "Six Sins or Less."

Among *New Yorker* cartoonists, Addams remained "completely different from anyone else," said Mischa Richter—"one of the pillars that held *The New Yorker* up." He was "beyond imitation," said Lee Lorenz, who considered Addams one of the half dozen most important comic graphic artists of the twentieth century. George Booth was happily upset by a 1983 Addams cartoon juxtaposing the innocent with the fantastic as only Addams could: As a man sits reading the paper by a window on a very dark night, his bland-looking wife stands outside the house in a shawl, leaving a long shadow that melts into the darkened shrubbery. "Maynard, I do think that just this once you should come out and see the

"Maynard, I do think that just this once you should come out and see the moon!"

moon!" she cries, as a gargantuan, pockmarked moon blocks out the night sky. "I couldn't sleep last night because of that moon cartoon," Booth wrote Addams in an uncharacteristic fan letter. Addams himself was sufficiently pleased with the cartoon to decline to sell the original.

Saul Steinberg—"Charlie's biggest fan," said Lee Lorenz—had long admired "the secondary ideas, which were creeping always into Charlie's work," the familiar things that in an Addams cartoon "became alarming." A 1983 Halloween cover by Addams had forever changed the way Steinberg saw taxis. On an eerily lit Upper East Side corner, a taxi has stopped in front of an apartment building. As the ordinary woman in brown pays the fare, both the cabdriver and the doorman stare at the small ghost, goon, clown, and witch who have just alighted. "But the real protagonist," Steinberg noted, "was the taxi cab." In Addams's palette of orange and yellow, the cab "looked like an American car, a normal American car, dressed up as a clown for Halloween."

In Addams's recent work, Steinberg was delighted by a "natural revolution toward the political," by which he meant "the sense of the conflict between the individual and the power," which he considered "a most important function of a cartoon in a magazine." He cited the cartoons in which Addams had abandoned Victorian architecture for "the corporation and bank architecture—what's called the Park Avenue Bauhaus." In an Addams drawing, "the familiar windows of a modern building" would "turn the corner—a spooky thing in itself," becoming "dangerous." One saw "the blinding lights" and "the emptiness" of modern architecture that "renders one short and inadequate."

"The most sinister place of all," Addams had said, "is a modernistic house that is going to pieces. It has a strange mausoleum quality, especially in the moonlight, all that blank dead-white cement with cracks running across it, those rusted iron pipes and huge glittering dead windows." Addams had followed his 1979 "no cause for panic" cartoon, showing prospective suicides positioned on the glass towers outside a stockbroker's window, with one set in a similar high-rise stockbroker's office, where a lifeboat hangs outside the window. In another captionless drawing, a mountain goat appears on a girder at a construction site towering above the mass of soulless architecture below. Addams "hated what was happening to the skyline in New York."

But let Steinberg intellectualize. "My cartoons don't have any political slant," Addams had said years earlier. "I'm not trying to say anything. I'm just trying to be funny." As for posterity, "if my drawings are remembered at all later on, I would think people would believe they reflected the period, and I think you do reflect your times."

Chapter Twenty-three

A Day with Frank Modell

O N   A   W E D N E S D A Y   M O R N I N G   I N   S E P T E M B E R   1988,   A D D A M S
and Frank Modell headed out to Connecticut to see a house Modell was
considering buying.

They had a long day ahead. After seeing the house, the old friends
planned to visit James Stevenson, who lived five minutes away from
Modell's current place in Guilford. They had been down this road before.
The last time Modell had brought Addams to see a house he wanted, he
had ended up not buying it, though he himself thought it was great. The
house was in the woods, observed Addams, and "very depressing."

Addams himself was living in a swamp now. By 1985, having become
unhappy with the development of the land on the other side of Burdett's
Creek, Tee had begun to make noises about moving. She had found a
much more private house she liked in nearby Sagaponack—a modest
shingled dwelling nestled in eighty-seven acres of conservation land,
much of it wetland. Addams didn't really want to move again. He loved
their slip of water at Toad Hall, the only water view he had now. And he
still enjoyed shooting rats along the creek. He took aim with a .22 from
the breakfast nook, then bragged that he was getting to be "a pretty good
shot." Tee had snapped a picture of him brandishing a rifle in one gloved
hand, dangling a rat by the tail in another. A copy of the photograph
hung on the wall next to the bar at Meghan's Pub in Water Mill, above a
message advertising the ratcatcher's services for $10 a day, plus carfare.

Still, Tee wanted to move. She promised that Charlie wouldn't have to do a thing. She would handle all the packing, everything; he would simply have to drive himself over to the new house. And she had been true to her word. On the appointed day, a grim-faced Uncle Fester in a suit took his place on the wooden raft before the four dogs, the solitary suitcase, and Morticia, who held the cat. He pushed a long stick through the waterways to their new home. "The Addams Family is moving to the swamp," Addams wrote in his neat hand below the drawing that Tee had printed as a change-of-address card.

On their first day in the new house, Addams had gotten up in the dark. From the surrounding swamp came bloodcurdling screams—the sound of possums mating, Tee later speculated, though it was perhaps a fisher, the dark-colored marten who stalked the wetlands, rooting rabbits from their nests. Addams returned to bed. "Someone is murdering babies in the swamp," he said. "Oh, darling," came the sleepy reply from the pillows, "I forgot to tell you about the neighbors."

"All my life I've wanted to live in one of those Addams Family houses, but I've never achieved that," Addams had recently told a reporter. "I do my best to add little touches," he said. "I have these stained glass windows." He was waiting for a bat house he'd ordered. Still, he conceded, "it's hard to convert a ranch-type house into a Victorian monster." He had had his bathroom walls painted black with a lacquer finish. He had been firm about the lacquer. When the workmen did it in buff, Tee made them correct it. Addams hung some old portraits he'd done of Pugsley and Morticia on one wall; in the strip between the bathtub and the window looking out on grass and trees, he placed his framed yellowing baby boots. To the right of the mirror over the sink, where he could see them as he shaved or reached for one of the white bath towels embroidered with large black *A*'s, he had arranged two obscene Cobean portraits of himself from the Signal Corps days, and a Steinberg sketch of a pointing hand. Inside the extended index finger were branching roots.

Along with the pleasure Addams derived from these sketches, they were touchstones from the old *New Yorker*. Steinberg was in the magazine "all too seldom now," Addams reflected. So was Whitney Darrow, Jr. But George Price was still at work; Addams spent an afternoon with him at the Metropolitan Museum. Charles Saxon, another artist Addams admired, was still publishing in *The New Yorker*. And Modell was still turn-ing up. In the sunny spare room that faced the front of the new house, his drawing room, he had hung an African cartoon by Darrow and a framed Modell from 1966 showing a grumpy man in a hammock, head raised ir-

The Addams Family is moving to the Swamp.

ritably from his book toward a bird singing his heart out on a branch. "All right, all right! Knock it off!" he cries.

THE *TIMES* THIS SEPTEMBER morning promised sunshine, with highs in the seventies, in both New York and Connecticut. The sun would scatter the patchy clouds and chase them out to sea. As Addams and Modell zoomed north in Addams's car, making detours off the beaten path and occasionally getting lost, Addams was in fine form. They talked about everything from the old Lackawanna railroad, whose 1907 Beaux Arts terminal was in Hoboken, New Jersey, to women, crossbows, and cars, a natural Addams progression of ideas. Quite apart from the women, Addams "had more toys than any grown man," Modell reflected, chuckling. (Seen another way, Addams's conversation was all of a piece, part of a wide-ranging aesthetic appreciation: the architecturally splendid Lackawanna terminal and its museum-worthy locomotives painted a memorable gray with maroon and gold trim were not such a stretch from etched and chiseled weapons, the sculptural lines of a classic car, or a beautiful woman.)

While they talked, Addams pushed jazz tapes in and out of the cassette player. He was driving an Audi turbo now—"the death car," as Tee called it—which had replaced the commodious "Benchley." The manufacturer had done a recall of the brakes, which made Tee uneasy about it. And then there was the matter of Charlie's reflexes, which were not as good as they had been. (Barbara Nicholls had been riding with him in his Aston Martin in a race a few years earlier when she saw a man on the track waving a flag and asked Charlie what it meant. "I don't know. I wasn't paying attention," he said.)

Tee had come to feel the way Alice did about riding with him; they finally compromised by taking separate cars when they went places together. Modell saw the advantage. "If you ever want to trade your Audi for my Dodge . . ." he would say. And Charlie, a forbidden cigar between his teeth, would give his little smile.

The day with Modell was just what Addams needed. Though he still spent the weekdays in New York, he wasn't having as much fun. Beginning the year after his marriage, he had experienced a series of reversals that curtailed his activities. First, another "ulcer upset," as he had put it in his 1982 datebook, had forced him to give up alcohol altogether. Then in 1983 came surgery for a blocked carotid artery. "He came out of it an old man," said Tee. And he suddenly began to look like one—a whiter, rounder version of himself. (Was it a coincidence that he had drawn himself and Uncle Fester into two angel cartoons published that year?) Even his handwriting changed; sometimes it was almost hard to read. More recently, he had acquired a hearing aid.

He had had a couple of scares when he became woozy in the car.

Along with monitoring his diabetes, he had to have his eyes checked regularly, perhaps because of the diabetes, which put him at risk for blindness as well as stroke, heart disease, and other maladies. The datebooks that had once been crammed with women's names and parties now read

Drawing for Tee.

like a roster for the American Medical Association: "4:15 Mirsky . . . 11:30 Dr. Coleman . . . 10:15 Dr. Paglia . . . 10:45 Fletcher . . . 4:15 Mirsky," went a typical series of entries. If he wasn't careful, he'd end up as "Sad Mary," as he called the *New York Times* writer Mary Cantwell. Every time she came out to Quogue to stay with Dona on the weekends, she seemed to have a cold or the flu; she would be bundled up and taking medication. "I've never seen anyone look sicker in my life," said Addams.

He had become one of the damned souls in his own 1983 cartoon, forever sentenced to look at, but never reach, the well-stocked bar across Hell's impassable divide. And so he socialized less often. Budd Schulberg ran into Addams at a party at Joe Loesser's, which they were both leaving early. It wasn't fun going to parties now that he couldn't drink, said Addams. The brief encounter saddened Schulberg. His old friend seemed "frail," he thought, "his days numbered." At *New Yorker* parties, Addams had even struck cartoonist P. L. Steiner as "kind of grumpy." (Not that Charles Addams should be interested in meeting *him,* said Steiner.)

And friends noticed that Addams had become prickly about politics. Since becoming a Republican, he had turned into "the most conservative of the conservatives." "This guy is bad news," he'd once said of Eugene McCarthy. And yet Addams "wasn't very political," said Arthur Schlesinger, Jr., who saw the Addams Republicanism as a response to the excesses of the 1960s.

Though he and Tee had given up the Heap, and he had "reluctantly" sold both the Aston Martin and the Bugatti—a passing he commemorated with a painting of a hearse pulling a Bugatti on a flatbed—there were good days, too, and trips. "Let's go!" he'd say at the sound of the town's fire alarm. In London that spring, he had "seemed just like his old self," thought a friend. In Washington, D.C., at the beginning of the year, where he was helping to promote a traveling show, "The Art of *The New Yorker:* A 60-Year Retrospective," which the magazine had been advertising with an Addams Family drawing done for the occasion, he hammed it up for Tee's camera. When Addams and the other *New Yorker* people were invited to meet President Reagan, Charlie "was up to no good," noted George Booth. Outside the White House, Addams regaled Booth with some off-color jokes he was going to tell the president.

However diminished, Addams still found much in which to rejoice. On his infrequent visits to the office of his new lawyer on Forty-second Street, he enjoyed studying the mansard roof of Grand Central Terminal. He had perhaps been contemplating the terminal's roof, which he never tired of looking at, when he turned up at John Sparkman's office one day to sign his new will, and forgot to bring a witness. (By now, Greenbaum, Wolff & Ernst had been dissolved.) At the last minute, Sparkman got the doorman in the lobby to serve. Addams "took nothing solemnly," said a delighted Sparkman.

Along with booze he had also virtually given up cigars—another pleasure fallen away, though it had worked wonders for his appearance. ("He turned pink," said Nancy Holmes, adding that he had been "gray, reeking of cigars," before.) Gone were the lazy lunches with drinks followed by an afternoon kibitz with Sidney Offit upstairs at Dunhill's. Having enjoyed the private humidors in the Rockefeller Center sanctuary, they would saunter down the sidewalk. "I'm not ready to sleep till I finish this cigar," the cartoonist would say in his drowsy Addams voice.

Throughout all of 1988, he wrote nothing in his datebook until September 15, when he recorded an appointment with Dr. Mirsky, whom he saw for his diabetes, and a one o'clock meeting on the twenty-seventh with a Knopf editor, Katherine Hourigan, who wanted to discuss a couple of prospective cartoon collections. Nor had he jotted down his recent visit to the zoo with Axie Whitney, when they caught up on news and laughed at the seals, or his lunch with Drue Heinz, also at the new children's zoo in Central Park, where Addams loved to watch the gorillas. He had played the role of tour guide, showing Drue all around the zoo. He offered to drive her out to Long Island to see Tee, but Drue was as little tempted as Tee to get into a car with Charlie, and she declined. "I just told you, I don't drink anymore," he said. "I drive like an angel." Finally they agreed that Drue would join him and Tee in Sagaponack during the weekend.

In the datebooks where Addams had long recorded the deaths of those important to him—"Katie dies," he had written on August 26, 1979; "New Dog dies," he wrote on August 2, 1982, after one of Tee's wonderful dogs drowned, an event Addams took hard (Steven Aronson remembered Charlie's eyes squinting up with tears); "Geraghty memorial," he scribbled sadly on April 23, 1983—the passing of Jack Heinz in 1987 was conspicuously absent. Along with Jim Geraghty, whose death had "most depressed" Addams, Heinz had been a close friend; if they had only one Monte Cristo cigar between them, they'd cut it in half. It wasn't like Addams to let such a passing occur without putting a marker in the little book, the nearest he came to a diary. But he had inscribed one death that year, a loss that perhaps accounted for all the white space he hadn't had the heart to fill. "Alice dies," he wrote in the block for June 11, 1987, and drew a simple cross.

After seventeen years together, they had both become softer and whiter. The wiry fur around Alice's face had become patchy and worn, like the moth-eaten coats of stuffed animals found in antiques stores; her

Addams and Alice.

eyes had taken on the urgent, glassy look of an old dog. Finally she had become incontinent, and Addams had had to put her to bed at night in his black bathroom. She could no longer make the weekly commute in and out of New York. Her traveling days over, she ran around and around the Sagaponack house in a slow lope.

Tee said it was time to put her down, but Charlie kept delaying it. Then without warning he came home one day and announced, "Alice B. Curr is dead." He had not stayed with her in her final moments, or waited to bring her home for burial in the pet cemetery Tee had transplanted from Toad Hall.

Chapter Twenty-four

—

The Stork Brought You

A S ADDAMS SOARED OUT TO CONNECTICUT WITH MODELL to the strains of Dixieland jazz, going eighty miles an hour in his silver Audi—"Charlie's cruising speed," noted another friend—his mood was lighthearted. He laughed openly. He was unusually talkative. If life overall wasn't as much fun as it used to be, there was still plenty to enjoy: old friends, a good car, places to investigate or revisit. He and Modell left the highways to find "historical sites and architectural landmarks"—a typical Addams drive in which getting there was the real fun.

These days, Addams mostly preferred to stick close to home, surrounded by his crossbows and armor. In this medieval shell that reminded him of a more romantic time, he kept his touchstones close at hand: Alice's personalized bowl, and the braided red and yellow leash Dona had bought for her in China. The scrapbook of Cobean's Signal Corps drawings, which "would no longer be considered unpublishable," an obviously amused Addams had pointed out to Mike Woolson. He kept various newspaper clippings, including an article on a "Toe-Kissing Suspect" who had been arrested in Massapequa. ("Thinking of you every minute," Addams's Long Island acquaintance Robert Parrish had written on it.) He kept the uncorrected proofs of a 1968 work, *The Rise and Fall of American Humor,* by Jesse Bier, who had attributed the fall in part to Addams. (Bier called the cartoonist "well ahead of the sick humorists who have seen the barbeque pit as the abyss.") Among his papers was an ad for Preparation H Suppository Bullets—"For those days when you have to deal with one inflamed asshole after another." An idea—"Title for my next book," Addams had written on a memo cover sheet, "STORMY WEATHER."

He had even saved a memento of a violent 1971 attack on his own life, from which he had managed to escape with only minor injuries. Back in his drinking days, on a late night in April 1971, Addams had been walking home from Elaine's—not too straight at one-thirty or two in the morning, he later admitted to Tee—after an evening with Al Hirschfeld and Art Buchwald. As he was passing the St. Regis on East Fifty-fifth Street, a car pulled up to the curb. Two women inside called out and propositioned him. He ignored them and kept walking. Soon he heard the clicking of heels on the sidewalk behind him. As he turned, the prostitute holding the liquid aimed for his eyes—getting one of his ears, part of his scalp, and the back of his neck and coat. The two women jumped back in the car and sped off. Soon Addams felt his skin burning. He reached his apartment, climbed into the shower with all his clothes on—and finally realized that he'd been doused with acid. He went to the nearest emergency room. The story ran as a blind item in two papers, including the *New York Post*, below a photograph of the buxom blonde Mamie Van Doren. "It could only happen to you, Charlie," said Hirschfeld. For years afterward, Addams kept the heavy raincoat with its acid holes hanging in a closet, where it served as a cautionary reminder.

Some years earlier, Addams had received a clipping from the *Times* of London that had particularly pleased him, as it had made one of his old cartoons seem prescient, and he had kept that too. Titled "Man-Sized Meal," it told of an Indonesian peasant who had been swallowed by a python "more than six yards long, too bloated to move. He was cut open to reveal the peasant's still-clothed body," Addams had recounted to Philip French. "So you see, it really does happen. And I thought I'd invented something. Perhaps they were influenced by my cartoon. Maybe the man wanted to be in the picture."

He called himself "a slippered pantaloon," and a look at his desk confirmed it. Among his papers were some photographs of his artifacts, including a Cheshire Cat–like cat-in-a-box painting he had done for an art auction, which George Plimpton had bought; Armor & Arms Club books; a letter from the Amilcar Register; a receipt in the amount of $281.00, written in French, from a Paris antiques shop; an account of a gruesome multiple beheading in 1442; and a request for a congratulatory letter to Dr. Helmut Nickel, who was retiring as curator of arms and armor at the Metropolitan Museum of Art.

Addams gave careful thought to what should happen to his treasures after he died. He did not want them to go to a museum, much as he valued museums. (He was very "sharing of his things," noted Jeffrey Vogel, who had bought Addams's Bugatti), and he wished other collectors to have the pleasure he himself had had from them. Just recently, for instance, there had been an actual crossbow shooting in New York. Addams happily expressed the worry "that he'd be considered a suspect."

As for his cartoons, apart from the fifty Barbara had wrested from him in the divorce agreement, he was willing them all to Tee, unless she died first. In that event, his executor was to divide them equally among the New York Public Library and the Lenox, Astor, and Tilden foundations of New York City, with the exception of the Addams Family drawings, which were to remain part of his residuary estate.

He didn't go out as much anymore. He was not exactly a hermit, and yet "reclusion is something I understand and always have," he had written to Geraghty. Now the man who used to turn to the novels of John O'Hara for comfort read more nonfiction than fiction, primarily biographies and history; he listened mostly to classical music, but also to Dixieland jazz. He often fell asleep nights listening to the radio. One day a reporter telephoned to update the Addams obituary for *The New York Times*. "Am I ill?" asked Addams.

And yet even a slippered pantaloon inevitably ran into people in New York. A while back he'd seen Cameron and Jean Argetsinger at the Madison Avenue Drinking and Driving Luncheon at Sardi's. This was perhaps in 1986. "You know who I think of when I see you?" asked Jean.

"Walter Matthau?"

"Sam Cobean."

"Of course," said Addams.

Though he submitted two or three roughs a week, he turned up at his *New Yorker* office infrequently. The art department had become big and computerized, losing the family feeling Addams had loved in the old days. And he hated the magazine's cover art under Robert Gottlieb, who had replaced William Shawn as editor in 1987. (Gottlieb's tastes ran to punning and surrealism, which had squeezed out some of *The New Yorker*'s superior cover artists, including Charles E. Martin and the painterly Arthur Getz, both of whom specialized in the Manhattan scene.) The other cartoonists tended to see Addams only on Tuesdays, when he arrived early for the 2:30 art meeting, still looking sharp.

In this casual age (too casual, Addams thought), he continued to dress for work. "I think men look better in ties," he had told Sidney Offit. "That little dash of color beneath the chin—it's the only thing that some of these guys have going for them." About the drab offices of *The New Yorker*, where the young people came on bikes and looked "slightly bohemian" in their "corduroy jackets, a lumberjack shirt, and some kind of a greasy sweater," noted Lee Lorenz, Addams remained a presence from another era in a "stark suit" or tweed jacket. (Though Michael Maslin did notice as he stood next to the *New Yorker* god in the elevator that the jacket was covered with dog hair. "God's coat had dog hair," he reflected.)

In the bearskin coat Addams wore on raw winter days—"with utter aplomb," noted Chip McGrath—this *New Yorker* legend could look formidable. (Budd Schulberg, who had known Addams since the early seventies, always thought he looked like a prizefighter: "so ferocious in the ring," and yet "so gentle.") But like Joe Mitchell, another living legend, Addams was approachable and friendly. Ed Koren, for one, enjoyed his "courtly interchanges" with Addams in the hall. Here he was, thought McGrath: His art "was the weirdest of all the cartoonists, and yet he was the least weird—well-dressed, a gent, shy."

Still, some of the younger artists were too intimidated to talk to the great Addams, even if they saw him eating alone in a restaurant at lunchtime. To them, he was THE *New Yorker* artist, incomparable, a genius.

Addams's own favorites of his cartoons were "Boiling Oil," his Valentine cover of the man locking his door as a heart slips below it, and his old octopus-in-the-sewer drawing, which he thought wouldn't be funny anymore. He had been pleased to learn that some critics had described his characters as "repulsively demonic [yet] constantly coping in appropriate ways with everyday situations."

"I think that's right," he said, smiling. "They're just getting along."

On the other hand, he was tired of people focusing on the black side of his humor. "I'm sick of people calling it macabre," he had told Drue Heinz. "It's just funny, that's all." He brightened when she told him that her favorite Addams cartoon was the 1960 drawing of a shepherd in an elevator that has opened onto the Elysian Fields.

Though some of the younger cartoonists had felt let down to learn that Addams had worked from bought ideas—suddenly the wizard wasn't a wizard—they had ultimately adjusted their thinking and come around to Mischa Richter's view of the old *New Yorker* practice: Addams was like "an actor doing a part" written by another person. Over the years, the influence of his Boy Scouts, little people, and murderous spouses would find its way into cartoons too numerous to mention.

And what did Charles Addams think of the current crop of cartoonists? "There don't seem to be many good young cartoonists," he said. But he appeared to be unfamiliar with the work of even such well-known graphic artists as Gary Larson and Gahan Wilson, though he spoke well of them personally, and in the spare room at home he kept a framed drawing of the Addams Family done long ago by a boy named Garry Trudeau.

Those who mustered the nerve to seek out the master found Addams encouraging and kind. Chip McGrath, who loved getting a peek inside Addams's office, where he thought he remembered seeing a skeleton or a piece of armor, was amazed at how patient Addams was with the younger generation. "Not all the old timers were," he said. "Do we sell to (perhaps) impecunious undergraduates?" Addams had queried Barbara Nicholls on a letter from a Harvard junior desperate to buy an Addams original. "Mort, I love your work," he'd said upon meeting Mort Gerberg years earlier. (Gerberg had sold some early drawings to *The New Yorker* for Addams cartoons.) The only cartoonist Gerberg ever met who was more gracious than Addams was Charles Schulz, who had carried on at greater length about the younger cartoonist's work. Addams liked *Peanuts*, he had told a reporter, "but I do not have Peanuts envy."

Having exchanged a couple of friendly notes with Addams (his cartoon god too), Mike Woolson telephoned one day to say he was coming to New York the weekend of April 15—"the anniversary of Lincoln's assassination and the sinking of the *Titanic,*" Woolson said on the phone. Addams chuckled. On the appointed day, Woolson arrived with a friend. Addams patiently looked through the fledgling cartoonist's portfolio, nodding and smiling at the drawings—highly derivative of Charles Addams, which he politely refrained from mentioning.

As Addams and Woolson's friend Andy drank scotch—Andy feeling as though he'd been hit by a truck "mid-way through [the] conversation"—Woolson, who had asked for "something a little milder," drank white wine with ice. (This after he answered Addams's offer of a drink with "milk, or a soda," and Addams repeated, "a *drink.*") Addams gave them a tour of his remarkable apartment, including the bedroom upstairs, where a work-in-progress lay on the drawing table. It was a little-people cartoon of a couple regarding a miniature subway on their home lawn. "Not your ordinary burrowing rodents, that's for sure," says the man.

Though Addams wasn't much interested in discussing his own work, he did observe that Steinberg called himself "an artist," while he himself "was only a 'cartoonist,' a distinction that seemed to amuse him more than it offended him," remembered Woolson. Ultimately, he thought, "we're all genetically cartoonists, but when you come to selling originals and you go to an art gallery, you like to call them drawings."

ADDAMS'S OWN RECENT WORK seemed to reflect what he called his "night worries," and his somewhat precarious state. Abraham Lincoln stands in the tall grass along a narrow, hilly country road, holding up a hitchhiker's sign reading GETTYSBURG. He wears a stovepipe hat, a frock coat, and a somber, cautious expression. As he heads for the great battlefield, a shawl covers his shoulders, as if he feels a chill. An unpublished cartoon in *The New Yorker*'s cartoon bank shows two businessmen talking outside an open elevator. Behind them, inside the elevator, stands a very sweet-looking Humpty Dumpty wearing a bow tie and pointy elf's shoes, his hands folded demurely behind his back. He waits below the lighted arrow saying DOWN, with a shy, wary expression not unlike Lincoln's. "I think I'll wait for the next elevator," says the conventional man on the far left. And then one notices the resemblance between the other, funny-looking man and the tentative egg. The man's ovoid head seems to be covered by a bad toupee, and he wears a look of stunned uncertainty, as though he himself is on the verge of falling to pieces.

Other cartoons followed the timeworn themes. He revisited the boat

"I think I'll wait for the next elevator."

pond in Central Park, where a tiny, ragged castaway drifted on a raft among the children's sailboats. He drew desert crawlers, a subject that *New Yorker* cartoonists had been playing with since the early fifties. He echoed his own groundbreaking "Congratulations! It's a baby" with a cartoon showing a similar balloon-headed, needle-nosed figure in a patent attorney's waiting room. "I'm the invention. The inventor should be along any moment now," he says. Botticelli's Venus rises from an oyster on the half shell. "I'm telling you the truth, sweetie—the stork brought

you," says the mother whose little boy is, on closer inspection, a wading
bird in a striped shirt, with a long beak and three-toed bird feet.

Occasionally Addams still tried something timely, such as a drawing
featuring boom boxes. An unpublished cartoon rough shows two women

"I'm telling you the truth, sweetie—the stork brought you."

regarding a mummylike man in a living room chair. "Somebody named
Christo appeared today and wrapped Harrison," says one of them.

He still worked often from bought ideas—"not a popular subject," realized Wilfrid Sheed when he once asked Addams about it. Addams
would paw through the *New Yorker* slush himself, take things out, and
make sketches, sometimes forgetting to note the name of the cartoonist
whose idea he was using, which complicated the matter of paying people,
said Lee Lorenz. Once, Addams remembered a rough from years before

that *The New Yorker* had rejected and thought he might be able to do something with it. Somehow Ann Hall tracked it down to John Jonik, and Addams turned it into one of his most haunting *New Yorker* covers: As the dark night air drifts in blue veils across a full Halloween moon over a pumpkin field, someone in one of the larger pumpkins carves it from the inside.

Though some cartoonists still refused to sell their work as a template—even for Addams or Price—others were willing, even honored. In 1986, *The New Yorker* had bought the rough of an unknown cartoonist named John Callahan—"the worst cartoon I ever drew; so lame it isn't funny," said Callahan—to be cannibalized by Addams. Callahan, who would soon dynamite the boundaries of black humor with his own highly original work (which he thought had been influenced by Addams), was paid $150 for his troubles. His rough became a 1987 Addams cartoon in which a bland blond wife comforts her weeping husband as they watch TV. "There, there, dear. It's only a commercial," she says.

FIFTY YEARS AFTER their debut in *The New Yorker*, and twenty-four years after their banishment from those pages, the Addams Family was again on the brink of revival. The characters had even been ushered back into *The New Yorker* by Robert Gottlieb, who did not share William Shawn's fastidiousness about television's polluting influence. First came a captionless 1987 cartoon of a hairy creature in sunglasses slumped over a coffee mug saying "It." Two drawings of Morticia and Pugsley with household repairmen followed in 1988, but they lacked the old seediness and wit. The jokes were tame, the sets too well lighted and cheerful. It appeared that someone had actually been using the vacuum cleaner Morticia had purchased in 1938.

The truth was, Addams's heart wasn't in them anymore—not in creating new ideas for them, anyway, which was no easier now than it had ever been. Perhaps their time had passed. And he was lamenting his latest dramatic deal, which would re-create the Family in *color*.

In November of 1987, Orion Pictures had taken an eighteen-month option for a theatrical production based on the Addams Family. The contract, negotiated by Barbara Colyton, carried a purchase price of

$450,000, with $250,000 to be paid up front. Barbara and Addams had split the advance fifty-fifty. Attached to the contract was yet another document Barbara had drawn up and Addams had signed, several months earlier, certifying that for her "good and valuable consideration given to me over a period of many years," Barbara Colyton owned 50 percent "of all rights and title in and to all characters known as the 'Addams Family' or the 'Charles Addams Characters.' This binding upon my heirs and assigns." Barbara wangled another $35,000 for herself "as a partial reimbursement towards her legal, general and administrative expenses for negotiations abroad." She also had Addams's power of attorney "coupled with an interest, to survive." This too was binding.

If Addams felt resentful of Barbara's cut—a percentage unheard of in an industry where writers and artists owned their own creations and 10 to 15 percent covered an agent's negotiations and administrative costs—he had stubbornly continued to shackle himself to her. "Look, she is fantastic about money, about the contracts, those movies, the IRS," he told Leila Hadley.

Each year he received Barbare Artists checks that added significantly to his income—$3,700, $5,000, $12,500, even $25,000—for deals Barbara had negotiated. (This in addition to the more than $36,000 he had earned from the Hanna-Barbera cartoon series, which had run on Saturday mornings for two seasons beginning in 1973 and generated new Addams Family merchandise.) In 1987, Addams earned an all-time high of $203,797, including the Orion advance.

Barbara also got a percentage of the gross on the Orion contract. Addams felt that "she had the golden touch," said John Sparkman. He paid all her travel expenses when she came to New York on Addams Family business—including tips to porters, taxi drivers, and maids, which were spelled out in oddly formal letters to Mr. Charles Addams and signed by Barbara, the Lady Colyton. And he griped about his old Madison Avenue lawyers, whose firm had now been dissolved: They were expensive.

When Jack Heinz congratulated Charlie on the movie deal, he simply waved it away. It was Barbara's, he said.

Thirty years had passed since Addams and Modell had sat in a bar commiserating about their wild women—Frank's "hysterical" actress and Charlie's lawyer girlfriend. "That's nothing," Charlie would say in response to a story about an attack on Modell with scissors. "Wait till you hear what mine did. . . ." And he would talk about the latest incident with Barbara.

But as the two cartoonists sailed north in the silver Audi, listening to jazz and talking, Addams was the picture of a happy man.

FOR SOME TIME, Addams had been convinced that he had been ill served by his lawyers on the television contract. More than twenty years after *The Addams Family* came to TV, the series was still going strong in reruns around the world. (Australia was particularly Addams-mad, with a Morticia Boutique Dress Shop and a Fester Brothers punk rock band.) David Levy had secured residuals when the show went into syndication—ultimately amounting to perhaps $200,000—but the Family's father was no longer earning anything. Addams had received his last Filmways check, in the amount of $179, in 1974.

Though Barbara demanded higher fees for Addams and got them—some of the time—she also lost deals, including a second planned cartoon series based on *The Addams Family,* which was canceled because of her unreasonable demands. Quite apart from the "horror stories" Eric Pleskow had heard about her during the feature film negotiations, tales about the money Barbara asked for were, according to one insider, "legion" in the entertainment industry alone. And she would resort to shameless tactics to get her way, including tears, illness, flattery, and repeated phone calls bordering on harassment.

But she was fiercely loyal in her way. At a time when she was sick herself, she flew into action to help him. Addams had been at a party at Jane Gunther's apartment on East End Avenue when he had the seizure that preceded his carotid artery surgery. Henry Colyton was also attending the party; he and Addams were to go to the Colyton apartment on East Sixty-fourth later, to have dinner with Barbara. (Tee was at home in Long Island.) When Addams suddenly vomited and fainted, no one at the party knew what to do. Colyton telephoned Barbara, and within five minutes, it seemed to Jane Gunther, Barbara had found a doctor and arranged for him to meet Charlie at Lenox Hill Hospital. She also telephoned Kay Leperq to fetch Alice from Charlie's car until Tee could get in from Long Island the next day. After his surgery, Charlie loyally had dinner at the Colyton apartment every night for about a month on the days he was in town. The special meals Barbara had prepared for him were served in the dining room, where several Addams drawings shared wall space with the very competent oversized courtroom sketches Barbara had done as a young lawyer. "Mr. Mitchell! You *know* you don't have kitchen privileges," says the disapproving landlady to the unhappy tenant with his head in the oven in the 1950 Addams cartoon on Barbara's dining room wall.

And yet she was manipulative, maddening, indefensible. Not long after their divorce, Barbara told Addams that before she married Henry, she had gotten him to sign over *his* house in England to her—the ancestral Netherton Hall, no less, surely destined for Colyton's son—a story that outraged Addams, though he loyally kept quiet about it. He had witnessed her grasping behavior about Henry Colyton's other possessions as well, and taken indignant exception to it. During one of her visits to New York, he accompanied Barbara to a bank vault, where she was presented with a huge pushcart loaded with Colyton silver and things she had had sent over from England. She would talk about other objects she was having shipped to her apartment in New York: "My Hepplewhite table," "my" this, "my" that, she called the Colyton heirlooms. Addams was furious about the way she talked about Colyton's things as her own. And yet he understood her impostures and her vulnerability; he knew that she didn't want a small life.

Drue Heinz saw Charlie's loyalty to Barbara as pity: She thought he felt sorry for Barbara because of her chronic ill health. And there is no doubt that he was touched by Barbara's suffering. Afflicted with one illness after another since at least the early 1960s, Barbara had finally been diagnosed with lupus, the potentially fatal immune disorder. She had telephoned Addams long distance after the diagnosis, and afterward he seemed genuinely concerned about her health.

Though Barbara's real powers were limited—she had not registered with the Office of Court Administration, and therefore could not legally practice law in New York—she remained intimidating. While she took credit for helping Addams in all kinds of ways, even in his creativity, her role in Addams's life was that of the bad fairy at the christening—of Bad

Barbara, never to be confused with Good Barbara. She was still mentally unpredictable; long years after her divorce from Addams, one could argue for a psychiatric diagnosis—though there is no question that she knew right from wrong. Perhaps Addams regarded her as an undiagnosed lunatic and decided to cut her some slack. Or maybe he was simply fascinated by Barbara: In his ongoing study of the abnormal, she had a special place in his gallery of misfits, as a moral freak.

He was not merely gentlemanly in public—"It wasn't really a bad marriage," he had told a reporter, "just sort of a battle of wills"—he was accepting. Friends who observed Charlie and Barbara together at dinners and parties with mutual friends saw a comfortable relationship, though they continued to fight from time to time. (How he regretted walking into that bar, he told Tee.)

As for Tee, she stayed as far away from "the old bat" as possible. For years she had watched Barbara take advantage of Charlie and upset him. And yet Charlie would not get rid of her. Tee found the entire relationship maddening and incomprehensible. While resenting and loathing Barbara, she was also a little angry with Charlie for letting that woman take and take from him. Though she liked Henry Colyton—everyone liked Henry, as they did Charlie—she would have nothing to do with Bad Barbara. When Charlie dined with the Colytons, Tee remained at home in Long Island.

The problem was that Tee would not come into New York at all. She had dug herself a hole in Long Island, and she refused to budge. She had been everywhere, done everything, she said; the city had little allure for her now.

But Addams had reached a point in his life where he wanted his wife with him more of the time. Without even Alice to keep him company now, he was lonely during the week. He talked a good game with reporters and other strangers, saying that he liked his unconventional domestic arrangement: "I live in New York City. My wife lives in the country. We see each other only on weekends. It's great," he cracked. Because they were apart so much, he was always happy to see her, he said. But such sentiments were only part of the Addams act. When Odette, now remarried to a Frenchman, came to New York, Addams walked arm in arm with her down Fifth Avenue, saying how much he wished Tee would come into town.

Even at home, Addams could seem lonely. "The trick when visiting Charles Addams at his house is keeping his hands off your knees," a woman told Dick Cavett.

At least one of Addams's friends blamed Charlie himself for his living arrangements. Al Hirschfeld, who had been married to the same woman for nearly forty years, thought Charlie should accommodate his wife. Though Hirschfeld enjoyed the bachelor-like Addams, whom he saw at Elaine's, he thought he "would not be an easy man to be married to."

But Addams "needed atmosphere" in order to work, to get ideas. And that atmosphere was New York.

Every Friday, he hurried back to Long Island in time for lunch. Shirley Baty, whom Addams had drawn as the stunned wife arriving at an island overrun with human-sized birds standing at attention in a 1982 cartoon ("Well, you wanted a place with more birds than people," says the cartoon husband), would already be at Meghan's Pub; Tee was always the last to arrive.

Though Addams had stopped drinking, and he needed to eat at regular intervals (as a diabetic, he had to maintain what Dr. Mirsky called "a structured life"), Tee made little effort to accommodate him. At home the dinner hour got progressively later. Kevin Miserocchi, who knew Tee through the volunteer work they both did for ARF, was at the Addams house for dinner one night when the cocktail hour went on and on. Addams wasn't drinking; Miserocchi finally said he himself couldn't have another one. It was now perhaps eight-thirty. Still Tee continued enjoying her own drinks and cigarettes, laughing and dancing alone in the kitchen while Addams did a slow boil. "This happens quite often," he told their guest, in obvious irritation. And he had not been amused when Tee turned up at Lenox Hill after his carotid artery surgery with a pair of silly animal slippers. "He was furious," said Leila Hadley. "He wanted sympathy, not a joke."

And yet he was a happy man. Visitors to the shingled gray house nestled in the swamp heard "a huge cacophony of barking . . . a dog would knock you down." Charlie would offer you a drink; both husband and wife were warm hosts, and they obviously delighted in each other's company. If marriage was a passé institution, marrying your friend of more than forty years had its consolations. He would walk to the car with a fake limp, making elaborate gestures as he fumbled with the door, and Tee would crack up. "My, Running Fox looks fine tonight," she would say in her fetching smoker's voice, admiring the way he had camouflaged his frayed cuffs with India ink. She kept bat's blood in the refrigerator and a stuffed albino cobra under a bell jar. She crowned the old dressmaker's form he'd found in an antiques shop with the Ringling Bros. papier-mâché head of Wednesday Addams, who had empty eyes and a dry black wig fanning out from her chalk-white face. And she knew just how to handle crank calls. "Hello, is Uncle Fester there?" asked the giggling child's voice on the telephone. "I'm sorry, he just stepped out into the garden," she would say, without missing a beat.

And the hours she spent bird-watching! She consumed endless rolls of film photographing the hummingbirds and swamp birds that came to the feeders she had placed behind the glass doors in the Bird Room, as she called the paneled addition she had had built off the kitchen. Addams drew himself as a bird approaching the window where an alarmed Tee stood. He called himself a "gimlet-eyed tit watcher," making her laugh.

She was his girl, after all, and he loved her. He took her to Kings Park to see the inmates, and to George Plimpton's annual fireworks display on Long Island. He drew her as Morticia confronting various guises of himself—as a Fester-nosed foundling at the front door, as a bird placing a tiny valentine among the feeders outside the glass sliders. Following a trip to France, where he photographed Tee standing among the white crosses at Normandy, he inked little red hearts onto the crosses and gave the picture to Tee for Valentine's Day.

Here was a fairly wealthy woman in her own right who loved a bargain. There was, for instance, the day Tee saw an ad for navy surplus binoculars—a steal at $11.99—and sent away for them. Then the binoculars came, and they were of course worthless—made of cardboard. They actually made things look *farther* away.

The couple picnicked in cemeteries and enjoyed the dogs. They read Thurber fables aloud to each other before bed, one each evening. But when Tee woke in the night to find Charlie reading *The Silence of the Lambs* (a book she had pushed on him after reading it herself, riveted), he said, "You know, this is not the sort of thing to read at night," and slapped it shut.

For his most recent birthday she had surprised him with a 1929 Model T Ford pickup, parked in back of Meghan's and festooned with Christmassy wreaths. It was a cold day. He was wearing the big black bearskin coat Tee had bought him at an antiques shop, looking as though he had just stepped out of the *Morte d'Arthur*—and he was delighted with his present. Later, he painted the words "Sagg Swamp" and a small dragon, a swamp thing, on the passenger side. He was soon sighted driving around town in the new jalopy wearing a Nature Conservancy cap.

At sixty-one, Tee was still braver than he was, and more mischievous. Once, on a trip to the Virgin Islands, he had become panicked while swimming in a heavy tide. After steadying him, Tee swam off to explore the caves alone, then came back for him. The year her friend Joan Baron planted asparagus for the first time, Tee realized that Joan expected the stalks to appear promptly, and she immediately saw an opportunity. She bought luxurious farm-stand asparagus and had Charlie drive her over at night to the Barons' in his Bentley. While he remained in the car, she crawled through the garden on her hands and knees like a commando, clutching the asparagus in one hand under cover of darkness—almost under the nose of Howie Baron, a doctor and sportsman who kept loaded rifles in the house. It was Charlie, not Tee, who gave the joke away when Joan walked into Meghan's Pub the week after the prank and saw his little smile.

It was a wonderful smile, thought Tee. In Charlie's drinking days, she had been able to tell by his smile how much he'd been drinking; his "mouth would twist. . . ." In the old days, when they were just friends, they'd run into each other at the funerals of mutual friends. He'd see her coming down the street and signal to the bar around the corner. After a couple of drinks they'd take their places on the church pews, and Tee quickly learned not to look at him. His belly would begin to tremble, and tears would trickle down his cheeks with his silent laughter.

There was no one like him; there never had been. Along with his sense of humor and his unique laugh was "that melodious voice" no one had ever quite captured in print interviews. How to capture Charlie? One day he told her with great glee that a dozen cockroaches could live at the bottom of a grandfather clock for ten years. "I've just dyed my feet," he said another time, after applying India ink to his skin through the holes in his socks.

There were the drawings and cards he made for her year after year; no Hallmark cards from him, unless they were printed with Addams cartoons. The day after Tee had been ripped off by the $11.99 navy surplus binoculars, an official-looking envelope with a CAR-RT SORT number in the upper left-hand corner, and addressed to Mrs. Charles Addams, arrived in the mail. Inside was a handwritten ad announcing

RICH LADIES SURPLUS
ONE TIME ONLY
GENUINE SYRIAN
PUBIC MINK*!*

Alongside a fourteen-inch drawing of a starry-eyed, bejeweled matron in a long fur—the antithesis of Tee, whose coat was more likely from Kmart—was a handwritten letter into which the name "Mrs. Addams" had been inserted. On the matron's left ankle was a sparkling bracelet reading "Chas."

"Happy Easter Aguinamo, and much love," he wrote above a little portrait of himself as a red Indian, "Chief Spotted Pants."

Charlie was a boy, after all—"All Boy, if not exactly All-American Boy or Youth's Companion," John O'Hara had said. When kids called the house and asked, "Is this Uncle Fester?" giggling, giggling, Charlie would adopt a gruff voice. "You're speaking to him," he'd say. And when they asked to borrow the Ringling Bros. heads of the Addams Family for Halloween, he would always lend them out—until the kids stopped returning them, and Tee put an end to it. (Charlie had himself stopped buying vanity license plates saying "Fester" after kids kept stealing them off his cars.) He had once worn the flaming red pajamas she'd given him—over his clothes, to a cocktail party. And that antique bathing suit! Charlie and Jack Heinz had each bought one—somewhere on the Riviera, Tee thought—then actually worn them, though they were unlined and showed everything.

Once, before Tee and Charlie got married, Charlie arrived at her Water Mill house from Westhampton Beach, where he'd been doing an interview. He was a little drunk. "You didn't!" she cried as he walked in wearing the ratty suit. "What?" he asked. "I'm not even married, and I'm going to divorce you!" she said. "Did you let them take—" "Oh, they took a lot of pictures," he said. And the photographs that ran with the published interview in a local paper had been every bit as "terrible" as Tee had imagined—"the whole thing [genitals] hanging out." It hadn't bothered Charlie "in the least." Afterward, when he would tell her over the phone that someone was coming for an interview, she'd say, " 'What are you wearing?' and try to steer him a little bit," but it was all pretty hopeless.

It was impossible to stay mad at him. Before their marriage they'd had perhaps their worst fight over whether there were seals in Long Island Harbor. Charlie insisted that he had seen one; Tee maintained that he couldn't have. He had stayed away for about a week. Then one day the doorbell rang, and there was a postman with a tiny painting Charlie had done of the seal he had seen in Long Island Harbor—just the painting, no note. Tee melted.

Though Addams would be seeing his "dear recluse" in a couple of days, before leaving for Connecticut with Modell he had mailed her a *New York Observer* picture of a monkey in a T-shirt signing something at an outdoor table. "Mr. Jiggs, described as the world's best known roller skating chimpanzee, was in Battery Park Sept. 15 to publicize Roll A Thon '88 for the Police Athletic League to be held in the park. . . ."

The pretty ghosts of his past sometimes floated into view—at the Plaza, for instance, just the other day, when Addams had met Drue Heinz at the children's zoo in the park. He pointed across the street. "You could get a room there for nine dollars," he said, remembering the old days.

There was Jackie, in town again after the death of Onassis. Charlie had encountered her at a Literary Lions dinner at the New York Public Library. Though he seldom saw her anymore, he was careful when he talked about her. As far as Tee knew, Charlie had never been more than an escort to Jackie. She never heard the slighting comments that had so wounded Charlie, which he had confided to Odette and Leila. Talking to Steven Aronson about Jackie, Addams had also held back. "She's not gonna tell you much; she never did," he said when asked about his past relationship with her. Joan Fontaine, on the other hand, told you too much. She had telephoned one day, complaining about getting old. "My pussy's getting bald," she said. "Get a merkin," Addams told her.

One day a couple of years earlier, he had stood in the open doorway of his tower apartment watching Bobby's grown daughter, Brooke Hersey, climb the stairs—a lovely, dark-haired echo of her mother, Charlie told Tee—come to get the Day family clock he still had. Long broken, it sat on top of his mother's antique secretary "where it remains something of a shrine," Charlie had written Bobby. And in the end he had not been able to part with it. He promised to leave it to Brooke in his will.

There seemed to be something wistful in a remark he made about Daphne Hellman's daughter, Daisy, born in 1946. "I always thought she was mine."

And yet if Addams regretted his childless state or his failed first marriage, he said nothing to Frank Modell. His one regret, Addams said as they drove over to Guilford, Connecticut, that afternoon to see Jim Stevenson, was that he had never gotten anywhere with Kay Leperq.

—

Chapter Twenty-five

Charlie's Dream

JAMES STEVENSON WAS STRUCK BY "HOW HAPPY" CHARLIE seemed that afternoon. He had a way of "wrinkling" when he laughed his noiseless laugh. The only time Stevenson had ever seen Addams "lose it and laughing" outright, really laughing, had been several years earlier, when the McMartin Preschool child molestation case in California was all over the news. The subject had come up at lunch at the Coffee House, and Charlie began his silent, shaking Uncle Fester laugh. "Awful things like that were hilarious to him," explained Modell. And yet in more than forty years Modell had never seen Addams "be rude or unkind or anything but gracious and generous to a fault." He had never seen a dark side of Addams. And when they were together, Charlie always picked up the tab.

The three cartoonists sat outside Stevenson's house enjoying the fine September day, laughing and talking and "pissing off the porch." One thing they never, ever talked about was cartoons. They talked about people. They talked about cars. They were jokey, said Stevenson, as old friends are.

That evening, they all went out to dinner. Then Addams and Modell returned to Modell's house to watch the Phillies beat the Mets on television, nine to three.

The next morning, Charlie sat at the kitchen table talking while

Modell fumbled with breakfast and made bad coffee—all thumbs, for some reason. Charlie talked about his dreams. One had concerned Dan Silverberg, of all people, who had been a friend of Harold Ross and a "champion of generations of *New Yorker* writers and artists," as the magazine's obituary had put it. In the old days, Silverberg had taken big parties to "21." He had bought a number of Addams cartoons, and borrowed others that Charlie wouldn't sell. When he died in 1984, he had still not returned them. In Charlie's dream, Silverberg was looking at him.

After breakfast, Charlie had a cigar. "I don't think one's going to hurt me," he said with a smile. Modell, who was remaining in Connecticut, gave him a gift to take with him, a French poster of an irascible bearded man over which a spider was superimposed. Charlie accepted it with his "sweet smile," put it in the Audi, and climbed in.

He had a busy day ahead—a cocktail party he was to attend with Steven Aronson, followed by a dinner at Denise Bouche's new apartment on Seventy-fourth and Fifth with some "glamorous women of a certain age," all of whom Charlie had slept with. And he wanted to work up a rough of a Herb Valen idea for the next art meeting. It was a variation on an old Family drawing of Lurch carrying a two-headed pig to the holiday dinner table; the pig has apples in both mouths. In the new Valen gag, two pigs stood outside the Victorian mansion peering through the window as the Addams Family partake of their Christmas dinner. On the dining room table is a silver tray holding a pig with an apple in its mouth. "He cleans up nice," says one of the pigs outside.

Charlie said something funny to Modell before driving off. He was wearing the solid gold belt buckle he always wore, which had belonged to Gerald Murphy. The day was sunny and cool, good driving weather like the day before. The forecast promised clear skies ahead.

By late morning, on Thursday, September 29, he had arrived at his destination. He did not break into a thousand tiny pieces, an egg shattered by a vibrational shriek at a theremin concert. His was an easy death. He was found slumped behind the wheel of his Audi in front of his apartment building, where he had had a heart attack. He was taken by ambulance to St. Clare's Hospital at 415 West Fifty-first Street, where he was pronounced dead in the emergency room.

Among his unpublished cartoons at home was a rough showing a newspaper office filled with telephones and reporters. There was the city desk, and there was the obituaries desk, at which a man sat taking information over the phone.

He was laughing.

Postmortem

"DON'T EVER DO THAT TO ME," CHARLIE TOLD TEE AFTER they had been to a funeral. She didn't. She gave him a party.

It was held in the New York Public Library on Friday, November 18, not quite two months after Addams's death. Tee got permission to use the library's recently remodeled Celeste Bartos Forum room, a gorgeous Beaux Arts confection.

Everything about the occasion would have pleased Addams. There was no sermon, no sitting up straight on hard wooden benches; no casket. Votive candles flickered on tables covered with rose-colored cloths, which were gathered café-style about a makeshift wooden stage. Tee had had catered food trucked in from Long Island; there was a well-stocked bar. Cocktail napkins were printed with "The Skier," and easels held a sampling of Addams cartoons, including his 1941 "cyanide" drawing of Morticia and the old hag next door, later known as Grandma Addams. As friends milled about the room, they told funny stories about the departed; little dramas ensued—"Marian Shaw and Bodie Nielsen circling each other like panthers," reported Kathie Parrish, who promised to tell Tee more, later. Daphne Hellman entertained on her harp; Lee Lorenz and his Dixieland jazz band played Addams's favorite tunes. Couples danced under the glass-and-cast-iron domed skylight, looking nothing like a Holbein mural.

"What a great party," Roger Angell told Calvin Trillin. "After this, this place is going to be booked for thirty years." And it was, almost.

Charles Addams seemed to be everywhere that day: in the architectural details of the room, whose soaring domed ceiling and Carrara marble walls must have delighted him; in his *New Yorker* colleagues and friends, some of whom he had loved; in "all the ladies who doted on him but whom he chose not to marry, loving you more," Leila wrote Tee. There was Dona Guimares, battling lung cancer and wearing a wig— "looking as if she will die," Kennedy Fraser later confided to her journal. Barbara Colyton was there, "all in black, playing the widow," sniffed Drue Heinz, who noted that Tee, by contrast, wore white, "with a lovely gold belt." Charlie's favorite cousin, Liz, Elizabeth Smith Shores since her second marriage, to whom he had willed $10,000, came with her mother and Craig Smith, her brother Dudley's youngest child. Charlie had gotten young Craig a job in *The New Yorker*'s art department; they had traded "Hi, Cuz," when they saw each other in the halls (Charlie always joking, with twinkling eyes, as Craig remembered).

Once when Charlie and Craig were out to lunch at The Century, the subject of Cuba had come up. "Ah! Used to go to Cuba on vacation," said Charlie. "Great place for a vacation; great brothels." And he told Craig about being in a bar with Hemingway—"Ernie," Charlie joked—who was called away to the telephone. "Ugh, this nut job, he's out in the woods and asked me for advice—this guy Fidel Castro," said Hemingway after returning to the bar. It was apparently after taking the call from Castro that Addams and Hemingway visited a brothel together, though Addams did not elaborate.

For the memorial, Tee had chartered a Hampton Jitney bus to bring in country friends such as the owner of Meghan's Pub; the plumber and his wife and son; June and Harvey Morris from the penny candy store in Water Mill, where Tee had bought Charlie's white chocolate skulls; and old McGee from the body shop. Tee saw to it that the bus was equipped with a bar and box lunches of steak sandwiches and pasta salad for the ride home.

Everyone had an Addams story. During the formal part of the party, John Astin talked about *The Addams Family* and the *New Yorker* cartoons he had hung on his dorm walls in college. Up next on the makeshift stage, Tony Duke told about Charlie at the charity auction, holding a Jackson Pollock to show the bidders—upside down. He talked about the time Charlie gave an impromptu talk to a group of juvenile artists—after pausing to don a gruesome fake eyeball, which he happened to have on him. He told how Charlie saved the day, and a would-be swimmer in shark-infested waters, with his humor and aplomb.

Saul Steinberg focused on the artist's work, particularly on the late cartoons and covers he himself had most admired. He was talking about the protagonist in Addams's drawings when, from somewhere in the library, a bell struck twice. He paused. "What was it?" he asked innocently in his Romanian accent, making the mourners laugh. He answered the question himself. "That was the protagonist," he said.

Lee Lorenz read a tribute by William Shawn, who was not there. (The occasion would have been too much for him, his wife explained.) The testimonials ended with a song written and performed by Burgess Meredith and his son, Jonathan, on guitar—"A Waltz for Charlie," about the mysterious sources of Addams's genius, "to be played only at dusk." They had worked on the ballad at the Algonquin in the eleventh hour while John Astin wrote his own eulogy to Charlie. "He took the writing of that song so seriously," Astin said of Burgess Meredith.

In its obituary, *The New Yorker* praised both the art and the man. The thirteen-hundred-plus cartoons and illustrations Addams had done for *The New Yorker*, which ultimately included sixty-four covers—distinguished by their "clarity, originality, artistic assurance, and abiding pleasure"—were the product of someone "elegant and uncontrived, [who] will be missed even more in our halls than in our pages, if that is possible," wrote Roger Angell in the unsigned tribute.

In the days and months that followed Addams's death, the tributes continued. "I celebrate in particular his luminous innocence," Kurt Vonnegut wrote Tee. "Charles was eminently useful to our civilization, and to me personally long before I considered it possible that I might be lucky enough to meet him." "It is too sad," wrote Lauren Bacall, who had called Addams "Chuckie Baby." "Am wearing my ARF sweatshirt as I write." Another friend, Ken Drake, wrote, "Everyone who knew him has special recollections of Charley; mine is the fact that—in an age where it seems to be impossible—he was truly a good man." Three people had masses said for Charles Addams; a little boy cried. "NEVER have I seen Sterling cry so hard as when I told him he had lost his beloved godfather," Lyda's daughter wrote Tee. "I weep, Tee," wrote Leila, "because I want to pick up the telephone and call Lone Tit 1-4016 and hear Charlie's voice saying it was all a dream what happened yesterday."

Long afterward, eighty-seven-year-old George Price remained too broken up to speak. "It was a real blow," explained his daughter, Susan Price, of Addams's death. Someone in Key West was also feeling a "tremendous" loss, and just now writing to Tee. "I know you were the one person who brought him real happiness," wrote Barbara Hersey, who confessed to feeling "awkward" about writing. "Though our marriage wasn't a good one, I always knew what a wonderful human being Charlie was, quite aside from his brilliant talent."

"Who could ever forget Charlie?" asked Barbara Gross. "He had such wide interests: train whistles, for Pete's sake, cameras, cars. . . ." Drue Heinz remembered Charlie taking her out to meet George Price at his home in Connecticut because she wanted to meet the man who did those cartoons. "I want you to see the way he lives," said Charlie. And Drue had been astonished to see a civilized and lovely house filled with antiques. Hedda Sterne recalled the first car she and Steinberg had bought at Charlie's direction—a convertible Packard, she thought, which the couple had driven to Vermont in 1947. (They couldn't have been more out of place with such a car and their accents, she added with a laugh.) Steven Aronson talked about the Maserati he had purchased with Charlie's guidance. "Ah, Steve, this car had cancer," Charlie said after the car turned out to be "the biggest lemon of all time."

People remembered Charlie's love for his dog—"She didn't actually go for the jugular, but she moved them along," he had admitted. There was his delight in his surroundings, his childlike enthusiasm. "This is Bugatti country," he had said of Long Island. Gardner Botsford, driving on a back road in the Hamptons, would look in the rearview mirror and see "a blue spider" which would then "roar past me." There were the travels with Charlie. Hedda Sterne recalled a time, decades before, when she and Steinberg had been in Venice with Charlie and the first Barbara. He disappeared and returned "with shiny eyes, so elated and full of happiness because he'd discovered the Piazza San Marco," which he had not known existed. Suddenly Hedda saw the Italian Renaissance buildings anew. "When you were with him, you saw things with his eyes, too," she said.

Success, fame—none of it had changed him. Once, a good-looking girl approached Addams in a restaurant. "Aren't you Charles Addams?" she said. "Well, I guess so," he said. "Don't you spell that with two *d*'s?" "Three *d*'s," he told her. "Are you still Hollyman?" he asked photographer Tom Hollyman when he ran into him after a long time.

"Who could forget Charlie?" Charlie and Nancy Holmes, 1980s.

He had remained the solid American boy he had always been, never taking himself too seriously. Once, when Steven Aronson told Charlie over lunch that he was meeting for drinks that evening with another Charlie Adams—Charles Francis Adams IV, the chairman of Raytheon and son of the famous secretary of the Navy, Charlie said, "You must tell him you had lunch with Charles Samuel Addams the First."

Who but Charlie would sing "bi-bi-opsy" to the tune of "Bye Bye

Blackbird"? Who but Charlie would record in his datebook the death of his hopeless old cleaning woman, Katie?

Who but Charlie lived so much in the world without making an enemy? "He was sui generis," said Philip Hamburger. "Everything about him was so original," said the art historian Rosamond Bernier. Frank Zachary, the former art editor of *Holiday*, for whom Charlie had done some assignments, called it "chiaroscuro." "He had a charm so strong, it was a kind of genius," said Steven Aronson. Barbara Nicholls was at a luncheon with perhaps six women when Leila Hadley looked around the table and said, "You know, I think Charlie's slept with every woman at this table." (Barbara piped up that *she* hadn't.) To Frank Modell, Addams was perhaps the only man he had ever known who was content with what he had. "He was a very happy man, I think," said Modell. "He loved his dog, he loved his wives—as much as you can love a wife," he added, laughing.

There was a lone dissenter. "He deserved to die," snapped Joan Fontaine to a shocked Gillis Addison when they ran into each other in New York soon after Charlie's death.

IT WOULD BE YEARS before Barbara Colyton could speak about Charles Addams without crying. When she did, she said, "He was like my brother, my arm." People heard a romantic tale of great lovers who had somehow made the decision to part. "He asked me to marry him in Westfield," said Barbara. "I remember it very distinctly. We had the most lovely day together. . . . I put flowers on his mother's grave. . . . And he told me he loved me and wanted to marry me." Their Haitian honeymoon, she said without irony, had inspired a 1955 cartoon. It showed a black native woman on the floor of her grass hut, sticking pins in the waxen human images surrounding her on the floor. "Can't you get along with *any*body?" asks her husband.

Forced to defend her actions, Barbara continued to dissemble and lie, telling wild, nonsensical, cruel stories in private, designed to make her look like a virginal victim. She said she had taken his Westhampton Beach houses "because of Charles's imprudence, and my innate knowledge that he required taking care of." Of the Addams Family rights, Barbara often repeated a story about Addams telephoning her in Africa, begging her to handle the television show when it had first turned up, which she had been unable to do. "He said that the Family was safe in my hands."

After Charlie's death, Tee tried to sort out his various contracts with Barbara. Having found no original documents pertaining to the *Addams Family* rights, she asked Barbara for clarification. Eventually, through her lawyer, Tee received two photocopies of the 1987 agreement made on the eve of the movie deal, with one crucial difference: The second version, dated May 7, 1988, said that Barbare Artists Inc. and Lady Colyton "are and have been the owners of 75%" of the Addams Family—a document Tee could not believe Charlie would have signed less than a year after giving Barbara 50 percent. (Looking at the Addams signature, one also noticed that though it was his, it did not align properly with the other signatures.)

The two women wrangled over the cartoons Barbara had gotten Charlie to sign over to her, which had, with the exception of a few, remained in his keeping. "In order to avoid an expensive lawsuit," said Tee, she and Barbara finally agreed to donate a number of them, including a few of Charlie's *New Yorker* cover paintings, to the New York Public Library.

As for the Westhampton Beach houses, Barbara held on to them for some years. At various times she talked of willing them to the New York Public Library, and promised them to the University of Pennsylvania. Though both of Charlie's houses became run-down, Barbara commissioned a brass plaque for the canal house; it was stuck to the water side of the now-ramshackle little place, attesting to the great cartoonist who had once lived there. In 2001 she sold both properties for $1.7 million. They were promptly demolished and replaced with new structures.

Until her death in 2004, Barbara Colyton continued to negotiate deals for Addams Family ventures and merchandise, including slot machines, costumes, and dolls. She sent Tee her 25 percent—though not always promptly—sometimes after holding on to checks for months. Other Addams income was withheld from Tee entirely. Without Tee's knowledge, she also contacted Hallmark Cards and other vendors with whom Addams had contracts independent of Barbara, and took them over.

Barbara kept some promises to Charles Addams. She established an annual art scholarship in his name, and in 2001 she became the founding donor of the Charles Addams Fine Arts Hall at the University of Pennsylvania, the first building of its kind at that institution. It bears a plaque with Barbara's name on it.

In 1991, three years after Addams's death, *The Addams Family* came to the big screen in a feature film directed by Barry Sonnenfeld and starring Anjelica Huston and Raul Julia. During the making of the movie, Paramount reportedly hired a woman whose sole responsibility was to take calls from Lady Colyton.

The movie was a hit, enjoying the eighth biggest three-day opening gross ever.

Barbara Colyton and Tee Addams shared their percentage of the gross for the movie and its sequel, which exceeded $3 million each.

Tee Addams continued to live quietly in Sagaponack, surrounded by dogs and cartoons. She oversaw the publication of a big collection of Addams cartoons, *The World of Charles Addams,* and in 1999 created the nonprofit Tee and Charles Addams Foundation to promote the study of the cartoonist's work through book collections, exhibits, educational programs, scholarly research, and merchandise. But she rarely left Long Island, and few people got down the wired driveway that rang a bell in the house when a car approached.

Charles Addams's cremated remains were buried in the little pet cemetery on his and Tee's property in Sagaponack, in great secrecy. Tee was so concerned about ghoulish Addams fans that she told almost no one about the location of her husband's remains, including family and close friends. Fourteen years later, in 2002, Tee herself came to rest beside Charlie in the secular graveyard where the possums and the fishers sing.

Acknowledgments

"WHILE YOU'RE OUT TODAY, I'll be looking in that bottom dresser drawer," I teased Tee Addams during one of my regular visits to her home in Sagaponack.

"Go ahead!" she said, meaning it.

In Tee Addams I found the most accommodating, generous, and delightful spouse of a subject that a biographer could ask for. Even in the midst of her failing health, and when confronted with an unwelcome Addams revelation, she remained wholly cooperative, friendly, and available. She insisted that I put every wart into the book, and that I not worry about her feelings. My gratitude is equaled only by my affection for her.

Also at the Addams homestead were Kevin Miserocchi and Robert Klosowicz. Without Kevin, who had the foresight to make a list of the contents of Addams's desk the day he died, and to photocopy certain documents before I came along, later locating them when they were lost, I would have missed a crucial piece of the Addams puzzle. His tireless and entertaining assistance during the years he himself was creating the Tee and Charles Addams Foundation was invaluable. Robert spoiled me with fabulous meals and warm hospitality, and offered friendship and emotional support.

Of those present at the conception, I am most indebted to my agent, Max Gartenberg, who believed in the project when almost no one else did, and to Stacy Schiff, whose enthusiasm for Chas Addams when he was only a gleam in his biographer's eye helped keep up my spirits during the long incubation. Stacy's judicious reading of the manuscript—pencil in hand—improved the book.

In Bob Loomis I found my dream editor, a marvel of patience, industry, and skill with a pencil, who was always available to me, always supportive, and somehow made me feel like the only author in the room. I also thank Bob's wonderful and amusing assistant, Cheryl Weinstein, and Random House senior editor Dana Edwin Isaacson for his editorial suggestions and interest. Emily DeHuff's marvelous copyediting did much to sharpen the book. My thanks also to Evan Camfield, production editor; to Laura Goldin, legal counsel; to Barbara M. Bachman for her superb design; and to Gene Mydlowski and Karen Lau for their inspired dust-jacket design.

For research assistance, information, hospitality, and friendship, I am indebted to Dudley and Liliane Smith, Bob Ward, Ryan Parker, Catherine Yanikoski, Joe Yanikoski, Michael Yanikoski, Ann Jones, Gary Monserud, Barbara Butterfield, Bob and Martha O'Brien, Ilene Goldstein, Stephen B. Oates, Sandra Katz, and Helen Sheehy.

A remarkable group of Addams's friends—Odette Terrel des Chenes, Leila Hadley Luce, Frank Modell, Nancy Holmes, Jane Gunther, Lyda Barclay Hall, Axie Whitney, and Steven M. L. Aronson—were indispensable sources who went out of their way for me. I cannot imagine having spun the Addams stories into whole cloth without each one of them.

An army of others also provided information and gave interviews, each contributing a piece to the puzzle. I hope they will forgive me for simply listing their names: David M. Adams (Adams Family Research Center in Reading, Pennsylvania), Craig Addams, Gillis Addison, Judith Applebaum, Cameron and Jean Argetsinger, Jared Ash (the Westfield Historical Society), John Astin, Mary Ann Bamberger (Jane Addams Memorial Collection, University of Illinois), Shirley Baty, Frederick W. Bauman (Library of Congress), Beatrice Benjamin, Christopher M. Benjamin, William E. Benjamin III, the Berks County (Pennsylvania) Historical Society, the Berks County (Pennsylvania) Register of Wills, George Booth, the Boston Public Library, Gardner Botsford, Ray Bradbury, the Bronx County (New York) Historical Society, Anneke Brook, Heywood Hale Broun, Jr., David Caldwell, John Callahan, A. S. Carroll, Dick Cavett,

Roz Chast, Audrey Cosden Chickering, Wendy Chmielewski and the Swarthmore College Peace Collection; Lil Colletta (Kittochtinny Historical Society), Barbara Barb Colyton, the Concord (Massachusetts) Free Public Library, Gerta Conner, Julia Moore Converse, Alistair Cooke, Frank Corwin, Leo Cullen, Fred Dahlinger, Jr., and the Circus World Museum, Mrs. Whitney Darrow, Jr., Bedford Davie, E. T. Bedford Davie, Liza Donnelly, Ann Bradley Donohoe, Wylie O'Hara Doughty, Anthony Drexel Duke, Ralph Fields, the Fitchburg State College Library, Celestine Frankenberg, Kennedy Fraser, Gordon E. Gale, Ira Gammerman, Eva Geraghty, Mort Gerberg, Tony Gibbs, Dorothy Gillette, Harvey Gochros, Ted Goodman (Avery Library), Ruth Ann Gordon, Robert Gottlieb, Julie Goucher, Barbara Gross, Jon Gross, Lee Gruver (University Libraries, Penn State), Ann Hall, Philip and Anna Hamburger, William Hamilton, Harvard University Libraries, Drue Heinz, Daphne Hellman, Barbara Hersey, Wolfgang A. Herz, Al Hirschfeld, Tony Hiss, Kitty Hoch, Jean Hollyman, Tom Hollyman, Patty Hopkinson, Ralph Jones (the Westfield Historical Society), John Jonik, Caroline Kennedy, Fran Kiernan, Harrison Kinney, Everett Raymond Kinstler, Ed Koren, Tom Kunkel, Lancaster County (Pennsylvania) Historical Society, David Langdon, Arthur Laurents, R. Willis Leath, Robert K. Levering, Cheryl Levine, Barbara Blackwell Locker, Bruce W. Lord, Lee Lorenz, Ron MacCloskey, Edna Maestro, Vittorio Maestro, Norman Mailer, Gordon Manning, Lou Marcus, Michael Maslin, Carol Matthau, Camilla McGrath, Chip McGrath, Walker McKinney, Joan Melloan, Helen Miller, Gina L. B. Minks (McFarlen Library, University of Tulsa), Joan Ford Mongeau, Muriel Oxenberg Murphy, National Archives and Records Administration, Patricia Neal, the New York Public Library, Barbara Nicholls, Caroline Nicholson, Johnny Nicholson, Sean D. Noel and Dr. Howard Gottlieb (Department of Special Collections, Boston University), Ken Norwick (National Archives and Records Administration), Sidney Offit, Denise M. Otis, Robert A. Parker, Sandra Payson, Bob Pilpel, Eric Pleskow, George Plimpton, Jim Pope, Daniel Gensemer Reinhold III, Mischa Richter, Lillian Ross, Jay Rutherford, Don Saltzman, John T. Sargent, Paula Schechter (Cole Free Library, Chambersburg, Pennsylvania), Arthur and Alexandra Schlesinger, Budd Schulberg, Marian Hall Segur, Peggy Hall Segur, Wilfrid Sheed, Annalee Pauls and

Margaret M. Sherry (Princeton University Library), the Shrewsbury (Massachusetts) Public Library, Rusty Smith, Claudia Solomon, John Sparkman, Jill Spaulding, Lydia Speir, Art Spiegelman, the Stark County (Ohio) District Library, the Stark County (Ohio) Historical Society, William Steig, P. L. Steiner, Hedda Sterne, James Stevenson, Carol Terry, Calvin Trillin, the University of Pennsylvania, Herb Valen, Gloria Vanderbilt, Norman Vockmann, Harriett Walden, Lisa Wallenda, Larry and Joan Ward, Ken Weatherwax, Nancy Wechsler, Penny Weeks, Amy Wehle, Nancy Whitney, Michael Wickes, Suzanne Wickham-Beaird, Edwin Wilson, Emmy and Bill Winburn III, Mike Woolson, Linda Yang, and Frank Zachary.

Last but always first, I thank my family—Chuck, Allie, and Randy—for welcoming yet another subject into our home, and tolerating my obsession with him as well as my absences. Without my tireless husband, Chuck Yanikoski, my best friend, cheering squad, and first reader, who also did most of the genealogical research on Addams, I couldn't imagine writing anything.

Notes

UNLESS OTHERWISE INDICATED, all of the art department notes and letters from and to *The New Yorker* are part of the *New Yorker* collection at the New York Public Library. This includes Charles Addams's letters to Katharine S. White and Wolcott Gibbs. The unpublished memoir by James M. Geraghty is from the James M. Geraghty collection at the library. With few exceptions, all the Addams correspondence, as well as family scrapbooks, Addams contracts, cartoon roughs, manuscripts, and the like belong to the Tee and Charles Addams Foundation, which also holds copies of most of the print interviews cited in this biography.

John Callaway's interview with Charles Addams, to which I owe much, aired on PBS on December 3, 1981. Steven M. L. Aronson shared with me an unpublished interview he did with Charles Addams. Some of my Aronson/Addams citations are from this interview.

Some spelling and punctuation errors in letters have been silently corrected.

CHAPTER ONE: Arrested at the Age of Eight

3 **"A charm to ward off"**: Patricia McLaughlin, "Charles the Imponderable," *Pennsylvania Gazette,* March 1973, 16.

4 **"eventually they'd get around"**: LHD interview with Calvin Trillin, February 21, 2000.

4 **"In Avignon"**: JMG/NYPL.

4 **"Are people ever disappointed"**: Marshall Ledger, "Charles Addams Comes to Campus," *Pennsylvania Gazette,* December 1979, 27.

4 **"a fat little man"**: Christopher P. Andersen, "The Real Grisly Addams Is Cartoonist Charles, Who Wants You to Get the Point," *People,* September 13, 1976, 90.

4 **("Just a matter of design")**: LHD interview with SA, April 5, 2000.

4 **"scary, grim"**: LHD interview with Mischa Richter, November 12, 1999.

4 **"the Van Gogh"**: *Time,* January 25, 1963, 33.

4 **"the Bela Lugosi"**: Hy Gardner, "Early Bird Coast to Coast," *New York Herald Tribune,* August 1, 1952.

4 **"the graveyard guru"**: Dolores Barclay, "Graveyard Guru Mellows with Age," *El Paso Times,* January 31, 1982.

4 **"American Gothic"**: *Literary Review,* September 1992, 14.

5 **"Well, it looked a bit like"**: "Mrs. Johnson Conducts TV Tour of LBJ Ranch," Casper (Wyoming) *Herald Tribune,* August 16, 1964.

5 **"purposeful charlady"**: CI.

5 **"It was of course rejected"**: LHD interview with SA, April 5, 2000.

6 **"Nazi concentration camps"**: Lee Lorenz, *The Art of The New Yorker 1925–1995* (New York: Alfred A. Knopf, 1996), 121.

6 **"The Gotham Rest Home"**: John Kobler, *Afternoon in the Attic* (New York: Dodd, Mead & Company, 1950), 3.

7 **"I woke up"**: Harry Altshuler, "Monsters Are His Best Friends," *New York World-Telegram and Sun,* August 30, 1965.

7 **"booby hatch"**: LHD interview with Daphne Hellman, December 6, 1999.

7   "Charlie, what about you?": LHD interview with Mort Gerberg, February 26, 2001.

7   "about seventy-five percent": LHD interview with Ralph Fields, November 14, 2001.

7   "the aberrations of life": LHD interview with Walker McKinney, June 8, 2000.

7   "the poor man's Bugatti": E. K., "Charles Addams, Cartoonist," *East-hampton Star,* 1988.

7   "Okay, let's get out": LHD interview with Denise Otis, May 12, 2000.

8   "Well, we'll stab them": LHD interview with AW, January 26, 2000.

8   "What a pity": "Nancy Woodward, 3128 Sheridan Ave, is agog of the New Yorker's monster-vampire cartoonist Charles Addams," unidentified clipping.

9   "Emily, have you ever": LHD interview with Emmy and Billie Winburn, June 24, 2000.

9   "the gentlest and kindest": *Time,* November 9, 1942.

9   "sinister figure prowling": to CSA from Katharine K. Sell, October 24, 1974.

9   "People expected him to look": LHD interview with Dick Cavett, March 1, 2000.

9   "Charlie, do you have any teeth?": LHD interview with MMA, April 1–5, 2000.

11   "The eyes aren't squinty enough": LHD interview with AW, January 26, 2000.

11   "twinkly": LHD interview with Everett Raymond Kinstler, October 15, 2004.

11   "his smile a rather villainous air": Peter DeVries, *Witch's Milk* (Boston: Little, Brown & Co., 1968), 204.

11   "looked so evil": LHD interview with ETBD, January 30, 2000.

11   "Thank God no one knows": LHD interview with MMA, January 16, 2001.

11   "like an elf": LHD interview with Mort Gerberg, February 26, 2001.

11   ("I try not to let it show"): Marshall Ledger, "Charles Addams Comes to Campus," *Pennsylvania Gazette,* December 1979, 27.

11   "You look like someone": LHD interview with Bill Leath, March 11, 2002; S. N., "Charles Addams 1912–1988," *Vintage Sports Car,* No. Two, 1988, 10–11.

11   "Mr. Matthau": LHD interview with MMA, November 1–5, 1999.

11   "side-of-the-mouth delivery": LHD interview with Sidney Offit, December 28, 1999.

12   "he looked like someone who": LHD interview with Lee Lorenz, December 10, 1999.

12   "as a kind of 1940s": LHD interview with Kennedy Fraser, April 4, 2000.

12 **faultless tailoring:** Patricia Coffin, "Charles Addams: Recluse About Town," *Single,* October 1975.

12 **"Surfwood walls":** "Celebrity Rooms on View," *New York Herald Tribune,* May 8, 1962, 18.

12 **ancient elevator:** "Appendix: Charles Addams Live!," unidentified type-script.

12 **"big black number 13":** Leslie Bennetts, "Charles Addams: He's Really Just a Normal Boy Who Craves the Grave," *Washington Star,* October 31, 1978.

13 **("a bargain at $700"):** Saul Pett, "Cartoonist Finds Humor in Repressed Violence," *Los Angeles Times,* October 11, 1953.

13 **"Don't worry":** LHD interview with Suzanne Wickham-Beaird, January 12, 2000.

13 **("It's not exactly"):** Andersen, "The Real Grisly Addams," 90.

13 **("It reaches inside"):** Bennetts, "Charles Addams: He's Really."

13 **("What was dried"):** Audrey Farolino, "Cartoonist Draws on the Macabre for Devilish Décor," *New York Post,* June 28, 1984.

13 **"a rather sinister stain":** Mark Matthews, "Westfield-Born Cartoonist Charles Addams," *The Courier-News,* August 10, 1974.

14 **"wiped out and tired":** LHD interview with Christopher Benjamin, June 22, 2000.

14 **"There was not a false note":** LHD interview with Shirley Baty, November 3, 1999.

14 **"sort of funny":** LHD interview with William Hamilton, November 15, 1999.

14 **"A throne should look":** LHD interview with Suzanne Wickham-Beaird, March 23, 2000.

14 **"quite beautiful":** CI.

14 **"like a walnut":** McLaughlin, "Charles the Imponderable," 18.

14 **("of the old Rolls-Royces"):** McLaughlin, "Charles the Imponderable," 18.

14 **"taken on a beautiful patina"** and following: CI.

15 **"a New Haven doctor":** Kobler, *Afternoon in the Attic,* 8.

15 **"the progenitor of":** Dolores Barclay, "Cartoonist Addams a 16th Century Man," *Daily Argus,* February 14, 1982.

15 **"I like to think":** Peter McKenna, *Bridgehampton Sun,* October 29, 1980, 10.

15 **"If I told you":** CI.

15 **"As very nice":** LHD interview with NH, April 29, 2001.

15 **"You're run out of the house":** McLaughlin, "Charles the Imponderable," 20.

16 **"because they want me":** CSA interview, *The Dick Cavett Show,* March 29, 1978.

16 **"People must feel":** John Grossman, "Charles Addams: Twenty-four Hours in the Life of the Creator of *The Addams Family,*" *TWA Ambassador,* September 1981.

16 **"perhaps childlike enthusiasms"**: McLaughlin, "Charles the Imponderable," 18.

16 **"a kind of cozy condition"**: *The Dick Cavett Show*, March 29, 1978.

16 **the water tower**: *The Literary Guild*, March 1977.

CHAPTER TWO: A Normal American Boy

17 **"drew skeletons"**: *Current Biography* (New York: The H. W. Wilson Co., 1954).

17 **"Are you Charles"**: Marshall Ledger, "Charles Addams Comes to Campus," *Pennsylvania Gazette*, December 1979, 28.

18 **"barely rolling"**: Mike Sweeney, "Cartoonist Recalls Boyhood Halloweens," *New Plains Courier*, October 31, 1972.

18 **"local bad boy"**: Ledger, "Charles Addams Comes to Campus," 28.

18 **"Separated at birth"**: *NYer*, May 4, 1981, 43.

18 **"I don't know whether"**: Ledger, "Charles Addams Comes to Campus," 28.

18 **"I was always aware"**: Patricia Coffin, "Chas Addams: Recluse About Town," *Single*, October 1975, 94.

18 **the streets of Westfield**: "Sergeant Jimmy Cannon Says: 'A Camel Bit Him,'" *PM*, January 1943.

18 **"Well, at least it was"**: Charles Addams, *Black Maria* (New York: Simon & Schuster, 1960), 63.

19 **"towering masses"**: *Westfield Leader*, May 13, 1914.

19 **"a good clean town"**: Henry Bellaman, *King's Row* (New York: Simon & Schuster, 1942), 3.

19 **"I know it would be more interesting"**: Ledger, "Charles Addams Comes to Campus," 28.

19 **"I'm one of those strange people"**: CI.

21 **"gobbled up the handsome young prince"**: *NYer*, April 14, 1951, 37.

21 **"could have been my Grandma Spear"**: CI.

22 **scare the wits out of her**: Eric Pace, "Charles Addams Dead at 76; Found Humor in the Macabre," *New York Times*, September 30, 1988.

22 **"stronger than he had expected"**: Sweeney, "Cartoonist Recalls Boyhood Halloweens."

22 **"mostly she was very kind"**: CI.

22 **"big arrest"**: CSA, "1912–1914: Memoir of a Prepuberty Wasp [*sic*]."

22 **"wore a different pair of shoes"**: *Current Biography*.

22 **"Charlie was the only person"**: LHD interview with LHL, April 6–7, 2000.

23 **"Get a load of the nose"**: LHD interview with MMA, April 6, 2000.

23 **"Oh, shit"**: Ron McCloskey interview with Ron Fullerton, 2001. Author files.

23   "Muff muff": LHD interview with MMA, June 12–16, 2000.

23   "Girlie" and following: Charles Huey Addams and Grace Spear Addams, 1931, 1930, 1924.

24   "I think [my father] saw": CI.

25   "I surely miss you": Charles Huey Addams to CSA, August 22, 1924.

25   "a dark red coat": CI.

26   "I think they'd have looked": radio interview, "The Haunt for Chas Addams: Charles Addams Talks with Philip French," August 15, 1978.

26   "a happy childhood": Gillian Reynolds, "A Man Too Good to Lose," *Daily Telegraph,* September 13, 1978.

26   "There was always a little group": LHD interview with Allison Mackay, January 5, 2001.

26   "I wouldn't have considered": "Chas Addams," *Look,* May 19, 1953, 99.

26   "cheese-like, pasty smell": Sweeney, "Cartoonist Recalls Boyhood Halloweens."

26   "very weird": LHD interview with Norma Hill Volckmann, December 21, 2000.

26   "I must have buried 50 treasures": Sweeney, "Cartoonist Recalls Boyhood Halloweens."

26   "Treehut": CSA, "1912–1924: Memoir of a Prepubescent Wasp [*sic*]."

26   "I lived in my imagination": "Phobias, Fears & Shinbones for Christmas," unidentified document.

27   "only exciting thing": LHD interview with MMA, August 7–8, 1999.

27   "I wasn't much for": CI.

27   "She is a wonderful mother": Charles Huey Addams to CSA, August 22, 1924, February 16, 1930.

27   "imagining the ghosts inside": Saul Pett, "Cartoonist Finds Humor in Repressed Violence," *Los Angeles Times,* October 11, 1953.

27   "imagine who was lying down there": CI.

27   "maybe I was trying to scare myself": Pett, "Cartoonist Finds Humor."

CHAPTER THREE: Be Prepared

28   "There's a legend in Westfield": "Sergeant Jimmy Cannon Says: 'A Camel Bit Him,' " *PM,* January 1943.

28   "damned the Kaiser": LHD interview with SA, April 5, 2000.

28   "had him stabbed": Virginia Sheward, "At Home with the Addams Family," *Holiday,* March 1973.

28   ("I think what talent I have"): Philip French, "Addams and the Monster Within," *The Listener,* September 21, 1978.

28   "Father drew well": Dwight Macdonald, "Charles Addams, His Family, and His Fiends," *The Reporter,* July 21, 1953, 37.

29   "moody backgrounds": *Quest* 3:4 (June 1979), 24.

29   "I don't care": LHD interview with BC, February 10, 2000.

29   "as a sort of pretty harpy": JMG/NYPL.

29   "necrophiliac artist": "The Compleat Charles Addams," NYPL exhibit publication, 1994.

29   "freckled to death": Harry Altshuler, "Monsters Are His Best Friends," *New York World-Telegram and Sun,* August 30, 1965.

29   "Your map of the lake": Charles Huey Addams to CSA, August 22, 1924.

30   "funny-looking people": LHD interview with Norma Hill Volckmann, December 21, 2000.

30   ("Very careless in Exam"): CSA report card, undated.

30   "She made class interesting": LHD interview with Helen Miller, December 4, 2000.

30   "a neverending source of interest": Westfield High School yearbook, 1929.

30   he was good-looking and following: to LHD from Dorothy Masenior Bass, January 2001.

30   "You should have seen him": *The Weather Vane,* 1929.

30   "You couldn't help but like him": LHD interview with Helen Miller, December 4, 2000.

31   scrawlings: LHD interview with SA, April 5, 2000.

31   "the counterpart of Chaplin": Gilbert Seldes, *The Seven Lively Arts* (New York: Harper and Brothers, 1924), 232.

31   "mauling clichés": Art Spiegelman, "When Grisly Horror Is a Family Value," *New York Times,* September 29, 1996.

33   "liked the feeling for the city": CI.

33   "Look out, Pete!": *The Weather Vane,* 1928.

33   "better forgotten" and following: CI.

34   "He amazed us": Westfield High School yearbook, 1929.

CHAPTER FOUR: Sex Fiend Slays Tot

35   "I would think": CI.

35   "Like everyone else": Cynthia Lowry, "Addams Family Made Jump from Cartoon to TV," *Long Island Press,* January 17, 1965.

35   "his interest in the bizarre": Dolores Barclay, "Graveyard Guru Mellows with Age," *El Paso Times,* January 31, 1982.

35   "It was a very tough business" and following: LHD interview with SA, April 5, 2000.

35   "practically everyone in Westfield": "Somewhat Gloomily Yours, Charles Addams," University of Pennsylvania *Almanac,* November 8, 1979.

35   "voluptuous nudes": "The Colgate Scene," Colgate University, November 1988.

36   "I hope Charlie is making progress": Charles Huey Addams to Grace Spear Addams, October 1930.

36   "as that helps a lot" and following: Grace Spear Addams to CSA, January 13, 1930.

36   a drifting year of hilarious times and following: Patricia McLaughlin, "Charles the Imponderable," *Pennsylvania Gazette,* March 1973, 16.

36   "They didn't let you touch color" and following: LHD interviews with LBH, December 10, 2001, November 3, 1999.

37   watching people: Leslie Bennetts, "Charles Addams: He's Really Just a Normal Boy Who Craves the Grave," *Washington Star,* October 31, 1978.

38   "the idea is important": Harry Altshuler, "Monsters Are His Best Friends," *New York World-Telegram and Sun,* August 30, 1965.

38   "I don't know if I'm happy": "Somewhat Gloomily Yours, Charles Addams."

38   Charlie was their "golden boy": LHD interview with LBH, May 8, 2000.

38   "thought he'd better get on": Ralph Jones interviewed by William H. Gordon, Westfield Historical Society.

38   "terrible" money and following: LHD interview with SA, April 5, 2000.

38   "the X where the body was found": Altshuler, "Monsters Are His Best Friends."

38   "with just a tad more blood": Dolores Barclay, "Cartoonist Addams a 16th Century Man," *Daily Argus,* February 14, 1982.

38   "This was just a job" and following: LHD interview with SA, April 5, 2000.

40   "an unfortunate scene": radio interview, "The Haunt for Chas Addams: Charles Addams Talks with Philip French," August 15, 1978.

41   "I think the money went to my head": CI.

41   "Why, hello, Otto": *NYer,* March 18, 1933, 11.

41–42   "He was always worried": Ron McCloskey interview with Guy Fullerton, undated, 2000.

43   "nervous penmanship": LHD interview with FM, August 8, 2003.

43   "Have you forgot": *NYer,* March 12, 1932.

43   "Geographic readers": *NYer,* June 29, 1935, 42.

43   "Something must be wrong": *NYer,* June 20, 1935, 20.

44   "better drawing": art meeting notes, January 23, 1935, NYC/NYPL.

44   "an ordinary Ride Playland" and following: Ron McCloskey interview with Guy Fullerton, undated.

44   "Alfred, look! Vultures!" *NYer,* August 17, 1935, 22.

44   "I gave up any thought": LHD interview with SA, April 5, 2000.

46   "It's nothing at all, really": *NYer,* September 5, 1936.

46   "He never knew what hit him": *NYer,* June 29, 1935.

46   "Now will you stop": *NYer,* October 26, 1935.

47   "Tough, gamy": *NYer,* December 14, 1940.

47   "ghastly in both thought and execution": Lee Lorenz, *The Art of The New Yorker, 1925–1995* (New York: Alfred A. Knopf, 1996), 33.

CHAPTER FIVE: Who's Talking?

For my understanding of *New Yorker* cartooning, I owe much to Lee Lorenz and his book *The Art of The New Yorker: 1925–1995,* and to Thomas Kunkel's biography of Harold Ross, *Genius in Disguise.* Joan Segur Fletcher interviewed her mother, Peggy Hall Segur, and then wrote the answers to my questions.

48   "Dear Mr. Gibbs": CSA to Wolcott Gibbs, August 16, 1935.
49   "collaborative effort": Thomas Kunkel, *Genius in Disguise* (New York: Random House, 1995), 326.
49   "We looked at 839": Linda H. Davis, *Onward and Upward: A Biography of Katharine S. White* (New York: Harper & Row, 1987), 114.
49   "Thurber's people have no blood": Kunkel, *Genius in Disguise,* 326.
49   "Next?": *NYer,* May 13, 1939, 15.
49   "It's broccoli, dear": *NYer,* December 8, 1928.
50   "the illustrated anecdote": Lee Lorenz, *The Art of The New Yorker, 1925–1995* (New York: Alfred A. Knopf, 1996), 48.
50   "NO Book drawings" and following: art bank notes, December 31, 1934, NYC/NYPL.
51   "Is that funny?": Lorenz, *The Art of The New Yorker,* 32.
51   "Pombo learn things quick": *NYer,* August 8, 1936, 14.
52   "ADDAMS: Scientist, astronomer in his observatory": NYC/NYPL, October 29, 1935.
52   "redrawn and the plate remade": Katharine S. White to Harold W. Ross, September 24, 1936.
52   "Oh, speak up, George": *NYer,* September 13, 1941, 27.
53   "who was sort of the paragon": CSA interview, *The Dick Cavett Show,* March 29, 1978.
54   a "swish" Manhattan dress shop: Peggy Hall quoted in e-mail to LHD from Joan Segur Fletcher, October 28, 2004.
55   "Are there many ahead of me?": *NYer,* March 23, 1940, 17.

CHAPTER SIX: Just My Idea of a Pretty Girl

56   "more or less something": radio interview, "The Haunt for Chas Addams: Charles Addams Talks with Philip French," August 15, 1978.
56   "just my idea": Carol Oppenheim, "Cartoonist Addams Is Nobody's Ghoul," *Chicago Tribune,* April 13, 1978.
56   "eyes slightly up-centered": CI.
56   "Vibrationless, noiseless": *NYer,* August 6, 1938, 9.
58   "You'll be surprised": *NYer,* May 22, 1937.
59   "okayed as an idea" and following: CI.
60   "scanty hair": CSA/AF.
60   "Oh, it's *you*!": *NYer,* November 25, 1939, 16.

60 "Congratulations!": *NYer,* November 9, 1940, 21.

61 "into reality": French, "The Haunt for Chas Addams."

61 "that haunting simile": *Time,* November 9, 1942.

62 "Surprised" by the public reaction: CI.

62 "A long treatise" in German: Randall Ross, "Charles Addams Confirms Family Resemblance," *The Polygon,* October 30, 1970.

63 "What's funny about this?": to CSA from Harriet Ray, to *NYer* from Harriet Ray, March 12, 1940.

63 a charming letter of his own: to *NYer* from Harriet Ray, May 18, 1940.

63 "Twenty-three thousand and one": *NYer,* June 29, 1940, 11.

64 "A round trip and a one way": *NYer,* January 18, 1941, 28.

64 "People always want to know": "Addams, Apostle of Happy Gloom, New Army Problem," *New York World-Telegram,* January 30, 1943.

CHAPTER SEVEN: One of the Great Comic Artists of All Time

65 "the pallor of angel cake": John Kobler, *Afternoon in the Attic* (New York: Dodd, Mead & Company, 1950), 9.

65 "I think she lived": CSA quoted in "Westfield-Born Cartoonist Charles Addams," *The Courier-News,* August 10, 1974.

65 "She was very, very lovely": LHD interview with Hedda Sterne, May 13, 2002.

65 sharp-minded and intelligent and following: LHD interviews with Philip and Anna Hamburger, December 6, 1999; JG, April 5, 2000; Cameron and Jean Argetsinger, May 12, 2003.

65 "She had a lovely little giggle": LHD interview with LBH, May 8, 2003.

65 "she was a real flame thrower": LHD interview with Gardner Botsford, April 30, 2003.

65 "Do you have one": *NYer,* January 16, 1943, 19.

66 "Gilbert Seldes hanging": CI.

66 "His mother [had] a fit": Ron McCloskey interview with Guy Fullerton, 2001, author files.

66 "had more friends": LHD interview with Jay Rutherford, February 1, 2000.

66 a "slightly fake" passport: "Saul Steinberg, Epic Doodler, Dies at 84," *New York Times,* May 13, 1999.

66 "a hollow-eyed man": CSA in radio interview with Heywood Hale Broun, undated, circa 1975.

66 "a quiet friendship": Saul Steinberg speaking at Charles Addams memorial service, NYPL, November 18, 1988.

66 one of four "zanies": Thomas Craven, *Cartoon Cavalcade,* 1942; quoted in "Charles Addams Is Dead at 76," *The Comic's Journal,* No. 125, October 1988.

67   "high priest in horror": *Look,* December 15, 1942, 60.

67   ("parted in the middle"): CSA quoted in *Interview* magazine 8:5 (1978), 22.

67   "Are you unhappy, darling?": *NYer,* November 14, 1942, 27.

68   "Nazi item": John Ruge to CSA, November 30, 1939.

68   "just exhausted": CSA to Daise Terry, January 16, 1943.

68   "a good shot": LHD interview with Lou Marcus, March 27, 2000.

68   "too young for World War I": LHD interview with Al Hirschfeld, February 5, 2001.

68   the "glandular" type of face: Michael Kimmelman, "His Hand Could Catch Your Essence in Flight," *New York Times,* January 26, 2003, 7.

68   "about to make a telephone lineman": CSA quoted in "Sergeant Jimmy Cannon Says: 'A Camel Bit Him,' " *PM,* January 1943.

70   "shadowy, ornate Georgian structure" and following: Kobler, *Afternoon in the Attic,* 9.

70   "to the Signal Corps": Gardner Botsford, *A Life of Privilege, Mostly* (New York: St. Martin's Press, 2003), 5.

71   "where we were ticketed" and following: Arthur Laurents, *Original Story by Arthur Laurents* (New York: Alfred A. Knopf, 2000), 28, 23.

72   "Go get 'em, boys!" and following: LHD interview with Lou Marcus, March 27, 2000.

72   "one of the great comic artists": Introduction, *The Cartoons of Cobean* (New York: Harper & Brothers, 1952).

72   "on a good day," joked Cobean: LHD interview with Cameron and Jean Argetsinger, May 12, 2003.

73   anything "bizarre": Johnny H. Admire, "Samuel E. Cobean: Creator of the Dream Drawing Cartoon," master's thesis, University of Oklahoma Graduate College, 1965.

73   "a great foil for Charlie": LHD interview with Jay Rutherford, February 1, 2000.

73   "about syphilis, or prosthetic devices": Russell Davies, "Addams and Evil," *Observer Magazine,* May 15, 1988, 27.

73   "a manual instructing the troops": Dwight Macdonald, "Charles Addams, His Family, and His Fiends," *The Reporter,* July 21, 1953, 40.

73   "the treacherous tactics": Admire, "Samuel E. Cobean."

73   "What talent you had" and following: LHD interview with SA, April 5, 2000.

73   "You fill the car up": LHD interview with Lou Marcus, March 27, 2000.

75   "the screwball days": John W. Sheeres to CSA, January 21, 1957.

76   "half-civilian, half-soldier": CSA quoted in Altshuler, "Monsters Are His Best Friends."

76   "alternative storyboard": Lee Lorenz, "Sam Cobean: A Forgotten Master," unpublished manuscript, author's files.

76   **"There was something about me"** and following: Introduction, *The Cartoons of Cobean.*

77   **"Tell him to clean these up":** Lorenz, "Sam Cobean."

78   **"remarkable . . . fantastic"** and following: LHD interview with Philip and Anna Hamburger, December 6, 1999.

78   **"at the crack of dawn":** CSA quoted in Michael Shnayerson, *Irwin Shaw: A Biography* (New York: G. P. Putnam's Sons, 1989), 119.

78   **"fame should increase":** Harold W. Ross to CSA, December 8, 1943, TCAF.

80   **"Contains glucose":** *NYer,* December 25, 1943, 9.

80   **"fascination with violence":** Macdonald, "Charles Addams, His Family, and His Fiends," 37.

80   **"preferred artists and idea men":** *NYer* telegram to CSA, December 8, 1941, TCAF.

80   **"You men will hear":** *NYer,* February 1, 1941, 9.

80   **"I thought perhaps he'd be good":** *NYer,* April 24, 1943.

80   **"It's just a simple case":** *NYer,* June 7, 1941.

81   **"weird Family":** Macdonald, "Charles Addams, His Family, and His Fiends," 37.

81   **"Well, don't come whining to me":** *NYer,* August 26, 1944, 29.

81   **"children are all kind of sadistic"** and following: "Westfield-Born Cartoonist Charles Addams."

81   **"the universal little boy":** CSA quoted in Carol Oppenheim, "Cartoonist Addams Is Nobody's Ghoul," *Chicago Tribune* April 13, 1978.

81   **"the kid next door":** CSA/AF.

81   **"couldn't bear to think of as married":** *Contemporary Literary Criticism,* Vol. 30 (Detroit: Gale Research, 1984), 11.

81   **"This is nothing":** *NYer,* March 8, 1941, 23.

83   **"Hey, Pop":** *NYer,* October 25, 1941, 27.

83   **"jokes of this sort":** *Berliner Illustrierte Zeitung,* quoted in Macdonald, "Charles Addams, His Family, and His Friends," 37.

83   **"It's a lovely spot":** *NYer,* September 30, 1944, 27.

83   **"We don't know who":** CSA/AF.

83   **"tasty little household":** Harold W. Ross to CSA, June 30, 1944.

83   **"souped-up 220 Merk":** *Mechanix Illustrated,* undated clipping.

84   **They gave wonderful parties:** LHD interview with Mrs. Whitney Darrow, February 2, 2000.

84   **"complete down to the last intestine":** John Kobler, *Afternoon in the Attic,* 5.

84   **"fly intimidator":** *True,* December 1949, 72.

84   **something "sinister-looking in the car":** LHD interview with Hedda Sterne, May 13, 2002.

85   **"It's all right":** JMG.

86   **"You know what?":** LHD interview with anonymous.

CHAPTER EIGHT: Boiling Oil

87 "Rhinebeck has a house": *Interview* magazine 8:5 (1978), 23.

88 "really a style developed by Mansart" and following: *Quest* 3:4 (June 1979).

88 "better for haunts": Carol Oppenheim, "Cartoonist Addams Is Nobody's Ghoul," *Chicago Tribune,* April 13, 1978.

88 four of the "weirdos": JMG.

89 "half circle of light" and following: LHD interview with Ed Koren, March 13, 2000.

90 "You mean you'd use that": JMG/NYPL.

90 "I don't think anyone": CSA to John Mason Brown, November 13, 1950, Houghton Library, Harvard College.

90 "It expresses their exact feeling": LHD interview with SA, April 5, 2000.

90 "Money is no problem" and following: CSA/AF.

91 "one for the road": CSA cartoon rough, TCAF.

91 "for possible re-rendering": George W. McKinney to CSA, November 25, 1953.

92 "My God!": Michael K. Duggan to CSA, April 1, 1954.

92 "That's really not the sort of thing": LHD interview with MMA, November 1–5, 1999.

92 " 'Well, what do you know?' ": to CSA from William Saroyan, September 10, 1949.

92 "a woman coming out of": e-mail to LHD from Arthur Laurents, March 16, 2005.

93 "dead white skin" and following: CSA/AF.

94 "not just a Family man": CI.

94 "A cask of Amontillado": *NYer,* November 23, 1946, 33.

95 told Pugsley to "kick Daddy good night": *NYer,* August 14, 1948, 31.

95 "Now kick Daddy good night": LHD interview with Wylie O'Hara Doughty, April 23, 2002.

96 "I firmly believe": Bennett Cerf to CSA, September 19, 1947.

96 "the strength of the whole Family": CSA/AF.

96 "an unsavory creature": CSA quoted in John Kobler, *Afternoon in the Attic* (New York: Dodd, Mead & Company, 1950), 9.

CHAPTER NINE: And Then the Dragon Gobbled Up
the Handsome Young Prince

97 "the most in love people": LHD interview with Carol Matthau, December 27, 2000.

97 "healthy and cheerful": John Kobler, *Afternoon in the Attic* (New York: Dodd, Mead & Company, 1950), 9.

97 "There was always someone having a drink": LHD interview with MMA, November 1–5, 1999.

98 "I am my own child": CSA quoted in Patricia Coffin, *Single* (October 1975), 93.

98 "the idea of children": LHD interview with Jessie Wood, June 5, 2000.

98 "find very young ones annoying": CSA quoted in Mark Matthews, "Westfield-Born Cartoonist," [page number missing].

99 "It's the children, darling": *NYer,* August 30, 1947, 20.

100 the Indy 500, "a sacred event": LHD interview with Wilfrid Sheed, October 24, 2003.

100 "begoggled rides": E. K., "Charles Addams, Cartoonist," *Easthampton Star* (1988).

100 "He was, in fact, absolutely terrified": LHD interview with Wylie O'Hara Doughty, April 23, 2002.

100 "Monte Carlo is thick": JMG.

100 "I'm so hungry" and following: LHD interviews with Audrey Cosden Chickering, April 14, 2000, October 9, 2002.

101 ("Charlie likes the monster in children"): Wolcott Gibbs quoted in Dwight Macdonald, "Charles Addams, His Family, and His Fiends," *The Reporter,* July 21, 1953, 38.

101 "a gleaming human skull": Wolcott Gibbs, Introduction to Charles Addams, *Addams and Evil* (New York: Random House, 1947).

101 "incredibly uncomfortable" machine: LHD interview with Tony Gibbs, June 11, 2000.

101 "wouldn't have minded": LHD interview with MMA, August 7–8, 1999.

102 "was mistaken for someone's grandmother": Johnny H. Admire, "Samuel E. Cobean: Creator of the Dream Drawing Cartoon," master's thesis, University of Oklahoma Graduate College, 1965.

102 "Sam could drink all night": LHD interview with Cameron and Jean Argetsinger, May 12, 2003.

103 "at a 53.6 clip": "Mike Lee Reports," Jamaica, N.Y., *Long Island Press,* September 12, 1957.

103 "animate scenery": Brad Herzog, "Driving Force," http://cornell-magazine.cornell.edu/Archive/SeptOct98/SeptWatkins.html.

104 There came a day when an older child: LHD interview with LBH, December 10, 2001.

104 "All right, children": *NYer,* June 9, 1951, 37.

104 possibly an alcoholic: LHD interview with anonymous.

104 "a very funny, witty fellow": LHD interview with Tom Hollyman, February 4, 2000.

104 "women were always falling for him": LHD interview with Gardner Botsford, April 30, 2003.

104   "the dragon gobbled up": *NYer,* April 14, 1951, 37.

104   "a marriage" between his poodle: CSA, Introduction to *The Cartoons of Cobean* (New York: Harper & Brothers, 1952).

105   "No Ears": LHD interview with Cameron and Jean Argetsinger, May 12, 2003.

105   "I didn't believe it": CSA, Introduction to *The Cartoons of Cobean.*

106   Bobby looked "great": LHD interview with Cameron and Jean Argetsinger, May 12, 2003.

106   "What a remarkably fine friendship": Anne Cobean to CSA, undated.

106   "she looked like a Japanese boy": LHD interview with LBH, November 3, 1999.

106   she didn't take "a nickel": LHD interviews with O, May 29, 2000, April 30, 2003, May 20, 2001.

106   "Mr. Straight Arrow": LHD interview with Gardner Botsford, April 30, 2003.

CHAPTER TEN: Everything Happens to *Me*

The Harriet Fleischl Pilpel memos quoted here are at the Tee and Charles Addams Foundation.

108   After Charlie's marriage ended: LHD interview with Tony Gibbs, January 11, 2002.

108   "organize[d] his own": *Current Biography* (New York: The H. W. Wilson Co., 1954).

108   "We'll use some of my cartoons": *Look,* May 19, 1953.

109   "a little tower": Harry Altshuler, "Monsters Are His Best Friends," *New York World-Telegram,* August 30, 1965.

109   ("I'm the only two-cupola man"): "May We Present," *Good Housekeeping,* July 1957.

109   "like being on a houseboat": "With Eleanor," unidentified magazine clipping, 1966.

109   "entrancing Irish brogue": Gardner Botsford, *A Life of Privilege, Mostly* (New York: St. Martin's Press, 2003), 212.

110   caught the word "bastard": Harrison Kinney, *James Thurber: His Life and Times* (New York: Henry Holt and Company, 1995), 961.

110   "Charlie Addams, you're a pig!" and following: LHD interview with Gardner Botsford, April 30, 2003.

110   Addams "was quite a catch": LHD interview with Philip and Anna Hamburger, December 6, 1999.

110   "there was always a very attractive woman" and following: e-mail to LHD from Arthur Laurents, March 16, 2005.

111 "YOU SHOULD BE HEARING": Elizabeth Hadlick to CSA, October 14, 1953.

111 "with that sweet slow smile" and following: LHD interviews with Gillis Addison, January 24 and 23, 2002.

111 "orange blossomish plans": Dorothy Kilgallen, "The Voice of Broadway," *New York Journal-American,* March 31, 1953.

112 The occasion was the premiere: "Dune Deck Unveils Charles Addams Mural," *Riverhead News* (N.Y.), July 10, 1952.

112 "Aren't they carrying this too far?": Rosemary Pettit quoted in Bob Sylvester [?], "Society Today," July 1959, unidentified newspaper clipping.

112 "I'm sure I defended that guy": Robert Sylvester, "A Large Artistic Weekend Reopens NY Barn Theatre," *Daily News,* July 2, 1952.

114 "a woman's body—built for action": LHD interview with NH, May 17, 2001.

114 "I could see the ocean": e-mail to LHD from Arthur Laurents, March 16, 2005.

114 "She was very spectacular-looking": LHD interview with JG, October 5, 2002.

114 She looked "like a beautiful showgirl": LHD interview with Hedda Sterne, May 13, 2002.

115 "a big, brassy number": LHD interview with Gardner Botsford, April 30, 2003.

115 People were astonished and following: LHD interview with JG, October 5, 2002.

115 "titled or wealthy persons" and following: "Legal Beauty Is Provided by Woman," *Milwaukee Journal,* February 7, 1954.

116 "a black ensemble" and following: *New York Herald Tribune,* March 4, 1939.

116 "girl lawyer": "Girl Lawyer, 23, Defends Man in Harlem Slaying," *New York Times,* March 14, 1939.

116 "a tort with tits" and following: LHD interview with NH, May 17, 2001.

117 "Spooky, that woman": LHD interview with LBH, November 3, 1999.

117 "Charlie just absolutely adored her": quoted in LHD interview with Jill Spaulding, March 30, 2001.

117 "Evidently, they didn't get along": LHD interview with FM, December 9, 1999.

119 "I really think I've had enough": LHD interview with ETBD, January 30, 2000.

119 "Charles Addams is now mixed up": *The Thurber Letters: The Wit, Wisdom and Surprising Life of James Thurber,* ed. Harrison Kinney with Rosemary A. Thurber (New York: Simon & Schuster, 2002), 633.

119 "Oh, my God, I'm married to a lawyer": LHD interview with Carol Matthau, December 27, 2000.

119 "Addams called and said": HFP memo, December 31, 1954.

120 "could barely walk": LHD interview with BC, June 2, 2002.

121 "I've lost our baby": LHD interview with MMA, March 6–10, 2000.

121 "a false miscarriage": LHD interview with JG, October 24, 2002.

121 "She told him she had no family": HFP memo, June 29, 1955.

121 "They're very nice people": LHD interview with JG, October 5, 2002.

121 "I'm going to see my family in B": LHD interviews with Drue Heinz, November 6, 2002; JG, October 5, 2002.

121 "I may even need your help": HFP memo, June 29, 1955.

122 "exquisite manners": LHD interview with JG, October 5, 2002.

122 intended to watch Barbara closely: HFP memo, June 29, 1955.

122 "Barbara Barb appears to be" and following: HFP memo, June 29, 1955. Also LHD interviews with MMA, May 28, 2002, May 16, 2002, June 12–16, 2000; LHL, June 7, 2002, May 10, 2002, June 1, 2000, February 28, 2000, April 6, 2000; FM, December 9, 1999; AW, May 29, 2002, January 26, 2000; Audrey Cosden Chickering, October 9, 2002.

123 Leila was furious: LHD interview with LHL, September 18, 2000.

123 "In a weak moment" and following: HFP memo, June 29, 1955.

123 "fifty per cent" and following: to Barbara Barb from John N. Wheeler, McClure Newspaper Syndicate, June 1, 1955.

124 "I urged him not to sign anything" and following: HFP memos, June 3, 1955, June 29, 1955, July 22, 1955.

124 "the sweetest girl in the world": LHD interview with Carol Matthau, December 27, 2000.

124 "al fresco lunches": LHD interview with BC, June 2, 2000.

125 "terrible dark passion" and following: LHD interviews with NH, June 20, 2002, May 17, 2001.

127 "Everything happens to *me*": Charles Addams, *Homebodies* (New York: Pocket Cardinal, 1965).

CHAPTER ELEVEN: I Am So Lucky

The cards to Barbara Barb Addams are at the Tee and Charles Addams Foundation.

128 "an ordeal because of his shyness" and following: LHD interviews with BC, February 10, 2000, June 2, 2002.

129 Barbara was "impossible": LHD interview with LHL, April 6, 2000.

129 who found Barbara "gay and good": LHD interview with Patricia Neal, September 15, 2004.

129 "Is the contract void": HFP memo, September 6, 1955.

129 "I like working" and following: Liva Weil, "Here 'Tis Always the Witching Hour," *Newsday*, October 3, 1955, 25.

130 "Addams called to say" and following: HFP memos, October 25, 1955.

131 **"is beyond his own depth"**: Harriet F. Pilpel, "The Job the Lawyers Shirk," *Harper's Monthly* 220 (January 1960), 67–71.

131 **the "female lawyer" he had married**: HFP memo, June 29, 1955.

131 **alabaster-skinned**: John Gilbert, *Opposite Attraction: The Lives of Erich Maria Remarque and Paulette Goddard* (New York: Pantheon, 1995), 258.

131 **never "dissembled or misled"** and following: LHD interview with anonymous.

131 **"great affection"** and following: LHD interview with Robert Pilpel, June 5, 2001.

132 **a rueful smile**: LHD interview with Judith Applebaum, May 25, 2001.

132 **"apparently to see whether she wanted"**: HFP memo, July 10, 1956.

132 **"I am so lucky"**: Therese Milstein quoted in LHD interview with Jill Spaulding, March 30, 2001.

134 **It *"isn't* Charlie"**: LHD interview with Audrey Cosden Chickering, October 9, 2002.

134 **called the letter "bullshit"**: LHD interview with AW, May 29, 2002.

134 **"coercion . . . a ransom letter"**: LHD interview with LHL, May 29, 2002.

134 **it read "like TV drama"**: LHD interview with FM, October 7, 2002.

134 **"totally high"**: LHD interview with O, May 27, 2002.

135 **"Lovers lie, too"**: LHD interview with NH, June 20, 2002.

135 **"afraid" was the whole key to Addams** and following: LHD interviews with Audrey Cosden Chickering, October 9, 2002, April 14, 2002.

135 **"Charlie was always being protected"**: LHD interview with LHL, April 6, 2000.

135 **he would have "done anything"** and following: LHD interview with MMA, May 16, 2000, June 12–16, 2000; interview with anonymous.

135 **"vocabulary, syntax, or language"**: LHD interview with FM, October 7, 2002.

135 **"My heart is so broken"** and following: BC to CSA, undated letter, May 30, 1962, December 24, 1962, undated letter.

136 **"was *not* a *happy* man"**: LHD interview with BC, June 2, 2002.

136 **"speedy decrees"**: "Cartoonist Addams' Wife Wins 45-Min. Alabama Divorce," *New York Post*, October 14, 1956.

136 **"a bona fide resident"**: Barbara E. Addams vs. Charles Samuel Addams, oral deposition, October 9, 1956.

136 **"BARE HALF-HOUR"**: New York *Daily News*, October 13, 1956.

136 **a "slinky, lank-haired Lawyer"**: *Time*, October 22, 1956.

137 **"Residents of the Hamptons"**: Dorothy Kilgallen, "The Voice of Broadway," *New York Journal-American*, October 17, 1956.

137 **"set what must be a record"** and following: Arthur Watson, "How Safe Is a Quickie Divorce?" *Sunday News*, October 21, 1956, C7.

137 **"migratory divorce"** and following: Harriet F. Pilpel and Theodora Zavin, *Your Marriage and the Law* (New York: Rinehart & Co., 1952), 329, 345, 330.

138 "Respondent denies each and every": CSA, answer and waiver to Barbara E. Addams vs. Charles Samuel Addams.

138 "in the same condition": BC to CSA, September 6, 1974.

CHAPTER TWELVE: The Tunnel of Love

The correspondence of Tee Davie—abbreviated as "MMA"—and E. T. Bedford Davie, along with the letters from Barbara Colyton to Charles Addams, is located at the Tee and Charles Addams Foundation.

140 "Charles Addams of New York": *Nashville Banner,* December 24, 1956.

141 ("It was lousy sexually"): LHD interview with MMA, December 8–14, 2001.

141 To begin with, they were known for and following: E. J. Kahn, "Powers Model," *NYer,* September 14, 1940, 26.

141 her own child made her "nervous" and following: MMA to ETBD, November 6, 1958.

142 "a wonderful lover, but a lousy husband": LHD interview with MMA, January 31, 2000.

142 "I can and will give up" and following: MMA to ETBD, undated (1958).

143 "It wasn't me, it was your father": ETBD to MMA, November 6, 1958.

143 "Here's your lover, and your dog": LHD interview with MMA, April 9, 2000.

143 ("Weather was Ghoulish"): *Nashville Tennessean,* December 26, 1956.

144 "I don't think you should": LHD interview with MMA, March 6–10, 2000.

144 "E. T. Bedford—Mortician": *NYer,* February 9, 1957, 27.

144 "It's too bad he had to use": LHD interview with MMA, March 6–10, 2000.

144 "not a cheerful place": LHD interview with O, July 7, 2003.

146 "And in three days": BC to CSA, November 28, 1957.

146 "the glamorous barrister": "Cholly Knickerbocker Says 'Romance No Forte of British Royalty,' " *New York Journal-American,* February 5, 1957.

146 "continue to represent her ex-husband": Leonard Lyons, "The Lyons Den," *New York Post,* February 15, 1957.

146 "Porker Bell" and following: BC to CSA, November 28, 1957, October 11, 1957, undated letter.

CHAPTER THIRTEEN: Dear Dead Days

Charles Addams's letters to Leila Hadley Luce are part of her collection at Boston University.

148 "Your picture of the family plantation": CSA to LHL, March 10, 1959.

148 "in an ever-rising, unbroken curve": Irwin Shaw to CSA, November 23, 1957.

148   **"Charles Addams has introduced a gothic element"** and following: Cecil Beaton, "Famous Names With Little-Known Faces," *The Observer* (1957), excerpted from Cecil Beaton, *The Face of the World* (New York: John Day Company, 1958).

149   **"Those flowers came too late"**: CSA quoted in Leonard Lyons, "The Lyons Den," *New York Post,* April 22, 1959, 1.

149   **"I revisited your old apartment"** and following: CSA to LHL, March 10, 1959.

149   **Here were photographs of dwarfs:** Charles Addams, ed., *Dear Dead Days: A Family Album* (London: Paul Hamlyn, 1959), 114, 64, 105, 122, 80, 87, 86, 85.

150   **"I have gotten a lot of letters"**: CSA quoted in "Charles Addams Dead at 76; Found Humor in the Macabre," *New York Times,* September 30, 1988, B-8.

150   **"I have heard of an undertaker's child"**: Homer Joseph Dodge to CSA, April 29, 1959.

150   **"I like the little top floor"**: E. B. White to CSA, April 12, 1959.

150   **"shoes for the entire family"**: radio interview, "The Haunt for Chas Addams: Charles Addams Talks with Philip French," August 5, 1978.

150   **"eliminating people with two heads"**: Bennett Cerf, "Try and Stop Me," *Los Angeles Examiner,* January 12, 1959.

151   **"have a refreshing conversational approach"**: "People," *Time,* November 3, 1961, 30.

151   **"that was where the blood"**: LHD interview with ETBD, January 30, 2000.

151   **"Saw 3 mutes, 2 dwarfs"**: CSA to LHL, undated.

151   **"fistheads"**: LHD interview with Nancy Whitney, February 7, 2000.

151   **"the good old days" of the electric chair:** LHD interview with SA, April 5, 2000.

151   **"anything weird, freaky, bizarre"**: LHD interview with Nancy Whitney, February 7, 2000.

151   **"a healthy escape"** and following: Charles Addams, "Movie Monster Rally," *New York Times Magazine,* August 9, 1953, 16–17.

152   **("It's hard to figure")**: CSA quoted in John Grossman, "Charles Addams: Twenty-four Hours in the Life of the Creator of *The Addams Family,*" *TWA Ambassador,* September 1981.

152   **"It doesn't take much"**: *NYer,* June 28, 1941, 9.

152   **"morbid suspicion"**: C. Anne Vitullo, "Somewhat Gloomily Yours, Charles Addams," University of Pennsylvania *Almanac,* November 8, 1979.

152   **"the idea of knowing there's an octopus"**: Marshall Ledger, "Charles Addams Comes to Campus," *Pennsylvania Gazette,* December 1979.

152   **a "doll-like" figure:** LHD interview with Lee Lorenz, December 10, 1999.

153 **"romantic, nostalgic"**: CSA quoted in Philip French, "Addams and the Monster Within," *The Listener,* September 21, 1978, 371.

154 **Addams had been "a presence"** and following: LHD interview with Tony Gibbs, January 11, 2000.

154 **"He had his feet up"**: Gardner Botsford, *A Life of Privilege, Mostly* (New York: St. Martin's Press, 2003), 181.

155 **"How great to see a freak"**: LHD interview with SA, April 5, 2000.

155 **"Shawn felt—said"**: French, "The Haunt for Chas Addams."

155 **"I can't imagine why anyone"**: Henry Schneiderman to CSA, July 3, 1964.

155 **"One word about *Dear Dead Days*"**: David Hogan to CSA, December 28, 1967.

156 **"Barbara (in a bizarre hat)"**: Evelyn Waugh to CSA, All Souls' Day 1959.

156 **"I think probably"**: French, "The Haunt for Chas Addams."

CHAPTER FOURTEEN: **Mr. and Mrs. and Mrs. Addams**

157 **"This is the kind of man"**: LHD interview with Carol Matthau, December 27, 2000.

157 **"always listened, interested"**: LHD interview with Barbara Gross, January 5, 2004.

157 **"come away feeling"**: LHD interview with George Plimpton, January 27, 2000.

157 **"not on his level"**: LHD interview with Barbara Gross, January 5, 2004.

157 **"co-conspirator"**: LHD interview with Jessie Wood, June 15, 2000.

157 **"He took an interest"**: e-mail to LHD from AW, February 28, 2000.

158 **"Are you limping"**: LHD interview with AW, February 16, 2000.

158 **"Spirits always soared"**: LHD interview with Arthur Schlesinger, Jr., December 6, 2001.

158 **"didn't perform, ever"**: LHD interview with Philip and Anna Hamburger, December 6, 1999.

158 **"reminded you of a summer meadow"**: "Charles Addams," *NYer,* October 17, 1988, 122.

158 **"his mumbly, rumbly voice"**: LHD interview with Drue Heinz, November 6, 2000.

158 **("It was almost like eavesdropping")**: LHD interview with Budd Schulberg, December 11, 2001.

158 **"Going skiing, no doubt"**: LHD interview with BC, February 10, 2000.

158 **"funny as hell"**: LHD interview with Philip and Anna Hamburger, December 6, 1999.

158 **"Any antique would fascinate him"**: LHD interview with Budd Schulberg, December 11, 2001.

159 **"had very true instincts"**: LHD interview with Arthur Schlesinger, Jr., February 6, 2001.

159 **"fascinated by O'Hara's eccentricities"**: LHD interview with Sidney Offit, December 28, 1999.

159 **"Oh, you're only doing that"**: LHD interview with Mischa Richter, November 12, 1999.

159 **"How could you talk"**: LHD interview with BC, February 10, 2000.

159 **"Let's go tell Frank!"**: LHD interview with FM, December 9, 1999.

159 **constantly used "you"**: LHD interview with Sidney Offit, December 28, 1999.

159 **"You're Charlie Addams"**: LHD interview with Philip and Anna Hamburger, December 6, 1999.

160 **"A fully clothed English nanny"**: CSA to NH, undated.

160 **"Do you go to every party"**: LHD interview with SA, April 5, 2000.

160 **"Mr. O'Hala"**: CSA to John O'Hara, September 1953.

160 **"the acquaintance who sucked his teeth"**: Marshall Ledger, "Charles Addams Comes to Campus," *Pennsylvania Gazette,* December 1979.

160 **"I came to see the *asp*"**: LHD interview with William Benjamin, June 15, 2000.

160 **("Now remember, act casual")**: *NYer,* July 26, 1952, 27.

160 **"A drawing instead of a plate"**: LHD interview with JG, April 5, 2000.

160 **"There's a silly sign"**: *NYer,* June 17, 1961, 31.

161 **"We went into a sort of stupor"**: Honoria Murphy to CSA, undated, 1964.

161 **"He was a *great* friend" and following**: LHD interview with Carol Matthau, December 27, 2000.

161 **"a certain kind of sophisticated talk"**: LHD interview with Lillian Ross, March 4, 2000.

161 **"I *wish*"**: LHD interview with Carol Matthau, December 27, 2000.

161 **"Charlie had a true interest in women"**: LHD interview with MMA, March 6–10, 2000.

162 **Charlie "flipped" and following**: LHD interview with Gerta Conner, April 6, 2000.

162 **"the hermit about town" and following**: John Bainbridge, *Garbo* (New York: Doubleday, 1955), 236.

162 **"a set of red woolen underwear"**: LHD interview with SA, April 5, 2000.

162 **"face concealing hat"**: Bainbridge, *Garbo,* 233.

162 **"he liked that her face"**: LHD interview with ETBD, January 30, 2000.

162 **"I am not feeling good"**: Bainbridge manuscript attached to letter to CSA, July 20, 1970.

163 **"Oh, Mr. Addams"**: LHD interview with SA, April 5, 2000.

163 **"The unlikeliest twosome"**: Sheila Graham, "Garbo, Addams Pair Off," New York *Daily Mirror,* September 30, 1960.

163 **"reached people very easily"**: LHD interview with JG, April 5, 2000.

163 **"She always says"**: CSA quoted in Bainbridge, *Garbo* (New York: Holt, Rinehart & Winston, 1971).

163   "the wrong time": LHD interview with SA, April 5, 2000.

164   ("Marsha wants a drink!"): LHD interview with MMA, November 1–5, 1999.

164   "adorable, frisky" Cousin Ronnie: LHD interview with LHL, June 1, 2000.

164   "suffering from a post Addams depression": Sloan Simpson to CSA, February 18, 1965.

164   "She had eight million dollars": LHD interview with SA, April 5, 2000.

164   "very statuesque": LHD interview with FM, December 9, 1999.

164   "the first Jewish Italian American princess": LHD interview with LHL, June 12, 2005.

164   the brilliant, stylish, never-married Dona Guimares: LHD interviews with MMA, November 1–5, 1999; Denise Otis, April 12, 2000; Linda Yang, June 5, 2000.

165   she would "visibly" shake and following: Howard Teichmann, *George S. Kaufman* (New York: Atheneum, 1972), 223.

165   "There was Charles Addams": Carol Bjorkman, *Daily News Record*, April 13, 1964, 4.

166   "nothing interfered with his work": LHD interview with O, June 24–25, 2000.

166   "Joan looked divine" and following: LHD interviews with MMA, January 4–7, 2000, June 12–16 2000, November 1–5, 1999.

167   "Now I'm careful": CSA quoted in Harry Altshuler, "Monsters Are His Best Friends," *New York World-Telegram and Sun*, August 30, 1965.

168   "the envy of London": Clive Fisher, *Cyril Connolly* (New York: St. Martin's Press, 1995), 290.

168   And she was absolutely wild and following: LHD interview with LHL, March 3, 2000.

168   "silvery laugh": Jeremy Lewis, "Pantherine," in Mark Bostridge, *Lives for Sale* (London: Continuum, 2004), 43–51.

168   "I would have preferred a splayed cane": Fisher, *Cyril Connolly*, 290, 319.

169   "became very aggressive" and following: Barbara Skelton, *Weep No More* (London: Hamish Hamilton, 1989), 84.

169   "Charlie just thought she was great": LHD interview with LHL, June 1, 2000.

169   "seems to be very curious": Barbara Skelton to CSA, October 10, 1960.

169   "as Charlie was scurrying naked": Barbara Skelton, *Tears Before Bedtime and Weep No More* (London: Pimlico, 1993), 322.

170   "Charlie was, on the whole, a passive man": Barbara Skelton, *Weep No More*, 84.

170   "a wonderful beau": LHD interview with LHL, February 28, 2000.

170   "a floating palace": Audrey Cosden Chickering to CSA, undated.

170   "the *New York Times*": O to CSA, undated.

170   "I've got something wonderful": LHD interview with anonymous.
171   "a sophisticated innocent": LHD interviews with LHL, June 1, 2000, April 6, 2000.
171   "absolutely rigid with boredom": e-mail to LHD from AW, May 29, 2002.
171   "I think he had the wrong operation": LHD interview with Audrey Cosden Chickering, October 9, 2002.
171   "My father was": LHD interview with NH, May 17, 2001.
172   "Mrs. Butterinsky": LHD interview with AW, February 28, 2000.
172   "My Husband Has Cancer": LHD interview with NH, May 17, 2001.
172   "lovely unexpected weekend": LHL to CSA, November 4, 1963.
173   "loved to climb up the trap door": Matthew Elliot to CSA, November 4, 1963.
173   "Oh, no, Mummy": LHD interview with LHL, April 6–7, 2000.
174   "made everything a little dirtier": LHD interview with MMA, March 6–10, 2000.
174   the ancient, "lumpish" black woman: LHD interview with LHL, April 6, 2000.
174   "Why don't you fire her?": LHD interview with MMA, March 6–10, 2000.
174   the Indy 500 was "a sacred event": LHD interview with Wilfrid Sheed, October 24, 2003.
174   "My dock seems to be on fire": LHD interview with MMA, March 6–10, 2000.
174   "child-like experience": LHD interviews with O, June 24–25, 2000, May 29, 2000.
174   "only babies have": LHD interview with LHL, March 30, 2001.
174   "blotted Victorian love poem": LHL to CSA, February 22, 1964.
175   "It's the little people": LHD interview with Audrey Cosden Chickering, October 9, 2002.
175   "he couldn't lie" and following: LHD interview with LHL, February 28, 2000.
175   "a joyous escape": LHD interviews with O, June 24–25, 2000, May 29, 2000.
175   "Charlie was the only man": LHD interview with LHL, February 28, 2000.

CHAPTER FIFTEEN: *Remarkably* Well Preserved

177   "How do you spell cunnilingus": LHD interview with LHL, February 28, 2000.
177   "hearty, easy, a lot of fun": LHD interview with JG, April 5, 2000.
177   ("witty, funny, mean"): LHD interview with Drue Heinz, November 6, 2000.

177 "had all the characteristics" and following: LHD interview with Gillis Addison, January 23, 2002.

178 "the best possible care of the star": Anne D. Mason to CSA, May 23, 1962.

178 "passionately attached" to Fontaine: Barbara Skelton, *Weep No More* (London: Hamish Hamilton, 1989), 102.

178 "So, Charlie, how's your love life?": Alistair Cooke, *Letter from America*, No. 2865 (January 22, 2004).

178 "We get our divorce any minute": "Mister Next for Elvis," *Hollywood Highlights* (1962).

178 "but no—too difficult": LHD interview with LBH, November 3, 1999.

178 "I am *remarkably* well preserved": LHD interview with LHL, February 28, 2000.

178 "get the vapors" and following: LHD interview with LBH, November 3, 1999.

179 "Charlie Addams, the famed cartoonist": Cholly Knickerbocker, *New York Journal-American*, July 22, 1962.

179 "I don't like you, piss face": LHD interview with LBH, November 3, 1999.

180 "It's such a wonderful friendship": *Time*, January 25, 1963, 33.

180 "I was afraid *I* was going to be": LHD interview with NH, May 17, 2001.

180 "The relief was almost": "Charles Addams: Recluse About Town," *Single*, October 1975, 39–40.

180 "never cruel about the lack of talent": LHD interview with LHL, April 6, 2000.

180 "while he tinkered" and following: Joan Fontaine, *No Bed of Roses* (New York: William Morrow, 1978), 263, 272.

180 "a bad investment": LHD interviews with LHL, February 28, 2000, March 8, 2002.

180 "As for La Fontaine": BC to CSA, undated.

CHAPTER SIXTEEN: The Addams Family

For this chapter I am greatly indebted to *The Addams Chronicles* by Stephen Cox, which told me virtually everything I needed to know about the *Addams Family* television show.

182 "I wanted to call him Pubert": Mark Matthews, "Westfield-Born Cartoonist Charles Addams," *The Courier-News*, August 10, 1974.

182 "smart black-and-white print fabrics" and following: *House Beautiful*, April 1963, 147.

183 ("Dear Mr. Addams"): Joan A. Pugsley to CSA, April 9, 1964.

183 "I just thought that up": John Grossman, "Charles Addams: Twenty-four Hours in the Life of the Creator of *The Addams Family*," *TWA Ambassador*, September 1981.

183   "Something really ought to be done": Wolcott Gibbs to CSA, undated (1947).

184   ("Rack" and "Ruin"): Richie Pew to CSA, February 19, 1961.

184   "powers that be in television": to CSA from Philip Stern, April 5, 1961.

184   the Family came across as "unsympathetic": Jo Coudert to CSA, May 22, 1963.

184   "Suddenly, I have a dreadful urge": *NYer,* December 15, 1962, 38.

185   "This is it speaking": *NYer,* October 12, 1963, 46.

186   "step by step": LHD interview with Don Saltzman, October 15, 2004.

187   Barbara fired off warnings to Filmways: HFP memos, February 25, 1964, February 24, 1964, February 26, 1964.

187   "of all sums due Owner": From *The Addams Family* TV show contract.

187   "She was interested in the money": LHD interview with Don Saltzman, October 15, 2004.

188   "Porker Bell," "Angel Porkerish": BC to CSA, May 30, 1962, July 10, 1962, July 25, 1962, December 24, 1962, December 13, 1962.

188   "that he *must* extricate himself" and following: HFP memos, October 30, 1959, January 6, 1961.

189   "in a seriously exposed": HFP memo, October 11, 1962.

189   "in the same condition": CSA to BC, October 13, 1962.

189   "He was suddenly frozen": LHD interview with O, May 27, 2002.

189   "Sea shell situation bearish": CSA to LHL, February 1964.

190   "a big friend of the Kennedys": LHD interview with SA, March 3, 2000.

191   "one of those very overcrowded": LHD interview with Arthur Schlesinger, Jr., February 6, 2001.

191   "stunned by, enchanted by Jackie": LHD interview with NH, May 17, 2001.

191   "He was really quite in awe": LHD interview with O, May 29, 2000.

191   "I can't stand it any more": LHD interview with MMA, January 31, 2000.

192   "astute and low-key": LHD interview with O, June 24–25, 2000.

192   "She did tell me how she felt": LHD interview with MMA, January 4–7, 2000.

192   ("Do you know, she had his *brains*"): LHD interview with anonymous.

192   "I love Pugsley and Lurch": Jackie Kennedy quoted in Christopher Andersen, *Jackie After Jack: Portrait of the Lady* (New York: Warner Books, 1999), 146.

192   playful and "very energetic": LHD interview with MMA, January 4–7, 2000.

192   "I drove her down to Pennsylvania": LHD interview with SA, March 3, 2000.

192   "Your friend looks just like Jackie Kennedy": LHD interviews with AW, January 26, 2000; MMA, November 1–5, 1999; SA, March 3, 2000.

192   **The adult Caroline Kennedy would remember:** to LHD from Caroline Kennedy, December 15, 2000.

193   **the food was "pretty good" and following:** LHD interview with SA, March 3, 2000.

193   **"should Miss Barb decide":** Jack Kaplan to CSA, April 20, 1964.

193   **"in high dudgeon":** HFP memo, February 18, 1965.

193   **"fuss with Filmways" and following:** HFP memo, February 18, 1965.

194   **"They almost fell off their chairs":** reprinted in Stephen Cox, *The Addams Chronicles* (New York: Harper Perennial, 1991), 22.

194   **"Now faced with doing introduction":** CSA to LHL, August 1964.

194   **"Just be easy—desinvolte":** LHL to CSA, August 29, 1964.

195   **"almost a typical suburban family":** "The Sixteenth Man," *Newsweek*, July 5, 1965, 81.

195   **emitted sudden screeches:** Cox, *The Addams Chronicles*, 22.

195   **Carolyn Jones was "enchanting":** *New York Post*, April 16, 1991.

195   **his "ruined beauty" and following:** CSA/AF.

195   **"romance be unceasing":** John Astin, foreword to Cox, *The Addams Chronicles*.

196   **"dedicated trouble maker":** CSA/AF.

196   **"Well, he certainly doesn't take after":** *NYer*, November 3, 1945, 31.

196   **"this isn't some boyish prank":** Episode 2, *The Addams Family*, September 25, 1964.

197   **" 'The Addams Family' is":** Brian Shane to CSA, undated.

197   **"in an age when non-conformity":** Cox, *The Addams Chronicles*, 145.

197   **"We almost had to do it":** Harry Altshuler, "Monsters Are His Best Friends," *New York World-Telegram and Sun*, August 30, 1965.

197   **"TV's Year of the Monster":** *Life*, August 21, 1964.

197   **"there wasn't too much of a clash":** CI.

197   **"poor [relation]":** Stephen Cox, *The Addams Chronicles*, 145.

198   **"invidious briars":** Virginia Sheward, "At Home with the Addams Family," *Holiday*, March 1973.

198   **"There's Charles Addams":** LHD interview with Denise Otis, May 12, 2000.

198   **"It's on at an awkward time":** *New York Post*, April 16, 1991.

198   **"Pretty awful":** LHD interview with Barbara Nicholls, January 17–18, 2000.

198   **"I guess he cut her up":** John O'Hara, *Elizabeth Appleton* (New York: Bantam Books, 1969), 20.

198   **"one correction, though":** CSA to John O'Hara, May 28, 1963. Penn State University Libraries.

199   **"disreputable children":** *Quest* 3:4 (June 1979).

200   **"was quite good":** CI.

200 "reached a lot of people": Randall Ross, "Charles Addams Confirms Family Resemblance," *The Polygon*, October 30, 1970.

200 As Shawn seemed to see it: Christian Williams, "The Father of the Addams Family," *Orlando Sentinel*, November 24, 1982, E-4.

200 "I don't think we want to revive them": LHD interview with SA, April 5, 2000.

200 ("No, this is not the 12:38"): *NYer*, September 21, 1986, 37.

201 "It must have been Moonglow": LHD interview with SA, April 5, 2000.

201 "but then the income": Patricia Coffin, "Chas Addams: Recluse About Town," *Single* (October 1975).

201 "made an indiscreet comment": C. David Heymann, *A Woman Named Jackie* (New York: Signet, 1990), 461.

201 "Well, I couldn't get married to you": LHD interviews with LHL, February 28, 2000; SA, March 3, 2000; O, May 29, 2000.

201 "*You* wouldn't know anything about that": LHD interview with LHL, April 6, 2000.

201 "Don't call him 'Jack' ": LHD interview with SA, March 3, 2000.

201 "Well, I'll be invited back": LHD interviews with AW, January 26, 2000, May 29, 2002.

202 "Let's go to bed": LHD interview with SA, March 3, 2000.

202 "One minute she is very sweet": Andersen, *Jackie After Jack*, 147.

202 "Why was Jackie whispering?": LHD interview with SA, April 5, 2000.

CHAPTER SEVENTEEN: Whatever the Gods Are, They Aren't Angry

203 Gomez is stretched out on the couch: unpublished roughs.

203 "think neurotic" and following: "The Sixteenth Man," *Newsweek*, July 5, 1965.

203 "Now this one was owned": *NYer*, January 28, 1961, 33.

203 "Every man is an island": CSA in undated radio interview with Heywood Hale Broun, circa 1975.

204 "Cannibals still exist": "Appendix: Charles Addams Live!," unidentified typescript.

204 "sort of in a state": *Contemporary Literary Criticism* 30 (Detroit: Gale Research, 1984), 11.

204 "You telephone 'Better Homes' ": *NYer*, May 25, 1963, 31.

205 ("You often wonder"): CI.

205 "really had it in for him": LHD interview with ETBD, January 30, 2000.

205 "Sometimes I ask myself": *NYer*, February 9, 1946, 21.

207 "There's enough hate": *NYer*, October 10, 1964, 51.

207 "Whatever the gods are": *NYer*, June 13, 1964, 35.

208 "an unsuccessful private eye's office": Charles Addams, *Homebodies* (New York: Pocket Books, 1965).

208 "**till an idea occurred to him**": LHD interview with Mischa Richter, November 12, 1999.

208 "**Frankly, I don't take much stock**": *NYer*, March 31, 1945.

208 "**Let's give Charlie the gray box**": LHD interview with Barbara Nicholls, January 17–18, 2000.

208 "**Bedford!**": LHD interviews with MMA, June 12–16, 2000; November 1–5, 1999.

209 "**No, no**": LHD interview with FM, December 9, 1999.

210 "**Your friend Barbara Barb**": Greenbaum, Wolff & Ernst memo, JP to HFP, December 21, 1966.

210 "**absolutely essential**": BC to CSA, December 9, 1966.

210 "**raised holy hell**": LHD interview with Nancy Wechsler, April 30, 2004.

210 **his lawyers had been "dilatory"**: HFP to CSA, February 2, 1967.

210 "**to retain the English**": HFP memo, December 21, 1966.

210 "**Pay her anything**": LHD interview with LHL, June 7, 2002.

211 "**misty, moisty morning**": Charles Addams, *The Charles Addams Mother Goose* (New York: Windmill Books, 1967).

212 "**purely a joke**": *New York Times*, November 1, 1967.

212 "**We all know**": David Hogan to CSA, December 28, 1967.

213 "**Why? What's wrong with it?**": LHD interview with Herb Valen, December 15, 2000.

213 "**oddly erect before the drawing board**": CSA, Introduction to *The Cartoons of Cobean* (New York: Harper & Brothers, 1952).

213 "**terribly embarrassed**": CSA to Jean Argetsinger, January 20, 1953; September 12, 1962.

214 "**Another quality roofing job**": *NYer*, July 29, 1974, 27.

214 ("**I see the cartoon as labored humor**"): CSA, *The Dick Cavett Show*, March 29, 1978.

214 "**maniacally, like a rug-maker**": LHD interview with FM, December 9, 1999.

214 "**with absolutely no anxiety**": LHD interview with Lee Lorenz, December 10, 1999.

215 "**search a little bit**" for the joke: *The Dick Cavett Show*.

CHAPTER EIGHTEEN: A Medium-Sized Dog

Charles Addams's postcards to Alice belong to Frank Modell and Alexandra Whitney, respectively. Tee's letters are the property of the Tee and Charles Addams Foundation.

216 "**She has a sweet face**": LHD interview with NH, May 17, 2001.

216 "**including her collar**": Patricia Coffin, "Charles Addams, Recluse About Town," *Single*, October 1975.

217 "Oh, I'm not ready for another dog" and following: LHD interview with FM, December 9, 1999.

217 "uncertain ancestry": Carey Winfrey, "Cartoonist Weds Dog Fancier at Private Cemetery for Pets," *New York Times*, June 1, 1980, 37.

217 "Nobody knows what she is": CI.

217 "something haphazardly fabricated": Patricia McLaughlin, "Charles the Imponderable," *Pennsylvania Gazette* 71:5 (March 1973).

217 ("also old ladies"): Coffin, "Charles Addams, Recluse About Town."

218 "When he took a step": LHD interview with Suzanne Wickham-Beaird, February 17, 2000.

218 "would eat anything": LHD interview with MMA, December 8–14, 2001.

218 "Where have I gone wrong?": LHD interview with Walker McKinney, June 8, 2000.

218 "a sweet dog": CI.

218 "breathed hard" into the telephone: LHD interview with Nancy Whitney, February 7, 2000.

218 "If you invite Charlie": CI.

219 "Well, let's wait and see": LHD interview with Audrey Cosden Chickering, October 9, 2002.

219 "Hope you are acting decently": CSA to Alice, May 28, 1971.

219 "It's just me and Alice": *The Courier-News*, August 10, 1974.

219 ("You know something?"): *NYer*, October 26, 1981, 55.

219 "Is Alice still shedding" and following: MMA to CSA, July 1, 1972, undated letter, 1972.

220 "Dear Red People": CSA to MMA, July 12, 1972.

220 "All right, 'Mr. Smartie'" and following: MMA to CSA, Friday, undated, 1972; July 12, 1972.

220 "The apartment sounds most interesting": CSA to MMA, July 12, 1972.

221 Shopping for meat was a challenge: MMA to CSA, undated letters from 1972.

223 ("Alice has collapsed"): CSA to MMA, July 19, 1972.

223 "had a continuing interest in this property": Harold Messing to Leo Rosen, February 6, 1970. TCAF.

223 "Can't work. But love you": CSA to MMA, July 19, 1972, July 20, 1972, July 12, 1972.

224 "When those anti-abortionists" and following: MMA to CSA, undated, 1972; Thursday, undated, 1972; August 3, 1972.

224 "made a hermit" out of him and following: CSA to MMA, July 20, 1972; July 19, 1972; Tuesday, undated, 1972; July 20, 1972.

225 ("Death ray, fiddlesticks!"): *NYer*, May 16, 1953, 25.

225　she was his "Creature": CSA to MMA, July 19, 1972; Tuesday, undated, 1972; July 20, 1972.

225　"I felt much better": MMA to CSA, August 8, 1972.

225　theirs was "light-hearted": LHD interviews with O, May 29, 2000; June 24–25, 2000.

226　("What is she?)": LHD interview with MMA, June 12–16, 2000.

226　"He was like the Dial-A-Dad": LHD interview with Christopher Benjamin, June 22, 2000.

226　"All right, I'll show you my teeth": LHD interview with William Benjamin, June 15, 2000.

226　"New York body": LHD interview with Christopher Benjamin, June 22, 2000.

227　"Viking-type": LHD interview with William Benjamin, June 15, 2000.

227　"What are your hours?": LHD interview with MMA, December 8–14, 2001.

227　"Dear Beatle": CSA to Beatrice Benjamin, spring 1968.

227　"Our friend O" and following: CSA to MMA, Tuesday, undated, 1972.

229　"If I couldn't have him": LHD interview with O, May 29, 2000.

229　"worse than jackhammers" and following: LHD interview with MMA, March 6–10, 2000.

230　"the haunted house" and following: Virginia Sheward, "At Home with the Addams Family," *Holiday*, March 1973.

230　"Oh, here comes Charlie": LHD interview with Frank Corwin, January 19, 2000.

230　"Well, you know what?": LHD interview with Bedford Davie, January 14, 2000.

230　USE THE KNOBS YOU SLOBS: LHD interview with Amy Wehle, June 13, 2000.

231　"No kids" and following: LHD interview with Bedford Davie, January 14, 2000.

232　"They will never see you!": LHD interview with MMA, March 6–10, 2000.

232　cooking up "little messes": Sheward, "At Home with the Addams Family."

233　"Alice looks just like me": LHD interview with Drue Heinz, November 6, 2000.

CHAPTER NINETEEN: Real Estate

234　"two unidentified wretches": *Pennsylvania Gazette*, April 1975.

234　"a little bit like visiting a monastery": CI.

235　Calling Addams "my oldest friend": Brendan Gill, *Here at The New Yorker* (New York: Berkley Medallion Book, 1976), 238.

235   "A lot of people took their raps": radio interview with Heywood Hale Broun, circa 1975.

235   "He said what people wanted to hear": "Appendix: Charles Addams Live!" unidentified typescript.

235   "Have you ever been to a party": LHD interview with SA, April 5, 2000.

236   "enormous party at Ben Sonnenberg's" and following: *Pennsylvania Gazette*, 17.

236   "If only *The New Yorker*": Judith Martin, "Cartoonists' Elite: Clubby Lunches and Just One Stop . . . Where Gags Are 'Ideas,' " *Washington Post*, January 23, 1972, F-1, 4, 5.

236   "I think the spirit of excellence": *Pennsylvania Gazette*, 17.

236   "an American landmark": *New York Times*, November 2, 1974.

236   "A good cartoonist": CI.

237   "Think of the things I used to do": Martin, "Cartoonists' Elite."

237   "Try to build a house like that": *NYer*, October 11, 1947, 37.

238   "Things are much more static here": CSA to James M. Geraghty, January 14, 1974. JMG.

238   "maybe three to five": Martin, "Cartoonists' Elite."

238   "Dear Mr. Adams [*sic*],": Morris Hurwitz to CSA, May 8, 1976.

238   "People send in little vultures": "Alumnus Creates 'Addams Family,' Uses Westfield House as Inspiration," *Westfield Hi's Eye*, April 2, 1965.

238   "Dear Mr. Ogilvy": CSA to Mr. Ogilvy, February 6, 1975.

240   "It's the opposite of when you see": LHD interview with P. L. Steiner, July 7, 2000.

240   IF YOU DON'T SEE WHAT YOU WANT: *NYer*, September 19, 1983, 42.

240   "giving the emptiness": e-mail to LHD from Michael Maslin, December 21, 1999.

240   "To . . . hell . . . with . . . yogurt": LHD interview with P. L. Steiner, July 7, 2000.

240   "quite good, rather seedy": LHD interview with SA, April 5, 2000.

240   "The drawings are indeed different": CSA to James M. Geraghty, January 14, 1974. JMG/NYPL.

240   "delicate and subdued" tastes: Lee Lorenz, *The Art of The New Yorker, 1925–1995* (New York: Alfred A. Knopf, 1996), 84.

241   "It was a doodle": CSA, *The Dick Cavett Show*, March 29, 1978.

241   "from closet sheep lovers": CSA to James M. Geraghty, May 20, 1975. JMG/NYPL.

241   "I was under the mistaken idea": *The Dick Cavett Show*.

241   "I think of my people as timeless": *The Courier-News*, August 10, 1974.

241   "that little bastard I draw": radio interview with Heywood Hale Broun, circa 1975.

242   "as someone dearer": BC to CSA, July 18, 1974.

244   "that were part of the contents": CSA to BC, October 10, 1974.

244 "Porker dear," she wrote from Monte Carlo: BC to CSA, November 19, 1974.

244 "All he wanted was that little house": LHD interview with MMA, May 28, 2002.

CHAPTER TWENTY: Mrs. Rupert Hutton

245 "Dear one": CSA to MMA, undated (March 1977).

245 she was "only the girlfriend": LHD interviews with MMA, August 7–8, 1999; August 15–18, 2000.

246 "fighting back to health": CSA to AW, undated (1973).

246 "Who's for a little drunken": LHD interview with Drue Heinz, November 6, 2000.

246 "It has a wonderful poisonous": Marshall Ledger, "Charles Addams Comes to Campus," *Pennsylvania Gazette,* December 1979.

246 "loaded" at parties: LHD interview with Lee Lorenz, December 10, 1999.

246 might be drunk "by midnight": LHD interview with JG, October 5, 2002.

246 "Charlie drank cheerfully": LHD interview with Budd Schulberg, December 11, 2001.

246 "disciplined" compared to other boozers: Burgess Meredith, *So Far, So Good* (Boston: Little, Brown, 1994), 79.

247 "a passé institution": Patricia Coffin, "Charles Addams: Recluse About Town," *Single,* October 1975.

247 The new Addams will: HFP memo, September 8, 1976.

247 "Then there's pretty Tee Davie": "Society by Suzy," unidentified clipping.

248 "Well, Charlie, what are we expecting": LHD interview with Drue Heinz, November 6, 2000.

248 "They are all old friends" and following: Coffin, "Charles Addams: Recluse About Town."

248 "little mushrooms": LHD interview with MMA, March 6–10, 2000.

248 "not poisonous": CSA to James M. Geraghty, January 14, 1974. JMG/NYPL.

249 "not ultra-serious about his condition": LHD interview with Stan Mirsky, March 1, 2000.

249 "If you could choose your end": George Plimpton, *Shadow Box* (New York: G. P. Putnam's Sons, 1977), 288–89.

250 "Addams is obviously uncertain" and following: HFP memos, September 9, 1976, May 18, 1977, October 20, 1977.

251 "network bureaucratic interference": Stephen Cox, *The Addams Chronicles* (New York: Harper Perennial, 1991), 154.

251 "an early sign of total reclusion": CSA to James M. Geraghty, November 9, 1977. JMG/NYPL.

251 "You look great in that beard": James M. Geraghty to CSA, November 2, 1977.

252 "looked like a baby hat": LHD interview with FM, December 9, 1999.

252 "An elderly friend": CSA, "Bugatti Lover," unpublished manuscript.

253 "no history of serious illness": Robert D. McFadden, "Rockefeller Is Dead at 70; Vice President Under Ford and Governor for 15 Years," *New York Times,* January 27, 1979, 1.

253 It was "fast work": LHD interview with LHL, April 6–7, 2000.

254 notorious and "child-like": LHD interview with FM, December 9, 1999.

254 "You must have—why not?": LHD interview with SA, March 3, 2000.

255 "There's no cause for panic": *NYer,* December 10, 1979, 47.

256 "Marry me, or else": LHD interview with Daphne Hellman, December 6, 1999.

256 "cut it out": LHD interview with MMA, August 7–8, 1999.

256 "I got rid of the girl": from Kennedy Fraser's journals; LHD interview with Kennedy Fraser, April 4, 2000.

CHAPTER TWENTY-ONE: The Way It Was

257 "appropriately gloomy skies": Carey Winfrey, "Cartoonist Weds Dog Fancier at Private Cemetery for Pets," *New York Times,* June 1, 1980, 37.

257 "eye flashes": CSA datebook, May 1980.

257 "and her dog, too": Winfrey, "Cartoonist Weds Dog Fancier."

258 "She looked lovely": CSA, *Today,* October 30, 1981.

258 "You either camp it up": LHD interview with MMA, November 1–5, 1999.

258 "Don't forget to bring the dog": LHD interview with Frank Corwin, January 19, 2000.

259 "everyone wanted to get in on it": LHD interview with MMA.

259 "in spite of having been married": LHD interview with Shirley Baty, September 17, 2002.

259 "You take blood" and following: LHD interview with MMA, November 1–5, 1999.

259 "I'm not sure it's a dog" and following: Winfrey, "Cartoonist Weds Dog Fancier."

260 "They were like kids": LHD interview with John Sparkman, March 6, 2000.

260 "ONE GIANT STEP": CSA and MMA to O, May 31, 1980.

260 "the beautiful and lucky ex–Mrs. Miller": Ralph Fields to CSA, June 2, 1980.

261 "Porker, darling!": LHD interview with MMA, May 28, 2002.

261 "Love you madly" and following: MMA to CSA, undated, summer 1980.

262 **"T. & Chas very cute together"**: from the diaries of John Sargent, unpublished, January 1, 1981, December 21, 1980.

262 **"had to work awfully hard"**: LHD interview with SA, March 3, 2000.

262 **"Are you going to get married?"**: LHD interview with ETBD, January 30, 2000.

262 **"Go ahead," Tee would say**: LHD interview with MMA, June 1, 2000.

263 **"She's a great girl"** and following: LHD interview with LHL, May 10, 2002.

263 **they were "inseparable"**: LHD interview with Johnny Nicholson, November 15, 2001.

264 **"It can be done with human bones"**: Joanna Ramey, "The Addams Family at Home," *The Bridgehampton Sun,* October 29, 1980.

265 **"half in the bag"** and following: LHD interview with MMA, September 7–8, 1999.

266 **"Living in the Heap"**: Glenn Collins, "Charles Addams's Idiosyncratic 'Heap,' " *New York Times,* June 11, 1981, C-1.

266 **"Let's rev up the Heap"**: LHD interview with MMA, September 7–8, 1999.

267 **"I wish I had an alligator"**: LHD interview with Barbara Gross, January 5, 2004.

267 **"The invitation said"**: LHD interview with MMA, March 6–10, 2000.

267 **"Why, just the other day"**: Christian Williams, "The Father of the Addams Family," *Orlando Sentinel,* November 24, 1982, 4–5.

268 **"She matched his wit"**: LHD interview with Drue Heinz, November 6, 2000.

269 **"We're having partridge"**: LHD interview with MMA, November 1–5, 1999.

269 **"Watch it!"**: Collins, "Charles Addams's Idiosyncratic 'Heap.' "

CHAPTER TWENTY-TWO: When It Stops Being Fun, I'll Quit

270 **"Dear Mr. Addams"**: to CSA from Robert Skirvin, November 11, 1973.

270 **"You look at George Price"**: John Grossman, "Charles Addams: Twenty-four Hours in the Life of the Creator of *The Addams Family,*" *TWA Ambassador,* September 1981, 72.

270 **"as long as I don't get arthritis"**: "Westfield-Born Cartoonist Charles Addams," *The Courier-News,* August 10, 1974.

271 **"What if my wife"**: Page Six, *New York Post,* July 9, 1981.

271 **He rose "fairly early"**: Grossman, "Charles Addams: Twenty-four Hours," 72.

272 **"a dry spell"**: Grossman, "Charles Addams: Twenty-four Hours," 75.

272 **"Then I happened to look"**: Grossman, "Charles Addams: Twenty-four Hours," 78.

272   a cover that "made me weep": Dorothy Schiff to CSA, February 23, 1981.

272   ("perhaps it becomes a mild obsession") and following: radio interview, "The Haunt for Chas Addams: Charles Addams Talks with Philip French," August 15, 1978.

272   "a small victory": Colin Covert, "The Way We Live," *Detroit Free Press*, circa 1982.

272   "great art" and following: "Somewhat Gloomily Yours, Charles Addams," University of Pennsylvania *Almanac*, November 8, 1979.

272   looked "exactly alike": CSA, *The Dick Cavett Show*, March 29, 1978.

272   "a complicated picture": CI.

273   "Inflationary pressures": *NYer*, March 31, 1980, 29.

273   "the brooding of the hand": "Saul Steinberg, Epic Doodler, Dies at 84," *New York Times*, May 13, 1999.

274   "was always terribly offended" and following: LHD interview with Al Hirschfeld, February 5, 2001.

274   "And the wizard has come out": *The Dick Cavett Show*.

274   "Budd is an expert on swans": LHD interview with Budd Schulberg, December 11, 2001.

275   "I think I have enough": Grossman, "Charles Addams: Twenty-four Hours."

275   "Unlike many cartoonists": LHD interview with Charles McGrath, October 30, 2001.

275   "I just do what I feel like": Grossman, "Charles Addams: Twenty-four Hours."

275   "a very poisonous little green snake": LHD interview with MMA, March 6–10, 2000.

275   "Yes, Charles, it's warmer": LHD interview with George Booth, November 4, 2000.

275   "I'm glad that it has become chic": French, "The Haunt for Chas Addams."

275   "After five minutes of looking at people": Eric Pace, "Charles Addams Dead at 76; Found Humor in the Macabre," *New York Times*, September 30, 1988, 1, B-8.

275   "was studying a display": Gardner Botsford to LHD, September 27, 2002.

276   "I live in my imagination": Leslie Bennetts, "Charles Addams: He's Really Just a Normal Boy Who Craves the Grave," *Washington Star*, October 31, 1978.

276   "More coffee, honey?": *NYer*, May 25, 1981, 37.

276   "It's going to be great!": *NYer*, January 26, 1981, 33.

277   "[getting] off a good one": *NYer*, October 18, 1982, 45.

277   "The T-Shirt of Dorian Gray": *NYer*, August 23, 1982, 25.

277   "Six Sins or Less": *NYer*, June 8, 1981, 45.

277   "completely different from anyone else": LHD interview with Mischa Richter, November 12, 1999.

277 **"beyond imitation"**: LHD interview with Lee Lorenz, December 10, 1999.

278 **"Maynard, I do think"**: *NYer*, July 25, 1983, 24.

278 **"I couldn't sleep"**: George Booth to CSA, September 13, 1983.

278 **"Charlie's biggest fan"**: LHD interview with Lee Lorenz, December 10, 1999.

278 **"the secondary ideas"** and following: Addams memorial service, November 18, 1988.

279 **"The most sinister place"**: Dwight Macdonald, "Charles Addams, His Family, and His Fiends," *The Reporter*, July 21, 1953, 37.

279 **"hated what was happening to the skyline"**: LHD interview with John Sparkman, March 6, 2000.

279 **"My cartoons don't have"**: Dolores Barclay, "Cartoonist a 16th Century Man," *The Daily Argus*, February 14, 1982.

279 **"if my drawings are remembered"**: Grossmann, "Charles Addams: Twenty-four Hours," 78.

CHAPTER TWENTY-THREE: A Day with Frank Modell

280 **On a Wednesday morning in September** and following: LHD interview with FM, December 9, 1999.

280 **"a pretty good shot"**: Joanna Ramey, "The Eccentric Charles Addams," *Women's Wear Daily*, March 31, 1988.

280 **"Someone is murdering babies"**: LHD interview with MMA, August 7–8, 1999.

280 **"All my life"**: Ramey, "The Eccentric Charles Addams."

280 **"all too seldom now"**: Christian Williams, "Playing It Ghoul," *Washington Post*, undated (1982).

282 **"All right, all right!"**: *NYer*, September 3, 1966.

283 **"had more toys"**: LHD interview with FM, December 9, 1999.

283 **"the death car"**: LHD interview with MMA, April 9, 2000.

283 **"I don't know"**: LHD interview with Barbara Nicholls, January 17–18, 2000.

283 **"If you ever want to trade"**: LHD interview with Kennedy Fraser, April 4, 2000.

283 **"He came out of it an old man"** and following: LHD interviews with MMA, November 1–5, 1999, May 23, 2000.

285 **His old friend seemed "frail"**: LHD interview with Budd Schulberg, December 11, 2001.

285 **"kind of grumpy"**: LHD interview with P. L. Steiner, July 7, 2000.

285 **"the most conservative"**: LHD interview with Denise Otis, May 12, 2000.

285 **"This guy is bad news"**: LHD interview with Barbara Nicholls, January 17–18, 2000.

285   "wasn't very political": LHD interview with Arthur Schlesinger, Jr., February 6, 2001.

285   had "reluctantly" sold: LHD interview with Jeffrey Vogel, January 29, 2003.

285   "Let's go!": LHD interview with Jessie Wood, June 15, 2000.

285   "seemed just like his old self": John and Joyce Nicholas to MMA, November 19, 1988.

286   "took nothing solemnly": LHD interview with John Sparkman, March 6, 2000.

286   ("He turned pink"): LHD interview with NH, May 17, 2001.

286   "I'm not ready to sleep": LHD interview with Sidney Offit, December 28, 1999.

286   "I just told you": LHD interview with Drue Heinz, November 6, 2000.

286   whose death had "most depressed" Addams: CSA to Eva Geraghty, January 19, 1983.

287   "Alice B. Curr is dead": LHD interview with MMA, January 4–7, 2000.

CHAPTER TWENTY-FOUR: The Stork Brought You

288   "Charlie's cruising speed": "Charles Addams," *NYer,* October 17, 1988, 122.

288   "would no longer be considered unpublishable": e-mail to LHD from Mike Woolson, March 23, 2003.

288   ("Thinking of you"): Robert Parrish to CSA, December 9, 1985.

288   "well ahead of the sick humorists": galley copy of Jesse Bier, *The Rise and Fall of American Humor* (New York: Holt, Rinehart and Winston, 1968), 201.

289   He had even saved a memento: LHD interviews with MMA, April 9, 2000; Gerta Conner, April 6, 2000; LHL, April 4, 2000, and April 6, 2000; Emmy and Billy Winburn, June 24, 2000.

289   "It could only happen to you": LHD interview with Al Hirschfeld, February 5, 2001.

289   "So you see": radio interview, "The Haunt for Chas Addams: Charles Addams Talks with Philip French," August 15, 1978.

289   "a slippered pantaloon": Joanna Ramey, "The Eccentric Charles Addams," *Women's Wear Daily,* March 31, 1988.

290   "sharing of his things": LHD interview with Jeffrey Vogel, January 29, 2003.

290   "that he'd be considered a suspect": e-mail from Mike Woolson to LHD, March 23, 2003.

290   "reclusion is something I understand": CSA to James M. Geraghty, November 9, 1977. JMG/NYPL.

290 "Am I ill?": LHD interview with MMA, November 1–5, 1999.

290 "You know who I think of when I see you?": LHD interview with Cameron and Jean Argetsinger, May 12, 2003.

291 "I think men look better in ties": LHD interview with Sidney Offit, December 28, 1999.

291 "slightly bohemian": LHD interview with Lee Lorenz, December 10, 1999.

291 a "stark suit": LHD interview with Roz Chast, November 11, 1999.

291 "God's coat had dog hair": e-mail to LHD from Michael Maslin, December 12, 1999.

291 "with utter aplomb" and following: LHD interview with Charles McGrath, October 30, 2001.

291 "so ferocious in the ring": LHD interview with Budd Schulberg, December 11, 2001.

291 "courtly interchanges": LHD interview with Ed Koren, March 13, 2000.

291 "was the weirdest of all": LHD interview with Charles McGrath, October 30, 2001.

291 "repulsively demonic": Russell Davies, "Addams and Evil," *Observer*, May 15, 1988.

292 "I'm sick of people calling it macabre": LHD interview with Drue Heinz, November 6, 2000.

292 "an actor doing a part": LHD interview with Mischa Richter, November 12, 1999.

292 "There don't seem to be many": unidentified article from a Hamptons publication, 1982.

292 "Not all the old timers were": LHD interview with Charles McGrath, October 30, 2001.

292 "Do we sell to (perhaps)": CSA to Barbara Nicholls, November 3, 1977.

292 "Mort, I love your work": LHD interview with Mort Gerberg, February 26, 2001.

292 "but I do not have Peanuts envy": *The Literary Guild*, March 1977.

292 "the anniversary of Lincoln's assassination" and following: e-mails to LHD from Mike Woolson, March 19, 23, 24, 2003.

293 "we're all genetically cartoonists": CSA, *Today*, October 30, 1981.

293 "night worries": MMA to LHL, undated draft.

293 "I think I'll wait": *NYer*, November 14, 1988, 39.

293 "I'm the invention": *NYer*, July 25, 1988, 28.

293 "I'm telling you the truth": *NYer*, October 19, 1987, 47.

295 "not a popular subject": LHD interview with Wilfrid Sheed, October 24, 2003.

296 "the worst cartoon I ever drew": LHD interview with John Callahan, March 24, 2004.

296 "There, there, dear": *NYer*, January 5, 1987, 29.

296 The contract, negotiated by Barbara Colyton: Orion Pictures Corporation to BC, November 11, 1987. TCAF.

297 "Look, she is fantastic about money": LHD interview with LHL, May 10, 2002.

297 "she had the golden touch": LHD interview with John Sparkman, March 6, 2000.

297 Frank's "hysterical" actress: LHD interview with FM, December 9, 1999.

298 "horror stories": LHD interview with Eric Pleskow, November 9, 2004.

298 "legion" in the entertainment industry: LHD interview with anonymous.

298 Colyton telephoned Barbara, and within five minutes: LHD interview with JG, October 5, 2002.

299 "Mr. Mitchell!": *NYer*, December 2, 1950, 49.

299 "My Hepplewhite table": LHD interview with JG, April 30, 2003.

300 "It wasn't really a bad marriage": Leslie Bennetts, "Charles Addams: He's Really Just a Normal Boy Who Craves the Grave," *Washington Star*, October 31, 1978.

300 "I live in New York City": Brad Darrach, "The Addams Family Loses Its Father, Charles, the Great Cartoonist Who Taught America to Love the Macabre," *People*, October 18, 1988, 142.

301 "The trick when visiting": LHD interview with Dick Cavett, March 1, 2000.

301 "would not be an easy man": LHD interview with Al Hirschfeld, February 5, 2001.

301 "needed atmosphere": LHD interview with SA, April 5, 2000.

301 ("Well, you wanted a place"): *NYer*, February 15, 1982, 40.

301 ("a structured life"): Stanley Mirsky, M.D., and Joan Rattner Hellman, *Controlling Diabetes the Easy Way*, 3rd ed. (New York: Random House, 1998), 16.

301 "This happens quite often": LHD interview with Kevin Miserocchi, September 13, 2000.

301 "He was furious": LHD interview with LHL, June 1, 2000.

301 "a huge cacophony of barking": LHD interview with Jeffrey Vogel, January 29, 2003.

302 "My, Running Fox looks fine tonight" and following: LHD interviews with MMA, October 6, 1999, January 16, 2000, January 4–7, 2000, August 7–8, 1999.

303 "that melodious voice": MMA to CSA, undated (1972).

304 "I've just dyed my feet": LHD interview with MMA, March 6–10, 2000.

304 "All Boy": John O'Hara, Introduction to *Charles Addams's Monster Rally* (New York: Simon & Schuster, 1950).

304 "Is this Uncle Fester?" and following: LHD interviews with MMA, August 7–8, 1999, March 6–10, 2000.

306   his "dear recluse": CSA to MMA, undated.

306   "You could get a room there": LHD interview with Drue Heinz, November 6, 2000.

306   "She's not gonna tell you much": LHD interview with SA, April 5, 2000.

307   "My pussy's getting bald": LHD interviews with MMA, January 19, 2000; LHL, March 8, 2002.

307   "Get a merkin": LHD interview with LHL, March 8, 2002.

307   "where it remains something of a shrine": CSA to Barbara Hersey, June 25, 1986.

307   "I always thought she was mine": LHD interview with MMA, March 6–10, 2000.

CHAPTER TWENTY-FIVE: Charlie's Dream

308   "how happy" Charlie seemed: James Stevenson to MMA, undated (1988).

308   a way of "wrinkling": LHD interview with James Stevenson, April 12, 2000.

308   "Awful things like that": LHD interview with FM, December 9, 1999.

308   "pissing off the porch": from Kennedy Fraser's private journals; LHD interview with Kennedy Fraser, April 4, 2000.

308   They were jokey: LHD interview with James Stevenson, April 12, 2000.

309   a "champion of generations": *NYer,* May 21, 1984.

309   "I don't think one's going to hurt me": LHD interview with FM, December 9, 1999.

309   "glamorous women of a certain age": LHD interview with SA, March 3, 2000.

309   "He cleans up nice": Herb Valen to LHD, April 4, 2000.

CHAPTER TWENTY-SIX: Postmortem

311   "Don't ever do that to me": Susan Heller Anderson, "The Late Charles Addams Gives Party and His Friends Praise Him," *New York Times,* November 19, 1988, 10.

311   "Marian Shaw and Bodie Nielsen": Kathleen Parrish to MMA, November 19, 1988.

312   "What a great party": LHD interview with Calvin Trillin, February 21, 2000.

312   "all the ladies who doted on him": LHL to MMA, November 21, 1988.

312   "looking as if she will die": From Kennedy Fraser's private journals; LHD interview with Kennedy Fraser, April 4, 2000.

312   "all in black, playing the widow": LHD interview with Drue Heinz, November 6, 2000.

312 "Hi, Cuz" and following: LHD interview with Craig Addams, May 25, 2000.

312 **For the memorial, Tee had chartered:** LHD interview with MMA, January 4–7, 2000, November 1–5, 1999; CSA memorial, November 18, 1988.

313 **Saul Steinberg focused on the artist's work:** Saul Steinberg, CSA memorial, November 18, 1988.

313 **"He took the writing":** LHD interview with John Astin, July 25, 2000.

313 **In its obituary,** *The New Yorker:* NYer, October 17, 1988, 122.

313 **"I celebrate in particular":** Kurt Vonnegut to MMA, September 30, 1988.

313 **"It is too sad":** Lauren Bacall to MMA, undated (October 1988).

313 **"Everyone who knew him":** Ken Drake to MMA, November 1, 1988.

314 **"NEVER have I seen":** Susan Ely to MMA, November 1988.

314 **"I weep, Tee":** LHL to MMA, September 30, 1988.

314 **"It was a real blow":** Glenn Collins, "For George Price, Art Imitates Life, Sort Of," *New York Times,* November 22, 1988.

314 **"I know you were the one person":** Barbara Hersey to MMA, November 12, 1988.

314 **"Who could ever forget Charlie?":** to LHD from Barbara Gross, February 7, 2004.

314 **"I want you to see":** LHD interview with Drue Heinz, November 6, 2000.

314 **"Ah, Steve":** LHD interview with SA, April 5, 2000.

314 **"She didn't actually go for the jugular":** Joanna Ramey, "The Eccentric Charles Addams," *Women's Wear Daily,* March 31, 1988, 16.

314 **"This is Bugatti country":** LHD interview with Jessie Wood, June 15, 2000.

314 **"a blue spider":** LHD interview with Gardner Botsford, April 30, 2003.

314 **"with shiny eyes":** LHD interview with Hedda Sterne, May 13, 2002.

315 **"Are you still Hollyman?":** LHD interview with Tom Hollyman, February 4, 2000.

315 **"You must tell him you had lunch":** LHD interview with SA, April 5, 2000.

316 **"He was sui generis":** LHD interview with Philip and Anna Hamburger, December 6, 1999.

316 **"Everything about him was so original":** LHD interview with Rosamund Bernier, February 18, 2000.

316 **called it "chiaroscuro":** LHD interview with Frank Zachary, January 24, 2000.

316 **"He had a charm so strong":** LHD interview with SA, April 5, 2000.

316 **"You know, I think Charlie's slept":** LHD interview with Barbara Nicholls, January 14, 2000.

316 **"He was a very happy man":** LHD interview with FM, December 9, 1999.

316 **"He deserved to die":** LHD interview with Gillis Addison, January 23, 2002.

316   **It would be years before:** LHD interviews with BC, February 10, 2000, June 2, 2002.

316   **"Can't you get along with *anybody*?":** *NYer,* April 21, 1956, 31.

316   **"because of Charles's imprudence":** LHD interviews with BC, February 10, 2000, June 2, 2000.

317   **"He said that the Family was safe":** "It's a Family Affair," *The Mail on Sunday,* December 15, 1991, 13.

317   **After Charlie's death:** LHD interview with MMA, August 7–8, 1999.

Credits and Permissions

Archival Material

Grateful acknowledgment is made to the following to reprint archival material:
Boston University and the Tee and Charles Addams Foundation: Quotations
    from Charles Addams to Leila Hadley Luce housed in the Leila Hadley

Luce Collection, Howard Gotlieb Archival Research Center at Boston University. Used by permission of Boston University and the Tee and Charles Addams Foundation.

Houghton Library, Harvard University and the Tee and Charles Addams Foundation: One letter from Charles Addams to John Mason Brown dated 13 November 1950, call number bMS Am 1948(29). Used by permission of the Houghton Library, Harvard University and the Tee and Charles Addams Foundation.

The New York Public Library and the Estate of James M. Geraghty: Excerpts from James M. Geraghty's unpublished manuscript (sections about Charles Addams and his work) housed in the James M. Geraghty Papers, Manuscripts and Archives Division, The New York Public Library, Astor, Lenox and Tilden Foundations. Used by permission of The New York Public Library and the Estate of James M. Geraghty.

The New York Public Library and *The New Yorker* / The Condé Nast Publications, Inc.: Unsigned art meeting notes for the following dates (MssCol2236): January 23, 1935, December 31, 1934, October 22, 1935, October 29, 1935; letter from Katharine S. White to Harold W. Ross dated September 24, 1936; letter from Harold W. Ross to Charles Addams dated June 30, 1935; letter from Charles Addams to Wolcott Gibbs dated August 16, 1935; letter from Charles Addams to Katharine S. White dated June 17, 1935. All material housed in *The New Yorker* Records, Manuscripts and Archives Division, The New York Public Library, Astor, Lennox and Tilden Foundations. Used by permission of The New York Public Library and *The New Yorker* / The Condé Nast Publications, Inc.

The New York Public Library and the Tee and Charles Addams Foundation: Letter from Charles Addams to James Geraghty dated July 12, 1949; letter from Charles Addams to James Geraghty dated May 20, 1975; letter from Charles Addams to James Geraghty dated November 9, 1977; and letter from Charles Addams to Miss Terry dated January 16, 1943. All letters housed in the James M. Geraghty Papers, Manuscripts and Archives Division, The New York Public Library, Astor, Lenox and Tilden Foundations. Used by permission of The New York Public Library and the Tee and Charles Addams Foundation.

The Pennsylvania State University Libraries and the Tee and Charles Addams Foundation: Correspondence between Charles Addams and John O'Hara housed in The John O'Hara Papers, Special Collections Library, The Pennsylvania State University Libraries. Used by permission of The Pennsylvania State University Libraries and the Tee and Charles Addams Foundation.

Index

—

Page numbers in *italics* refer to illustrations.
CA = Charles Addams

ABOUT THE AUTHOR

—

LINDA H. DAVIS is the author of *Onward and Upward: A Biography of Katharine S. White* and *Badge of Courage: The Life of Stephen Crane.* She and her husband, Chuck Yanikoski, live in Harvard, Massachusetts, with their two children and a dog named Addams.

CPSIA information can be obtained
at www.ICGtesting.com
Printed in the USA
BVHW030349300921
617773BV00001B/7

9 781684 426904